'With exceptional skill and deep unde[rstanding, Xiaoming Huang] offers a very fine study of international [relations of East Asia. Empirically] and theoretically rich, this book is highly recommended for all students of East Asian studies: it will have a long lifespan on our bookshelves. East Asian IR have undergone fundamental transformation and the region is exceptionally important for global politics, international security and in predicting future patterns of global governance.'

—**Weixing Hu, University of Macau**

'This is a much needed and anticipated book on a timely and important topic: the International Relations of East Asia. Huang provides a comprehensive look on the IR of East Asia by thoroughly examining various issues of history, security, geopolitics, political economy, domestic politics, culture, and transitional challenges.'

—**Hun Joon Kim, Korea University**

'This major new text finally does justice to the field of international relations of East Asia, by highlighting their inherent peculiarities and dynamism. The volume represents an insightful investigation into East Asia's acquired centrality in global politics, economy and governance and is a refreshing and powerful contribution. Highly recommended.'

—**Antonio Fiori, University of Bologna**

'This excellent, comprehensive textbook on international relations of East Asia is written from a truly East Asian perspective and based on many years teaching experience in this field. I recommend it to both undergraduate and postgraduate students new to the region.'

—**Fumihito Gotoh, University of Warwick**

'In this fascinating book, Xiaoming Huang treats the international relations of East Asia as a distinct subject, and embarks on a theoretically innovative and empirically rich study of its various aspects. Realpolitik, rapid industrial growth, and bifurcated cultural identities are seen as the driving forces behind the IREA, shaping the institutions and international order prevalent in the region, and leading to possible development of a new system. No one can understand the world today, a time of US-PRC competition, without understanding the IREA. Huang's book is a must for such understanding.'

—**Yu-Shan Wu, National Taiwan University**

'An excellent text which provides a highly readable, comprehensive and theoretically-grounded introduction to the international relations of East Asia. Superbly applying theories of international relations to East Asian practice, Xiaoming Huang illustrates admirably how geopolitical, institutional and civilizational forces have jointly shaped the evolving international order of a region that matters hugely to the future of the world.'

—**Jian Zhang, University of New South Wales, Canberra**

'*International Relations of East Asia* is a comprehensive source of knowledge on the patterns and logic of interstate interactions in one of the most important regions of the world. It is unique in that it considers international relations of East Asia as a domain in its own right.'

—**Alexander Korolev, University of New South Wales, Sydney**

'A remarkable text that brings together both the rich past traditions and most recent scholarship on East Asia to provide a comprehensive survey of the development of the region. The volume integrates the intersecting perspectives of power politics, culture and political economy. The result is a book that will be of central importance and use to students and researchers of the East Asian region for many years to come.'

—**Christopher Hughes, University of Warwick**

'This well-structured text has excellent teaching strategies and is built on the latest research. It offers a brilliant introduction to the increasingly complex international relations of East Asia and the impact of the events of that region on global affairs.'

—**Niall Duggan, University College Cork**

'*International Relations of East Asia* offers a compelling account that captures intelligently the complexity of structural and institutional changes of East Asian international order since the end of World War II. Theoretically informed, it adds valuable alternative perspectives in understanding the dynamics of East Asian international relations today.'

—**Yongjin Zhang, University of Bristol**

'This is the most comprehensive text on East Asia and its international relations. The book not only examines the topic with a carefully developed theoretical framework, but also explains clearly the complexities of the region. This is a very well written book for readers to understand the past, the present and the future of East Asia.'

—**Jing Men, College of Europe**

INTERNATIONAL RELATIONS OF EAST ASIA

Structures, Institutions and International Order

Xiaoming Huang

© Xiaoming Huang, under exclusive licence to Springer Nature Limited 2020

All rights reserved. No reproduction, copy or transmission of this publication may be made without written permission.

No portion of this publication may be reproduced, copied or transmitted save with written permission or in accordance with the provisions of the Copyright, Designs and Patents Act 1988, or under the terms of any licence permitting limited copying issued by the Copyright Licensing Agency, Saffron House, 6–10 Kirby Street, London EC1N 8TS.

Any person who does any unauthorized act in relation to this publication may be liable to criminal prosecution and civil claims for damages.

The author has asserted his right to be identified as the author of this work in accordance with the Copyright, Designs and Patents Act 1988.

First published 2020 by
RED GLOBE PRESS

Red Globe Press in the UK is an imprint of Springer Nature Limited, registered in England, company number 785998, of 4 Crinan Street, London, N1 9XW.

Red Globe Press® is a registered trademark in the United States, the United Kingdom, Europe and other countries.

ISBN 978-1-352-00872-2 hardback
ISBN 978-1-352-00868-5 paperback

This book is printed on paper suitable for recycling and made from fully managed and sustained forest sources. Logging, pulping and manufacturing processes are expected to conform to the environmental regulations of the country of origin.

A catalogue record for this book is available from the British Library.

A catalog record for this book is available from the Library of Congress.

Contents

List of Figures ix
List of Tables xi
Acknowledgements xiii
Abbreviations xv

1 Introduction **1**
   What is and what drives IREA? 1
   IREA as a field of study 3
   Why we study IREA 4
   Theory, scholarship, and policy analysis 5
   Learning strategies 6
   Further reading 9

2 Theorizing IREA **11**
   Conventional framings of IREA 13
   Nation and state in war and peace 16
   Bipolarity 17
   Regional industrial diffusion 20
   East Asian theories 21
   "IR Theory with Chinese characteristics" 23
   Does Japan have an IR theory? 26
   "Korea between empires" 29
   Regional identity and an ASEAN IR theory 31
   National theories and a theory of IREA 33
   A framework for IREA 34
   Further reading 36

3 Historical International Orders **39**
   International orders and order transformation 40
   The warring states 40
   The Chinese world order 42
   European colonial governance 45
   The greater East Asian sphere of co-prosperity ... 51
   Imperial orders and modern transformation 55
   Further reading 57

4 War, Peace, and Geopolitical Dynamics **59**
   The Cold War and hot wars 60
   War over state constitution 60
   War over state boundaries 65

	War and transborder nations	66
	Geopolitical drivers	69
	Japan and China in East Asia	70
	Rise of China in post-Cold War East Asia	75
	US engagement with East Asia	77
	Between great powers	80
	Further reading	84
5	**The Bipolar Structure**	**87**
	International structure in a regional system	88
	Power vacuum	91
	The Yalta vision	92
	Concentration of power	93
	Organization of collective forces	95
	The bipolar structure in IREA	98
	Correction, disturbance, and structural shift	99
	A historical pattern or a generic structure	102
	Further reading	103
6	**Culture in IREA**	**105**
	Culture in International Relations	106
	Confucian authority structure	110
	International policy and behavior, Japanese style	112
	National identity	115
	Religion as a political force	118
	Third-wave democracy	119
	China's evolving international identity	122
	The ASEAN way and the Asia-Pacific way	124
	The normative structure of IREA	125
	Further reading	127
7	**Industrial Development**	**129**
	East Asian growth	130
	The lead goose	132
	Akamatsu's original model	134
	"Four little dragons" and newly industrializing economies	135
	A theory of East Asian growth	137
	The rise of China, economically	140
	Debating Smith, Wallerstein, and Kant	144
	Further reading	148
8	**Economic Regionalism**	**151**
	Regionalization and regionalism	152
	Market forces and institutions as drivers	154
	Visions of a region	156

	PBEC, APEC, and Pacific business cooperation	162
	"Funerals," "weddings," and the noodle bowl	164
	APT, EAS, and ASEAN centrality	169
	TPP, RCEP, and BIFURCATION of a region?	171
	Principal movers and shapers	177
	Multilateral institutions of economic regionalism	183
	Further reading	186

9 Cooperative Security — 189
- An "after-victory" moment — 190
- China and ASEAN rapprochement — 192
- Concept and theory — 196
- Politics of multilateral engagement — 197
- Institutionalizing an East Asian security order — 199
- East Asian security architecture — 202
- Balance of power or institutions and community? — 205
- Further reading — 208

10 Transnational Challenge — 209
- Transnational issues — 210
- Ethnicity, religion, and the nation-state — 213
- Rights movement and transnational activism — 217
- Environmental security — 221
- International institutions of transborder governance — 223
- States and interstate politics — 226
- Further reading — 228

11 Domestic Structures — 231
- The "second image" problem — 232
- Three types of domestic structures — 233
- Regime types and IREA — 234
- International policy of the developmental state — 235
- Liberal states, pacific community, and democratic peace — 237
- Social ideas, economic interests, and national identities — 239
- When Duterte became President — 241
- Mechanisms of domestic and international linkage — 242
- Further reading — 244

12 East Asia in the World — 247
- East Asia as a civilization — 248
- International society and East Asia — 250
- Triple transformations — 252
- Industrial revolution, East Asian style — 253
- Democratic transitions — 256

Civilizational identity of the region	259
Three challenges	261
Agent, structure, and East Asia as a platform	262
Further reading	264

13 Conclusion: Futures of IREA — **267**

Key dynamics of IREA	267
Three key areas to watch for future IREA	269

Bibliography 273
Index 293

List of Figures

2.1	Theorizing structural bifurcation in IREA	19
3.1	Illustration of Fairbank's Chinese world order of the nineteenth century	43
3.2	Tambiah's depiction of the galactic polity of Ayutthaya, Thailand, seventeenth century	47
3.3	Spheres of imperial influence in East Asia, early twentieth century	50
3.4	Japanese Empire in East Asia, 1942	54
4.1	US defensive perimeter and strategic engagement with East Asia	79
5.1	Lake's conception of international economic structures	90
5.2	Illustration of hub-spoke alliance systems in East Asia in the 1960s	96
7.1	East Asian growth: National income level, 1950–2016	130
7.2	Japan's real GDP annual growth and high-speed-growth period (1951-2014, percentage, shaded area)	133
7.3	Illustration of Akamatsu's flying geese pattern of national industrial development	135
7.4	Illustration of flying geese model of industrial difusion in East Asia	139
7.5	China's real GDP annual growth and high-speed-growth period (1982–2014, percentage, shaded area)	140
7.6	Change in weight of national economies in East Asia (1950–2016)	141
8.1	Geoeconomic areas of East Asia and the Asia-Pacific	157
8.2	Baldwin's depiction of noodle bowl syndrome in East Asian regionalism	169
8.3	In search of a region: a "noodle bowl" of multinational economic institutions in East Asia	172
9.1	Huang's depiction of Communist states in continental East Asia and Communist forces in Southeast Asia, 1950s	193
12.1	Structural shift in global distribution of national wealth and economic capabilities (1860s–2010s)	254

List of Tables

7.1	Waves of rapid growth of East Asian economies (1951–2014)	136
7.2	China's exports and FDI outflows to world regions	142
7.3	China's exports and FDI outflows to East Asian economies	143
8.1	Weight of international economic groupings in East Asia in world economy (%)	154
8.2	Institutions of East Asian regionalism	176
8.3	Weight of major economies' FDI outflows to East Asia (2009–2017) (%)	179
8.4	Weight of major economies' exports to East Asia (1980–2017) (%)	179
12.1	Political change in East Asian states from 1980s	257
12.2	Governance quality of East Asian states	258
12.3	Value distribution in East Asian countries (%) (2011–2014)	261

Acknowledgments

I wanted to write a book on international relations of East Asia 25 years ago when I first started teaching the subject at the School of International Relations at the University of Southern California (USC) in Los Angeles, before I moved on to spend a year as a visiting fellow at the Program of International Politics and Economy at the East-West Center in Honolulu. Professor James Rosenau, then at USC, stimulated my interest in the theory and practice of international relations in East Asia or simply in the possibility of such a field of inquiry. Jim's intense curiosity, almost like that of a philosopher, inspired me to take this journey of intellectual exploration. Are IREA an instance of how international relations work? Is there a pattern of repeated occurrence of certain types of state action, behavior, and relations in IREA? If so, what shapes such a pattern? Do these forces transcend East Asia? And will the pattern persist?

While many have encouraged and influenced the idea of such a book, including James Rosenau, Mike Mochizuki, Francis Fukuyama, Stephen Chan, Takashi Inoguchi, Zhao Baoxue, Wang Jisi, Michel Oksenberg, Harry Harding, Charles Morison, David Shambaugh, Yun-han Zhu, Chih-yu Shih, Seiji Endo, and Yongjin Zhang, early on and along the way, it was not until the autumn of 2018 that I managed to sit down, in an elegant and beautiful office at Ryukoku University in Kyoto to concentrate on writing this book, thanks to Professor Kosuke Shimizu. That research visit was made possible also by a grant for sabbatical leave from my home university, Victoria University of Wellington.

I have been able to write this book now, after so many years, partly because of the publisher's persistent encouragement, from Steven Kennedy, Stephen Wenham, Lloyd Langman, and Andrew Malvern in particular; partly because of the fact that I have been teaching this subject for the past 20 some years and accumulated substantial scholarly material and intellectual understanding; and partly because of the fact that I have had ongoing difficulties referring students to an authoritative book of knowledge on the subject.

International relations in East Asia have undergone profound changes, and the dynamics that have constantly generated distinct patterns in IREA have had ample time and occasion to manifest. I have also had opportunities to engage in the practice of IREA in various capacities and in national and international settings. This has enabled me to develop broad and in-depth empirical knowledge of the working of IREA. There is much richer empirical material available now to satisfy scholars' theoretical curiosity and eagerness for a body of knowledge on IREA. All of these factors helped me better understand how politics operates at the interstate level in the shaping of IREA and allowed me to become more effective in isolating factors, identifying patterns, articulating the logic, and explaining unique patterns in IREA. What follows in this book is not a set of my opinions on issues in IREA or a national position in IREA; it is a body of knowledge on this academically challenging subject.

I dedicate this book to those who have explored and contributed to the development of the field before and along with me, including those mentioned earlier. I know many of them personally. There are too many of them to name each one individually. But their pioneering work and very thoughtful explorations helped pave the way for much of the material incorporated in the book you now hold. I also want to dedicate the book to my students, particularly those in the courses I taught over the years on this very subject. They have been a primary source of inspiration and discipline for my work on this project. Finally, I want to thank my wife, Dr. Kyongju Kim, who carefully read all the chapters and made invaluable comments. Many of the ideas in the book reflect the influence of conversations we have had regularly on issues significant for the world and for East Asian nations.

Xiaoming Huang
January 30, 2019
Gojo and Fukakusa
Kyoto, Japan

Abbreviations

ACFTA	ASEAN-China Free Trade Agreement
ADB	Asian Development Bank
AIIB	Asian Infrastructure Investment Bank
AJFAT	ASEAN-Japan Free Trade Agreement
AKFTA	ASEAN-Korea Free Trade Agreement
AMU	Asian Monetary Unit
APEC	Asian Pacific Economic Cooperation
APT	ASEAN Plus Three
ARF	ASEAN Regional Forum
ASEAN	Association of Southeast Asian Nations
BLOs	Border Liaison Offices
BRI	Belt and Road Initiative
CEA	Continental East Asia
CEPA	Closer Economic Partnership Arrangement
CPTPP	Comprehensive and Progressive Agreement for Trans-Pacific Partnership
CSCAP	Council for Security Cooperation in the Asia-Pacific
CSIS	Center for Strategy and International Studies
DPRK	Democratic People's Republic of Korea
DRV	Democratic Republic of Vietnam
EAEG	East Asian Economic Group
EAG	East Asian Growth
IREA	International relations of East Asia
EAS	East Asian Summit
ECFA	Economic Cooperation Framework Agreement
ECLAC	United Nations Economic Commission for Latin America
EU	European Union
FDI	Foreign direct investment
FTAAP	Free Trade Agreement in the Asia-Pacific
GDP	Gross domestic product
ISIS	Institutes of Strategic and International Studies
JETRO	Japan Export Trade Promotion Organization
JIIA	Japan Institute of International Affairs
LDP	Liberal Democratic Party
MEA	Maritime East Asia
MITI	Ministry of International Trade and Industry
MMP	Mixed member proportional
NAFTA	North American Free Trade Agreement
NATO	North Atlantic Treaty Organization
NGO	Nongovernmental organization
NIE	Newly industrializing/industrialized economy

PAFTAD	Pacific Trade and Development Conference
PBEC	Pacific Basin Economic Council
PRC	People's Republic of China
PTA	Preferential trade agreement
RCEP	Regional Comprehensive Economic Partnership
RGDPPC	Real GDP per capita
ROC	Republic of China
ROK	Republic of Korea
ROV	Republic of Vietnam
SCO	Shanghai Cooperation Organization
SFIA	Seoul Forum for International Affairs
SPT	Six-Party Talks
SRV	Socialist Republic of Vietnam
TAC	Treaty of Amity and Cooperation in Southeast Asia
TPP	Trans-Pacific Partnership
TPPA	Trans-Pacific Partnership Agreement
UNDCP	United Nations International Drug Control Program
UNTAC	United Nations Transitional Authority in Cambodia
USSR	Union of Soviet Socialist Republics
WATO	Warsaw Treaty Organization

1 Introduction

> In This Chapter...
>
> - What is and what drives IREA?
> - IREA as a field of study
> - Why we study IREA
> - Theory, scholarship, and policy analysis
> - Learning strategies

International Relations in East Asia (IREA) have experienced significant changes since the early twentieth century. The impact many countries in East Asia now have in world politics, international security, the global economy and development, and global governance is far greater than it ever was. More importantly, the international order in the region has transformed dramatically over the past 150 years, from the Chinese world order to European colonial governance and imperial competition, and to the Japan-led greater East Asian sphere of influence; and from the Cold War bipolar order to the US-led hegemonic order, and now to an increasingly bipolar order of China-US competition and engagement. Not only have the principal movers and shapers and their power relations changed, but the institutions, normative practices, and operation platforms they use to organize IREA have changed as well. To understand the direction in which IREA are moving, we must understand what has been driving the changes. This book explains the dynamism in IREA and how it has driven IREA to unfold and evolve in the way they have.

WHAT IS AND WHAT DRIVES IREA?

IREA are a complex set of international relations in and over East Asia that include both Northwest and Southeast Asia. This system of international relations has evolved in modern times through a series of distinct patterns and manifested in a constant shift of the international order in the region. Curiosity, inquiry, and theorizing over what drives IREA to evolve and take shape has been an important part of the field of study. Much of the attention has concentrated on the external interests and forces in the shaping of IREA. This tradition sees the influence of the geopolitical dynamics of great power competition or, more rigorously, the effects of the international power structure on IREA.

Growing attention is also seen in the role of industrial growth and economic development in IREA and the national and regional systems of organizing production and trade. Industrial growth and economic development after 1945 added significant substance and dynamism in contemporary IREA and enabled East Asian states to engage with broader international relations. We have traditionally focused on the role of East Asian culture and civilization in the formation of the international identity of East Asian states and developed an analytical tradition that looks at IREA in a binary framework of international society versus East Asia in analyzing IREA. Traditional East Asian culture and civilization have changed with the new national and international political and economic conditions. This has led to a shift in the normative structure in IREA and complicated how East Asian states identify with international society and pursue a particular set of IREA more so than others. A normative structure in IREA is a pattern of distribution of institutional, normative, and civilizational identities of states in IREA. We will discuss this further in Chapters 6 and 12.

These single factor–focused explanations, however, explain some aspects of IREA in isolation. How do these distinct sets of forces relate to one another in a logical relationship? How do they together provide a coherent explanation of what IREA are and what has driven IREA to evolve in the patterns and sequences we have seen? In addition, these single factor–focused explanations identify three key variables in the development of IREA: the material power and capabilities of states and their international distribution; institutional arrangements, normative practices, and cultural identity that reflect, support, rationalize, and influence the power relations; and a set of authority relations among the states in IREA that form the international order in IREA. An analytical framework to stipulate the possible causal relations between these three variables will not only help connect the various aspects of IREA but also help us to think about IREA theoretically and holistically: what are IREA, how do they work, and what drives their development?

This text organizes the content and material in IREA within such a framework. Chapters here aim to demonstrate that the international structure in IREA, i.e., the systemwide distribution of power and interests of the states in IREA, is fundamental in enforcing an international order in IREA. An international structure is unique in the interstate power distribution. It can be hegemonic and hierarchic or multipolar and competitive. Each state has a different position in the structure in relation to the others. Change in the capacity and interests of a state or states leads to shifts in the international structure, i.e., change in the power relations among these states. This in turn results in changes in the effectiveness of the structure on the behavior, action, and interaction of the states.

An international structure enforces an international order through international institutions and normative practices, such as sovereignty, international treaty, tribute system, mechanisms of conflict settlement, hub–spoke alliance system, collective security arrangements, forms of transborder industrial production, rules on trade and transborder flow of capital, products, and people. The distribution of institutional, normative, and civilizational identities among the states forms the normative structure in IREA. These international institutions, normative practices, and cultural identity convey the effects of the power structure on individual states. They reflect, support, and legitimize the power structure, and rationalize, motivate, and constrain action and interaction among states.

Significant shifts in the international structure will eventually lead to the transformation of the international order. In IREA, the international order has undergone major transformations in the past 150 years: from the Chinese world order up to the mid-nineteenth century, to the European system of colonial governance and imperial competition, Japan's greater East Asian sphere of co-prosperity, the bipolar international order during the Cold War, the US hegemonic hierarchic order in post-Cold War East Asia, up through an increasingly bipolar order in more recent years. An international order is a set of authority relations among states. These relations are supported by the underlying power structure and the associated institutional arrangements and normative practices. An international order is stable when these institutions and norms are observed in state actions and interactions.

Chapters in this text will show how these structural, institutional, and civilizational dynamics have been instrumental in the development of IREA and, more specifically, in the shaping and transformation of international order in IREA. We will show the working of this dynamism in individual functional areas – geopolitics, industrial development, international security, regional community – through discussions in individual chapters. More importantly, each chapter forms a part of the discussion of the unfolding of the structure–institutions–international order dynamism in the overall development of IREA. Overall, the text will show how structural shifts and institutional and normative dynamics have led to the rise and transformations of the international order in East Asia in the past 150 years and how they are influencing IREA to evolve and develop going forward.

IREA AS A FIELD OF STUDY

East Asian international relations constitute a system of relations among nations actively engaging with one another in the region of the eastern part of Asia bordering on the Pacific Ocean. This book introduces students to IREA and offers access to knowledge and scholarship on this critically important subject. While discussing key concepts and issues, analytical frameworks, theories, and research methods, as well as forms and sources of material and data, the book focuses on a unique set of forces and dynamics that drive nations to engage with one another in politics, economics, security, and war, peace and development in East Asia. We investigate the unique power structures, patterns of economic competition and cooperation, and the institutions and normative practices that emerged from their engagement, interaction, and exchange that have helped shape the international order in modern East Asia. In discussing these systemic and functional issues in IREA, the book will cover the international policy and strategy of key countries of significant engagement and influence in IREA.

Treating IREA as a stand-alone subject is not without its challenges. In the first place, the boundary around the discipline of international relations is always contested. Different views exist as to whether international relations should be part of political science or the other way around, that international politics includes national politics. There is also the question of whether regional politics should be part of comparative politics or part of international politics. In a fully developed discipline of international relations, regional studies are always a very prominent subfield.

We treat IREA here as a subfield of international relations. This, however, is complicated, or enriched, by two interesting features of IREA studies. First, studies of IREA often lead us to investigate the forces and factors at the national level that have uniquely shaped relations and interactions in IREA. Quite a bit of scholarship on IREA has developed in the knowledge system of political science, political economy, development studies, sociology, area studies, and cultural studies.

Moreover, the field also draws on knowledge and scholarship from other subfields in IR, such as international security, foreign policy analysis, international political economy, and international diplomacy and history. Consequently, the subfield is influenced by the research focuses, theoretical frameworks, and research methodology in these other areas of the IR discipline.

As we will show in this book, the study of IREA is a study of a miniature system of international relations. Our focus, though, is on the underlying structure of IREA, the institutions and norms that sustain the structural relations, and the dynamics of stability and change in the international order that have shaped war and peace, and poverty and development in East Asia. This focus is manifest in our treatment of an individual functional area of IREA in each chapter, as well as in the theoretical explanation of IREA overall that fashions individual chapters into a coherent thesis.

WHY WE STUDY IREA

There are reasons why IREA has emerged as a popular subject area of study. East Asia is the last area in the world to be affected by the global expansion of the modern international system. It is an area that might have had its own coherent and distinct system that governs the actions of states and structures relations among them. The modern transformations of international order in East Asia in the past 150 years involved not only shifts in the interstate power structure in the region, but also changes in the institutions and normative practices in the conduct of international relations in East Asia. We are interested in how these different sets of dynamics shaped the evolution of the international order in IREA.

Moreover, the system, i.e., the way IREA are structured and organized, may have a role to play in producing some high-impact "East Asian miracles" in industrial development, political modernization, and cultural change in the twentieth century. We are interested in how IREA operate, what drives them, and what influences their development in different functional areas of IREA: in international security, industrial growth, trade, and culture and civilization. We intend to understand all of these in the broad context of established theories and practical experiences as to how a set of international relations progresses and operates in modern times.

Furthermore, there have been a significant number of "system-changing" international events and developments of global significance in post-1945 East Asia; for example, three major wars in the Cold War, waves of rapid industrial growth, and political liberalization in the 1980s and 1990s. Issues stemming from these events and developments decades ago remain high on the agenda in the practice of IREA. They have attracted a great deal of scholarly interest as well as policy efforts to analyze and forecast IREA for nations' more effective engagement with East Asia. Politicians, policymakers, and policy analysts, as well as business practitioners, social groups, and an engaged public, require knowledge and expertise on IREA and analysis and explanations on these issues.

Finally, as students of international relations, we are naturally interested in what we can learn from IREA about how the general international system works. IREA are a rich set of empirical content that can help us consider concepts and theories established in IR in explaining how international relations are shaped by whom or what, in what mechanisms and on what platforms, and to what ends. We are interested in how general IR knowledge is useful for us to understand IREA. On the other hand, with the rich practice and experience of East Asian states in international relations, our knowledge on IREA can make an important contribution to the development of IR as a body of knowledge.

THEORY, SCHOLARSHIP, AND POLICY ANALYSIS

The reasons for our interest in IREA also point to some of the challenges we face. The first challenge is how to balance between "seeking truth" from empirical material and using established concepts and theoretical frameworks and applying them to the empirical setting. This is a broad challenge for the social sciences generally, not just IREA students. But there is an element of uniqueness in this challenge to IREA studies. IREA are often seen as "non-Western" international relations, and as such, non-Western approaches might be required for explaining and interpreting IREA (Hoffman 1977; Holsti 1985; Acharya & Buzan 2010; Chan & Moore 2009). Identifying where these non-Western approaches come from, though, has been a challenge for attentive scholars and theorists for decades: from the East Asian intellectual traditions or from the ever-evolving practice of IREA? Our focus in this text is to scope knowledge on IREA rather than a non-Western theory of international relations. For this purpose, we engage established theories and concepts, Western or non-Western, to help us understand the empirical patterns and trends in specific functional and issue areas of IREA. We also explore the inherent logic underlying the patterns and driving their change in IREA and use this to frame the rich body of empirical material of IREA. The rich empirical material allows us to think about IREA theoretically. Chapter 2 will discuss this overall approach in greater depth.

The broad scholarly and policy interest in IREA also influences the focus and methods of research and the standards of scholarship in IR. There are pressures from various directions that combine to compel scholars to be more active and impactful and engage in policy issues, writing op-ed pieces, commissioned reports and community contributions, and to be active and effective in scholarly inquiry in systematic investigations on issues important for knowledge development on the subject. Both avenues of activity have their value in contributing to the development of knowledge and expertise under the current research environment. It is a challenge to ensure that both contribute to the growth of knowledge and the impact of our research.

This challenge can be further complicated by the politics of international policy with East Asia in the national capital where a different approach by the current administration can brush aside much of the research focus, knowledge products, and networks of knowledge production on IREA. As a student of international relations, we will want our knowledge and scholarly work to be useful for policy analysis and general practice of international relations. Understanding the dynamics of knowledge development and skill building in this regard would be useful for us to meet the challenge.

LEARNING STRATEGIES

In light of the preceding discussion, how do we go about studying this subject? More practically, how do we use this book for our classroom learning? Knowledge on IREA is organized in this text around a key "middle-range theory" in each chapter about what drives IREA in that functional area. In each chapter, you will learn to apply theoretical perspectives to the analysis of IREA in functional areas. These theoretical perspectives focus on geopolitical competition, structural dynamics, cultural and normative factors, transborder industrial integration, multilateral institutions, nontraditional challenges, domestic structures, and global structure and international society, and how they have influenced the shaping of the international order in a particular functional area of IREA.

Chapter 4 looks at geopolitics in East Asia in the analytical tradition of classical realism. It focuses on the unique causes of war and conditions for peace in IREA and the role of geopolitical competition of the major powers in the shaping of contemporary IREA: Japan, China, United States, ASEAN, and middle powers. Chapter 4 represents a conventional account of IREA and an application of one of the middle-range theories to IREA. In the overall framework explaining IREA, it forms part of the investigation of the forces in the power distribution in East Asia.

Chapter 5 takes this discussion of power distribution in IREA in a more rigorous structuralist direction. It focuses on the formation and transformation of the international structure in IREA and its defining character. The chapter asks whether there was an international structure in IREA and how these structures emerged and evolved in the context of Cold War East Asia. More importantly, it asks whether the bipolar structure that developed was the effect of the structural dynamics in the historical evolution of the power structure in IREA or that of the unique sets of conditions during the Cold War. In exploring this topic, the chapter highlights the organization of alliances and partnerships in each camp as evidence for the role of institutional arrangements and normative practices in the shaping of the bipolar structure.

Chapter 6 investigates the cultural, normative, and civilizational dynamics that have shaped IREA and the emergent normative structure that sustains the international order in IREA. In particular, the chapter works carefully to consider "East Asian culture," or civilization, and its contemporary development and transformation. East Asian culture is believed to be an important variable defining the distinct character of IREA. Chapter 6 shows that culture, social values and national identity have significantly changed in East Asian nations. This has blurred the traditional boundary between East and West and replaces it with a divide between "liberal" and "conservative" that aligns states into different groups. The chapter explains why and how culture matters in IREA today.

Chapter 7 discusses the growth of national capabilities of East Asian states. This distinct growth in their industrial, financial, and trading capabilities adds new dynamics to the power distribution in IREA and influences the power structure underlying the international order. Moreover, the chapter explores the institutions and normative practices of national and transborder organization of industrial production in East Asia. The flying geese pattern of industrial development and flying geese model of regional industrial diffusion are the focus of the chapter's discussion.

Chapter 8 focuses on the building of multilateral institutions for such an economic community in East Asia in the past 30 years. We use methods and frameworks of institutional analysis and employ concepts and theories of multilateral institutionalism to assess how regional economic cooperation and integration have been achieved. Chapter 8 discusses the politics of East Asian regionalism and engages the debate over the role of multilateral institutions and market forces of industrial development in regional economic cooperation and integration.

Chapter 9 discusses the role of multilateral institutions in shaping the international security order in East Asia. The chapter examines the rise of the movement of multilateral institutionalism and the shaping of a new international security in post–Cold War East Asia. It investigates the challenge of institutionalizing commitments to common security and building confidence and trust among dialogue partners and the piecemeal, accumulative process of reaching agreement on the rules and norms of states to act for a security order in East Asia. The chapter discusses the dependency of institutions on the power structure for their effectiveness in ensuring a regional security order.

The unique form and substance of transnational challenges in IREA and the rise of international institutions to organize regional governance to meet those challenges are discussed in Chapter 10. The chapter uses a range of practical cases to show that growing transborder ethnic, religious, civilizational, and economic interests and activities are increasingly requiring some form of effective management and governance for the security and wellbeing of people in the region. The state-centric international institutions are inadequate in meeting this challenge. New institutional arrangements and norms are developing to form an international order on transnational issues.

Chapter 11 investigates the domestic sources of international behavior of East Asian states and the impact of the state's "internal structures" on the international order in the region. Structural effects and institutional dynamics transcend state boundaries. The chapter explores how domestic structures, institutions, and normative practices in domestic politics influence state behavior, action, and policy and, ultimately, how the domestic power structure translates into international institutions and policy, and influences the shaping of the international order.

Chapter 12 analyzes the changing relations between East Asia and the international system. East Asia itself has transformed significantly in the twentieth century. The chapter examines the general claims that IREA have been significantly shaped by the world power structure, international society, and the current global international order. It discusses in detail how and to what extent the forces of IREA influence the world power structure, international society, and the global international order. It suggests a two-way influence between IREA and global IR. But more importantly, the chapter highlights the original sources of the shaping of the international order in East Asia.

The two chapters immediately following this frame the foregoing material into a coherent theme on the dynamism of IREA. Chapter 2 looks at various different theories, largely nationally privileged perspectives, on the structure, institutions, and order of IREA and lays out a framework that centers on the mutually constitutive roles of the international structure and institutional and normative dynamics in the shaping of the international order in IREA. This theoretical framework helps connect discussions in the individual chapters into a logical process of the historical evolution of IREA: the power distribution and its shifts, development in institutional arrangements and normative practices, and the stability and transformation of the international order.

Chapter 3 investigates the historical instances of the transformation of international order in East Asia. It presents more empirical material on what is explained in our explanation of IREA. The chapter discusses the distinct interstate power structure and institutional arrangements and normative practices that underlay each of these international orders and shows the effects of the dynamics of the interstate power structure and institutions and norms on the transformation of one international order into another. In this exercise, the chapter highlights some of the key indicators and methods in the analysis of international orders and their transformation.

There seems to be a historical sequence in the subject matters these chapters deal with. This in a way helps us to understand the dynamic nature of IREA and the logical relations between the different aspects of IREA. Structural shift, institutional change, normative adaption, and the transformation of the international order take time to connect and effectuate. There has been a distinct pattern of transformation of the international order in East Asia over the past 150 years. The development of the different ways IREA are organized and different mechanisms in which IREA are enabled brings us back to the central questions: Have IREA evolved to improve the way they are organized in the historical shifts in the power structure and institutional and normative dynamics of IREA? Have IREA moved from one set of power relations and institutions to another? Are all of these forms of power and influence still available in the toolbox of IREA? Do these forms of power and influence and the patterns of change in IREA constitute a distinct system of international relations? We hope to provide some answers to these questions over the course of the chapters that follow.

The text here presents a large amount of material and evidence, as well as scholarship, on these issues and topics. For a learning strategy, the reader may focus on one or two particular functional areas – security and military dynamics, great powers and geopolitics, regional political economy and geoeconomics, cultural dynamics and national identity, values and normative structure, transnational challenges, multilateral institutions, domestic structures, East Asia in international society, and so forth. One could also focus on the theoretical side of these topics and investigate whether there are such things as international structures, institutions, and orders and, if so, how they might work and how one has influenced the others in the evolution of IREA. You will take structuralist, institutionalist, or cultural theories, for example, to task and critically examine them in the working of IREA. Or you might come up with something of your own making.

The text is also written within a context of a changing scholarly environment and system of material, information, and content distribution. In a traditional scholarly environment, detailed material and information are often essential as evidence presented in texts on a specific subject matter. However, such materials are increasingly available in digital form, with instant accessibility, on fully developed content holding platforms and, best of all, in the public domain. This text would serve as a guide on locating and assessing these contents and materials while leaving more space for the text itself on analysis, interpretation, discussion, and overall framing. The text, after all, is aimed at enabling the reader to acquire solid knowledge on the significant experiences, events, and developments in IREA, an ability to identify patterns in IREA in a particular region, a set of skills to interpret or explain a particular pattern as an instance of how an international system works, and, from there hopefully, some ability to forecast the unfolding of these patterns in the years or decades to come as IREA continue to evolve as we look on.

Further Reading

Acharya, Amitav, 1997. "Ideas, Identity, and Institution-Building: From the 'ASEAN Way' to the 'Asia-Pacific Way'?" *The Pacific Review* 10(3):319–346.

Gilpin, Robert, 1981. *War and Change in World Politics*. Cambridge: Cambridge University Press.

Goh, Evelyn, 2013. *The Struggle for Order: Hegemony, Hierarchy, and Transition in Post-Cold War East Asia*. Oxford: Oxford University Press.

Ikenberry, G. John, 2015. *Power, Order, and Change in World Politics*. Cambridge: Cambridge University Press.

Inoguchi, Takashi, and Edward Newman, 2002. "Towards an East Asian IR Community?" *Journal of East Asian Studies* 2(1): 11–20.

Katzenstein, Peter J., 2002. "Area Studies, Regional Studies, and International Relations," *Journal of East Asian Studies* 2(1): 127–138.

Lake, David A., 1984. "Beneath the Commerce of Nations: A Theory of International Economic Structures," *International Studies Quarterly* 28(2):143–170.

Lake, David A., 2009. *Hierarchy in International Relations*. Ithaca: Cornell University Press.

Pekkanen, Saadia, John Ravenhill, and Rosemary Foot, 2014. *The Oxford Handbook of the International Relations of Asia*. Oxford: Oxford University Press.

Waltz, Kenneth, 1979. *Theory of International Politics*. New York: McGraw-Hill.

2 Theorizing IREA

In This Chapter...

- Conventional framings of IREA
- Nation and state in war and peace
- Bipolarity
- Regional industrial diffusion
- East Asian theories
- "IR Theory with Chinese characteristics"
- Does Japan have an IR theory?
- "Korea between empires"
- Regional identity and an ASEAN IR theory
- National theories and a theory of IREA
- A framework for IREA

Learning Objectives

By the end of this chapter, you will be able to
- Understand early scholarly attempts to develop an understanding of IREA
- Understand key middle-range theories that explain IREA in a particular functional or issue area
- Understand that national theories of international relations in East Asia are not a theory of IREA
- Understand how IREA scholarship relates to policy analysis and the practice of IREA
- Use the analytical framework developed here to identify your research interests and analyze IREA.

While the field of IREA is relatively young, efforts to understand the distinct patterns and character of IREA and their historical transformations are substantive. Questions are often raised over whether there is an East Asian theory of international relations or if there is an IR theory in East Asia (Acharya & Buzan 2007; Inoguchi 2007; Qin 2007; IRAP 2017). The perceived "poverty of theory" in IREA may have a lot to do with the paradigmatic dominance of the "American social science of international relations" (Hoffmann 1977; Holsti 1985). This dominance has left little space for genuine IR theory to develop on a distinct set of international relations such as IREA.

This, though, has not prevented scholars from applying established frameworks and approaches to the study of IREA and developing useful knowledge on how IREA works in a functional area or in the practice of a nation in IREA. The field has been influenced by scholarship in other disciplines such as history, culture, sociology, law, and economics, for example. This influence has contributed to the development of knowledge and understanding of IREA in functional areas and to the development of distinct methods and frameworks in the scholarly analyses. National theories of international relations in East Asia have witnessed rapid growth. This seems to be a response to anxieties over the lack of a "non-Western theory" of international relations. These national theories partially focus on IREA as seen particularly from the perspective of a given country and show the close connection between IR knowledge and the analysis of international practices of the state.

As will be shown in this chapter, there have been plenty of theoretical activities in search of a theory of IREA. Because of their different disciplinary and paradigmatic traditions as well as national focuses, these activities are not connected in an analytically meaningful way to form a coherent theory of IREA. More importantly, it seems unclear as to what might be the focus of such an IREA theory. Shih Chih-yu, for example, identifies several "local schools" of international relations in Asia that include those of Beijing, Kyoto, Delhi, Sydney, Seoul, and ASEAN schools of international relations (Shih 2010, 2013) and considers them as "civilizational perspectives" of international relations. Shih dislikes seeing them as "national" and believes they are not "international." Critically, these "local schools" are not about IREA; they are about IR.

Takashi Inoguchi (Inoguchi 2007), on the other hand, confirms the existence of activities theorizing international relations in Japan as early as the 1920s and 1930s. Inoguchi identifies Nishida Kitaro's constructivist thinking on the ontological nature of international relations, Tabata Shigejiro's theory based on international law and individual freedom, and Hirano Yoshitaro's theorizing on regional integration as three representative cases of the "middle-range" theories of international relations in Japan. Inoguchi clearly sees IR theories in Japan as more of an extension and pluralist development of the social science in the "American academy" (Inoguchi & Bacon 2001: 1). These middle-range theories are not national theories of international relations; they are theories of international relations in a functional or issue area. They may represent a theory of an aspect of IREA.

In a project designed to explore the possibility of an Asian IR theory, Amitav Acharya and Barry Buzan surveyed subregional IR theory activities and found that Western IR theory dominated in Asia and that "the likely main movement in Asia was toward national schools of IR" (Amitav & Buzan 2007: 342). They saw the danger that the discipline could "fragment." Ten years on, when they revisited the issue, they found that the trends remained intact but also that new developments had emerged in connecting local IR theory to the development of a global IR. It is here, though, that interest in an East Asian theory of international relations is most likely mixed up with an interest in a theory of IREA. Acharya and Busan, like Shih and many others in the field, are not interested in a theory of IREA. They are interested in an East Asian theory of international relations.

These surveys of IR theories in East Asia highlight a dilemma or challenge for a theory of IREA, and the aforementioned theoretical activities are driven by a powerful desire to develop different theoretical perspectives – East Asian, Asian, non-Western, Chinese, Japanese – to international relations, in response to the dominance of the American social science of international relations and a strong belief in a more pluralist global research community of IR theory. They mostly focus on explaining why and how an East Asian nation thinks and acts in terms of international relations, presumably differently from their counterparts in American or British social science schools. What seems to be missing in these theoretical activities is the subject of IREA itself, the matters that a theory of IREA is to explain: What is IREA? How has it changed? And what has driven those changes?

On the other hand, these theorizing activities concern primarily the international relations involved with East Asian nations or East Asia overall and their impact on those nations. They help frame IREA and are relevant to a theory of IREA. These national or functional theories are all "middle-range" theories that explain some aspects of IREA in a functional area – geopolitics, industrial development, security, institutions – or a distinct set of IREA – national, cultural, civilizational, transnational. These middle-range theories serve as building blocks for a theory of IREA and help us to think about IREA theoretically: what is IREA, how does it work, and what has influenced its development?

This chapter aims to guide the reader through some of these significant perspectives and activities. National theories are examined to show influential national perspectives and theorizing activities in IREA and how a particular set of IREA, for example, China's relations with the United States, is rationalized. Selected middle range theories in functional areas will be briefly discussed to show how they possibly contribute to a theory of IREA. These will be fully discussed in the chapter on IREA in this particular functional area.

Discussions here lay the groundwork for a discipline-based framework to help us think about IREA theoretically and holistically. The chapter ends with a fuller discussion of the theoretical framework touched on briefly in Chapter 1. This theoretical framework will serve to help connect the various "middle-range theories" on different aspects of IREA and explain the overall patterns and dynamism of IREA. In doing so, the framework will help integrate discussions in different chapters in this text into a coherent argument on what IREA is and what drives IREA.

CONVENTIONAL FRAMINGS OF IREA

The first group of those scholars was composed of historians, international law specialists, and growth economists who were intrigued primarily by how modern international relations emerged in East Asia. This does not seem to be that unusual in the development of knowledge of international relations as a discipline. For different reasons, these scholars from various disciplines brought in well-established frameworks and insights from international practices of Europe and North America, and applied them to the rich empirical content of interstate activities, interactions, and relations in and on the Far East.

The primary contribution of their theorizing activities to a theory of IREA is they represent early attempts to scope out and conceptualize an entity of East Asia and bring the notion of "international" and "civilizational" to the well-established world order in this region. In doing so, these scholars have built up a theoretical framework that sees IREA as being shaped more by forces external to the region in the practical interaction between European powers and institutions on the one hand and the East Asian world order on the other. This analytical tradition also emphasizes, particularly in its later and more recent developments, the role of modern international institutions and norms as an important set of enabling mechanisms in the organization of IREA and the shaping of the international order in IREA. This analytical tradition captures the dynamism and tension in the transformation of the traditional East Asian world order in a modern international order in IREA from the late nineteenth century.

John K. Fairbank, a historian at Harvard University, looked at the Chinese world order in East Asia and described vividly the structure and institutions of that world order in the nineteenth century. European powers encountered the Chinese world order in their advance to continental East Asia (Fairbank 1968). A world order is different from an international order. The latter is informed primarily by the institutions of the modern nation-state system. Fairbank explains how China's relations with other polities were structured and institutionalized in nineteenth-century East Asia. He identifies two particular sets of institutions and mechanisms that sustained the Chinese world order: a set of concentric circles of different types of political relations between "China" and other polities in East Asia and beyond, and a set of institutional arrangements and normative practices that support the tributary relations. The tribute system is a set of institutionalized interstate practices in which representatives of countries went to the Chinese capital and paid tributes in ceremonial form to the Emperor of China in recognition of the moral and spiritual connections between Heaven, the Chinese Emperor, and the tribute state, and the political and economic connections between the Chinese state and the tribute state.

Fairbank believes this is how China related to other polities in the world and managed its relations with them. This represents perhaps one of the first systematic attempts in modern scholarship in English to conceptualize the structure and institutions of interstate relations in East Asia and theorize about the rise of the hegemonic and hierarchic world order in East Asia. This scholarly tradition has further developed and expanded in recent years considering the rise of China today in its capacity to shape and influence the region and how China organizes its efforts to that end (Cohen 2000; Kang 2010; MacKay 2015; Lee 2017). This intellectual tradition prompts scholars to consider the scope, structure, and institutions of IREA and to recognize that there was a self-sustained system of interstate relations in East Asia then and that system, given the particular intellectual resources it draws on to analyze, was more a product of the interaction between China and "the world" around it.

This tradition of framing IREA is carried on by scholars of the English school of international relations theory in a different way, more from the perspective of the global spread of the prevailing institutions and norms of international society. A key concept in the English school explaining the rise and expansion of the modern international system, –international society is a community of nation states who conduct their relations within a framework of widely accepted norms, and settle their disputes, conflicts, and wars among themselves by a set of agreed-on principles and rules.

As the Europe-originated modern international system expanded globally (Bull 1977; Bull & Watson 1984; Watson 1992), it encountered more states from outside the system. The way in which these states, presumably following distinct sets of rules and norms of their own in conducting interstate relations, learned to follow the rules and norms of international society in their engagement with the international system represented a challenge. Garry Gong, for example, investigates the "standard of civilization," and how the rules and norms extended to Asia, and how non-Western nations, Japan, China, Thailand, and Turkey in his case, learned diplomacy, practiced international law, and entered international society by accepting and internalizing the rules and norms of diplomacy, conflict resolution, and international treaties in their conduct of interstate relations (Gong 1984). While Gong sees this as being about the "standard of civilization," it is really about international law and legal practices in Gong's case studies. These are the core institutions of modern international relations.

The concept of international society is central to this exercise and to the English school's theorizing about the rise of modern international relations in the non-Western world. The English school's application to IREA demystifies the notion of East Asia and the institutional basis of modern IREA. This tradition has continued to serve as an influential framework for explaining contemporary IREA and advanced further in two different directions: first in the possibility of an international society of East Asia (Zhang and Busan 2014) and second in how IREA fits in with the shaping of global governance and global international society (Clark 2014; see a fuller discussion of this in Chapter 12).

Beyond the institutional core of the analyses, both the Chinese world order and the standard of civilization involve looking at IREA as a civilization and seeing how different polities relate to one another under this civilizational framework. Civilization here is taken as a large ethnic, religious, and cultural community that develops over a long historical period with a distinct set of social structures, institutions, and normative practices in organizing the political economy of the community. This civilizational tradition goes back as far as Arnold J. Toynbee (1934), who treated China, Japan, and Korea as part of Far Eastern civilization, one of the four third-generation civilizations in human history. Taking China, Korea, Japan, and Vietnam as part of East Asian civilization, influential scholars have investigated in detail the civilizational substance of East Asia and the institutions of state and interstate organization (for further discussions in Chapters 6 and 12). These included John Fairbank and Edwin Reischauer, with their Harvard project on East Asian tradition (1960), and William Theodore De Bary and Shmuel Eisenstadt, with their project on East Asian civilizations (De Bary 1988; Eisenstadt 1997).

The scholarly tradition of East Asian civilization theorizes a more organically interconnected human experience in East Asia larger than the nation and explains the unique institutional arrangements of interstate relations therein. Civilization is a prevalent form of large-scale political economic organization informed by the natural and technological conditions of the time. The East Asian civilization thesis adds a significant cultural element to the conceptualization of the structure and institutions of polity organization in East Asia. In doing so, it exposes the historical and institutional roots of the distinct form in which political economy in East Asia is organized and how interstate relations are structured and institutionalized.

IR scholarship has grown on the basis of analyses of state behavior and action and patterns of interstate interaction, exchange, and organization from traditional disciplinary areas such as history, international law, society, culture, and civilization. There is no exception to this in the growth of knowledge of IREA. In the development of scholarship on IREA, however, history has come to shape it in a way that theories and frameworks built on European experiences are not always equipped to capture the rich empirical content of IREA. Institutions in which European states encountered East Asian states in the nineteenth century did have significant effects on the shaping of IREA. It is, however, the development of geopolitics and political economy in East Asia before and after the nineteenth century that has lent important dynamics to the growth of the structure and institutions in IREA and to the transformation of international orders in East Asia. This is an area we will revisit with an in-depth investigation in subsequent chapters, Chapter 12 in particular.

NATION AND STATE IN WAR AND PEACE

Inquiries into the patterns of war and peace in contemporary East Asia led to the rise of a nation-state theory of IREA that centers around the indeterminacy of both the nation and the state in their capacity, identity, and authority, and around how political efforts to determine them led to a series of civil and international conflicts and wars in the early decades of the post-1945 East Asia. This theoretical perspective developed from empirical research on the causes of wars and conflicts in post-1945 East Asia. It argues that civil tensions over statehood for a newly independent nation further divided the nation. With each political force in national politics allied with external powers, civil conflicts became international conflicts. This mixture of forces of civil and international conflict led to the wars in Korea, Vietnam, over the Taiwan Straits, and in many Southeast Asian countries during the Cold War.

This theoretical perspective has contributed to a theory of IREA. Unlike the conventional framings pointed out in the preceding discussion, these perspectives look for forces internal to East Asian states as the primary forces that drive war and peace in IREA. In particular, they focus on the contention of political forces at the national level over the structure and institutions of the state. These political dynamics influence the shaping of both the state and the nation. With the long list of countries that went through this process in post-1945 East Asia, the outcomes of these processes significantly determined the structure and institutions of IREA.

European powers came to East Asia and brought new global geopolitical and geoeconomic dynamics to the region. After World War II, newly emerging nation-states were set up in East Asia and accepted by political forces of all persuasions as the only legitimate units in organizing the political world in East Asia. We witnessed continual tensions, conflicts, and repeated instances of large-scale wars in East Asia, from the Korean War in the early 1950s to the Vietnam War in the 1960s and 1970s, as well as conflicts across the Taiwan Straits in the 1950s. There were small-scale conflicts as well, between China and the Soviet Union in 1969, between China and India in 1962, between China and Vietnam in 1979, and between China and the United States over the South China Sea in 2010s. Various internal and transborder conflicts and tensions also erupted in and among the new states of Southeast Asia, in addition to various low-intensity wars among the states and various ethnic, religious, and ideological communities and populations.

IR scholars asked questions. Was East Asia more prone to traditional geopolitical conflict and war? If so, why? Bruce Cummings took up the challenge of investigating why we had the Korean War. That war is a case of how political structure influences national identity and shapes the institutions of the state; it also illustrates the tension between nation and state in the formation of new East Asian states. In his 606-page thesis on the origins of the Korean War (Cumings 1981), Cumings shows us that it was the domestic political conflict between two ideologically opposing political forces, the progressive and conservative forces in Korea, that led to the emergence of two states out of the Korean nation, and the tension between the two states, and between one nation and two states, that led to the Korean War and lasting tensions and conflicts afterwards (see the more detailed discussion on this in Chapter 4).

Analyses and investigations of the causes of war and sources of geopolitical conflict in East Asia also mushroomed over the Vietnam War, the conflict in the Taiwan Straits and conflicts in Southeast Asia. Earlier analyses of IREA largely looked for causal factors or motivating forces from outside East Asia and the ways in which East Asian states interacted with and responded to the world to understand developments in IREA. The new studies look at the enabling forces of war and peace in East Asia and within the countries themselves and the tension between nation and state that uniquely developed in early postwar East Asia. In doing this, such studies show that the substance of IREA is generated from within East Asian nations as much as they are influenced by global geopolitical forces, and there has emerged a repeated pattern of progressive and conservative forces contesting state power in these states.

This tension in nation building and state making at the same time (see further discussions in Chapters 4 and 10) drove much of the civil and international conflict in East Asian countries over the identity, boundaries, or authority of nation and state that we would otherwise consider the effects of conventional geopolitics or nationalism. Investigations into the problem of mutual constitution of nation and state, often by scholars of comparative politics, East Asian (country) studies, and modern state building, form a strong intellectual tradition that uniquely explains war and peace in East Asia.

BIPOLARITY

Inquiries into the patterns of war and peace in contemporary East Asia and, further, into the dynamics of great power politics and the organization of collective forces for security in post-1945 East Asia have also led to the rise of a structural theory.

This theory focuses on the pattern of a bipolar distribution of power in continental East Asia and maritime East Asia over the East Asian crescent. This power distribution brought about not only the three large-scale armed conflicts along the East Asian crescent in the early Cold War years but also the subsequent *longue durée* of "East Asian peace."

Structural theory is not new in IR theory. But Kenneth Waltz has never had a real empirical test of his structural theory of international relations. The fact that IREA can be more effectively analyzed in a structural theory not only enriches structuralism in IR theory; it also makes a unique contribution to a theory of IREA. It argues that an international structure can be operative in a confined set of international relations, for example, in IREA. What drives or shapes IREA can be reduced to the measurable and observable pattern of distribution of power of states and their effects on state actions and relations.

The bifurcation of political forces in East Asian states extended to force a pattern of distribution at the regional level. This suggests the existence of a parallel bipolar, region-wide distribution of force that shapes the structure, motivates the states, and rationalizes interstate institutions and normative practices in IREA. Was there a set of East Asia–wide dynamics that structured the distribution of interests and capability of states to go to war? Focused research on IREA during the Cold War seems to suggest a yes to that question. Michael Yahuda, in his pioneering work on IREA (Yahuda 1996), spent a large part of the book to trace the rise and development of the bipolar structure in IREA during the Cold War.

The bipolar national political structure between conservative and progressive forces in East Asian states manifested at the regional level where political interests, relations, and war fighting capabilities were lined up through alliance and partnership to balance the opposition between communist continental East Asia and anticommunist maritime East Asia. Figure 2.1 illustrates the bipolar structure and pattern of actual distribution and networking of forces and capabilities of states in IREA at the high point of the Cold War in the 1960s.

The East Asia crescent in Figure 2.1 is a zone of engagement between the two collective forces where the three major wars and conflicts in East Asia were located. This brings in a different theory as to why states and nations waged these wars in East Asia. The international structure here is a unique set of power relations that collectively exert effects on states and pressuring them to act in a certain way in international relations, for example, to use force or seek alliances for national survival and security (see the full discussion of this theory of IREA in Chapter 4).

Seeing IREA in this way vindicates, among other things, the notion of East Asia as a substantive system of international relations where the underlying international structure is clearly identifiable and effective at instigating international activities and strategic action and interaction among states in IREA. More importantly, it theorizes the pattern of states' intentions and engagement in war and peace in East Asia, which are significantly influenced by the power of the bipolar structure.

Moving from traditional geopolitical analysis of the patterns of IREA to a more structuralist analysis of IREA echoes the development of mainstream IR theory

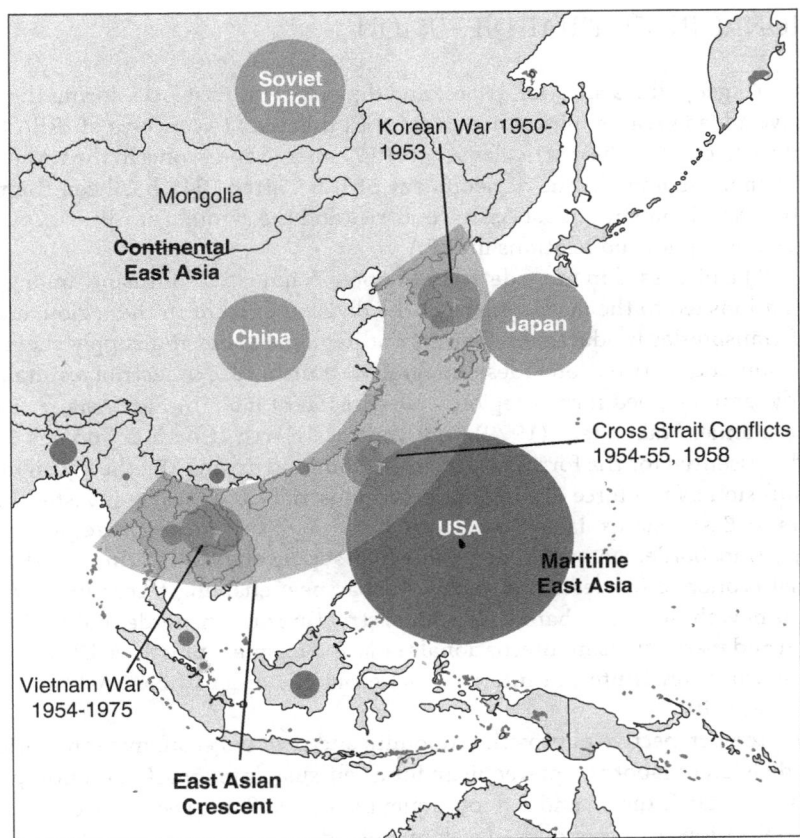

Figure 2.1 Theorizing structural bifurcation in IREA
States geopolitically located and networked in two large blocs in continental and maritime East Asia. The size of a country's circle illustrates the relative size of its international interests and capabilities, as measured in real GDP in 1969
Data source: PWT9.0 (2017)

from realism to neorealism in the 1970s and 1980s. When the Cold War ended, IREA scholars continued to ponder whether the same geopolitical logic operates in East Asia as in Europe in the nineteenth century (Friedberg 2003), about the precise nature of the structure of IREA (Cha 2010; Goh 2007), about whether the Cold War structure was a permanent feature of IREA and would continue to shape IREA, and whether the frameworks centered on traditional geopolitical logic and structure ignored something important in IREA in explaining war or its absence (Acharya 2003b). We will present a full discussion of structural theory and how it explains IREA in Chapter 5.

REGIONAL INDUSTRIAL DIFFUSION

Traditional geopolitics and war, peace, and diplomacy in East Asia during the Cold War have added great empirical material for IR theorists to conceive of IREA theoretically: what makes this particular set of IREA emerge and evolve in the way it has? What is more striking in the development of IREA after 1945 has been the rapid industrial development of East Asian countries and the significant role of economic and trade dynamics and relations in IREA.

As will be discussed in more detail in Chapter 7, industrial diffusion among East Asian nations led to the development of the division of labor in the region and the rise of transborder production networks and regional value and supply chains for production and distribution. These integrative transborder industrial, capital, and trade dynamics helped form a region-wide division of labor in East Asia, a process that Immanuel Wallerstein (1979) and Douglass North (North & Thomas 1976) consider essential for the formation of an economic structure. The theory on industrial diffusion as the force driving national industrial capital to be invested across borders in East Asia explains how East Asian states seek to organize production through transborder networks, and value and supply chains. It brings to the fore national economic interests and capabilities as new enabling forces in IREA and explains how these forces shape the regional structure of transborder industrial production and institutions in international trade and business practices. Ultimately, it explains what constitutes an international economic order in East Asia and what causes it to shift.

From the perspective of growth economics and regional economic integration, a single division of labor is a prerequisite for a self-sustaining market economy. East Asian industrial diffusion and the consequent so-called flying geese pattern of rapid industrialization and economic development added a new set of self-generated dynamics to the region, which had been dominated by great power politics and geopolitical tensions and conflict. Those who work on institution building for regional economic integration and cooperation (see full discussion in Chapter 8) and on the long East Asian peace (Chapter 4) theorize that these new integral dynamics are what's driving the persistent efforts of nations to institutionalize economic cooperation and led to the long peace and prosperity in post-1949 East Asia.

Furthermore, the integrative economic forces encountered the prevailing "international institutions" and national institutions, that is, the institutions of national sovereignty, currency exchange, taxes, banking, dispute settlements, and multilateral regulations. These institutions influence and structure the movement of economic interests and capabilities across borders. Transborder division of labor is a form of production organization where different growth inputs – capital, labor, technology, resources, markets – are connected to a single production process in a wider transborder area where efficiency gains are possible with production in different countries having their own comparative advantage. A large body of scholarship in the field has investigated the conditions and consequences of East Asian regionalism and the international political economy of organizing transborder production and service provision. We will discuss this topic in greater detail in Chapter 8.

The question for those who see the new dynamics shaping the international order in East Asia is whether East Asia has emerged as an economic community with a single and system-wide division of labor. The debate continues. Scholars debate the scope of "East Asia" – whether that includes Northeast Asia and Southeast Asia or whether it is East Asia proper or Asia-Pacific that includes a greater number of Asia-Pacific countries. They also debate the integrative nature of the division of labor – whether this is just a scholarly construct – and how empirically we can identify the boundary of the single division of labor in East Asia. But these scholarly explorations and debates add up to something of theoretical significance. Beyond geopolitics, which is traditionally believed to be the primary force responsible for shaping structures and institutions in IREA, homegrown economic dynamics have significantly influenced the play of IREA and shaped the international order in the region.

This is particularly significant for the development of an IREA theory. In conventional geopolitics-centered frameworks, IREA are often seen more as the effect of the interaction of external stimuli and East Asian responses. The new approach to regional economic growth recognizes a very important set of new, "endogenous" dynamics in the shaping of IREA and draws our attention to how the logic of industrial development brought the large region of East Asia together and guided it toward the formation of an economic community.

EAST ASIAN THEORIES

Investigating the forces enabling IREA and extending the focus on external, structural factors to internal and economic forces has enabled us to gain a broader and fuller understanding of IREA, of what drives IREA, and how these factors help shape an international order in IREA. It is worth noting that major perspectives and analyses of IREA come from academics and researchers trained in an English-speaking scholarly environment. This is part of the large phenomenon Staley Hoffman tried to bring to our attention decades ago. In an essay in 1977, Hoffman reminds us that international relations have become "an American social science" (Hoffman 1977: 41), because, for one thing, the field in different countries is dominated by academics trained in the United States.

US dominance in IR studies is not just about where the researchers are trained but also the logical expectation that they were more likely to use the theoretical frameworks and methods with which they are familiar through their training, in search of patterns and explanations in IREA. Teaching, Research, and International Policy (TRIP) Project surveys have over the years followed this issue and assessed the development of the discipline in different countries around the world. In its latest survey (2014), it still confirms "US hegemony" in global IR teaching and research (Maliniak et al. 2018).

The report is ambiguous on the problem of the lack of diversity. Diversity in its investigation is measured by the extent to which national identity is manifest in the frameworks, theories, and methodologies academics use in their teaching and research in these different countries. The latest survey does not make clear the extent to which IR teachers and researchers in East Asian countries use their own content and frameworks, from their own perspectives, and for their own purposes. This itself is not a problem as many strong national IR theorists have feared. In a way, it is simply how the modern discipline of IR has historically evolved, reflecting the pathway by which the empirical part of the subject has developed.

A question it raises, though, is whether IR can be a discipline like physics where its content and knowledge respects no national boundaries or scope or whether knowledge of the discipline centers around the position of a nation-state that significantly engages with the world given the very nature of *international* relations. Early on, the English school attempted to provide an answer to this question, as have the French tradition before it and the Danish school in more recent times.

In East Asia, the rise of national theories of international relations is particularly strong. This is reflected not only in the general assessment of the discipline (Tickner & Wæver 2009) but also in the waves of debate among IREA scholars themselves over the nature of an East Asian theory of international relations (IRAP 2017; Acharya & Buzan 2007, 2010, 2017). A tension is visible in the debates and discussions over a theory of IREA versus an East Asian theory of international relations. A theory of IREA is an analytical framework explaining the forces that drive or shape the development of IREA. An East Asian theory of international relations is an IR theory in East Asian states and by their scholars, which tends to become nationally focused. These national perspectives theorize, to the extent they do so at all, international relations, not IREA, from the perspective of the East Asian nation. The development of a theory of IREA has been weak because of the dominance of not only the American social science but also national theories of international relations in East Asia.

Several reasons explain the dominance of national theories in the development of an IREA theory. First, the rise of national IR theories seems to be a response to the problem of the global dominance of American IR theory. The criticism of the American dominance in IR theory is based on the premise that IR theory is and can be organized nationally. This logically called for strengthening of IR theory by other nations. East Asian states have been mostly active in post-1945 international relations. East Asian states have been principal participants in the global dramas of international relations that played out in East Asia. They draw great insight from these unique experiences as to what modern international relations are and how geopolitics, industrial development, international institutions, identity, and norms work. This provided rich and dynamic empirical material for theoretical analyses and investigations from the perspective of East Asian states.

More importantly, East Asian countries have a long-standing professional tradition in which academics work for their country in terms of the purpose and perspective of IR research and analysis and for the state in terms of policy input and impact, a scholarly tradition in East Asian states that Xiaoming Huang calls the state-centric tradition in modern studies of international relations (Huang 2007). National theories of international relations in these East Asian countries have developed for the practice of international relations of the state.

This is an aspect of the development of the IR discipline Hoffman noted in his original thesis that the American IR discipline is strongly connected with and influenced by US international practices at the time. The IR profession in East Asian countries is institutionally and socially structured to connect a country's theories and analysis of international relations and its practice of international relations. National identity and purpose are naturally influential in IR scholarship and the profession. In the sections that follow, we discuss several representative national IR theories in East Asian states to show the rich activities of theorizing international relations in East Asia and how these states theorize international relations to guide their practice in international relations. In doing so, we will show how their theories cover only partially the patterns and dynamics of IREA.

"IR THEORY WITH CHINESE CHARACTERISTICS"

A national theory of international relations is nowhere more evident than in China. The notion of "the Chinese theory of international relations" or "an IR theory with Chinese characteristics," as many Chinese IR scholars would put it, started to emerge in the 1990s. Over the 30 years of its development, the search for a Chinese theory of international relations has developed the field of IR theory in China into an enterprise almost like the "American social science" of international relations (Hoffmann 1977: 41). Competing theoretical perspectives mushroomed to theorize international relations as China sees it. Representative perspectives include the theory of moral realism of Yan Xuetong (2018), the relational theory of world politics of Qin Yaqing (2018), the Tianxia system of Zhao Tingyang (2011), and many other "theories" intended to frame major policy initiatives of the state, such as the Three World theory, peaceful rise theory, human community theory, Belt and Road theory, and so forth. The first set of theories uses theoretical resources from American social science and Chinese intellectual traditions. "Theory" in the second group has somewhat different connotations, and its function is closely related to China's practice and policy in international relations of the time.

One of the earlier attempts to "theorize" international relations from the national perspective of China was Mao's Three World theory in the 1970s. Though it is labeled a theory, the Three World theory was largely a policy guideline for China's strategic engagement with different parts of the world in the 1970s and 1980s. It is a worldview that informed Mao's thinking about China's position in the world political structure and its strategy to strengthen its position. This worldview stated that the world is divided into three parts: The United States and USSR were in the First World, most developing countries were part of the Third World, and between them were countries of the Second World, mostly developed countries. The Three World theory provided a policy justification for China's international strategy of working with those in the Third and Second Worlds against the hegemonic powers of the First World. As a theory, though, it recognizes the effect of the international power structure on the shaping of international interests and strategy of China.

Efforts in Chinese IR scholarship for a Chinese theory of international relations (Qin 2007, 2011; Zhang & Chang 2016) intensified from the 1990s and 2000s. Much of the effort focused on the debate in global IR scholarship that increasingly emphasized China. Popular mainstream IR theories and approaches from the United States were introduced into the Chinese context. Qin Yaqing, for example, translated Alexander Wendt's work on social constructivism (Wendt 1999) into Chinese. In working out his own relational theory of world politics (Qin 2018), Qin goes beyond Wendt's social constructivism he helped introduced to China. Drawing on the notion of culture and relationality from Chinese intellectual traditions, Qin argues for a relational theory of international relations that would understand state actions as being in a cultural community. Relations affecting the actors involved are crucial for one's understanding of international relations. This relations-based theory reflects the Chinese approach to thinking about international relations, in contrast to individual rationality–based "Western mainstream international relations theory" (Qin 2016: 33).

Joseph Nye's thesis of soft power (Nye 2005) and John Mearsheimer's offensive realism (Mearsheimer 2001) had a significant influence on the research agenda in Chinese IR scholarship and policy analysis in the 2000s. Yan Xuedong's moral realism is a good example. Critiquing Mearsheimer's offensive realism (Yan 2016), Yan argues that China has practiced a different kind of realism in its rise in the hierarchic international system. For Yan, economic and military power is important for a nation to pursue its interests in international relations. However, it is the sense of moral responsibility and organizing capabilities of the nation that determine whether it can achieve these interests and how. Morality-based political leadership allows China to rise in the international hierarchy. Yan's notion of morality is developed from his investigation of the notion of "humane authority" (王道) in traditional Chinese ways of governance.

The use of intellectual resources from Chinese political traditions is also reflected in another major development for a Chinese IR theory. Zhao Tingyang's work on the *tianxia* system develops an analytical framework to rethink the ontological nature of international relations. Tianxia (天下 or "under Heaven") is an established concept in traditional Chinese thought on polity and state. It is close in meaning to "domain" or "imperial world order." In this *tianxia* system the nation state is not a fundamental unit of human activities. The *tianxia* system, according to Zhao, is an all-inclusive society with universal humanity and a set of institutions that govern and regulate the various relations. This system can better accommodate differences and avoid conflict than the dominant world orders as envisaged by Hobbes, Locke, and Kant.

Intensive efforts to interpret, explain, and forecast China's international policy and behavior have been a critical part of the rich development of a Chinese theory of international relations from the 1990s. This paralleled the "rise of China" in the international system. The rise of China refers to the rapid increase and large-scale expansion in China's international interests, capabilities, and influence in the international system in the late twentieth and early twenty-first centuries. The scholarly and policy debate this rise has generated have dominated mainstream IR scholarship and influenced policy options of states in response. It also reflects the close, dynamic link between IR research and theoretical development and the evolving practice of a country in international relations.

The scholarly and policy debate over the rise of China focuses on the nature and forms of Chinese power, China's international interests, vision, and strategy, and the ways in which the rising China influences the shaping of international order. It initially centered on the question of whether China was a revolutionary, status quo, or revisionist state (Johnston 2003) and the nature and forms of Chinese power (Shambaugh 2018). This was to ascertain whether China was rising to the position of a power of global influence.

The debate then shifted to focus on China's intentions, purpose, and strategy in international relations. China was considered to have adopted a strategy of neo-Bismarckianism (Goldstein 2003) or 韬光养晦 ("to keep a low profile") (Yan 2014), aimed to avoid being unnecessarily provocative, rely on multilateral diplomacy to make friends rather than enemies, and create an international environment that would not disrupt China's continual growth and rise. As time went on, the debate further shifted to determine whether China had changed its course to become more "assertive" and "proactive," intending to "strive for achievements" in international relations.

The debate further focused on whether the rise of China would be peaceful and lead to international order or be hostile and lead to disorder (Busan 2010; Toje 2018) and whether China's rise represented a disturbance to the existing power equilibrium and a challenge to the liberal international order (Root 2013; Ikenberry 2014, 2018). Finally, the debate also concentrated on determining the best strategy to meet the challenge of China's rise. More specifically, for policy advice in Washington, whether the United States should seek to contain the rise of China before it was too late or engage with China so as to influence the country and its integration with the international system (Tunsjø 2017; Campbell & Ratner 2018).

The development of Chinese scholarship toward a Chinese theory of international relations has been actively engaged in these debates. The search for a Chinese theory of international relations has turned out to be the development of theories of Chinese international relations. There are different possible or even conflicting ways of interpreting or explaining China's international relations. These theories focus on the purpose, interests, vision, identity, and strategy of China in international relations. The Chinese theory of international relations seemed to be sandwiched between mainstream IR theory and the evolving forms and dynamics of rising international relations that seek scholarly recognition and appreciation.

No one single theoretical framework seemed to have emerged to dominate the field and define what a Chinese theory of international relations might be. David Shambaugh summarizes the empirical basis of this "theoretical ambiguity" in Chinese IR theory (Shambaugh & Ren 2012). This theoretical ambiguity arose out of conflicting national identities and worldviews as the nation rose in an ever-shifting position, interests, and capabilities in world politics, economy, and society. The dynamic tension between the scholarly world of IR theory and the practical world of profound international political change is not unprecedented or unexpected in the history of the rise and fall of great powers. In the Chinese case, though, the theoretical ambiguity has gradually faded away as the vision and strategy of China in international relations have been more clearly articulated and more forcefully laid out in recent years.

On the other hand, perspectives on a Chinese theory of international relations serve to demonstrate the extent of theorizing activities in China. What these perspectives try to theorize about, though, are international relations as the Chinese see them; they are not primarily about IREA. To the extent they are concerned with IREA, these theoretical perspectives offer different ways to conceptualize, rationalize, or justify China's relations with the world and its approach to international relations. Its contribution to a theory of IREA is that IREA or, more precisely, the relevant part of IREA, can be explained by a national theory, but only to the extent of the nation's influence on IREA. In China's case, this influence is quite significant.

DOES JAPAN HAVE AN IR THEORY?

Intellectual enthusiasm for a theoretical framework to locate a nation's position in the world structure came much earlier for Japan. A broad view of how Japan should position itself in the world of imperialist competition and relate itself to different groups of countries to advance its interests and influence emerged in the mid-nineteenth century. Reflecting a belief that the world was being taken over by nation-states with immense power, modern institutions and technologies, and appealing social norms and culture, this theoretical framework called for Japan to adopt the systems of political economy of Western countries, focus on industrial development and modern state building, and engage with East Asia as the European powers were doing.

This theoretical perspective significantly influenced Japan's international policy and strategy from the late nineteenth century and its political, economic, and military activities in IREA in the first half of the twentieth century. The perspective has not developed further into a more systematic theory, and IR theory stopped after Japan's defeat in World War II. In more recent years, there has been growing policy analyses and public debate on Japan's role and identity in international relations, its relations with the United States and East Asian countries, and the challenge to become a "normal state" again in the world. But IR theory in Japan remains very weak.

The rise of modern Japan, of a magnitude and global significance similar to that of China today, happened in the late nineteenth century. The Meiji Restoration from 1868 enabled Japan to become as strong, rich, and capable an international power as European, Chinese, Russian, and American powers that operated in East Asia at the time. Fukuzawa Yukichi (福澤諭吉) was considered one of the first in Japan to contemplate Japan's purpose and position in world politics and how Japan related to the world in major power relations.

Fukuzawa's *"out of Asia to become like Europe* (脱亜入欧)" thesis (Fukuzawa 1887) represented a popular and powerful conception of how Japan should relate to the world and how this in turn could help Japan's industrial growth, modern state development, and emergence as a nation of wealth and strength like European nations. It is an idea or a strategy that Japan should learn from Europe how to organize national industrial development and modern political economy and act like a European power in world politics. This "theory" rationalized a major shift in Japan's international identity, from being one of those in the chaotic, decaying, and China-dominanted Asia to becoming a rich, strong, civilized, European-like nation-state.

This is the first major intellectual thought on Japan's strategic choice to position itself in the world beyond Asia. European institutions and normative practices in industrial development, modern state building, and international competition have significantly influenced the way Japan emerged as a great power in the twentieth century. This shift in Japan's international identity and the practical programs it has pursued in national development and international expansion in the twentieth century has set a model for latecomers, particularly from the non-Western world, in the rise and fall of nations in world politics. Japan competed with European powers by learning their methods and adopting their successful institutions and policy regimes in organizing industrial development, modern state and society, and international competition.

"Asia" for Japan, then, refers largely to East Asia (東洋, 東亜), that is, today's continental East Asia. This "abandoning Asia" thesis was part of the debate on the basis of which Japan was to modernize, transform, and develop into an internationally strong and effective modern state. Those of the "Asia-rejuvenating" (興亜) school of thought, on the other hand, advocated building a rich and strong modern Japan based on a reorganized and rejuvenated East Asia. These thoughts on Japan's relations with the world closely interacted with the policy and international practice of the Japanese state, which fell increasingly under the influence of the military and industrial capital that envisioned an East Asia–wide political and industrial reorganization as the basis of Japan's rise and further development.

Takashi Inoguchi, a prominent IR scholar playing a significant role in bridging the global and Japanese IR studies, discusses the influence of "Staatslehre, historicism, Marxism, and positivism" (Inoguchi 2007: 370) on the shaping of Japanese theory of international relations in the 1920s and 1930s and three representative theories that emerged from this early movement for a Japanese IR theory. The influence of Staatslehre, historicism, and Marxism focused early Japanese IR scholarship on the central question of modern state organization and how to reform the state to support the nation so it could rise in the world of competitive powers.

Of the three representative works, Nishida Kitaro, a constructivist philosopher, takes up the problem of Japan's identity "between East and West." Tabata Shigejiro, socialized in international law, focuses on the concept of national sovereignty as the basis of the international system. Hirano Yoshitaro, a Marxist economist, argues for regional integration higher than state sovereignty. These are issues that featured similarly in many other countries in the early decades of the development of the IR discipline. While Inoguchi sees them as three theories, they clearly define some key aspects of the challenge for Japan as a rising power, particularly Japan's vision and interest and its relations with East Asia and the West.

This intellectual and policy debate regarding a Japanese theory of international relations was abruptly interrupted at the end of World War II with Japan's defeat in the Pacific theater. Post-1945 scholarly, or theoretical, thinking on international relations was significantly limited. Japan was constitutionally limited as a state in its interest and capability to act in international relations. Japan's IR studies have been known for their lack of strategic and theoretical thinking but being more effective in technical analysis of specific issues. A 2001 survey of the field by Takashi Inoguchi and Paul Bacon found that Japanese IR scholarship was very light in "theoretical investigations" and contrasts with the American social science of IR (Inoguchi & Bacon 2001: 15). Japanese IR studies concern themselves more with practical issues, policy analyses, and regional and historical issues (Shimizu et al. 2008: 78).

However, efforts to fashion a Japanese theory of international relations continued, in a set of quite varied scholarly frameworks, or in what Kosuke Shimizu calls the cultural tradition of Japanese IR (see further discussion in Chapter 6). A generation of scholars in post-1945 Japan focused their inquiries on an understanding or an explanation of Japan's international identity and the forms in which such an identity influences its international relations. Akira Iriye is a leading scholar who pioneered the exploration of the impact of culture and cross-cultural communication on the direction of Japan-United States relations during the Japanese American war (Iriye 1981). Inoguchi has done significant work in bridging US/global and Japanese IR scholarship, transplanting key concepts, theories, and research frameworks from one context to the other. Inoguchi published widely in mainstream IR scholarship, introduced Japanese IR scholarship to the English-speaking IR community, and established two influential journals based in Japan, *International Relations of the Asia-Pacific* and *Japanese Journal of Political Science*.

The cultural theory of Japan's international relations became a model of scholarly inquiry into the development of national IR scholarship in other East Asian countries (IRAP 2007, 2018). This line of work has not only helped generate similar interests, scholarship, and professional networks in Japan, Korea, China, and Southeast Asia on international relations theory and practice, but also helped create an intellectual tradition across East Asian countries that focuses on the nation's relations with the world, with the West in particular, and on a national theory of international relations engaging with global IR scholarship. The cultural theory of IR in Japan is a continuation of the intellectual tradition of the 1920s and 1930s that focuses on Japan as a rising nation-state and its shifting relations with the international system in terms of identity, interests, and methods of its international conduct and pursuits.

Further conditions pressuring Japan to think about its position and role in world politics emerged in the 1980s. These included the rise of Japan again, this time largely in economics, trade, and industrial development; shifts in the domestic political, economic, and social basis of Japan's international interests and policy; and the growing need for theoretical and strategic thinking and policy analysis of Japan's role and strategy in international relations. Major scholarly research into this called for the "internationalization of Japan." This resonated well with the thoughts of the leading politician at the time, Prime Minister Yasuhiro Nakasone, and his nationalist vision of Japan in the world. Debate on the most effective way to make Japan a "normal state" went on between those who wanted to get "out of the Yoshida doctrine to become a normal state" and those who saw the need to strengthen or upgrade the Yoshida arrangements (see further discussion in Chapter 3). The Yoshida

Doctrine was a set of policy guidelines for a preferred political, economic, and international orientation of the newly restored Japanese state after 1945. It was formulated in a series of government policies associated with then-Prime Minister Shigeru Yoshida. With the LDP-dominant governing political institutions established in 1955 and the US-Japanese security alliance enforced in 1961, the Yoshida Doctrine called for Japan to focus on economic development while its national security would be looked after under the auspices of the US-Japanese security alliance.

The debate was not resolved until the mid-1990s, when politicians and policymakers arrived at a consensus that moving closer to the United States and strengthening the US-Japan alliance, rather than moving away from it, seemed a realistic and effective way of transforming Japan into a normal state. This reset was facilitated by the strong political leadership under Junichiro Koizumi and Shinzo Abe in the 2000s and 2010s. This very significant development in the practice of Japanese international relations has attracted much less attention in scholarly discussions and theoretical debates than it did on earlier occasions or in the case of China around the same time. Perhaps much of the role of theoretical thinking and scholarly debate is overshadowed by policy bureaucrats and politicians, or IR academics in Japan are indeed more practical than theoretical. But the Japanese theory of international relations led by politicians and policy bureaucrats reflects the conventional model of national politics and policy in Japan.

It is hard to say whether Japan has a theory of international relations, though there is a clear and distinct pattern in Japan's international relations. Japan is a very practical nation. Much of what might be considered theoretical perspectives of Japan are in fact patterns of how Japan identifies with the world and conducts itself in international relations. Japan has developed a unique system and behavioral pattern of how to organize industrial development, engage with international society, and mitigate external political and cultural influences. These Japanese international relations are a legitimate and important part of IREA. We will discuss some theoretical attempts to explain the patterns and character of Japan's international policy and behavior: cultural explanations in Chapter 6, an institutional explanation in Chapter 7, and a civilization explanation in Chapter 12. These theoretical perspectives contribute to a theory of IREA in different ways, with a distinct focus on culture, civilization, or institutions as important factors influencing Japan's international behavior and policy.

"KOREA BETWEEN EMPIRES"

The close "mutually constitutive" influence (Wendt 1987: 360) between theory and practice of the state's international relations is also seen in South Korea, though in Korea the theory side is much heavier. IR theory in Korea is strongly influenced by its "inferior" position in the hierarchic power structure in Northeast Asia and its experiences of suffering as a national state under the tributary system of the Chinese world order, the colonial rule of Japan, and the condition of a divided nation and a divided state since the Korean War. Dominant theoretical perspectives emphasize the ethnic integrity of the Korean nation and the original Korean qualities of the state institutions. More importantly, they rationalize the Korean nation and the Korean state in the framework of the modern international system: sovereignty, equality, diplomacy, and the nation-state.

There is one underlying theme in the Korean theory of international relations: the security and identity of a small country in a large geopolitical structure. Korea is often seen as being sandwiched between the forces of two major geopolitical powers at any given historical time. In the early attempts to understand the origins and causes of the Korean War, for example, much attention was focused on the geopolitical structure and great power politics surrounding Korea. Samuel Kim was one of the early IR scholars to consider the issue of Korea and the world and the structural forces that influenced what happened on the Korean peninsula and Korea's position and identity in the great power structure (Kim 2000, 2003, 2004, 2006; Armstrong et al. 2005).

This tradition has been substantially enriched by works in two other clusters of research. One set of work focuses on the development of Korea's statehood, sovereignty, and identity from the traditional imperial system in East Asia (Schmid 2002; Shin & Robinson 1999). Andre Schmid, for example, contributes a historical narrative on the shaping of the Korean nation, national consciousness, and national identity in the evolving and complex institutions and relations of empire and colonial governance in East Asia. The idea is taken further to investigate the unique state institutions for Korea as a sovereign state in and out of an imperial and colonial interstate system in the region (Palais 2014) and the problem of sovereignty and international status of countries such as Korea in IREA (Park 2017).

The other line of inquiry takes up the problem of the structure and institutions of the East Asian interstate system at the time and explores how they helped shape Korea's relations and identity with the world. Theoretically, this concerns the effects of the geopolitical structure and institutional forms of IREA organization on individual states. "Korea between empires" (Schmid 2002) has been an enduring theme in contemporary Korea's international identity and practice. It explains Korea's strategic options but also justifies some of its very innovative moves in regional geopolitics and geoeconomics. Scholars seeking to demonstrate structural effects often refer to the Confucian structure/Chinese world order, Japan's empire and imperialism, and the Cold War geopolitical structure in East Asia for evidence of the structural effects of these "empires." David Kang (Kang 2010, 2012), for example, investigates the traditional China-dominated interstate system in East Asia in the past 500 years. Victor Cha, on the other hand, considers the formation and institutional and normative foundation of the US-centric alliance system in East Asia (Cha 2016).

The Korean theory of international relations focuses on the nature of the Korean state and its position in the violent geopolitical structure in East Asia it found itself in. Focusing naturally on the popular issues in general IR theory, such as nation-state, sovereignty and autonomy, divided nation, and national identity, the Korean theory of international relations provides an explanation of the structural condition for the difficulties in Korea's attempt to be a nation and a state on its own. It builds this claim on the primary institutions of the modern international system and helps policymakers in Korea to frame Korea's national interests in IREA and approach different countries in IREA involved in Korea-related issues.

Contributing to a theory of IREA, the Korea theory highlights a key challenge in theorizing IREA. East Asian nations were largely on the peripheries of the hierarchic structure of interstate power in IREA. A profound concern of a theory of IREA is what rationalizes the thinking and action of East Asian countries to survive and develop in such a structure and international order. The Korea theory appeals to modern institutions of international relations, sovereignty, national state, and equality to ensure Korea's survival and development as a nation-state. This theoretical perspective enjoys broad appeal in many East Asian countries participating in IREA. This theory expects modern institutions to be an important force in pluralizing the structure of IREA and constraining the behavior of great powers that have much greater capacity to influence IREA. Here the institutions are expected to influence the power structure, in the hope that this will lead to a different international order.

REGIONAL IDENTITY AND AN ASEAN IR THEORY

Taking institutions as an important force influencing IREA is a significant contribution to a theory of IREA. This is also seen in another set of activities theorizing IREA. Scholars theorizing a collective identity of ASEAN as an important mechanism in East Asian regionalism have a great expectation of the transformative effects of ideas and identity on the shaping of an international order in IREA. Moreover, the institutions and normative practices in associating these small national forces into a large collective force in a region constitute an important part of the normative structure that supports regional networking and incorporation of national forces. In this theory, institutional arrangements, normative practices, and state identities are considered the primary shapers of the interstate power structure and international order in IREA.

Adding to the proliferation of national theories of international relations in IREA is a stream of theoretical thinking and scholarly publications by academics of Southeast Asian background working on the problem of regional international relations from the perspective of Southeast Asian states. Amitav Acharya is one of the thinkers and writers developing a distinctive framework for considering international relations in the region. Aaron Frieberg and David Kang published two influential articles in the 1990s and 2000s that generated an interesting debate on the nature of the international order in East Asia.

Friedberg's classical realist analysis saw East Asia moving toward a multipolar pattern of power relations that were "ripe for rivalry" (Friedberg 1993/4). Kang's advice for attention to both the power structure and cultural identity suggests the peace and stability of IREA under a hegemonic hierarchic order such as the Chinese world order (Kang 2003). In response, Acharya argues (Acharya 2003) that modern institutions and norms have been developing in East Asia in such a way that they can provide a form of constraint on East Asian states in the playing out of the geopolitical and historical normative dynamics as suggested by Frieberg and Kang.

This debate reveals the scholars' different views on what drives IREA and the structural and institutional conditions of the international order in East Asia. Acharya's institutionalist framework lies at the core of a large body of literature on the theory and practice of the *ASEAN way* of regional international relations (see Chapter 9 for a fuller discussion). The ASEAN way refers to a set of principles and normative practices that developed among ASEAN countries for managing their relations and resolving conflicts and reducing tensions among themselves during the Cold War.

In explaining the mode of ASEAN regionalism, Acharya in his 1997 essay (Acharya 1997) highlights the importance of ideas, a collective identity, and multilateral institutions for ASEAN, as well as the development of a shared identity as the basis for an ASEAN community. This quickly grew into a significant area of scholarship, with works by Muthiah Alagappa and Amitav Acharya (Alagappa 1998, 2001; Acharya 2001a, 2001b, 2007, 2013). These works provide the theoretical framing and empirical substance for a Southeast Asian approach to international relations and lend intellectual support to the practice of ASEAN-centric multilateral institutionalism in post-Cold War East Asia.

There is some difficulty in naming this "Southeast Asian" approach a "national" theory in our discussion of national theories of international relations in East Asia. It is certainly not "national" as we know it. However, collective identity is so essential for Southeast Asian states to be effective in IREA. It reflects more of a shared position of Southeast Asia countries in the structure of IREA than common material interests they have in IREA. An ASEAN theory of international relations is about ASEAN as a consequential actor in IREA, as a collective entity in the IREA structure, and as an effective form in which ASEAN states influence IREA and advance their interests on critical issues in IREA.

Taking East Asia in this way as the primary platform for international relations of ASEAN states is supported by the fact that much of the international relations of the ASEAN states are for political, economic, and social-cultural interaction, exchange, engagement, and integration in the wider region, particularly with Northeast Asia. This is also evidenced in the theorizing efforts themselves. Acharya and Busan (Acharya & Busan 2007, 2017) found no sufficient material and intellectual substance in Southeast Asia for an ASEAN theory of international relations. IR thinkers there were mostly concerned with how to connect local contents and material to the global IR theory. They also found that the practice and scholarship of "Confucian hierarchic structure" in East Asia (Acharya & Busan 2017: 364) may provide a basis for a distinct East Asian theory of international relations that includes both Northeast and Southeast Asia.

Acharya's focus on a regional identity, norms, and the ideas of a region in an ASEAN IR theory is clearly influenced by the popular constructivist theory at the time. The spread of ideas, the formation of a collective identity, and a set of shared norms and practices as the primary forces shaping IREA represent a perfect instance of the theory of how ideas, norms, and identity influence the shaping of an international order as constructivists envisage. Constructivism, in the fashion of Alexander Wendt (Wendt 1992, 1999), focuses on the process whereby aspects of international relations are socially constructed rather than driven primarily by human nature or the international structure, as realists and neorealists have popularly claimed.

The ASEAN theory of international relations reveals how the ASEAN way has developed in the practice of ASEAN states engaging multilaterally to manage and reduce conflict among themselves. It also shows how a collective identity can emerge from this "socialization" exercise among ASEAN states over their mutually accepted norms of handling conflict and dispute. This in turn provides the necessary normative foundation for ASEAN as a security community.

NATIONAL THEORIES AND A THEORY OF IREA

In our discussion of the "national" theories of international relations in East Asia, we have seen some interesting patterns. First, these national theories are generated around the idea of the national actor in international relations, its identity with other states or groups of states, its strategic interests, its capacity to influence the movement of relations, and its strategy to deploy these interests and capacities to achieve a set of strategic purposes. Many of these theories are more guidelines for a nation's international actions and policies than a set of causal mechanisms as in conventional theories of international relations.

These national theories, however, can be useful for explaining what states do and why they act the way they do in IREA and forecast their actions into the future. These theories, however, do not take IREA as something they try to explain. They tend to focus on one particular set of IREA related to the given country. To the extent that the international relations they theorize are important parts of IREA, these national theories contribute to our understanding of IREA. Moreover, the methods and frameworks scholars employ to develop their theories are good cases in which we can learn how these intellectual resources can be utilized in analyzing and explaining IREA. For example, the relational theory, tianxia theory, or the theory of moral realism explaining Chinese international relations and the institutional-constructivist theory explaining the ASEAN regional identity are useful for thinking about IREA in terms of the role of these forces in the shaping of IREA.

The analytical and empirical focus of these national theories is global as well as national. The theories are the response primarily to the growing desire of scholars to formulate indigenous content and theory on international relations and overcome the hegemonic dominance of Western IR theory, American social science, or the English school. The empirical and analytical focus is not regional, not on IREA per se. Many theories are indeed very much opposed to the idea of seeing IREA as a coherent system of international relations or as the primary focus of their scholarly inquiry and policy analysis.

This brings us to the purpose of this book and the need for a coherent framework that would help us explain what IREA are, how they work, and what drives their development. The theoretical perspectives discussed earlier include many significant "middle-range" theories and national theories. Individual chapters in the book will fully discuss these middle-range theories and use them to explain IREA in the functional area or make sense of the patterns and their change in this specific set of IREA. The national theories will also be further discussed and explained in the individual chapters where a nation's international relations and its international strategy and identity are discussed.

The challenge here is to see how these different sets of IREA in distinct functional areas are related and how they together serve to explain, in a coherent and logical form, the overall pattern of IREA and their transformation over time. Such a challenge, as we touched briefly on in Chapter 1, calls for a theoretical framework that can help unpack the underlying dynamism of IREA that connects different parts of IREA and drives IREA to develop, evolve, and take form as a coherent system of international relations. This framework directs us to think about IREA theoretically and to look for the power structure and structural shifts, institutional arrangements and normative practices, and international orders as the core dynamics of IREA and understand how they affect one another.

A FRAMEWORK FOR IREA

Taking IREA as a distinct field of scholarly knowledge and inquiry, IR scholarship is motivated in particular by two questions: whether IREA are shaped by a set of organizing principles different from those presumably underlying other international systems and whether nations and peoples in East Asia conduct and organize their relations differently because of their particular historical, cultural, religious, civilizational, ethnic circumstances or because of their particular set of material and institutional interests and motivations. Inquiries along these lines have developed into various theories and frameworks in explaining IREA: from cultural and historical determinism to the imperatives of modern political economy; from institutional primacy to various dichotomous theories built on opposing forces believed to drive IREA: structure and agent, East and West, state and nonstate actors, regime types, and traditional and modern platforms and institutions of interstate relations. Above all, intellectual curiosity comes to focus on the system itself: is there a distinct set of dynamics and patterns that collectively define IREA? If yes, what are they?

Efforts to theorize IREA discussed in this chapter have identified some of the primary forces that shape IREA. If the outcome of this shaping is an international order, then the forces that shape the international order and the way they do are what we are theorizing about: geopolitical forces, international structure, culture and civilization, and the dynamics of industrial and economic growth, transnational economic integration, transformative power of multilateral institutions, nontraditional security challenges, national politics of international policy, and the influence of the global environment. All these forces are believed to motivate, influence, or constrain states to act, deploy resources, and pursue certain types of relations with others. These actions, interactions, strategic alliances, and partnerships shape the structure of IREA.

International institutions are formally agreed-upon rules, and international norms are widely accepted standards and normal practices for organizing interstate activities and relations. The prevailing structure generates international institutions and normative practices to sustain and support the distribution of interests and capabilities of states in the system. Together the power structure and institutional arrangements and normative practices determine an international order that satisfies and prioritizes the interests of states in specific ways and rationalizes their course of action. An international order tends to be stable where there is equilibrium in the distribution of material interests and capabilities and effective institutional and normative motivations and constraints on states to act in relation to that order.

A critical mechanism that triggers the transformation of an international order is the shift in the underlying power structure. This shift is caused, as Robert Gilpin and George Modelski explained long ago (Gilpin 1981; Modelski 1987), when a nation sees a relatively faster rise in power – its military, industrial, financial, and technological capabilities. This breaks the equilibrium in the power distribution and leads states of different positions in the structure to react differently, and these collectively drive the states to seek a new equilibrium.

Any new equilibrium, as John Ikenberry has shown (Ikenberry 2000, 2014), requires a unique set of institutional arrangements and normative practices to support. They sustain and legitimize the power structure and ultimately make that structure operationally effective for the states involved. The specific pattern of power distribution and the unique set of supporting and legitimizing institutions and norms constitute, or contribute to, an international order. This international order represents a set of authority relations that stipulate the obligations and responsibilities of, as well as benefits to, the participating states in taking a course of action under the given structural effects. The transformation of an international order therefore entails a shift in the underlying power structure with the rise and fall of powers, tensions over the institutions and norms reflecting different dynamics of power distribution, and the changing ability of those authority relations to allocate responsibilities and deliver benefits.

This dynamism of IREA is not a brand-new theory. Certain aspects of it – international structures, institutional and normative dynamics, and international orders – are addressed in mainstream IR scholarship separately in various ways. It is an analytical framework that connects these different parts of IREA in a logical way and in a cause-and-effect fashion to explain patterns and changes in IREA. This framework suggests that what we intend to explain in IREA are the patterns and their changes in the set of international relations in and over East Asia. More specifically, it concerns a series of international orders in East Asia, their transformations, and the forces that drive this transformation.

IREA experienced significant shifts in the underlying power structure and profound transformations of the international order over the past 150 years and offers great empirical material on how power is distributed in IREA and how this structure shifts because of the rise and fall, and in and out, of different powers of systemic significance in IREA. Moreover, inherent tensions in IREA have arisen in connection with the system's institutional, cultural, and normative identities. East Asia has comprised a set of nations that were not originally part of the Westphalian system of international relations and European global imperial competition. They have developed complex relations with the US-led liberal international order at the global and regional levels. This framework allows us to see the complex impact of institutional arrangements and normative practices on the shaping and transformation of the international order in IREA.

Finally, post-1945 has seen significant transformations of the international order in East Asia, from a bipolar, communist–anticommunist order to a common security and development community arranged through multilateral institutions. With the rise of China and the renegotiated US-dominated order, all critical forces defining the international order in East Asia have come into full play. This framework is useful for understanding what forces influence what arrangements in the shaping of the international order and the possible scenarios of IREA development going forward.

Study Questions

1. Theorizing of IREA has experienced shifts in its focus from external-stimulus explanations to internal-dynamics explanations, from classical realism to structural institutionalist explanations, from geopolitical to geoeconomic explanations. Discuss these shifts and how they relate to the practice of IREA.
2. Why are there many national theories of international relations in East Asia? Use one example to discuss whether these national characteristics are more influenced by the international structure a country finds itself in or the political, economic, and cultural conditions in the country.
3. What is the problem of nation and state in IREA theorizing? Why is this a significant issue for a theory of IREA?
4. Use one country case study to discuss how "the economy" influences the development of a theory of IREA.
5. There is a close link between IR scholarship and policy analysis in East Asian countries. How does this affect the quality of the IR profession in East Asian countries?
6. The state in East Asia has been strong, though often contested, in its legitimacy and constitution in post-1945 IREA. Does this influence the thematic focuses and scholarly approaches in IR theories in East Asia?

Further Reading

Amitav Acharya, and Barry Buzan, 2007. "Why Is There No Non-Western International Relations Theory? An Introduction," *International Relations of the Asia-Pacific* 7(3): 287–312.

Acharya, Amitav, and Barry Buzan, 2010. *Non-Western International Relations Theory: Perspectives on and Beyond Asia*. Abingdon: Routledge.

Hoffmann, Stanley, 1977. "An American Social Science: International Relations," *Daedalus* 6(3): 41–60.

Holsti, K. J., 1985. *The Dividing Discipline: Hegemony and Diversity in International Theory*. Boston: Allen & Unwin.

Huang, Xiaoming, 2007. "The Invisible Hand: Modern Studies of International Relations in Japan, China, and Korea," *Journal of International Relations and Development* 10(2): 168–203.

Ikenberry, G. John, and Michael Mastanduno, 2003. *International Relations Theory and the Asia-Pacific*. New York: Columbia University Press.

IRAP, 2017. "Why Is There No Non-Western International Relations Theory? Ten Years On," *International Relations of the Asia-Pacific* 17(3): 341–370.

IRAP, 2018. "Theorizing China's Rise in and Beyond International Relations, Special Issue," *International Relations of the Asia-Pacific* 18(3): 289–311.

Johnston, Alastair Iain, 2012. "What (If Anything) Does East Asia Tell Us About International Relations Theory?" *Annual Review of Political Science* 15 (June): 53–78.

3 Historical International Orders

> **In This Chapter...**
>
> - International orders and order transformation
> - The warring states
> - The Chinese world order
> - European colonial governance
> - The greater East Asian sphere of co-prosperity
> - Imperial orders and modern transformation
>
> **Learning Objectives**
>
> By the end of the chapter, you will be able to
> - Understand the basic character of the historical international orders in IREA
> - Understand the structural and institutional dynamics of their transformations
> - Understand the challenges in the development of modern IREA in the twentieth century
> - Analyze how these historical international orders influence the patterns of contemporary IREA.

IREA have seen distinct patterns of change over the thousands of years of their evolution. Scholarship today considers these patterns as a series of international orders. An international order is a set of authority relations among states that shapes and works on a structure of power distribution among the states, and the institutional arrangements and normative practices that support, moralize, and transmit the effects of the power relations on states. Since the emergence of early states in continental East Asia, IREA has experienced the period of Warring States, a Chinese world order, the European colonial treaty port system, the Japanese sphere of influence, the Cold War bipolar order, and the post-Cold War US hierarchical hegemonic order. These international orders appeared consecutively and swung between two general types: the multistate system and the hegemonic hierarchical system. This chapter examines the historical international orders in East Asia before 1945, the underlying power structures and the institutions and normative practices that sustained them, and the conditions for their transformation from one to another.

INTERNATIONAL ORDERS AND ORDER TRANSFORMATION

These international orders all relate to something that happened in IREA and still exert an influence on the development of contemporary IREA. We are interested in the historical structures, forms of polity, and institutions and norms of interstate relations in East Asia. Interstate relations are relations between polities that may or may not be constituted on the basis of a single dominant national population. Nation-state-based international relations is a modern concept that equates interstate relations with international relations and has some difficulties in explaining certain types of interstate relations, particularly those in premodern times. Some of the orders here therefore have been called "world orders," suggesting that they transcend national boundaries. Examining all these international orders along the lines of historical evolution allows us to explore the transformation of the international order in East Asia from one embedded in imperial institutions and practices to one based on the nation-state system.

More importantly, these international orders, as we explore briefly in early chapters, are patterns of IREA that the theoretical framework developed in this text aims to explain: what international orders are, how one particular order transformed into another, and what drove the transformations. If the international order was a set of authority relations shaped by the power structure, as well as by institutional arrangements and normative practices, we want to know in each of these international orders the pattern of the power structure, mechanisms of institutional and normative support, and how the power structure shifted in such a way that led to its tension with the established institutional arrangements and normative practices. Erosion in the effectiveness of the normative structure or its collapse and the emergence of new institutional arrangements and international practices created the conditions for order transformation.

This theoretical proposition frames much of the discussion of contemporary IREA in individual functional areas in subsequent chapters. This chapter focuses on the large patterns in the overall IREA before 1945. We investigate the power structure and its shift, the unique institutional arrangements and normative practices, and different patterns of IREA in these individual orders. We are interested in revealing the organizing principles and mechanisms that structured the interstate orders in IREA.

THE WARRING STATES

The "Chinese world order" was a categorical label for the traditional interstate structure and institutions in East Asia. Before it set in, states emerged in continental East Asia. Organized political entities developed in the greater Yellow River region in the central eastern part of today's China. It was a long period of time, hundreds of years, in which a cluster of states, or "warring states" as historians later called them, emerged out of the breakup of a centralized, unified Kingdom, the *Shang* (1600–1046 B.C.). The warring states engaged with each other politically, militarily, and diplomatically in conducting war, resolving conflict, negotiating settlements, and reinstalling interstate order among themselves following war and conquest. Yongjin Zhang makes the case that the Warring States system had all the qualities of a multistate system that we usually think only emerged after the Westphalia settlements (Zhang 2001).

A multistate system comprises a set of institutions and normative practices that govern the operation and management of interstate relations based on principles of power, diplomacy, interstate agreement on engagement, and settlement among sovereign states. More importantly, though, recognizing the Warring States as an interstate system and as a principal form of international order in continental East Asia opens up an intellectual space where the complex and dynamic process of formation and dominance of the contending forms of the governing order in continental East Asia can be properly analyzed. These forms indeed concern the structure, institutions, and norms of an international order.

While these states were soon to be conquered and incorporated, by one of them, into a larger polity, the first Chinese empire, Qin, the institutional transformation from the multistate system to the imperial system that governed the Qin Empire happened in the East Zhou era before the imperial system of Qin was formally imposed on the new Chinese empire. Ever since that time, the evolution of the interstate order in East Asia has alternated between a multistate system and a multinational imperial system where a hierarchical set of institutional arrangements and normative practices sustained a centralized structure of authority and political order in the domain. Structurally, the interstate order evolved between a form of diffused power distribution and that of centralized power and authority.

In the period of transition and changeover, there was a third form of arrangements for distribution of power and authority in the polity, the enfeoffment regime (分封制). The arrangement is more like a "federal" system, but the power and authority sharing between the states and the empire came not from the states' willingness to surrender their sovereignty to a newly constituted federal state, but from the breakdown of a united centralized imperial polity. In the case of the Warring States emerging out of the large Shang Kingdom, when Zhou conquered Shang and took over its territories, the king deployed princes and dukes to these territories and bestowed on them title to the territories, and they ran the territory as semiautonomous fiefdoms. As time went by, the king replaced the enfeoffment regime with a prefecture-county system (郡县制) in part to strengthen the connection between the court and these territories. In this prefecture-county system, the governance of the territories became part of the imperial system, and the court appointed state officials and bureaucrats to govern the states as prefectures and counties at the different levels of the integral centralized imperial system.

During the Zhou period, a comprehensive system of ceremonies, music and art, education, and social norms and values also developed, assisted by the great efforts of Confucius, a senior royal counselor then, to restore political and social order in a changing and expanding society over various "national" groups and social classes, and moralize the centralized, hierarchical imperial structure of restored political power.

The prefecture-court system was unable to hold off the centrifugal dynamics built in the enfeoffment regime. In a fiefdom, the transfer of political authority went beyond the royal house lines. Military chiefs often gained independent power and a capacity to claim authority over the fiefdom, which tended to evolve anew into an independent and competitive state. The empire would then break up once again into separate states. This pattern of warring states transforming into fiefdoms in a federal state and subsequently becoming incorporated into a centralized, hierarchical imperial state until the imperial state broke up would repeat itself again and again in the thousand years of the evolution of the governing political structure and institutions of interstate relations in continental East Asia, often with a couple hundred years in each period. Alternations between a multistate system and a multinational imperial system defined the pattern of international political change throughout premodern times. The same pattern of state formation and contending states seeking incorporation into a large empire was also seen on the Korean peninsula, the Indochina peninsula, and the Japanese archipelago.

THE CHINESE WORLD ORDER

The previous section showed that for thousands of years, interstate relations in East Asia have evolved amid tensions between two dominant sets of dynamics that influenced the way these interstate relations were organized: the imperial structure, with institutions often embedded in a multinational empire possessing extensive territories within its jurisdiction and authority; and the Warring States and associated institutions, normative practices that defined an interstate order in East Asia.

Significantly, the imperial forms and institutions, particularly those associated with the Ming and Qing Empires, are identified in the scholarly literature as the principal form of interstate relations in East Asia. In a landmark collective study by thirteen scholars that popularized the term "Chinese world order," historian John K. Fairbank looked at China's relations with non-Chinese polities (Fairbank 1968). In search of a concept that could explain the pattern of China's "foreign relations" during the Qing Empire (1644–1912), Fairbank found a set of different types of relations between China and non-Chinese states in East Asia (Fairbank 1968: 12–13): relations to control through military and administrative means, to attract through culture, ideology, and religions, and to manipulate through material interests and diplomacy.

These different types of relations were developed through different sets of institutions and norms that governed China's interactions with individual "foreign areas." They formed three sets of "concentric zones" of bilateral relations, as we can observe on a real geopolitical map in Figure 3.1: the Sinic Zone, with Korea, Vietnam, *Liuqiu*, and Japan; an Inner Asian Zone, with Mongolia, Tibet, and Central Asia; and an Outer Zone, with Russia, Sulu, Portugal, Holland, and England. These zones are concentric around the center, the Middle Kingdom, or China Proper, as the connecting point between Heaven and anything under Heaven, or *tianxia* (Zhao 2006, 2011; Wang 2017). This is the structure of power and authority underlying the Chinese

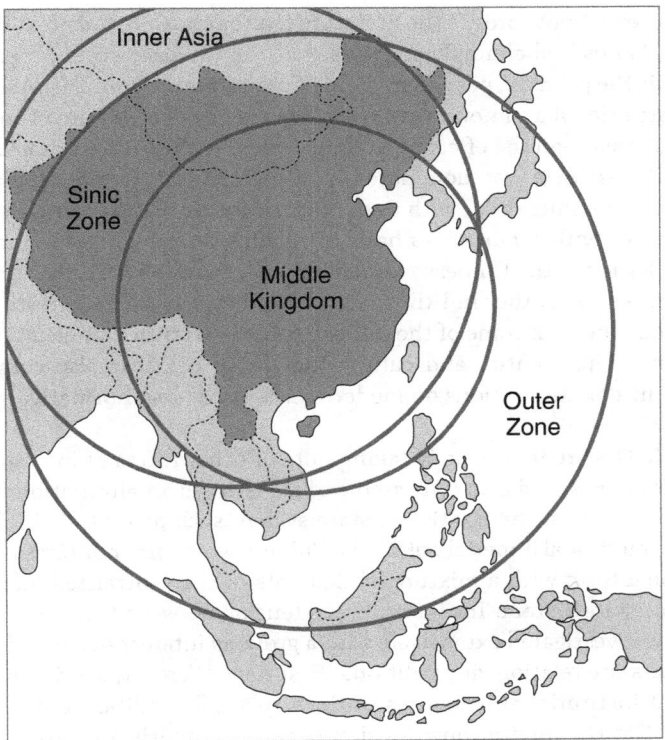

Figure 3.1 Illustration of Fairbank's Chinese world order of the nineteenth century
Based on Fairbank's description in Fairbank 1968: 12–13.
Graph credit: Huang 2009: 235

world order. The hierarchical political structure determined the authority relations among states in the domain and was legitimized through the moral power of Heaven transmitted in the deeds and acts of the Emperor, "Son of Heaven."

In this overall hierarchical and centripetal imperial order, institutions and normative practices developed to shape China's relations with other polities. Fairbank discusses at length the tribute system that operated between China and polities around China in his original work (1968). Extensive scholarship (Cohen 2000; Kang 2010; Lee 2017) has since elaborated on the tribute system as a defining element of the Chinese world order and of the institutions and norms of interstate relations in East Asia under the Chinese world order.

This makes the notion of the "Chinese world order" and the associated debate particularly relevant for the theory and practice of IREA. In IREA practice, does this concept reflect a dominant or principal structure of IREA? Did this China-centric, hierarchical, and centripetal structure influence interstate relations in East Asia at that time and for much of IREA's premodern history? Was this a guideline or a grand design for China's practice in IREA, or this is an instance of the mutual influence of international structure and the institutions and norms of interstate relations in the shaping of an international order? The literature (Fairbank 1968; Cohen 2000; Kang 2010; Wang 2017) overwhelmingly suggests that the Chinese world order, or the *tianxia* system, is the primary, persistent form of interstate order in East Asia, and it is more the institutional and normative consequence of the structure of interstate relations in East Asia than the effect of a grand design by the Chinese empire.

The fact that East Asia was dominated by a hierarchical, China-centric power structure and an interstate order with a set of institutions that sustained a pattern of China's relations with other states has far-reaching implications for contemporary IREA. The legacy of the Chinese world order influences how China, and Korea, Japan, Vietnam see each other in IREA today; how they see their interests and the intensions of the others on some of the critical issues in territory, international alliance and partnership, identity and cultural norms in IREA. It also complicates efforts to build interstate relations on modern institutions and normative values in postwar East Asia.

However, scholars are increasingly taking note of other forms of interstate relations in traditional East Asia, as discussed earlier. There is an alternation between the two dominant forms, the multistate state system such as that of the Warring States, and the traditional imperial polity, the Chinese world order or *tianxia* system, and a transitional form with a mixture of elements of the centralized hierarchical system and multistate system. The institutional tension between the forms of interstate relations is investigated extensively with a growing interest in a broader range of forms of interstate relations in traditional East Asia. Were these different forms indeed different institutional responses to the structural condition in power relations in IREA? Did the institutional tension between a multistate system and an imperial interstate order exist in IREA long before the clash between the Chinese world order and the Westphalian system?

Much of the scholarship on the forms of interstate relations in East Asia focuses naturally on the dominance of the Chinese world order and its inevitable clash with the Westphalian system as that system expanded into East Asia and the institutions of modern international system were introduced as European powers moved into continental East Asia in the nineteenth century. The Chinese empire began to crumble from the mid-nineteenth century, and the Chinese world order started to collapse, with tributary states either being taken over by other imperial states or becoming independent from China in the Westphalian sense. The monarchy not only lost its appeal to and influence over tributary states but increasingly lost control and governing effectiveness over the Chinese polity itself. Around the world, there was a global movement from the imperial system to the nation-state form of polity in a whole slew of countries, and many existing imperial polities broke down (Kumar 2013; Wang 2014). The collapse of the Chinese empire allowed different interstate forces to fill the power vacuum. The question is whether the new forces to replace the Chinese world order would organize IREA differently.

All signs pointed to the likelihood that the new forces would organize things differently. The two great sets of forces emerged to be the most effective challenges to the China-centric interstate order in East Asia: the West and Japan. The West, as seen in East Asia in the late nineteenth and early twentieth centuries, included West European powers, Russia, and the United States, and represented the most effective and influential forms of political economy, polity, and interstate relations at the time. As shown in Fairbank's original work and subsequent scholarship (Fairbank 1968; Gong 1984; Zhang 2001), they represented a direct challenge to the Chinese empire and the Chinese world order. The rise of Japan and its expansion to East Asia added a significant reinforcement of the pressures being brought to bear by the European powers on continental East Asia, on the Chinese world order, and on the Chinese empire itself. Japan reorganized itself from the Meiji Restoration (1868) and built a Meiji imperial system, recentralizing its power structure away from the Tokugawa "feudal" system.

There is some debate over the exact nature of the interstate system European powers practiced and advanced in East Asia in their move into continental East Asia in the nineteenth century. It is also unclear what type of interstate systems Japan would have built in the areas it conquered and controlled in its move into continental East Asia and maritime East Asia in the first half of the twentieth century. It is useful, therefore, to look into the interstate political structure they helped to shape and the international order the two sets of political forces intended or effected to advance in IREA. This will allow us to gain a better understanding of the transformation of the Chinese world order into the Cold War structure and international order and the logic of structural and institutional development behind the transformation.

EUROPEAN COLONIAL GOVERNANCE

Colonialism as a scholarly issue has been covered well in the literature in a broad range of areas. Understanding the impact of European colonial governance and imperial competition is crucial for understanding postindependence development of the former colonial polities and the structure and institutions of the international order in contemporary East Asia. For our discussion here on the structure and institutions of the European state–dominated international order in East Asia, we focus our examination on the expansion of political, economic, and territorial interests of European states in East Asia and the development of political, economic, and social institutions to manage the relations arising from expansion and interaction.

All European states involved in IREA had a clear intention to develop some form of "constitutional arrangements" for a political order in the territories over which they gained control. This would enable them to connect territories to the imperial polity back home in Europe. Our interest here is to explore the political structure and "state" institutions that sustained the European colonial interstate order in East Asia. While research on the structure and institutions of colonial governance in Southeast Asia is more advanced, there is a debate over whether European powers brought the Westphalian system or imperial system into Northeast Asia (Fairbank 1953; Zhang 1991; Suzuki 2009). We look at these and hope to draw a fuller picture of the interstate order in East Asia dominated by European states. This will help us better understand the formation of the modern international system in East Asia and the critical forces that shaped it.

European powers came to East Asia starting in the sixteenth century in several waves and established presences in East Asia. The Portuguese, Dutch, and Spanish came to East Asia first in the sixteenth century in search of the "East Indies." The Portuguese and Dutch came via the East Atlantic route around Cape Town over the Indian Ocean and to South and Southeast Asia. They set up controlling ports on the trade routes and networks. Spain crossed the Pacific Ocean to establish settlements in today's Philippines around the same time. Portuguese trading ports in East Asia spread throughout the whole "East Indies" and went as far as Macau in today's China. Dutch trading ports concentrated in today's Indonesia but also reached as far as Nagasaki, Japan, and Taiwan. These expeditions were led largely by their East India Company. This enterprise became the primary organizer of trade relations between the European nation and its colonial settlements in Southeast Asia.

Worldwide rivalries among European powers over the new world quickly halted Portuguese and Dutch colonial advances in East Asia. The successful industrial revolutions at home and the crowning of India drove the British colonial movement further down south and east from the South Asian continent. The British established strait settlements around the mid-nineteenth century in Malacca, Dinging, Penang, Singapore and British Malaya, Borneo in the large area of today's Malaysia, and Burma in the north connecting with British India. British colonial advances in East Asia also operated under the British East India Company. With the colonial government of India being formally transferred from the British East India Company to the Crown in 1858, the colonial territories were formally integrated into the British Empire. This was accompanied by French efforts to establish direct colonial rule in Cochinchina and indirect rule in other parts of the large Indochina Peninsula. The United States took over the colonial rule of the Philippines from Spain.

Once the presence of European countries was established in East Asia, efforts were made to develop some form of "constitutional arrangements." European empire building enabled the development of a set of governing institutions in Southeast Asia. Much of the existing polities in Southeast Asia then were loosely organized "galactic" polities" (Tambiah 1976: 137), "mandalas" (Wolters 1982), "solar polities" (Lieberman 2003), or even simply a dual-sphere structure of the court and villages loosely related (McCloud 1995). Figure 3.2 is Stanley Tambiah's depiction of the galactic polity of Ayutthaya in the seventeenth century in today's Thailand. The galactic polity is a form of polity found in traditional Southeast Asia where regions are loosely connected to the court and influenced and controlled by the court only to varying degrees. There is an evolving political order in the polity where political power and authority are diffused, and the polity is still evolving to grow into separate states or a larger multinational state. This is a logic similar to that discussed earlier on the early forms of states in continental East Asia. These polities usually have no clear boundary between the internal and the external in the sense of territory and sovereignty in modern interstate institutions and no clear institutionalized structure for the distribution of power and authority within the polity.

European incursions into East Asia, particularly in the British and Dutch cases, usually started with trade expeditions by a purposely organized national trading company. As the settlement stabilized, the trading company would then be incorporated by the home government into a semistate institution that performed certain

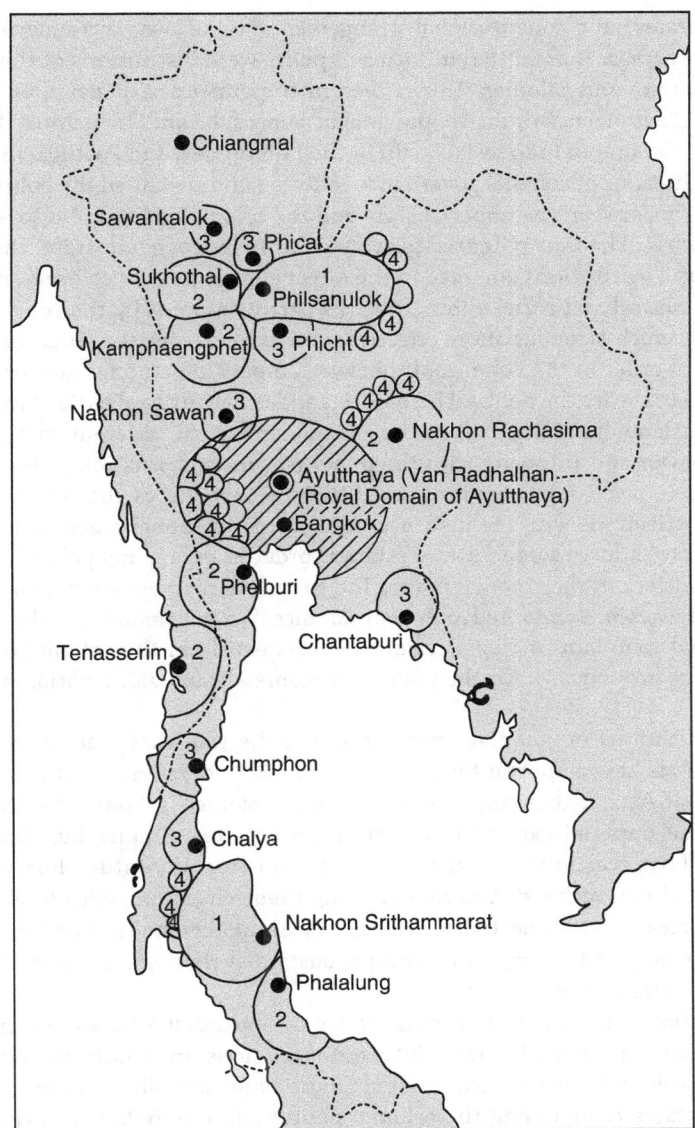

Figure 3.2 Tambiah's depiction of the galactic polity of Ayutthaya, Thailand, seventeenth century
Graph Credit: Tambiah 1976: 137

government functions in the settlement. In the next step, the colonial government would be transferred to "the Crown" from the trading company and a governor general would be sent to govern the territory on behalf of the empire. This is a typical course of development, as seen in the case of the British colonizing India. In Southeast Asia where European advances into East Asia initially concentrated,

European states built "constitutional arrangements" in various ways and with varying degrees of success. These different forms of polity were institutions of the relations between empire and colonies. This is seen in the imperial expansion of European powers in East Asia: Britain in the Malay Peninsula and Indochina, France in Indochina, Holland in Indonesia, Spain in the Philippines, and Portugal in Timor.

The institutions of colonial governance reflected and sustained the political structure not only between the imperial state and the colonial polity but also within the polity, which still had the potential to evolve into an independent state. The political structure and institutions emerged in the direct engagement of colonial enterprises and local political and social elites. This was partly enforced by the colonial forces, which were much stronger, more effective, and better organized. This shaped colonial political order in the colonies. Intensive competition among European powers drove them to clarify the political boundaries and constitutional basis of these newly claimed settlements. Each of them developed somewhat different institutions to organize power and authority with the polity (see more discussion in Huang 2009: 26–18). The European powers influenced the development of the "national" structure and institutions with the institutions and organizational practices used in the home state to enforce some form of political order in organizing politics, the economy, and society in the colonial polity. The British parliamentary system is a good example. It was widely adopted in British colonies. What is important, though, is the institutional foundations that developed subsequently in the colonial polity that prepared the groundwork for the polity to become a stand-alone nation-state after World War II.

The institutions of colonial governance and the way they were established in Southeast Asia have important implications for our understanding of the interstate order in East Asia at that time. First, European colonies in Southeast Asia largely reflected the imperial expansion of European empires. Empire building is state building, a form still popular in the world of the nineteenth century. European powers competed in Southeast Asia more among themselves than with local elites for territory, access, and connectivity. Each colony in the region was substantively connected vertically to the empire in Europe, sustained through exclusive trade relations and political arrangements.

The relationships among European states in Southeast Asia were competitive, exclusive, and influential. Thus, interstate relations in Southeast Asia under European colonial governance existed more substantially among competing European states than among the colonial polities, and more between the colonial power and its colonies. The institutions of the Westphalian system operated mostly among European powers themselves than among or with the territories they competed to possess. Principles of equality, sovereignty, and diplomacy were applied more to European states themselves while the relations between a European power and its colonies were mostly pursued as part of the organizing principles of the empire.

Second, European states built the structure and institutions for a form of colonial governance and incorporated their colonial territories in Southeast Asia. The way they achieved this is a classic model of polity formation in human history. A strong and powerful state rises up to conquer fellow polities in a domain. The empire incorporates conquered polities in two different ways: enfeoffment and centralization. We discussed this earlier in the case of the Warring States system and the Chinese world order. The two models have two distinct sets of institutional arrangements. European colonial governance in Southeast Asia is more like polity formation at the enfeoffment stage where power was still shared between the European empire and the colonies, and these colonies could be either further incorporated and eventually integrated into the centralized, hierarchical empire. The colony could also expand its own power base and remain a district polity itself.

The forms of European colonial governance supported the unequal power structure between European empires and colonies but equal and competitive relations among the European powers themselves. The effects of these institutions were ambivalent in the direction of further development of the polities involved. These forms faced great difficulties when European powers advanced further up to Northeast Asia and into continental East Asia where the potential target for European colonial advances was of an empire itself.

European powers moved to Northeast Asia from the mid-nineteenth century, extending imperialist competition into continental East Asia. Around that time, Japan's Tokugawa Shogunate of the Edo period, China's Emperor Kangxi of the Qing Dynasty, and Korea's Joseon Dynasty all adopted a policy of maritime ban on trade and human traffic (鎖国sakoku/ 쇄국swaegug /海禁haijing). Unlike their efforts in Southeast Asia, European powers joined hands, with additional powers – Russia, Germany, Japan, United States, and others – joining in a collective effort to face a very strong, well-established polity. As in Southeast Asia, European powers started by establishing trading ports around the coast of continental East Asia, the East Asian crescent. Initially they were confined to Yokohama in Japan and Guangzhou in Qing China. Japan took the opportunity to open up the country. Emperor Meiji, with power restored, initiated a series of internal changes in state institutions.

In China, resistance to European encroachment proved to be much stronger and persistent. European powers decided to force their way in. In 1842, Qing China signed the Treaty of Nanking on the British warship HMS *Cornwallis* anchored outside Nanjing city. Among other things, the treaty opened up four more "treaty ports" and granted some extraterritorial rights to British subjects in these ports. This led to a series of similar treaties between China and other powers and eventually to the 1901 Peace Agreement between the Great Powers and China after the eight-power coalition occupied Beijing. As Figure 3.3 shows, these treaties established a series of trading ports along the coast of continental East Asia where European powers, as well as Japan and the US, were granted extraterritorial rights and privileges. Imperialist competition and further advances in China, together with political change in China itself, led to the collapse of the Qing Dynasty and the rise of the Republic where various political forces competed for state power, territories, and the scope of the new polity. More importantly, though, the First World War broke out and drew much attention of the European powers back to their home continent.

Discussions about the forms of interstate relations emerged from the advances of European powers in Northeast Asia, the treaty port system more specifically, are at the core of the empire-nation state debate, or imperial-Westphalian debate, on the nature of European practices in IREA in the nineteenth century. The treaty

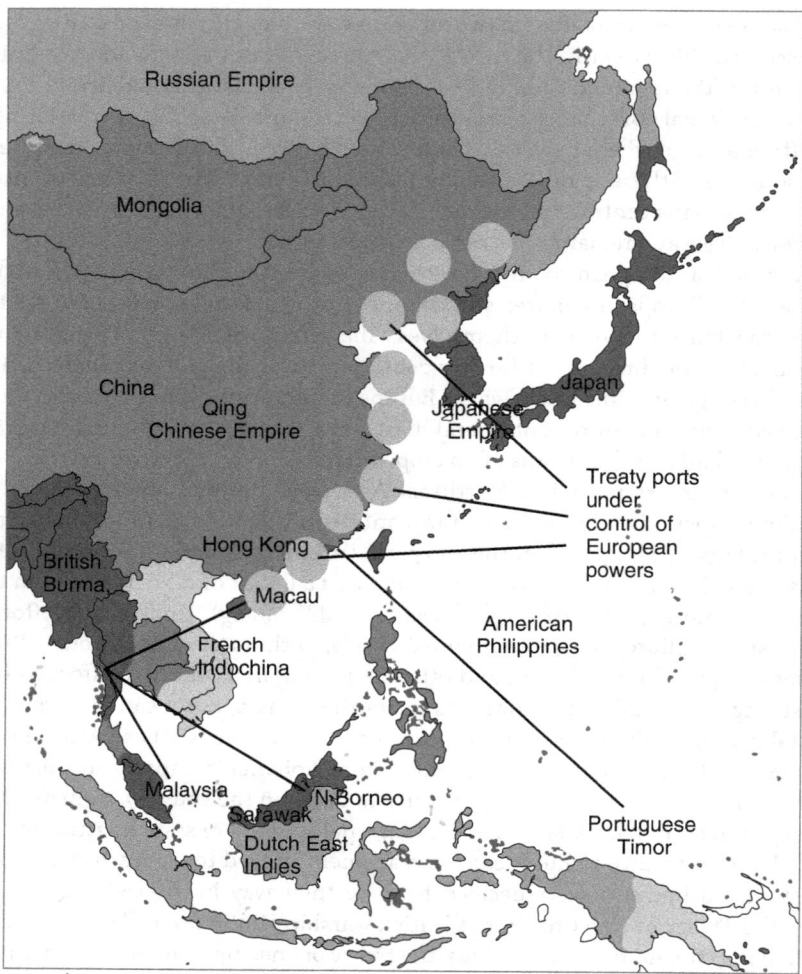

Figure 3.3 Spheres of imperial influence in East Asia, early twentieth century

port system is a unique set of institutions of interstate relations established through international treaties between European powers, and China and Japan. The system extended the authority of European states to their subjects in Chinese ports that they had gained possession of for trade. In Fairbank's original discussion, the treaty port system is seen as the working of the international law and diplomacy of the Westphalian system over the Chinese tribute system for trade (Fairbank 1953).

If we look at the complexity of the dynamics that shape power relations and institutions, we see the same pattern of a mixture of Westphalian institutions and imperialist methods of empire building. Unlike polities in Southeast Asia, Qing China and Japan were seen as imperialist powers themselves and subject to the use of international law, diplomatic protocols, negotiation, and treaty for settling international disputes (Gong 1984). For the "territories" the imperialist powers took control over from China or Japan, however, imperialist logic and institutions prevailed. The institutions of extraterritorial rights were certainly not an ideal instance of Westphalian principles and norms. These institutions legitimized an international practice whereby the home law of the imperialist state was applied to its nationals in a newly possessed foreign land of another state.

European interests and presence in Northeast Asia gradually withdrew over time. China collapsed as an empire and sought a way to rebuild itself as a modern state. European powers were not able to further develop in China the type of colonial governance they had in Southeast Asia. Japan, on the other hand, took the initiative to "mimic" state institutions and organize state power and authority, following largely the European models, and transformed itself into a great power. Even though the collapse of the large empires in Europe led to the rise of modern states there, European empire-building efforts in East Asia did not lead to the rise of a significant alternative in the forms of polity and institutions of interstate relations, following the decline and collapse of the Chinese world order in the late nineteenth and early twentieth century.

European empire building in East Asia did have an influence on subsequent developments in IREA and the emergent structures and institutions that defined the international order in post-1945 East Asia. This influence was most visible in the East–West dichotomy that arose in IREA in the sense of the world structure of geopolitical and geoeconomic power between developed and developing states and the national structure and institutions of the state. This dichotomous set of dynamics drove the political development of East Asian countries for much of the twentieth century.

Moreover, different outcomes of European empire building in Southeast and Northeast Asia provided part of the historical foundation for the bipolar structure that developed in IREA, and this will be discussed in Chapter 5 in greater detail. The fact that European powers moved northward from the south in East Asia further advanced the structural and material connection between continental and maritime East Asia. Finally, European empire building in Northeast Asia and imperial competition did not lead to an effective alternative to the Chinese empire model of polity but, rather, almost replaced the Chinese world order with the European powers' own order. This complicated the "grand transformation" in East Asia from an imperial world order to a nation-state system, as Samuel Kim envisaged (Kim 2008). This grand transformation would materialize in East Asia as the empire of Qing China collapsed and the Chinese world order declined. It further intensified the tension between these two forms of polity and associated modes of interstate relations.

THE GREATER EAST ASIAN SPHERE OF CO-PROSPERITY

Accompanying the movement of European powers to continental East Asia in the late nineteenth century were three other powers: Russia, Japan, and the United States. These three continued to shape the structure, institutions, and international order in IREA for much of the twentieth century.

Japan's attitude toward the intensifying great power competition in continental East Asia in the late nineteenth and early twentieth centuries was ambiguous. As Akira Iriye suggests, Japan's ambiguity was largely driven by two contending views and the political forces behind them in Japan at the time over the role of Japan in East Asia – the Wide Ocean Society view "advocating that Japan should make itself the leader in Asia" and Other People's Rights view "insisting the nation should help other Asian countries achieve freedom and independence" (Iriye 1997: 9). These views were part of the "Pan-Asianist orientation" in political and intellectual circles in Japan against a backdrop of "the government's preoccupation with the West." Chushichi Tsuzuki, in his analysis of Japan's engagement with East Asia (Tsuzuki 2000), also found a mixture of different forces that drove Japan's imperial expansion to continental East Asia and beyond: "to rival China" as the leader of the East Asian order and the Meiji reform and change to make Japan a European-like nation. In Jon Davidann's investigation of Japan's vision of East Asia in relation to both European and US efforts in East Asia (Davidann 2003), Japan is seen as being motivated by itself being the real different "citadel of civilization" to save East Asian civilization.

The Pan-Asianist orientation is further part of the larger set of contending views of Japan's relations with East Asia and, more specifically, with the Chinese world order. Some argued for more active engagement in East Asia and an active role in the shaping of the structure, institutions, and order in IREA. Others wanted to focus on the internal development of Japan and let the West fight in continental East Asia. The Pan-Asianist orientation informed the growth of continentalism in Japan's strategic thinking in IREA. Continentalism was a dominant strategic vision of Japan's role and purpose in East Asia in the early twentieth century. It advocated for a broad focus in continental East Asia rather than a narrow focus on oceanic Japan as the base for its further growth and development. It argued for a concentration of efforts and resources in its imperialist expansion in continental East Asia and further north. The latter part of this was reshaped in the 1930s and 1940s when Japan moved instead southward to take Southeast Asia and the Pacific as the strategic focus of its East Asian order building.

The government took a more "realistic" stance on the declining order in continental East Asia and growing great power competition for spheres of influence. It opted for more active participation in the great power competition in continental East Asia. Japan actively engaged with Korea first in the late nineteenth century to gain influence and a stronghold on the edge of continental East Asia. Japan challenged Korea's traditional relations with China under the Chinese world order and an increasingly aggressive Russia in the region. Japan defeated Qing China in the first Sino-Japanese War in 1894–1895. The Treaty of Shimonoseki in 1895 settled the conflict between Qing China and the Empire of Japan, and China relinquished its suzerain rights over Korea and ceded Liaodong Peninsula, Taiwan, and the Penghu Islands to Japan. Japan further defeated Russia in the Russo-Japanese War in 1904–1905 over the sphere of influence in Manchuria, Liaodong Peninsula, and Korea. In the Treaty of Portsmouth that ended the war, mediated by US President Theodore Roosevelt, Russia accepted Korea as part of Japan's sphere of influence, agreed to withdraw from Manchuria, and ceded interests and rights in southern Liaodong and the Sakhalin Islands to Japan.

Japan's intentions were quite clear and direct with regard to the new "territories" over which it gained control. Taiwan was directly ceded to Japan after the Treaty of Shimonoseki. Korea became independent (from China) after the treaty in 1895 but a protectorate of Japan in the Japan-Korea Treaty of 1905 and recognized as such in the Treaty of Portsmouth of the same year. Japan formally annexed Korea in the Japan-Korea Treaty of 1910. Japan further moved into Manchuria. In 1931, Japanese troops seized Manchuria and formally set up Manchuguo, with the last emperor of Qing as its head of state and emperor. In 1937, the Japanese advanced to northern China that triggered the Second Sino-Japanese War. This allowed Japan to expand its "sphere of influence" to northern and eastern parts of China. There was a pattern of three-step assimilation and annexation in Japan's expansion in continental East Asia. It seized polities one at a time, severing their connection with the Chinese imperial system. It then turned those polities into some form of a protectorate of Japan and organized the political economy in the polity. Institutional and material infrastructures were set up so the polities could be assimilated into Japan. Then the polities were formally incorporated into the Japanese Empire.

With the Pacific War between Japan and the United States breaking out in 1941, Japan's continentalism shifted to the wider ocean of the West Pacific, taking over control of a long list of European colonial territories in Southeast Asia. These included Malaya, Burma, Hong Kong, New Guinea, and the Solomon Islands from the British Empire, Indonesia from the Dutch Empire, and Indochina from the French Empire. It completed the process of seizing control over all of East Asia (Figure 3.4) in 1942.

Japan's military control of Southeast Asia was brief. The new territories were placed largely under temporary war time military administration. The Great East Asian Sphere of Co-Prosperity was a term Japan used in the 1930s and 1940s to promote the idea of a community of East Asian nations centered around Japan and a term to describe Japan's sphere of influence in East Asia that included these new territories. It was not clear whether this would be a traditional sphere of influence with loose "colonial arrangements" connecting various non-Japanese territories with Japan, a "feudal system" of Tokugawa Japan of the pre-Meiji time, or an imperialist polity that incorporated these territories into a centralized state system. It was a classic problem that troubled China in its attempts to build an empire in continental East Asia and the European powers in building their imperial presence in this part of the world.

Regardless of the possible scenarios for an effective governing structure and legitimizing institutions to emerge in and over these former European colonial territories, this was the first time that continental and maritime East Asian countries were brought together under a single polity framework or a single hegemonic power. Charles A. Fisher describes this as "a remarkable demonstration of the ever-present antithesis between landward and maritime concepts of empire" (Fisher 115(1/3): 1). In the long history of interaction and connection between continental and maritime East Asia, the political, economic, social, cultural, and religious influence had largely flowed from continental East Asia to maritime East Asia. This was driven by the expansion of the influence of the Chinese empire and the Chinese world order. Japan's expansion moved in the opposite direction, from maritime to continental

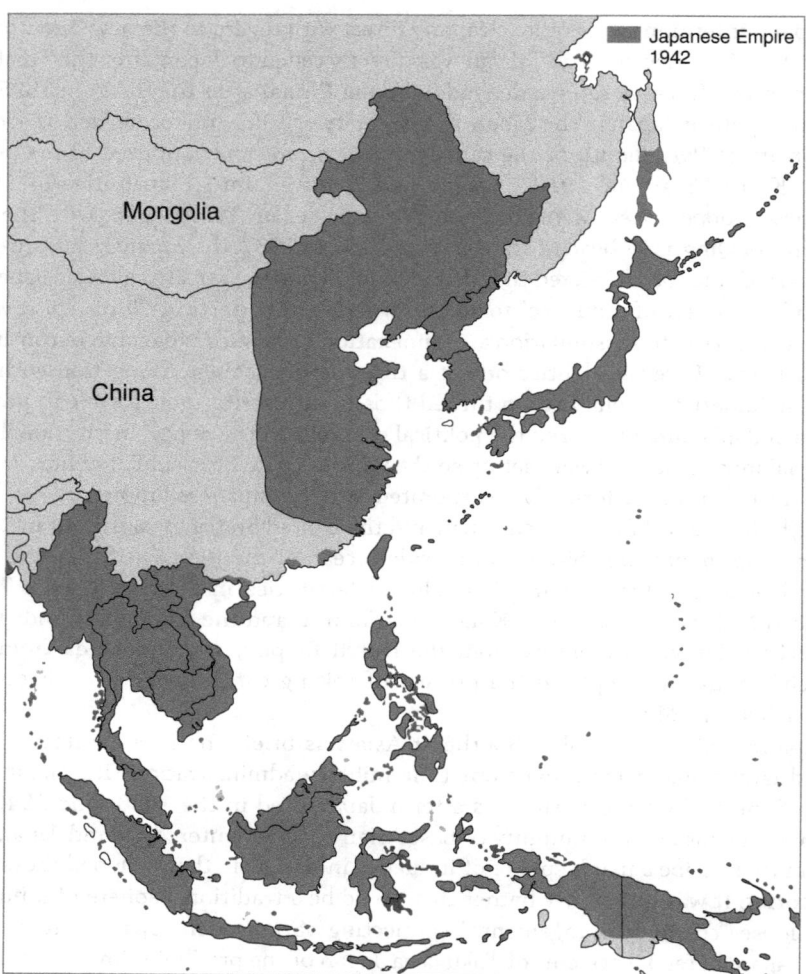

Figure 3.4 Japanese Empire in East Asia, 1942

East Asia. Its advances in the region brought material and institutional substance to East Asia as a unit of political authority and order. As seen in the extensive literature (Myers & Peattie 1984; Moore 2013; Peattie 1988; Hata 1988; Cox 1988) on how Japan organized its rapidly expanding empire, institutions of systematic assimilation in governance, political economy, and society and culture were set up in the formal colonies in Northeast Asia. In the rest of the "sphere," particularly in maritime East Asia, ad hoc policies, programs, and temporary arrangements dominated.

Japan's imperial expansion in East Asia was part of the trend for some time in East Asia whereby nation-states organized industrial development across national boundaries. Japan expanded its political economic interests and production activities to Korea, Taiwan, and Manchuria, reorganized the political economy in these colonies, and connected them to industrial development in Japan. This formal economic integration had not yet extended to China proper and Southeast Asia by the time the Japanese Empire suddenly collapsed at the end of the Pacific War. But the institutions that developed to shape political economy in these polities and their connection with Japan remained and would have a significant impact on postwar industrial development and economic growth in East Asia.

Japan's imperialist expansion in the first half of the twentieth century brought about the complete collapse of the Chinese world order and interrupted European powers' attempts to extend their spheres of influence there. Because this itself was a form of empire building and imperial expansion, it did not lead to an alternative to the traditional hegemonic hierarchical structure in East Asia, except that the hegemonic power sustaining the hierarchical structure was different. In a significant way, it was still an imperialist solution to the problem of interstate order in East Asia – building an international order through imperialist competition, expansion, and conquest by a hegemonic power.

The rise and fall of the Japanese Empire in the first half of the twentieth century further influenced the interests and actions of the other major players, notably that of the United States, and its strategy to engage with East Asia. Japan's effective advance seriously affected the equilibrium of international power in East Asia. With the European powers withdrawing from the region, and China continuing to be pushed inward with the further worsening of internal tensions and conflicts, organizing an effective force on continental East Asia to counterbalance Japan seemed strategically imperative. In the years leading to the Pacific War, US primary interests in the region lay largely in engaging with the political forces in continental East Asia, bringing the Communists and Nationalists together in China, and hoping these efforts would help at least to retain some form of power balance in East Asia against Japan.

IMPERIAL ORDERS AND MODERN TRANSFORMATION

Interstate relations in East Asia have been dominated by the Chinese hegemonic, hierarchical, imperial structure and "world order" for centuries. Even in the *longue durée* of Pax Sinica, however, the Chinese empire was not the only form that dictated interstate relations in East Asia. Pax Sinica describes the long interstate peace under the Chinese world order and China's hegemonic reign in East Asia. It has also been used in more recent debates to question whether the rise of China would return the hegemonic Chinese world order to East Asia and whether that would further contribute to peace in IREA. We have shown in this chapter that in continental East Asia, "China" itself was a group of warring states at one point, a multinational empire at another, and something between at many other points. Some periods of the Chinese empire, Qing China or Yuan China for example, were not ruled by Chinese. Many of the states during the Warring States period were all ruled by the Han Chinese.

The types of state were more complicated in East Asia then. It is hard to use today's concepts and frameworks to ask whether there were Westphalian style international relations in premodern East Asia (Zhang 2001). But it is clear that in the long historical evolution of interstate relations in East Asia, there has been constant tension between the Warring States system and the imperial system. This tension was driven by dual dynamics of change in the power structure and institutions and norms that support the interstate order. Our discussion has shown that these dynamics drove the interstate order in IREA to transform from one order to another.

There has been debate over what caused the Chinese empire, and the Chinese world order, to collapse from the mid-nineteenth century. One popular view, based on the original Fairbank thesis, suggests it was the arrival of European states in East Asia that instigated response of the empire and stimulated change within the empire. Another popular view, informed by the works of Bull and Watson and the English School in general, argue that it is probably the advance of the Westphalian nation-state institutions that prevailed over the imperial system of interstate relations in East Asia (see further discussion in Chapter 12).

More recent scholarship (Zhang 2001; MacKay 2015; Kumar 2013; Wang 2014) urges us to see the decline of the Chinese empire as part of the playout of the long cycles of alternating forms of polity in East Asia between state and empire, a process further complicated by the worldwide "transformation" of polity from empire to republic/nation-state in the nineteenth and twentieth centuries. Whether an alternation between the imperial and multistate system or a modern transformation from empire to nation-state, the dominant responses to the decline of the Chinese empire and the collapse of the Chinese world order from the late nineteenth century were still very much imperialist in nature. These included the European movement to continental East Asia to establish a presence in Northeast Asia and Japan's attempt to establish its own empire in East Asia.

In this long procession of international orders in East Asia, we see the power of the structural and institutional conditions in the shaping of patterns in IREA. These conditions would continue to influence the shaping of the international order after 1945. First, with the collapse of the Chinese world order, the failures of the European powers to establish an imperial presence in continental East Asia, and the swift collapse of the Japanese empire itself, there emerged a significant "power vacuum" for competing forms of polity and interstate relations to fill in. East Asia would look for more effective ideas and forms to organize not only their national political economy but also interstate relations. This would likely be very contentious as each "state" that emerged in East Asia from the ruins of World War II was contested and disputed.

Moreover, while the Europeans and Japanese failed to build alternative structures and institutions in IREA, the trade interests, activities, and industrial development they brought to and generated in East Asia left a significant material basis for a region-wide drive for industrial development. This provided a level of connectivity and an initial impetus for the division of labor that further industrial development could build on after 1945.

Finally, the outcomes of the imperialist competitions in East Asia gave the USSR and US significant leverage to play dominant roles in the shaping of IREA at the end of World War II. The USSR and US were the two "superpowers" that emerged out of the brutal world wars, each with a clear and well-articulated ideological framework as well as the material and institutional capacity to pursue building their own world order. They also involved themselves in the shaping of IREA with a position different from those of the "Old World" and, of course, from those in East Asia.

Study Questions

1. Discuss the tension between the imperial form and multistate system in the evolution of IREA. What principally influenced the rise and fall of these forms?
2. Were the "warring states" at different historical periods in East Asia a distinct system of interstate relations? Why or why not?
3. Discuss the institutional consequences of European expansion in East Asia in the late nineteenth and early twentieth centuries. Were they the working out of the Westphalian or imperialist system?
4. Discuss the implications of the structure and institutions of polity formation in East Asia for contemporary IREA. Are IREA destined for a hierarchical and hegemonic international order?
5. Discuss the transformations of international orders in East Asia. Use the logic of structure–institution–international order to explain the transformations.

Further Reading

Beasley, William G., 1987. *Japanese Imperialism, 1894–1945*. Oxford: Oxford University Press.

Chow, Kai-Wing, Kevin M. Doak, and Fu Poshek, 2001. *Constructing Nationhood in Modern East Asia*. Ann Arbor: University of Michigan Press.

Cooley, Alexander, and Hendrik Spruyt, 2009. *Contracting States: Sovereign Transfers in International Relations*. Princeton: Princeton University Press.

Crump, Thomas, 2007. *Asia-Pacific: A History of Empire and Conflict*. New York: Hambledon Continuum.

Duus, Peter, 1988. *The Cambridge History of Japan: The Twentieth Century*. Cambridge: Cambridge University Press.

Fairbank, John K., 1953. *Trade and Diplomacy on the China Coast: The Opening of Treaty Ports, 1842–1854*. Cambridge: Harvard University Press.

Fairbank, John K., 1968. *The Chinese World Order*. Cambridge: Harvard University Press.

Goldman, Merle, and Andrew Gordon, 2000. *Historical Perspectives on Contemporary East Asia*. Cambridge: Harvard University Press.

Jensen, Richard, Richard Jensen, Jon Davidann, and Yoneyuki Sugita, 2003. *Trans-Pacific Relations: America, Europe, and Asia in the Twentieth Century*. Westport: Praeger.

Kang, David, 2010. *East Asia Before the West: Five Centuries of Trade and Tribute*. New York: Columbia University Press.

Kim, Samuel, 2008. "The Evolving Asian System: Three Transformations," pp. 35–56, in David Shambaugh and Michael Yahuda, *International Relations of Asia*. Lanham: Rowman & Littlefield.

Lee, Ji-Young, 2017. *China's Hegemony: Four Hundred Years of East Asian Domination*. New York: Columbia University Press.

MacKay, Joseph, 2015. "Rethinking the IR Theory of Empire in Late Imperial China," *International Relation of the Asia Pacific* 15(1): 53–79.

McCloud, Donald G., 1995. *Southeast Asia: Tradition and Modernity in the Contemporary World*. Boulder: Westview Press.

Modelski, George, 1987. *Long Cycles in World Politics*. London: Macmillan.

Montgomery, Evan Braden, and Evan B. Montgomery, 2016. "Japan and the Creation of a New Order in East Asia, 1894–1902," pp. 75–101, in *In the Hegemon's Shadow*. Ithaca: Cornell University Press.

Moore, Aaron, 2013. *Constructing East Asia: Technology, Ideology, and Empire in Japan's Wartime Era 1931–1945*. Stanford: Stanford University Press.

Myers, Ramon Hawley, and Mark R. Peattie, 1984. *The Japanese Colonial Empire, 1895–1945*. Princeton: Princeton University Press.

Park, Seo-Hyun, 2013. "Changing Definitions of Sovereignty in Nineteenth-Century East Asia: Japan and Korea Between China and the West," *Journal of East Asian Studies* 13(2): 281–307.

Park, Seo-Hyun, 2017. *Sovereignty and Status in East Asian International Relations*. Cambridge: Cambridge University Press.

Schmid, Andre, 2002. *Korea Between Empires, 1895–1919*. New York: Columbia University Press.

Spruyt, Hendrik, 1994. *The Sovereign State and Its Competitors: An Analysis of Systems Change*. Princeton: Princeton University Press.

Steinmetz, George, 2013. *Sociology and Empire*. Durham: Duke University Press.

Tsuzuki, Chushichi, 2000. *The Pursuit of Power in Modern Japan 1825–1995*. Oxford: Oxford University Press.

Wang, Yuan-kang, 2013. "Explaining the Tribute System: Power, Confucianism, and War in Medieval East Asia," *Journal of East Asian Studies* 13(2): 207–232.

Wang, Hui, 2014. *China from Empire to Nation-State*. Cambridge: Harvard University Press.

Zhang, Yongjin, 2001. "System, Empire and State in Chinese International Relations," *Review of International Studies* 27 (1):43–63.

Zhao, Tingyang, 2006. "Rethinking Empire from a Chinese Concept 'All-Under-Heaven'," *Journal of Social Identities* 12(1): 29–41.

Zhao, Tingyang, 2011. *The Tianxia System: An Introduction to the Philosophy of World Institution*. Beijing: China Renmin University Press.

4 War, Peace, and Geopolitical Dynamics

In This Chapter...

- The Cold War and hot wars
- War over state constitution
- War over state boundaries
- War and transborder nations
- Geopolitical drivers
- Japan and China in East Asia
- Rise of China in post-Cold War East Asia
- US engagement with East Asia
- Between great powers

Learning Objectives

By the end of this chapter, you will be able to
- Understand the unique conditions, particularly the problem of nation building and state making, for war and peace in East Asia
- Understand the impact of international geopolitical dynamics on war and peace in IREA
- Understand the role of China, Japan, and the United States in great power politics in contemporary IREA
- Use a traditional, state-centric geopolitical framework to analyze the problem of war and peace in East Asia.

Why do states go to war and how do they make peace? This seems to be a foundational problem that your IR 101 class should have addressed. But how does this problem manifest in East Asia? Are wars sources of the problems in IREA, or they are solutions to problems? What are those unique forces that drive states to engage in conflict and war? What are the unique sets of participants involved over a distinct set of issues? What are the unique East Asian ways in which tensions are reduced and peace restored or, looking at it from the opposite perspective, tensions escalate and real war breaks out? Do these together inform a pattern of war and peace among states in IREA and a coherent set of explanations?

East Asia is a unique region that can provide useful knowledge on these questions. There is a debate on whether East Asia is more peaceful and stable or more "conflict ridden." David Kang (2010) argues that East Asia has been very peaceful and stable for much of the last 500 hundred years when major wars plagued Europe and impacted the world. Muthiah Alagappa, though, observes that "post 1945 Asia has been conflict ridden. Between 1945 and 2010, there were a total of 71 major wars (in which battle deaths exceed 1,000), of which 15 were inter-state wars, 47 intrastate wars, 6 wars of liberation against colonial rule, and 3 non-state wars. There were also approximately 23 minor inter-state wars (25 to 999 battle deaths) and 24 military incidents (less than 25 battle deaths). In all, about 2 million combatants were killed in interstate wars, 1.9 million in intrastate wars, and about 400,000 in anti-colonial struggles" (Alagappa 2014:1). Alagappa also cites further evidence from Ben Goldsmith's investigation on political institutions and interstate conflict initiation in determining the conflict level in IREA. Goldstein's evidence (Goldsmith 2007: 10, also 2013) suggests a much higher level of interstate conflict initiation in post-1945 East Asia.

There also seems to be a general view in the literature that the number of conflicts has been significantly reduced in more recent decades in East Asia. While international wars and conflicts notably intensified in other parts of the world, there has been an "East Asian peace" (Tønnesson 2017; Weissmann 2012) in IREA. East Asian peace here refers to a distinct period in more recent decades in IREA where there has been a significantly lower level of conflict, in contrast to that in the region during the Cold War where major wars and conflicts raged and in other parts of the world where international wars and conflicts intensified. However, scholars differ on when the East Asian peace started to set in and what enabled it.

In this chapter, we investigate, through a series of significant case studies in IREA, a particular set of causes that drive states and nations into war and conflict in East Asia, a unique set of conditions for tension reduction, conflict management and war settlement, and the role of traditional geopolitics, diplomacy, and great power politics in war and peace in East Asia.

THE COLD WAR AND HOT WARS

There seems no dispute that there was a significantly higher level of interstate conflict in East Asia during the Cold War. Three large-scale wars and armed conflicts of global significance during the Cold War took place in East Asia: the Korean War, Taiwan Strait conflicts, and the Vietnam War, all on and across the East Asian crescent. These three wars followed a similar pattern of development in terms of what caused the open conflicts that involved large-scale armed force and firepower and destruction, coalitions of national and international forces, and the background of the global confrontation of two groups of geopolitical and ideological forces – the Cold War between the US and USSR and their allies. The outcomes of the wars were different and their impact on the nation, states, and interstate relations varied.

WAR OVER STATE CONSTITUTION

The Korean War broke out in 1950 after years of efforts by allied powers to secure a settlement ending World War II in East Asia failed over the Japan islands and the Korean Peninsula. This was largely attributed to the hardening of the position of the

United States and the Soviet Union on the postwar global international order. It is often common, therefore, for people to think of the global strategic and ideological competition between the United States and the Soviet Union, or the global Cold War, as the primary cause of the tension and conflict on the Korean Peninsula. The literature overwhelmingly frames the Cold War in East Asia as a structural effect of the global Cold War, the geopolitical and ideological confrontation between the USSR and US.

Bruce Cumings was one of the leading scholars to look at the internal forces, national politics, and civil war as the causes that drew different states into conflict on the Korean Peninsula, confrontation over state power and legitimacy, and institutions of state organization for the newly independent Korean nation (Cumings 1981, 1990, 2010). While the communist and progressive forces established dominance in the north and set up a government structure there, the Democratic People's Republic of Korea (DPRK) in September 1948, the nationalist and conservative forces did so in the south and set up new state institutions, the Republic of Korea (ROK) in May 1948. The armistice was ratified in 1953 by the United Nations Command and the Command of the Korean People's Army and the Chinese People's Volunteers for "a complete cessation of hostilities and of all acts of armed force in Korea until a final peaceful settlement is achieved." This final peace settlement has not been achieved to this day, more than 60 years after the armistice.

The Korean War made a great impact on IREA and the world. The war caused more than a million battle deaths on all sides and more than 1.5 million civilian deaths in Korea on both sides. The war delayed social economic development in Korea and economic development in Korea and China. The war is considered to be the onset of the worldwide Cold War or the first major instance of how the Cold War manifested in a regional theater. The war reshaped the geopolitical order in East Asia. Most importantly, the war cemented the division of the Korean nation into two states, DPRK and ROK, and added a significant dynamic to the Korean problem that has been high on the agenda of IREA ever since. It turned the Korean Peninsula into an active theater in which international and national politics would play out.

The Korean War, like many other wars around the same time in East Asia, was motivated, at least initially and partially, by opposing political forces in Korea to build a new Korean state. The conflict was turned into an international geopolitical exercise by major powers that envisaged an ideologically informed global grouping of international forces and interests. The unfolding of the Cold War in East Asia turned the Korean Peninsula into a primary zone of contention for global ideological forces. Over time this reinforced the two-Korea arrangements, even beyond the end of the hot war and, further, beyond the end of the Cold War itself. A peace treaty for a unified Korea has been incredibly difficult to initiate in this prolonged bipolar confrontation in East Asia.

If the Korean War is one more effect of the global Cold War and geopolitical and ideological confrontation, tensions would have relaxed and conflict lost its purpose when the global ideological confrontation collapsed as the Cold War ended. The fact that the tension continued, and even escalated to open conflict from time to time, with no peace settlement having been achieved thus far, suggests the original tension over state structure and institutions for the Korean nation has not be resolved.

With the structure and institutions of two Korean states and even two Korean "nations" being perpetuated in the 70 years of development of the Korean nation and state, a settlement on the original intentions and interests that drove parties into the Korean War seems to be increasingly complicated and difficult to achieve.

The same pattern of a civil war turning into interstate conflicts was also seen in a series of conflicts over the Taiwan Strait in the 1950s and a prolonged tension between PRC and the US for many of the post-WWII decades. A long civil war over state power, authority, and institutions of the Republic of China (ROC) between the Communists and the Nationalists ended following the end of World War II in East Asia and China's victory in the second Sino-Japanese war (1937–1845). Chinese Communists, led by Mao Zedong, established the People's Republic of China (PRC) on mainland China in 1949, and the Nationalists, led by Chiang Kai-shek, moved the ROC to the Taiwan islands.

International forces and interests were involved in the civil war from the very beginning. Stalin's Soviet Union had great influence on Sun Yat-sen's Republican revolution that had both the Nationalists and Communists behind it. Japan failed to win over Chiang Kai-shek's Nationalists while the United States built positive relations with Chiang's Nationalists and Mao's Communists. The establishment of the PRC on mainland China with the full support of the Soviet Union and the Communist International and the relocating of the ROC government to the Taiwan islands reinforced the interstate dynamics in the intrastate conflict. The intertwinedness of these two sets of dynamics laid the ground for continual tension and conflict across the Taiwan Strait.

In the ensuing decades, the tension and armed conflicts between the PRC and USSR on the one hand and the ROC and US on the other intensified. The Taiwan Strait became a primary site of interstate tension and conflict in East Asia. Tensions shifted to direct clashes in the 1950s between PRC and ROC over some of the offshore islands close to the southeast coast of the mainland that were under ROC control. In the first Taiwan Strait crisis in the winter of 1954–1955, a PRC military campaign took over control of some of the islands and pushed ROC forces back to the Taiwan main island. In the second Taiwan Strait crisis in 1958, ROC troops were able to sustain a People's Liberation Army attack on Kinmen and Matsu islands and consolidated its control there. On the surface, the clashes were over the legitimacy of the PRC and ROC over China and, hence, the continuation of the civil war between the Communists and Nationalists. In the long-term strategic thinking of both the Communist and Nationalist decision makers, these were attempts to prevent the civil war from turning into an interstate conflict.

The PRC-ROC feud was not settled but continued to be a cause of tension and conflict in IREA. The tension and conflicts have managed to be confined by all parties as a civil war for a long time. The direct casualties of the conflicts were limited, but as in the case of the Korean War, their impact on the political, economic, and social development of both the PRC and ROC was profound. Much of the politics, policy, and resources on both sides were concentrated on managing the tension and influencing its further development. Internal political developments in recent decades in both ROC and PRC have made efforts to contain the tension and resolve disputes more complicated and difficult. Separate economic, social, and political developments on both sides shaped the development of a different political economic basis that drives relations to move further from a civil conflict to an interstate conflict.

A third major war in East Asia since World War II was the Vietnam War – which broke out on a set of dynamics very similar to that seen in the Korean War and the Taiwan Strait conflicts. The Vietnam War was part of a series of Indochina wars over the form, jurisdiction, and legitimacy of the states that emerged from the collapse of French Indochina in World War II. Vietnam gained its independence at the end of World War II, after the surrender of Japan. It took the first Indochina War (1946–1954) for Vietnamese nationalists to defeat the attempts of the French to restore its colonial rule to Indochina. The Battle of Dien Bien Phu was a decisive military engagement between French forces and Viet Minh that ended the first Indochina War in 1954.

As in the Korean War, from the very beginning the Vietnam War (1955–1975) involved elements of both a civil war and an interstate war. This seems to be a pattern for new states gaining independence from their colonial rulers. The war was officially between the Democratic Republic of Vietnam (DRV), or North Vietnam, and the Republic of Vietnam (ROV), or South Vietnam. The Geneva Conference in 1954, attended by France, Viet Minh, the USSR, the PRC, the US, and Great Britain, ended the first Indochina War, divided Vietnam into two temporary zones, and recognized the authority of the DRV in the north and the ROV in the south, as well as the Kingdom of Cambodia and the Kingdom of Laos. This prepared the groundwork for the two national political forces to engage in a civil war to claim state authority and constitutional power in the promised new state of Vietnam.

At the same time, the breakup of French Indochina, instigated largely by the national independence movement associated with the Communists from the north, left the door open to a restructuring of regional interstate order in Indochina. The actual Vietnam War, the principal part of the Second Indochina War, started immediately after the Geneva Conference, with civil conflicts across the Indochina Peninsula, in Vietnam, Laos, and Cambodia, but largely between North Vietnamese forces backed by the Soviet Union and China, on one side, and South Vietnam forces backed by the United States, on the other. Direct, close engagement by the Chinese and US military forces started to become substantive in the mid-1960s. There is no debate that the conflict incurred huge human costs. Direct military and civilian casualties in the war were in the millions, plus the significant impact on political, economic, and social development in Vietnam, Indochina, and IREA. The conflict, of both an interstate and an intranational nature, was brought to a close in 1975, with the success of North Vietnam at extending state power to and establishing authority in the south, the withdrawal of US and PRC forces from direct military engagement from Indochina, and the collapse of the ROV.

Geopolitics continued after the end of the Vietnam War. Communist state authority was established in all three Indochina states: Vietnam (now the Socialist Republic of Vietnam, SRV), Cambodia (Democratic Kampuchea), and Laos (Lao People's Democratic Republic, LPDR). The Sino-Soviet split, however, added different dynamics to regional interstate relations and intensified the civil war in Cambodia. In 1978, Vietnam, backed by the Soviet Union, sent troops to Cambodia to bring down the

Khmer Rouge regime backed by China and reorganized Cambodian state institutions. This led to tension and direct military conflict with Thailand over the border and a brief war in its northern provinces with Chinese military forces in 1979.

This Third Indochina War ended through diplomatic negotiations at the Paris Peace Conference (1989–1991), brokered by the five permanent members of the UN Security Council. The four main political forces in Cambodia agreed on a way to rebuild state institutions and government for a unified, independent, and sovereign Cambodian state. The Paris Peace Accords ratified in 1991 formally ended the Cambodia-Vietnam War and established the United Nations Transitional Authority in Cambodia (UNTAC) to organize the establishment of the new state of Cambodia.

The three major wars of global significance in contemporary East Asia suggest a close connection between intranational and interstate conflict. Interstate conflicts stirred up domestic tensions, and civil conflicts were used as a platform for effective international engagement and interaction. Civil rivalries sought to engage international forces to reshape power structures in the civil conflict and hence transformed a civil conflict into an interstate conflict. National rivalry over the organization of the polity in each case connected well with the global rivalry over the form and substance of interstate order in the region. The three wars involved both elements of a civil war that was evolving to become an interstate conflict and a civil conflict that was part of a large geopolitical interstate confrontation.

Second, in these three wars, intranational dynamics dominated interstate developments, but the outcomes in nation and state building have been different. National independence and state authority are not only a national issue but also an international problem. Nation and state are not only both the focus of war and conflict in IREA; they are mutually constructive in the rise of nation-states in post-1945 East Asia. The end of the Vietnam War avoided the perpetuation of the two states over a divided nation. The Korean War has led to two states over a divided nation, which over the decades has evolved into two increasingly distinct political, economic, and social communities. How this will evolve from here and whether one polity will emerge for the Korean nation and in what forms is not entirely clear. The same applies to cross-strait relations. The civil conflict between the PRC and ROC has been so far confined to being intranational, but the development of political relations between the PRC and ROC and the changing geopolitical structure in the region presents a scenario whereby the conflict can be pushed into an interstate one.

Third, diplomacy and negotiations are always alternative avenues for settling international conflict and making peace. However, these efforts are complicated by the two large sets of factors in IREA. First. these wars were in a significant way civil conflict over the structure and institutions of state power and authority. Unless these conflicts are resolved, diplomatic efforts will be less effective in bringing peace to the warring parties. Peace remains elusive 70 years after the two Koreas set up their own states, and relations in connection with the Taiwan Strait remain tense. In the case of the Vietnam War, it was what ultimately ended civil rivalry. Moreover, different forms of international conflict resolution are also influenced by great power politics. Unless the great powers involved arrive at some agreement among themselves on the nature of interstate order in the region, diplomacy and negotiations will have little effect.

WAR OVER STATE BOUNDARIES

Along with these major wars, there have been a great number of low-intensity, religious, ethnic, ideological, and territorial wars and conflicts in post-1945 East Asia. One set of these wars and conflicts surrounds the border areas of China that form a circle around China, along with the Korean War, Taiwan Strait conflicts, and the Vietnam War, as discussed earlier. These include India-China war in 1962, tensions with the Soviet Union and Mongolia in the 1970s in the northern border areas, and direct military engagement in the border areas at the tip of the Chinese northeast Asia corner. There is also a heightening of tensions over the Sengaku/Diaoyu Island between Japan and China, over the South China Sea between China and Vietnam, the Philippines, and Indonesia, and between the United States and China.

All these tensions, and the actual wars and conflicts are primarily over the territorial disputes between China and the countries bordering Chinese territories around the borders of the traditional Chinese empire. This is a classic example of how the transformation (rather than collapse into "warring states" or being taken over by other imperialist powers, as discussed in Chapter 3) of a traditional imperial polity into a nation-state in the modern international system has made the boundaries of its territories problematic. In the Chinese case, the boundaries shifted inward or outward over time. Some were not clearly demarcated or others were not institutionalized as expected in modern international law.

There are more China-related territorial disputes that could have led to more interstate conflicts and wars. Bilateral negotiations between China and these states settled many of these disputes. These include China's territorial demarcation agreements with North Korea in 1962, Myanmar in 1963, Pakistan in 1963, Vietnam in 1999, and Russia in 1991. Research has shown that China has been selective in approaching territorial disputes with neighbors. Taylor Fravel, for example, finds that China is "more likely to compromise" in territorial disputes when confronting internal threats to "regime security" (Fravel 2005: 46) but more resistant on other claims. The territorial approach is also influenced by the strategic dynamics in the international environment where China's large strategic interests can supersede the narrower territorial considerations in the bilateral relations. The settlement of territorial disputes in one form or another prevented them from developing into interstate conflict and war. But these cases suggest that disputes over state boundaries are important sources of tension and conflict in IREA.

However, many remain unsettled, notably the one between India and China. With the rise of China, which is removing China's traditional concerns over regime security and strategic concerns, China can take a firmer position on disputes and not shy away from solving disputes by all means. There are also emerging territorial disputes where a dispute develops because of the changing international conditions. Notably among these are the East Sea dispute, the Senkaku/Diaoyutai Island dispute, and the tension and conflict over the South China Sea. Different views of Japan and China on the legitimate extent of their special economic zones in East Asia and who has territorial rights over the Senkaku/Diaoyu Islands (尖閣諸島/钓鱼岛) have always been there. The gas fields found in the disputed area in the East Sea and the new United Nations Convention on the Law of the Sea (UNCLOS) of 1985 have not helped to resolve differences and foster arrangements on the disputes. Both sides see ownership of the island as a critical issue involving state sovereignty. In the shifting international environment where strategic alignment or realignment in East Asia intensified from the mid-1990s, these disputes became an important part of the strategic engagement and interaction.

Territorial disputes in the South China Sea are another example of how practices of international relations meet contemporary institutions for organizing interstate relations. South China Sea disputes refer to a set of overlapping territorial claims by the Philippines, Vietnam, Malaysia, and China over their extended continental shelf in the South China Sea, which has led to heightened tension and clashes between claimant states and confrontations between the US and China in the 2010s. There are multiple claimants in multiple sets of disputes over the South China Sea. These claims were formally made by the Philippines, Vietnam, Malaysia, and China in 2009 in their submissions to the Commission on the Limits of Continental Shelf (CLCS) on the outer limits of their extended continental shelf (Nguyen & Amer 2011; Jayakumar et al. 2014). Some of the claims overlap, which drives the tension among the claimant countries.

Unlike those in other types of territorial disputes, these are claims on something that has not been regulated by modern international law until very recently. These claims are part of the first wave of exercise of the new UNCLOS to clarify ownership of the waters and seabed floors in the South China Sea. International institutions developed in a specific international political environment. Tensions among the claimants were quickly framed in the larger context of US-China strategic competition in the Asia-Pacific, with the rise of China to extend its power and influence in South China Sea and the Pivot to Asia of the United States to uphold its dominance and freedom of movement. The two sets of dynamics combined to drive the escalation of tension to clashes and armed confrontation among claimant countries and between China and the United States.

In sum, territorial disputes are an important source of interstate tension, war, and conflict in East Asia. As East Asia was traditionally under the influence of the Chinese empire, or the Chinese world order, these disputes and associated conflicts were concentrated around the border areas of the Chinese empire of the past or where the tribute relations used to rule. As such, they are often related to the broader context of the structural transformation of IREA discussed earlier, where structural dynamics sufficiently influenced the development of the disputes and ways of their escalation or resolution.

WAR AND TRANSBORDER NATIONS

A third set of wars and conflicts are largely found in Southeast Asia in and across Southeast Asian nations. These wars and conflicts are often categorized as "ethnopolitical conflicts," wars of "people against states," "internal conflicts," "intrastate conflicts," "communal conflicts," and "tribal conflicts" (Gurr 1993, 1994; Reilly 2002). Ben Reilly notes that the "Asia-Pacific region has both the highest incidence of ethnic conflict and the highest number of ethnopolitical groups" in intrastate conflicts, mostly in Southeast Asia (Reilly 2002: 8). An ethnopolitical group is a population in a state with shared ethnic traits that are distinct from those of the majority national population the nation state is based on.

In East Asia, ethnopolitical groups are often part of the larger national group across boundaries in neighboring states, and these ethnopolitical groups have no recognition or representation as a collective entity in state institutions. The new states often inherit a political order where the boundaries of their territories either are not clearly defined or cut through various national groups or over areas where there was a mixture of ethnopolitical groups. Ted Gurr believes that "the post-Cold War surge" in a rebellion of "people against states" is "the continuation of a trend that began in the 1960s" (Gurr 1994: 347). Gurr argues that the main issue in these "ethnopolitical conflicts is the contention for state power among communal groups in the immediate aftermath of state formation, revolution, and efforts to democratize autocratic regime."

As was shown in Chapter 3, most states in Southeast Asia were all new states set up after World War II. The new states were built on the successful independence movement from European colonial rule and the victory of majority national groups in their respective countries in gaining political power over other ethnopolitical groups. The new state would usually take steps to clarify or establish its boundaries. Confrontation between Indonesia and Malaysia in 1963 over the formation of Malaysia is an example of how tension can build up among states because of the ambiguity or overlapping of the authority of the state in relation to an ethnopolitical group. The tension between Malaysia, Indonesia, and perhaps the Philippines was clearly driven by their contention over the status of Sabah and Milan in the newly proposed Malaysia, as each saw the ethnopolitical groups there as part of the national population of their own state. This ethnopolitical source of the civic and interstate tension impacted the stability of state institutions and the legitimacy of the state and interstate relations. Indonesia, Malaysia, the Philippines, Singapore, and Thailand formed a group in 1967, now known as the Association of the Southeast Asian Nations (ASEAN), to collectively deal with the tension and prevent it from escalating into open hostility and war. The principle of nation-state faced difficulties in practice.

The instance of conflict and tension ASEAN states faced was exacerbated by a large problem in IREA at the time that generated region-wide interstate tensions and conflict: the communist movements and antistate activities. In Northeast Asia, communist forces successfully came to take over state power, in North Korea, North Vietnam, and Mainland China. In maritime East Asia, the Communist Party of Indanones (IDP), in collaboration with the nationalist force led by Sukarno, was almost on the edge of taking over state power in the mid-1960s. IDP was much more influential than the more radical Islamic state forces then.

Communist forces were a significant challenge to state power of the newly established states. In Singapore, Malaysia, Thailand, and the Philippines, communist activities and Chinese ethnopolitical forces were almost inseparable. Because of the significant size of Chinese ethnic groups and the complex national basis for the newly established state, communism from the north via ethnic Chinese groups was perceived as a real threat. Many of the armed campaigns by the states against communist forces were carried out in the gray area between civil war and interstate war. After the Indonesian army destroyed the communist and nationalist forces in 1965, and the military in the Philippines, Thailand, and Myanmar controlled state power, "guerrilla war" between the communist forces and the military went on for decades in the Philippines, Thailand, and Myanmar. Communist/Chinese ethnopolitical forces were also marginalized and neutralized under the strongman's rule of Lee Kwan Yue in Singapore and Mahathir in Malaysia.

In these wars and conflicts against communism throughout Southeast Asia, the influence of ethnopolitical forces was visible. Ethnopolitical conflict and interstate conflict went beyond the Communist/Chinese threat from the north. In the Philippines, there has been continual tension between the state and armed ethnopolitical forces. For decades, government forces aimed to eliminate these political forces, though at times they tried to negotiate a peace settlement with various armed ethnopolitical forces. The latest instance is the government-organized military campaign to destroy Islamic militant groups in Malawi in 2017.

A similar pattern of tension, conflict, and war is also seen in the southern part of Thailand that borders with Malaysia where the ethnopolitical group is ethnically more part of the Malay population spreading across the borders in Thailand. In the northeast part of Myanmar bordering with China, ethnic and religious groups there have closer ties with the populations across the border in China. This is also seen in the eastern border areas with Thailand, the northwest part with India, and in the state of Rakhine, where the Muslim Rohingya population resides with the majority Buddhist population (for further details of these cases as transnational security challenges, see Chapter 10). Tensions and conflicts between the Myanmar state, the military, and these various ethnopolitical forces have been going on for decades.

In all these past and ongoing tensions and conflict, restoring or establishing ethnic unity and integrity and matching state institutions with their ethnopolitical basis in the state has been a key theme in national politics in these countries. Tension is high and conflict breaks out from time to time, particularly in cases where the ethnopolitical groups in question are part of a large national population across borders in neighboring states. This connects and complicates intrastate and interstate politics. Irredentism is an ideology based on national solidarity across state boundaries. It usually implies the notion that the home country of some large national group seeks to recover its "lost" territories over the entire "nation," and this often leads to interstate conflict as we saw, for example, in Northeast Asia. This is not always the case in Southeast Asia. In all these cases, nations learned to accept the state boundaries. To avoid tensions from escalating into interstate conflict seems to be a guiding principle for these Southeast Asian countries. Post-1945 experiences show that the ASEAN way – to organize conflict resolution and tension reduction among ASEAN states or among the states involved in the dispute – is an effective way to prevent civil conflicts from escalating into interstate wars.

This last set of wars and conflicts is a prevalent form of international conflict in East Asia. Some of them are not usually included in discussions of interstate wars and conflict. These international conflicts, however, say quite a bit about a unique combination of forces that drove interstate relations in East Asia to escalate into open conflict. These territorial, ethnic, religious, ideological, and institutional forces or factors and their combined effects at a given historical time are very East Asian. It has been a condition that underlies relations among East Asian states. Most of them were newly established states that emerged out of a very complex interplay of ethnic, religious, and communal factors. Both the national/ethnopolitical groups and the state have an instinct to close the gap between state and nation. This leads to violence and political resolutions to disputes between the state and ethnopolitical groups. Because the state always has the upper hand in the long run, these ethnicity-based intrastate and interstate conflicts mostly end with the ethnopolitical groups being incorporated into the state institutions.

This set of conflicts in IREA also helps us understand the unique pattern of how interstate conflicts are managed in IREA. Because of the incoherent national basis for most of the states and the generally risk- or conflict-averse East Asian culture, states tend to avoid open conflict with one another but are more determined to confront ethnopolitical forces as the organizer of an intrastate solution to the tension. The security and legitimacy of the state is paramount in these states' management of ethnopolitical conflicts.

Finally, this set of conflicts in IREA suggests a close relationship between national politics and interstate relations, a subject we will look into in more detail in Chapter 11. The problem of these conflicts is both intrastate and interstate – a phenomenon we found to be distinctly strong in wars and conflicts in Northeast Asia in our earlier discussion. Because of the indeterminacy of both the nation and the state of these new East Asian states, intrastate conflict over the constitution, institutions, and legitimacy of state authority engages the interests and objectives of the states in the larger interstate geopolitical environment. On the other hand, imposition of state institutions and boundaries across national boundaries is itself an interstate exercise. Here we see a much more complex set of dynamics that drives states or nations to war and peace, than the simple theories of nations seeking to break away from the state, or the state to enforce itself on nations or part of a nation can explain.

GEOPOLITICAL DRIVERS

The preceding discussion of war and peace in East Asia shows the dual nature of the major wars and conflicts in post-1945 East Asia. In these wars and conflicts, there was a close intertwinedness of intrastate and interstate political dynamics, exacerbated by the problem of mutual constitution of nation and state in violent forms. Interstate geopolitics played a significant role in the formation of the state. This is not a new problem and certainly not one that is unique to East Asia. Charles Tilly (Tilly 1990), for example, has been influential in exposing different forms of political economic organization in historic Europe that led to different types of states to develop. Ja Ian Chong (Chong 2014), on the other hand, takes that analysis a step further to investigate how geopolitics, great power rivalry, and foreign intervention influenced state formation in East Asia.

In interstate relations where the state itself is in search of a power structure, material basis, and communal and institutional infrastructure, external power rivalries and interests can have a great influence on the shaping of the state, and its internal and external relations, and on the distribution of international interests and capabilities supporting the emergent state. Because both the state and nation were contentious in post-WWII East Asia, geopolitics and interstate rivalry had greater influence in state formation, power distribution, and capability endowment. External influences engaged in intrastate contestation helped enforce a political order, shaping the direction of further development of the nation-state tension.

Geopolitics is made up of geographically conditioned activities and relations of influential states that seek to influence the power distribution and enable an international order of strategic significance. In the long history of IREA, geopolitics often means great power politics since great powers of global significance had the interests and capabilities to influence IREA, and these great powers have been both from within East Asia and, more often, from outside East Asia in modern times. The specific powers active and influential in IREA have changed over time with the rise and fall of great powers of global influence as well as changes in technology and forms of political economic organization. These changes in turn affect the way geographic conditions enable, motivate, or constrain states in IREA. In many ways, the systemic changes in IREA discussed in Chapter 3 reflect the way the unique set of great powers and their rivalry influenced war and peace in East Asia at any given time.

Geopolitics is also a traditional form of interstate politics that focuses on state intentions, interests, and strategic actions. To understand how great power rivalry affects war and peace in East Asia, we need to understand how the great powers geographically or strategically, positioned among themselves and in relation to the issue, target states and their interstate relations for geopolitical impact. All geographical conditions – distance, situation, forms of transport, movement and deployment of forces and capabilities, and partnerships in force coordination – influence the assessment, calculation, and operation of great powers.

Geopolitics therefore often operate in specific sets of relations, bilateral or multilateral. Geopolitical relations are often strategic because it often takes a long-term and a broad perspective in thinking of the relations and activities at a given time as building blocks for a grand geopolitical order on an issue or situation. All these are critical mechanisms and dynamics that connect global political and strategic relations to war and peace in IREA. But we will start first in what follows with one set of geopolitical relations that have shaped war and peace in East Asia for the past 150 years.

JAPAN AND CHINA IN EAST ASIA

China and Japan are the two most influential great powers in East Asia. Their geopolitical relations and strategic interaction have had a profound impact on the development of IREA. Japan grew into a substantive polity in East Asia on the edge of the Chinese imperial system in continental East Asia. After Yamato unified Japan over its own warring states into a centralized state in the sixth century in the western part of modern Japan, the organization of the polity, political economy, and urban life was very much modeled after that of the Tang imperial system of China, with strong influences in trade, religion, society, culture, and governance from China via the central eastern coast of continental East Asia.

At the same time, Japan was largely excluded from being an integral part of the Chinese world order. This was partly because Japan fell back to warring states from the twelfth century, with no central state to interact with China and China itself evolving into different forms of polity and being dominated by different peoples at different times (see our discussion earlier in Chapter 3). More importantly, there was a similar pattern of alternation or tension in the polity between the warring states system (or a "feudal system" in a Japanese version) and the imperialist system, as Japan continued to evolve, expand, and incorporate polities in the whole Japan archipelago.

The same dynamism of traditional polity organization came to dominate the institutional selection of the form of the Japanese polity. Warring states were incorporated through conquests into a large polity and organized into a system mixed with institutions of centralized bureaucratic state and feudal domains. In Japan's case, the political power of feudal domains, rather than the imperial court, became much stronger and fully institutionalized in the Tokugawa system of governance. Under the Tokugawa system, the ruling clan of a feudal domain had an independent authority for the governance of the domain while the strongest clan, the Tokugawa clan, exercised imperial power and authority on behalf of the emperor. The inherent tension between the two sets of dynamics in the organization of the polity has been central to the development of the Japanese state in its transformation from the Tokugawa polity to Meiji Restoration and to the rise of the modern Japanese state. In this general historical perspective, Japan seems to have its own version of "world order" that influenced Japan's approach to China, East Asia, and the world after the Meiji Restoration as Japan continued to develop and expand.

Japan's interaction with China was the working of the same logic that drove China and other Eats Asian states (Korea and Vietnam, for example) to search for an imperial form of polity organization. Besides engaging with China, Japan advanced northward to exert an influence on the Korean Peninsula, particularly when polities on the peninsula, the three kingdoms in particular, were fighting for a unitary state. Japan also developed very active trade activities in the East Sea rim surrounded by Korea to the north, East China to the west, and South Japan to the east, particularly in the sixteenth century after the arrival of the Portuguese in East Asia, and in Taiwan in particular.

Japan's activities in establishing a presence in the East Sea rim shifted in the nineteenth century when European powers advanced to Northeast Asia. Under the banner of 尊王攘夷 ("respect emperor and resist foreigners"), the Meiji Restoration in Japan from 1868 returned governing authorities from the clans to the emperor, restored the system of an imperial, centralized state, and focused the nation on industrial development and fending off foreign invasions. This enabled Japan to transform into a modern state and opened a new stage for Japan to work out the form and scope of the Japanese polity in twentieth-century East Asia.

Japan's imperialist expansion emerged with the imperialist moves by European powers into continental East Asia. These imperialist moves saw the French empire in

Indochina; Great Britain in Hong Kong, Myanmar, and Tibet; Germany in Shandong; and Russia in Manchuria. Japan moved along its historical route to continental East Asia through Korea. The first major direct military engagement with China in 1898 over Korea destroyed the Chinese navy, ended China's special relationship with Korea, and took over Korea and Taiwan.

China experienced serious internal tensions between the ruling Qing imperial system and Chinese society, and the state was in disarray and unable to organize an effective response to the intrusion of these imperialist powers. This further intensified geopolitical competition among major powers in continental East Asia. At the same time, great power politics in Europe gathered momentum and finally got to the point where profound tensions had to be settled through large-scale wars. Most European powers were drawn into the First World War, and this significantly weakened their ability to compete or even sustain their presence in East Asia.

Moreover, Japan saw itself as a leading force of Asian nations rebelling against European colonialism. Japan's success in modernizing its industrial production and military capability, its defeat of the traditional Chinese empire and European imperialist power, Russia, in major international warfare, and the idea of Pan-Asianism under the newly acquired industrial, intellectual, and cultural leadership gave Japan all the motivation and justification for rapid and large-scale movement into continental East Asia and then to maritime Southeast Asia.

In China, the Qing imperial system finally collapsed in 1911. The new Republic of China was established, and the transformation from the imperial system to a republican system was completed, at least formally. However, state institutions for the new polity were still being established and a constitution was yet to be drafted. The challenge of organizing a national government was constantly contested by different political forces of which the Nationalists and Communists finally emerged to dominate. China in the early twentieth century was turned into a state of disorder, more like the warring states in its own history or even more closely, the Tokugawa system. Out of this political chaos, Nationalists and Communists emerged as two major political forces contending for state power and authority and fighting to organize the new Chinese state in their own way. This internal rivalry provided a great operational environment for Japan to establish presence, influence, and power in continental East Asia. After years of Japan's expansion from Korea to Manchuria and to central northern China, China under the Nationalist government finally declared war on Japan in 1937.

Japan's war on China forced the Nationalist government to retreat to the southwest corner of China and the Communists to northwest China, and the Chinese state was on the edge of collapse. This situation was stabilized when Japan opened a second war front, the Pacific War, against the United States in 1941. The Pacific War was a major interstate war from 1941 to 1945 between Japan, on one side, and the United States and Allies, on the other, in the western Pacific and Southeast Asia – the Far East theater of World War II. The war not only was a turning point in Japan's imperialist expansion in East Asia but also changed the geopolitical dynamics of IREA. These new dynamics connected Northeast Asia, Southeast Asia, and the United States in the structural transformation of IREA. Japan moved a significant amount of resources and war capabilities to Southeast Asia and the western Pacific.

Japan's imperialist expansion in the first half of the twentieth century clearly had the potential to replace the collapsing Chinese world order and the European colonial order in East Asia with a Japanese world order (see further discussion in Chapter 3).

The end of World War II brought all these issues back almost to where it all started in the late nineteenth century. Japan was reduced to a state of limited constitutional capacity and international rights but retained the centralized state model. Japan's international activities were limited to those nonpolitical in nature and nongeopolitical entirely. State capabilities were concentrated largely in industrial recovery and economic development. Chalmers Johnson summarizes the Japanese state and its way of organizing industrial development as the developmental state. The dynamics of industrial development and upgrade, generated under this developmental state, extended to the region for production, cooperation, and integration (see full discussion of this topic in Chapter 7).

The direction of the flow and regional distribution of integrative industrial activities was significantly influenced by the interstate political structure in which Japan found itself in the early postwar decades. The historical route to regional outreach to continental East Asia via Korea and Taiwan was complicated by the political realities of two-Korea rivalry, PRC-ROC rivalry, and a China of complete different ideology, political economy, and governance system in continental East Asia. This seems to have prompted Japan to focus its interests in regional economic and industrial development with Southeast Asia. The Fukuda Doctrine of 1977 highlights Japan's vision on the foundation of Japan-Southeast Asia economic cooperation and partnership for regional industrial integration. The Fukuda Doctrine was a set of principles meant to guide Japan's post-1945 relations with Southeast Asia. Declared by then-Japanese Prime Minister Takeo Fukuda in 1977, the Fukuda Doctrine indicated Japan's intentions to build its relations with Southeast Asian states on new ground given that the region suffered under European colonial governance and the Japanese empire itself.

Such a vision of Japan's geopolitical role in the region could not possibly work without the engagement of the United States. As we will show in what follows, the United States saw Southeast Asia as a very important platform for its engagement with East Asia. The San Francisco system it led to provided the parameters for US-Japan relations such that the United States would look after the political side of Japan's international role and interests. The San Francisco system was an interstate order equipped with a set of institutions that emerged from the conclusion of the peace treaty with Japan and the US-Japan Security Treaty, both signed in 1951 in San Francisco. The system entailed special US-Japan relations and a network of US-led bilateral alliances for the postwar international order in East Asia. Consequently, Japan's vision regarding East Asia shifted more toward the Asia-Pacific. It engaged the United States politically and focused on trade and industrial development with Southeast Asia as the two core elements of its framework for regional engagement.

This was further reinforced by a shift in the 1990s in Japan's strategic thinking on its relations with the United States and its approach to becoming a normal state in the international system. The effectiveness of the campaign by then-Prime Minister

Yasuhiro Nakasone for the internationalization of Japan in the 1980s was weakened by trade tensions with the United States. This forced Japanese policymakers to reconsider the role of US-Japan relations in Japan's efforts to become a normal state. This led to a series of efforts by the Japanese government to "upgrade" its relations with the United States to a strategic partnership, starting with a reformulation of the guidelines for US-Japanese defense cooperation in 1997 and a further major revision of the guidelines in 2015.

Japan has established a way of engaging in geopolitics in East Asia decades after its defeat in World War II when the imperial state was reduced to a limited national state and its power and influence were confined to the Japan islands. The platforms that Japan has been building to engage in IREA have been largely economic and trade focused and the way it operated was largely nonconfrontational. More recent times have seen increasing efforts to take part in geopolitics in East Asia, through its high-profile engagement on Korea-related issues and a more proactive role in strategic alignment in IREA for more substantive involvement in the shaping of regional interstate order.

The post-1945 transformation of Japan has not produced a regional condition where a Japan-centric regional geopolitical order is likely. It has, however, certainly reconnected the traditional dynamics of the tension in East Asia between a China-dominated regional order and a Japan-dominated regional order. This can be seen more clearly in how China is shaping its international interests and capabilities, its vision for geopolitical relations in East Asia, and its approach to Japan.

In China, the Communists established themselves as the dominant force of the state, and the Nationalists relocated the ROC to Taiwan. The challenge of building a new China out of the traditional Chinese empire was just getting started, in the hands of the Communists. China, in the words of Fairbank, "is a civilization pretending to be a state" (Fairbank 1992: 235). Fairbank explains that "the story of modern China could be described as the effort by both Chinese and foreigners to squeeze a civilization into the arbitrary, constraining framework of the modern state." In the language of international relations, this suggests that there is an inherent tension in the shaping of China's international identity, purpose, and strategy. This tension is driven by the structural and institutional pressures for China to be "a nation-state in the family of nations," and the accumulative political economic, social, and cultural forces and practices of "Chinese civilization" had supported the Chinese imperial system and the Chinese world order. This tension influenced in a significant way China's search for its position in IREA, how it related to the new states in post-1945 East Asia, and how it responded to geopolitical developments in IREA.

The PRC engaged directly with events shaping the regional interstate order: the Korean War, the PRC-ROC conflict, the Vietnam War, confrontations with the Soviet Union (1960s and 1970s), war with India (1962), and the Nixon shock (1971). It exerted a significant influence on the shaping of the regional geopolitical order simply by direct involvement with these developments, which at the same time were largely the effects of the ideological structure in post-1945 East Asia. While internal politics in China and the alliance of the communist states put a large constraint on China's external relations and interests, it was not clear that Chinese activities and efforts were driven by a coherent vision about what it wanted to achieve in IREA. Its role and impact on the regional international order was consequently incoherent, and increasingly ineffective, toward the end of the 1970s.

Along with the collapse of state institutions and the political economy model in the mid-1970s, the PRC found itself almost unable to sustain the centralized state system and to influence what was happening outside its borders. This great tension between the traditional structure of the polity and its very limited capability to influence geopolitics in East Asia led to the growing pressure for China to reorient itself. This shaped what China was to become in the following decades – a process that is so classic yet so profound in the type of international political change explained by Robert Gilpin (Gilpin 1981).

RISE OF CHINA IN POST-COLD WAR EAST ASIA

The post-1945 development of China's geopolitical profile and posture in East Asia made a significant turn from what they were in the 1980s. In the "short" 40 years since then, China has transformed its political economic system, built a new industrial power of global significance, and actively engaged in international relations globally, with a focus on IREA. China has achieved an ability to influence the development of international relations in general and critical issues and challenges in IREA. This "rise of China" has been quickly recognized as a textbook instance of the rise and fall of great powers in world history, a historical pattern that A. F. K. Organski, Robert Gilpin, Paul Kennedy, and George Modelski have explained over the years (Organski 1958; Gilpin 1981; Kennedy 1987; Modelski 1987). A key element that propelled the rise of China as part of the great powers' "motion" or "circle" in the international system was China's ability to transform itself with systemic and institutional innovations that enabled national growth in wealth and power.

Moreover, China's rise is fully connected with the structural dynamics of the international system. The rise can be seen as the effect of the structural function of the system, part of the progressive transformation of the structure itself, or the consequence of the working of the modern capitalist political economy in a particular form (Wallerstein 1979; North & Thomas 1973; Kennedy 1987; Arrighi 2009). In the theories and predictions derived from the influential scholarship on national growth and the structural change of the world system, drawn largely on the rise and fall of great powers of the Western world, one found that China's rise fits very well with the pattern. These theories and forecasts, though, seem to be less helpful for attentive watchers to understand whether the rise of China would be peaceful or confrontational and how and why China as a great power again will be a force for peace and stability.

Taking the rise of China as a positive change in China's ability to influence international relations, and hence in its position in the international structure in relation to other great powers, the debate focuses on the nature of Chinese power, measuring that power, and whether China has gained the stature of global influencer (Yan 2006; Shambaugh 2018). Given the newly enhanced capabilities, how China will use them and for what strategic purposes becomes critically important. Much of the debate, particularly in the early years, focused on ascertaining China's strategic intentions, China's grand strategy, or China's world vision (Goldstein 2003; Yan 2014; Buzan 2014; Schweller & Pu 2011). Clarifying China's intention, vision, and strategy for its rise is important because it will help us to see how China's rise affects the existing international order. Here the debate goes beyond the early focus on material power and structural change associated with China's rise and investigates the institutional and normative mechanisms of international order where the effects of China's rise on the international system can be better determined (Lake 2017; Ikenberry 2018; Clark 2014; Root 2013; Wohlforth 2018; Zhang 2015).

The rise of China and the scholarly and policy debates it has generated is particularly relevant for our discussion here. Great power geopolitics has a critical role in shaping war and peace in East Asia. There was a wide expectation that the rise of China would significantly change the geopolitical dynamics and strategic postures of states in the region. A huge amount of scholarship and policy analysis from the 1990s has focused on the possible effects of China's rise on states in IREA and the strategic responses of East Asian states (Friedberg 1993, 2011; Kang 2003, 2007; Acharya 2014; Goh 2013, 2017). Aaron Friedberg, for example, argues that the rise of China will transform Asia into a multipolar order that, by the logic of structural realism and on the basis of our knowledge of a similar pattern seen in the European experiences in earlier centuries, would lead to tension, conflict, and interstate rivalry. This is a unique challenge for East Asia because it lacks the type of institutions and normative practices that developed in Europe for conflict reduction and management (Friedberg 1993).

David Kang, on the other hand, believes such analyses miss the dimension of international norms and identity in informing state action and interstate interactions. As shown in the long history of IREA, a hegemonic China provided a stable institutional and normative framework in which states in East Asia were related and incorporated (Kang 2003, 2007). Amitav Acharya and Evelyn Goh take the debate a bit further and argue that relations among states are dictated not only by the power structure but also by the institutional and normative dynamics in an international order. For Acharya (2003b), the regional institutions and economic interdependence that developed in contemporary IREA would serve to mitigate the effects of material power hierarchy and its shift in East Asia. For Goh (2013), the power and normative structure underlying the international order in East Asia, however hierarchical and hegemonic, is resilient and durable because of the enduring power of the normative structure, a view that resonates well with the growing interest of mainstream scholarship on the issue (Ikenberry 2014).

The rise of China, therefore, has led to a mixture of effects on IREA, and on the geopolitical relations in particular. It sees limits on the extent to which the rise of China can lead to a fundamental change in the prevailing geopolitical order in East Asia. It also sees the possibility that tension will intensify and possibly escalate into open conflict because of the rapidly growing power and influence of China in the structure and geopolitical order in IREA, where US hegemonic power has been dominant since the end of the Cold War. There are different scenarios in which these new great power dynamics can play out – to develop in a scenario of "mutual acceptance" or "power sharing" (White 2012), or irreconcilable differences would push them to a more dramatic form of interaction and settlement. We will nevertheless see a period of mixed effects of the structural shift on the geopolitical interests and relations of states in East Asia.

The rise of China has led to a profound change in the empirical environment for scholarly analysis and policy debate on critical issues in IREA. "The elephant in the room" is often a talking point in discussions that refers to the unavoidable influence of a hegemonic power on every specific delicate issue or problem in IREA. The question is, or the debate often centers on, who that elephant is in IREA in the 2010s.

US ENGAGEMENT WITH EAST ASIA

Discussions of geopolitics and strategic interactions of great powers and their impact on war and peace in East Asia cannot be meaningful without an understanding of the role of the United States in post-1945 IREA. Much of the US rise to dominance in the international system in the twentieth century has had a lot to do with its interests, relations, and activities in East Asia; its strategy and vision to advance these interests and relations; and the particular methods, platforms, and mechanisms it utilized to articulate these interests, cultivate relations, and implement the strategy. The international policy and activity of the United States has decisively influenced the shaping of interstate relations, geopolitics, and war and peace in IREA.

United States' substantive engagement in East Asia started in the late nineteenth century as industrialization also enabled it to reach out beyond its borders for trade and other international interests and benefits. The geopolitical game in East Asia had been largely monopolized by the old European powers that now moved into East Asia as the final frontier of their global expansion and competition. As a latecomer along with Japan, Russia, and Germany, the United States approached East Asia with a set of slightly different rules of engagement and principles of interaction.

As competition among major powers in continental East Asia intensified toward the end of the nineteenth century, the United States pushed forward with an open-door policy in China in a series of notes by then-Secretary of State John Kay that promoted equal opportunity for everyone involved in business and trade in China. The open-door policy was a general guiding principle favored by the United States in the early twentieth century in great power competition in China. The policy stipulated that trade and investment privileges and benefits should not be monopolized by a few, but be open to all. While US Perry's Black Ship arrived in Japan in 1853 to open Japan up for such trade opportunities, the United States signed Korea's first international treaty in 1882 with special trade and consular privileges. The United States waged war with Spain and gained control of the Philippines in 1898, and it brokered a peace treaty between Japan and Russia in Portsmouth, New Hampshire, in 1905 that settled the Russo-Japanese War over Korea and Manchuria.

The United States managed to be part of international agreements by European powers with China on the principles of most favored nation and equal opportunity: the Treaty of Wangxia of 1844 after the Sino-British Treaty of Nanking in 1842; the Treaty of Tientsin of 1858 along with Great Britain, Russia, and France; and the

Boxer Protocols of 1901 with eleven other great powers. The United States also played a leading role in the post-World War I peace settlement for the "Far East." This was when President Woodrow Wilson proclaimed the historic "Fourteen Points," the guiding principles of the US to negotiate a peace settlement to end World War I. The Fourteen Points emphasized free trade and freedom of the seas, open diplomacy, national self-determination, and general association of nations. These principles set the US apart in its approach to international relations and contrasted with that of the Old World.

These general principles influenced or further sharpened US strategic vision on East Asia. Added to the open-door policy and a vision of a new world order in East Asia was the growing US concern over the real threat to the United States across the Pacific from East Asia. The "strategic defensive perimeter" in East Asia (as seen in Figure 4.1), laid out by then US Secretary of State Dean Acheson after the war with Japan in World War II, established the United States' forward defense posture in the western Pacific close to continental East Asia. With the end of World War II, US strategic aims in East Asia became clearer: to prevent the rise of great powers in East Asia that could pose a serious national security threat to the United States.

Around this strategic defensive perimeter, the Philippines and Japan became key strongholds on the first line of defense at the end of World War II. As new states emerged, European colonial influence retreated from the region, particularly from Southeast Asia, and the Communists took over state power on continental East Asia, the United States increasingly engaged in political development in those countries and developed a security zone further westward from the defensive perimeter in East Asia.

There are three critical defining moments in the evolution of the US postwar geopolitical interests and strategic posture in East Asia. Framing US posture in East Asia in the strategic defensive perimeter was the first defining moment before the Korean War. This was quickly overshadowed by a more proactive and offensive strategic posture for the shaping of a geopolitical order driven by a set of broader, global strategic concerns.

A second moment was 1969, when President Nixon put forth in Guam what is now known as the Guam Doctrine or Nixon Doctrine. The Guam Doctrine was a new US global strategic framework where US geopolitical engagement with East Asia was scaled down with more security responsibilities to be shifted to security partners in the region. President Nixon declared that the US was now prepared for one and a half wars at the same time globally rather than two wars simultaneously, one in Europe and one in East Asia. The half war was the scope of US geopolitical and strategic commitment to East Asia. It signaled "strategic (re)balancing" in US global commitments and operations and a scaling back of US direct operational involvement in East Asia.

While the Guam Doctrine reflected Nixon's cost-effectiveness calculation over extensive US security commitments to counties in East Asia in the first two decades of the Cold War, it also reflected Washington's consideration that the truly serious security threat to US and to East Asian states was from the Soviet Union. East Asian states could take up their own responsibilities to meet the security challenge, and

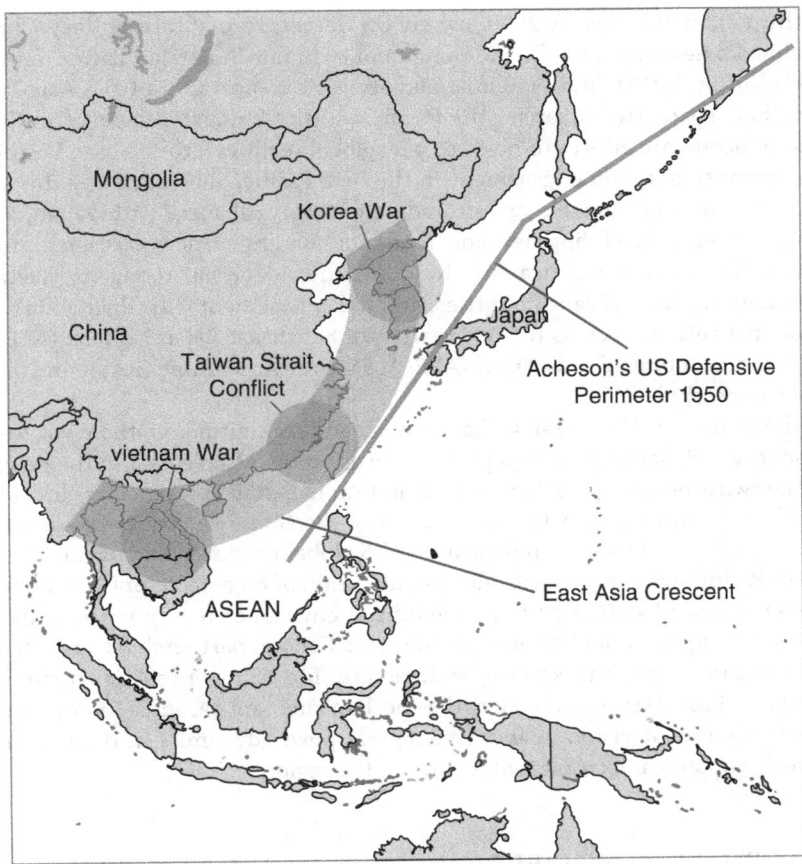

Figure 4.1 US defensive perimeter and strategic engagement with East Asia: Dean Acheson delivered a speech in 1950 stating that the US would defend Japan, the Ryukyu Islands and the Philippines, but not South Korea or Taiwan. The East Asian Crescent saw the beginnings of American strategic planning for containment in Southeast Asia. Circles represent areas of conflict.

they, including China in Dr. Henry Kissinger's mind, could together form a force of deterrence with the United States against the Soviet Union. The Guam Doctrine suggested that the United States would continue to honor its treaty commitments to its allies but provide a "nuclear shield" to its allies and expected the East Asian states to "assume the primary responsibility of providing the manpower for its defense" (Nixon 1969: 8). The declaration of the Guam Doctrine was followed by the US opening up relations with China in an attempt at a strategic alignment of the US, Pakistan, China, and Japan against the aggressive expansion of the geopolitical influence of the Soviet Union in the region. This led to a notable change in the geopolitical landscape in East Asia in the 1970s and 1980s.

A third moment was in 2011, when US Secretary of State Hillary Clinton proclaimed a new direction for US foreign policy in her "America's Pacific Century" article (Clinton 2011). The economic and strategic importance of the Asia-Pacific region that "spans two oceans – the Pacific and the Indian," compels the United States to "accelerate efforts to pivot to new global realities": to increase US investment, commitment, and engagement in the Asia-Pacific. Substantiating this strategy of "forward deployment" are an update of treaty alliances with Japan, South Korea, Australia, the Philippines, and Thailand; building of new partnerships with China, India, Indonesia, Singapore, New Zealand, Malaysia, Mongolia, Vietnam, Brunei, and the Pacific island countries; and full engagement with the region's multilateral institutions such as the Association of Southeast Asian Nations (ASEAN), Asia-Pacific Economic Cooperation (APEC), East Asian Summit (EAS), and Trans-Pacific Partnership (TPP).

In the context of US overall global strategy and commitments, the pivot to Asia represents a "rebalancing" from a primary focus on the Middle East in the new century, the twin-theater operations in Iraq and Afghanistan in particular, and a "correction" to the strategic posture in place since the Guam Doctrine. Operationally, the pivot to Asia envisaged a refocusing of US global resources and partnerships to the Asia-Pacific and, more specifically, a reallocation of 60 percent of US naval forces to the Asia-Pacific by 2020. At the same time, it envisioned incorporating, integrating, and developing more "theater" resources, alliances, partnerships, and regional institutions into a regional security architecture. The US pivot to Asia redefined US interests in East Asia and updated the mechanisms and resource endowment to enable this strategic vision. It intensified great power dynamics in the region and reshaped geopolitical relations with states in the region.

BETWEEN GREAT POWERS

One of the key features of post-1945 and particularly post-Cold War IREA is the rise and fall of other geopolitical forces in the region. The first group of these other geopolitical forces is the European states. European states largely retreated from East Asia following very brief attempts to reclaim their possessions in East Asia after World War II ended. Germany's presence in East Asia collapsed after World War I. The French and Dutch failed to retain their presence in East Asia after World War II. Colonies of Great Britain transformed into self-government and newly independent states in the 1960s. Great Britain's relinquishment of its colonial arrangements in Hong Kong in 1997 marked the end of a European formal institutional presence in East Asia. With the dominance of the United States in East Asia, the individual European states have shown scant interest and taken little action toward establishing geopolitical influence in the region.

Another group of geopolitical forces are those bordering on East Asia and increasingly active to engage with East Asia. The process of shaping the post-1945 international order in East Asia involved various states of geopolitical significance in the greater "Asia-Pacific" area in different ways and through different mechanisms and processes. These include Russia, Australia, and India. The growing geopolitical and economic importance of East Asia as well as the shift in the geopolitical landscape in the region, particularly after the Cold War, presented a challenge to these countries to connect with this region. There has been great debate in each of these countries over "whether we are part of the Asia-Pacific," what the country's interests in East Asia are, and what platforms would be more effective for engaging with East Asia. The debate gradually shifted from whether "we are part of the Asia-Pacific" or "Look East" to more specific aims and methods for these states to engage with East Asia, or "Act East," and on how to address the power shift and trade competition. These and other discussions provide a rationale for these countries to stake out a position in relation to the power structure in the region and motivate them for closer engagement with geopolitics in East Asia.

Against the backdrop of its tense competition with Japan and China over influence in Northeast Asia ever since the nineteenth century and the collapse of the Soviet Empire at the end of the Cold War, Russia seems to have accepted the shifting geopolitical realities in East Asia. The fact that China has become an increasingly influential force globally works well for Russia, which has found itself increasingly isolated from a united front of Europe and the United States. Russia's interests in East Asia have shifted from containing China in the 1970s and 1980s to working with China in the 2010s. Its precise geopolitical interests, though, would need to take further shape in the years to come.

East Asia is much more important strategically for India. In the early years of the post-1945 Asia, strong dynamics developed among Asian states to bring a new international order in the vacuum created by the collapse of colonialism in the region. India, China, Indonesia, and Egypt were the four leading countries spearheading such a course of great international significance. The Bandung Conference in 1955 was one of the platforms that emerged for advocating solidarity among developing countries in Asia and Africa against colonialism and the great power politics of pre-1945 Asia. The Cold War largely excluded India from playing an active role in East Asia and from connecting South China to East Asia in strategic and functional areas of international relations. This situation was worsened by a brief war between India and China over their border disputes in 1962. Much of India's international interests and attention were focused on relaxing tensions and conflict and building a new state in South Asia.

When India embarked on economic reform and openness in the early 1990s, it found a very dynamic, competitive, and prosperous East Asia where ASEAN was playing a role in integrating the region. The Look East policy was established by Prime Minister Rao in 1991 as a shift in the strategic direction of India's international policy. It reflects India's strategic interests in engaging with East Asia for its economic reform and development. The outlook was further upgraded by Prime Minister Modi in 2014 to the Act East policy. This is a more proactive and operational strategy that calls for more concrete and specific actions to advance India's interests and relations in the region and a broader framework that connects its interests and actions to strategic conditions in East Asia.

Australia's relations with East Asia underwent a similar shift from Cold War participation to twenty-first-century engagement. Australia's geopolitical interests and activities in post-1945 East Asia were shaped by different sets of geopolitical dynamics. On the one hand, Australia was part of the US-led collective action against the communist threat in East Asia, with direct involvement in war efforts in Northeast Asia and security operations in Southeast Asia. Australia was itself in the midst of a transformation into a sovereign nation, a process that involved adjustments in its relations with the old Europe, the British Commonwealth, the new global power of the United States, and, most importantly, the former European colonies turned newly independent states in Asia, mostly in South and Southeast Asia – India, Malaysia, Singapore, and Indonesia. These diverse sets of geopolitical dynamics prompted Australia to cement a significant position of influence in the geopolitical order in the Asia-Pacific.

Australia's geopolitical interests in the region since the Cold War evolved in three directions to its north: eastward to ASEAN, northward to China and Japan, and westward to India. With the rise of China, ASEAN's hedging, India's Look/Act East, and US periodic strategic reorientations with East Asia, these strategic factors naturally connected in Australia's conception of its role and purpose in the shaping of regional geopolitical structures. In this strategic thinking, South Asia, Southeast Asia, and the Pacific feature prominently, as do China, India, and Japan. Cabrera moved to take on a more active role in East Asian geopolitics than simply being a supporting part of the US-centric regional order. Key to such strategic thinking is a strategic balance of power between India, China, and Japan; between Northeast Asia and Southeast Asia; and among core parties of interests and capabilities in South Pacific. In such a balance of power, Australia's geopolitical interests and capabilities would be not only relevant but also effective in the shaping of East Asian geopolitics.

The third group of geopolitical forces are those "middle powers" or "emergent powers," in East Asia, sandwiched between the large consecutive sets of binarily contentious geopolitical forces that have dominated the region: those between the Chinese empire and European colonial powers in East Asia; between the Chinese world order and the Japanese empire, and between China and the United States. Korea, Vietnam, and Singapore have all been through these historic moments where their survival and security were strongly influenced by great power geopolitics. "Middle" powers here are more in the sense of their critical position in the binarily contentious geopolitical structure of IREA than in the size of their military and scope of their economic power and influence. Great power geopolitics generated large-scale movements of forces and shifts in relations, as well as intensive competition over these on-the-edge polities.

Great power geopolitics, however, is also a platform for these middle and small powers to create space for their existence, survival, and development. Opposing forces in great power geopolitics can also cancel or neutralize each other and open up geopolitical space for their rent-seeking and strategic compensation in geopolitical grouping. Often, there are three different strategies pursued by those middle powers in IREA or three different patterns of how these states position themselves and operate vis-à-vis the competing great powers. The first is to "take sides," to align themselves with one great power in alliance or partnership. This led to the shaping of the balance of power during the Cold War.

A second strategy is to *hedge*. With the great uncertainty in the nature of the threat to their security and wellbeing, and their limited ability to defuse potential threats on their own, these states chose "a middle position" that forestalls their having to choose one side at the obvious expense of the other. Such a middle position allows them to invest in relations with both great powers and avoid being a "chip" in the great powers' bargaining game or an easy target for punitive actions against them. With the predominantly binary nature of the distribution of geopolitical forces in East Asia and the political culture of pragmatism of East Asian peoples that guides them to avoid offending either side in opposing relations, the hedging strategy seems to have been adopted more often. We have seen this particularly among ASEAN states in the perceived strategic competition between China and the United States in recent years.

The third strategy for the middle powers is to take the second strategy a step further: not only to avoid being played by the great powers but also to engage in the geopolitical game themselves, as "honest brokers" between opposing great powers or simply "facilitators" for geopolitics to develop in a desirable direction. Recent developments leading to the Trump-Kim summits in Singapore and Vietnam are good examples of how middle powers can play a role and have useful input in the positive development of geopolitical relations. Singapore's long political engagement with both the United States and China allows it to have a critical role in facilitating tension reduction and peacemaking in East Asia. The same applies to Vietnam. At the same time, all the progress shows that North and South Korea were able to influence the development of geopolitics in East Asia.

The rise of the second and third groups of geopolitical forces in IREA in the importance of their geopolitical interests and capabilities and the influence they have on the development of great power politics in East Asia is an interesting feature of the post-Cold War development in geopolitics in IREA. While much of the scholarship, policy analyses, and public debate on issues in IREA focus extensively on great power politics, the role these states play in the shaping of the international order and war and peace in East Asia should not be underestimated.

Study Questions

1. What are some of the unique features of major wars and conflicts in post-1945 East Asia? What made tension reduction and conflict management in East Asia difficult?
2. How have the wars and conflicts in East Asia influenced post-1945 development of IREA in terms of structure, institutions, and international order?
3. How have the changing relations between China and Japan affected the international order in East Asia? Do you think China and Japan have similar or different geopolitical interests and influence in IREA?
4. How has the rise of China changed the geopolitical landscape in East Asia?
5. Discuss the evolution of US strategy and geopolitical influence in East Asia.
6. Discuss different types of geopolitical forces in IREA and the forms and mechanisms of their influence on IREA.
7. Discuss global, regional, and national dynamics in war and peace in East Asia.

Further Reading

Ang, Cheng Guan, 2018. *Southeast Asia's Cold War: An Interpretive History*. Honolulu: University of Hawaii Press.
Arase, David, 2016. *China's Rise and Changing Order in East Asia*. New York: Palgrave.
Bailey, Jonathan, 2007. *Great Power Strategy in Asia: Empire, Culture and Trade, 1905–2005*. London/New York: Routledge.
Black, Jeremy, 2016. "Geopolitics Since 1990," pp. 211–259 in *Geopolitics and the Quest for Dominance*. Bloomington: Indiana University Press.
Chong, Ja Ian, 2014. *External Intervention and the Politics of State Formation: China, Indonesia, and Thailand, 1893–1952*. Cambridge: Cambridge University Press.
Christensen, Thomas J., 1999. "China, the US-Japan Alliance, and the Security Dilemma in East Asia," *International Security* 23(4): 49–80.
Cumings, Bruce, 2010. *The Korean War: A History, Modern History*. New York: Modern Library.
Dent, Christopher M., 2008. *China, Japan and Regional Leadership in East Asia*. Cheltenham: Edward Elgar.
Emmers, Ralf, 2009. *Geopolitics and Maritime Territorial Disputes*. London: Routledge.
Ralf Emmers, and Sarah Teo, 2015. "Regional Security Strategies of Middle Powers in the Asia-Pacific," *International Relations of the Asia-Pacific* 15: 185–216.
Friedberg, Aaron, 1993. "Ripe for Rivalry: Prospects for Peace in a Multipolar Asia," *International Security* 18(3): 5–33.
Goh, Evelyn, 2013. "The Hierarchical East Asian Order," pp. 202–226 in *The Struggle for Order: Hegemony, Hierarchy, and Transition in Post-Cold War East Asia*. Oxford: Oxford University Press.
Green, Michael J., 2017. *More Than Providence: Grand Strategy and American Power in the Asia Pacific Since 1783*. New York: Columbia University Press.
Hack, Karl, and Geoff Wade, 2009. "The Origins of the Southeast Asian Cold War," *Journal of Southeast Asian Studies* 40(3): 441–448.
Hook, Glenn D., Julie Gilson, Christopher W. Hughes, and Hugo Dobson, 2011. *Japan's International Relations: Politics, Economics and Security*. London: Routledge.
Jager, Sheila Miyoshi, 2014. *Brothers at War: The Unending Conflict in Korea*. London: Norton.
Koo, Min Gyo, 2010. *Island Disputes and Maritime Regime Building in East Asia: Between a Rock and a Hard Place*. London: Routledge.
Lawrence, Mark Atwood, 2010. *The Vietnam War: A Concise International History*. Oxford: Oxford University Press.
Logevall, Fredrik, 2001. *Choosing War: The Lost Chance for Peace and the Escalation of War in Vietnam*. Berkeley: University of California Press.

Ross, Robert S., 1999. "The Geography of Peace: East Asia in the Twenty-first Century." *International Security* 23(4): 81–118.

Ross, Robert S., 2003. "The U.S.-China Peace: Great Power Politics, Spheres of Influence, and the Peace of East Asia." *Journal of East Asian Studies* 3:351–75.

Sullivan, Michael P., 2015. *The Vietnam War: A Study in the Making of American Policy*. Lexington: University Press of Kentucky.

Taylor, Fravel M. 2009. *Strong Borders, Secure Nation: Cooperation and Conflict in China's Territorial Disputes*. Princeton: Princeton University Press.

Tønnesson, Stein, 2017. *Explaining the East Asian Peace*. Copenhagen: NIAS Press.

Tucker, Nancy B., 2008. *Dangerous Strait: The U.S.-Taiwan-China Crisis*. New York: Columbia University Press.

Weissmann, Mikael, 2012. *The East Asian Peace: Conflict Prevention and Informal Peacebuilding*. Basingstoke: Palgrave Macmillan.

5 The Bipolar Structure

In This Chapter...

- International structure in a regional system
- Power vacuum
- The Yalta vision
- Concentration of power
- Organization of collective forces
- The bipolar structure in IREA
- Correction, disturbance, and structural shift
- A historical pattern or a generic structure

Learning Objectives

After studying this chapter, you will be able to
- Use structural theory to explain some of the unique patterns of IREA
- Understand whether the bipolar structure is an enduring feature of IREA or a transitional one among many patterns of IREA
- Understand what forces helped shape the bipolar structure during the Cold War in East Asia
- Understand what forces ultimately drive the structural movement in IREA.

The collapse of the Chinese world order and the unsuccessful attempts by European powers and the Japanese empire to establish a new world order in East Asia drove chaos and disorder in East Asia through the end of World War II. What emerged out of the war debris in IREA has been debated. Conventional analysts, particularly IREA watchers and policy analysts, see the playout of classic great power geopolitics, as discussed in the previous chapter. Investigating the working of a traditional balance of power, some note the effects of a persistent pattern of interstate power distribution that shaped the international policy and strategy of states in IREA. Michael Yahuda, example, details the evolution of bipolarity in the Cold War structure in East Asia (Yahuda 1996: 43–104) and explains the strategy and alliance of the great powers in this context. A similar framework of bipolar structure is also seen in John Mearsheimer's investigation of how the distribution of power would play out in East Asia between the land power, China, and its "offshore balancers" and argues that "it is the structure of the international system that forces states" (Mearsheimer 2001: 2) to turn great power politics into a "tragedy."

For some, taking IREA as a set of structure-driven international activities and relations may not be particularly meaningful or even useful, as this is not very different from how conventional realists interpret and analyze structures. However, the Cold War structure is often highlighted in scholarly discussions and policy debate on IREA as a unique force that influenced IREA to evolve in a tragic direction during the Cold War and, as witnessed by many, increasingly so in more recent times. It would be useful to see what precisely that structure is in IREA and how it drives states to seek power and confront each other with force. Moreover, neorealism or structural realism has successfully asserted itself as a theoretical approach distinct from classical realism in explaining state behavior and interstate relations (Waltz 1979; Keohane 1986). The persistent effects of the international structure in IREA is a great empirical instance in which we can explore how international structure works and investigate whether an international structure can be regional and whether the working of the international structure requires more than the distribution of power.

This chapter therefore investigates the shaping of the Cold War structure in IREA, its defining character, and, from here, whether the pattern of power distribution and normative relations is generic to the system of IREA. In the broad context of different sets of significant forces enabling IREA we intend to investigate in this text, we focus on one set in this chapter, that of structural forces. The chapter examines whether there is a distinct and stable pattern of distribution of power and interests of states in IREA, the key features and character of that distribution, and how this pattern influenced the regional interstate order. Assuming this structure is dynamic, we are also interested to see how the structure that started to form as interstate forces from continental East Asia and maritime East Asia substantively engaged and interacted over the East Asian crescent from the nineteenth century has continuously evolved beyond the Cold War decades.

INTERNATIONAL STRUCTURE IN A REGIONAL SYSTEM

Before we discuss the Cold War structure in East Asia and how it has helped shape the international order in post-1945 East Asia, let us first look at some key concepts and the underlying logic of how an international structure affects a state's behavior and interstate action. Ever since the publication of Kenneth Waltz's *Theory of International Politics* (1979), the structural theory of international relations has been widely appreciated as a powerful framework for understanding war and peace among nations and the patterns of their interactions and relations. The structural view of the causes of international conflict and order is different from traditional realism and geopolitical frameworks. In the structuralist framework, the international structure is a system condition (Waltz 1979: 93). Structural causes and effects therefore must be manifested and operative system-wide.

Moreover, it is the material capabilities of the state that can have "economic and military effects" on states (Waltz 1979: 91) and they are what is measured specifically in the "distribution." In interstate relations, an international structure is a system-wide distribution of capabilities of states in an "anarchic" international system of sovereign states. It is the power relations embedded in the distribution that decisively influences a state's calculation of its interests and the costs and benefits of the various courses of action. The anarchic condition is necessary for the structural force to exert influence as there is no other forces that can effectively constrain or motivate states under such an anarchic condition. The power relations must dynamically evolve toward hierarchy to be effective on states.

A state's position in the power distribution is therefore important. It is also what is used to measure and determine the power distribution and also to identify changes in the power distribution and forecast structural shifts. David Lake deals with the challenge of measuring or describing this "system condition" in some way in his pioneering work on international economic structures and regional international structures (Lake 1984, 2009). Taking Waltz's framework a step further, Lake (1984) argues, as shown in Figure 5.1, that an international structure is a hierarchical distribution of capabilities of influential states. A significant change in the positions of these states in the hierarchy results in a different international structure. A change is significant when a new great power takes over the position of hegemonic leader. In another study, Lake identifies several regional security structures under the US hegemonic power and authority that are often "hidden by a formal legal approach" (Lake 2009: 57): North America, South America, West Europe, East Asia, South Asia, post-Soviet area, the Middle East, and Southern Africa.

Lake links an international structure to the international order in a region and makes a strong case that an international structure in a region is not only an empirical reality but also theoretically necessary because this is where people find an explanation for the international order in a region. Lake's work here also makes the concept of international structure "thicker" or more sophisticated in that "hierarchy" is where structural power is legitimized as an international authority through institutions and normative relations that together sustain the international order.

This latter point features more widely in the growing scholarship on international structure, institutions and norms, and international order and in the significance of the hierarchical and hegemonic international order in the post-1945 international system in general and in East Asia in particular. Structural effects occur when (1) a particular pattern of interstate power distribution brings about a particular set of different international behaviors of states depending on their positions in the structure of power relations and (2) the pattern of distribution changes where the rise of a great power in the structure, or the formation of a collective body of states, leads to disturbances in the power relations and, hence, the states to redefine their interests, recalculate their power relations, and reposition themselves.

Efforts to reposition and to reestablish a favorable equilibrium in power distribution can come in various forms: increase one's own power; build alignments, alliances, and partnerships; form a collective body of greater power with other states; or confine, reduce, or break up the other great power(s). When a new equilibrium is established, the updated power structure and the institutional and normative mechanisms sustaining the structure form an international order (Ikenberry 2014: 83–106). And, as Gilpin suggests, this equilibrium of interstate power stabilizes the

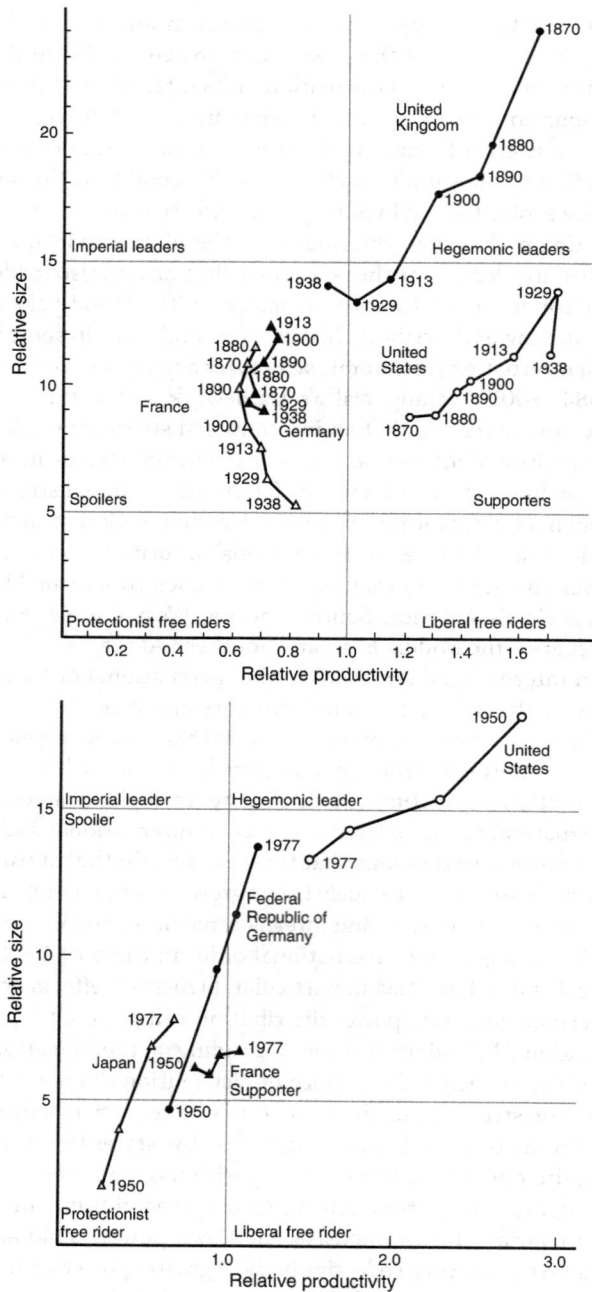

Figure 5.1 Lake's conception of international economic structures: 1870–1938 (top) and 1950–1977 (bottom)

Different positions of states at different times in the respective distribution of national capabilities, as measured in relative size of the economy (measured by a country's proportion of world trade) and relative productivity (measured by national output per man-hour relative to the average national output per man-hour in the other middle and large sized nations) (Lake 1984: 159, 163).

international order until the next significant disequilibrium occurs (Gilpin 1981). An international order therefore is a distinct set of authority relations among states, defined or shaped by the ever-evolving interstate power distribution and the institutional and normative dynamics that sustain and legitimize the power relations (Ikenberry 2000; Lake 2017). Because of different types of power structure and "normative structure" (Goh 2013: 12), there are different types of international order.

This theory of international structure helps explain how the distribution of power of states forms a material structure in their relations, and the influence of one state on others is determined by their relative positions in the structure. An international structure in IREA gives the region a significant level of connectivity. This in turn enables the meaningful movement and incorporation of material forces, eventually into an equilibrium of opposing collective forces at the system level that would neutralize the coercive effects of the others' force.

The land power in continental East Asia has always had a hegemonic dominance. This has mobilized states to form a collective force offshore from maritime East Asia to counter or neutralize land power. This has influenced the bipolar dynamism of the international structure to form and operate in East Asia since the nineteenth century. Moreover, the formation of collective force requires intensive institutional and normative processes to incorporate states into the collective framework of power. These processes allow the common interests of these states to develop, shape their international identity and role, and cultivate the transactional aspects of collective action and pubic goods within the framework. In the case of post-1945 East Asia, these institutional and normative processes involved the development of alliances, partnerships, and other forms of power networking.

POWER VACUUM

To understand the shaping of the international structure in post-1945 East Asia, its distinct and context-specific characteristics, and its effects on IREA, we must start with the disorder following the collapse of the existing international order. As discussed in Chapter 3, the Chinese world order started to crumble with the break-up of the Chinese empire from the late nineteenth century. The Chinese world order collapsed with the shift in the underlying power structure and supporting institutions and normative practices in interstate relations, and with the advance of European powers as well as Japan and the United States into continental East Asia.

More specifically, as shown in Figure 2.1, great powers with hostile and zero-sum intentions encroached on the power structure and supporting institutions of the Chinese world order along the East Asian crescent on the edge of continental East Asia. This was the first time new forces engaged from maritime East Asia in the established power distribution in East Asia. The stalemate in force movement suggests a balance of power could be established over this zone of engagement. But the power shifts were driven by states with interests larger than the crescent area. As forces of European powers retreated to the European continent, they started increasingly to operate against each other rather than cooperating as a collective force in continental East Asia. Japan emerged as a fast growing and expanding power, destroying much of the power base and social and institutional fabric of the Chinese world order. At the end of World War II, with the Chinese empire no more, the new power structure failed to establish itself. East Asia found itself in a political vacuum waiting for some power to fill in the void, for new states to establish a presence and connect to the power structure, and for interstate arrangements to materialize.

THE YALTA VISION

In February 1945, anticipating the imminent surrender of Germany and the end to the conflict in Europe, President Franklin Roosevelt of the United States, Prime Minister Winston Churchill of the United Kingdom, and General Secretary Joseph Stalin of the Soviet Union met in Yalta, Crimea, to discuss the postwar settlements and international order in Europe. On the side of the main business, securing the Soviet Union's entry into the war against Japan, the Big Three agreed to Moscow's political conditions for its entry: preservation of Outer Mongolia's status; return of Russia's rights in southern Sakhalin Island, lost in the 1904–1905 war with Japan; restoration of Russia's rights and interests in the port of Dairen and railways in Manchuria; and hand-over of Kuril Islands to Soviet Union. The "Far East Agreement" (Davidson 1969: 55) was preceded by the Cairo Declaration from the Cairo Conference among the United States, United Kingdom, and China in 1943, followed by a Soviet-China agreement and the Potsdam Declaration in 1945.

The Cairo Conference was aimed at wartime operation coordination and the postwar order in the Far East. On the postwar settlement, the Cairo Declaration states that (1) "Japan shall be stripped of all the islands in the Pacific"; (2) "all the territories Japan has stolen from the Chinese, including Manchuria, Formosa, and the Pescadores, shall be restored to the Republic of China"; (3) "Japan will also be expelled from all other territories"; and (4) "in due course Korea shall become free and independent," (NDL 2003a). The Soviet-China agreement in 1945 largely confirmed the Yalta Agreement on the Far East. The Potsdam Declaration, issued by the US, UK, and ROC in 1945, laid out the terms of Japan's surrender. In addition to changes required of the Japanese state, Japan's territorial sovereignty was limited to its four main islands (NDL 2003b).

This series of stipulations about the postwar international order in East Asia reflects the changing power relations in response to the structural shift between China and European powers and between China and Japan. This shift in power relations was driven primarily by the growing interests and influence of the United States and Soviet Union in East Asia and the structural logic of the need to have a balance between China and Japan for an international order in East Asia.

The Yalta vision, as this has commonly been referred to since, envisaged a permanently limited state of Japan; a strengthened, sovereign, and effective China; a greater stake and influence for the Soviet Union in East Asia, particularly in the

Mongol-Manchuria area; and strengthened security and influence for the United States in the western Pacific around Japan, the Philippines, and Southeast Asia. Power relations that had shifted significantly after the two world wars in East Asia required a new set of institutional arrangements to support the power structure and ensure the development of institutional and normative dynamics to stabilize the new power distribution in the long term.

The Yalta vision remained a vision. It is more a vision than an effective policy framework as the postwar settlement in East Asia went in a slightly different direction, more to the effect of forming a power balance between continental and maritime East Asia. The developments in the years immediately following the end of the war in East Asia threw many of the assumptions behind the Yalta vision into question. The Yalta vision assumed, for example, that the reorganization of power relations in East Asia would provide the necessary basis for cooperation among the United States, United Kingdom, Soviet Union, and China for a new international order. This proved to be not exactly the case. The United States and Soviet Union quickly turned into two leading powers, each with a different set of allies and partners, collectively opposing each other, primarily in East Asia. The wartime idealism for postwar settlement seemed not to have paid enough attention to the fundamental dynamics of IREA where bipolar structuration in the power distribution between continental East Asia and maritime East Asia drives the pendulum moves of structural shift across the East Asian crescent.

CONCENTRATION OF POWER

In classical structuralist analysis, power concentration and redistribution are enabled by the extraordinary growth and expansion of great powers in size and capability (Modelski 1987; Gilpin 1981; Lake 1984). Such concentration and distribution can also be generated by issues of international interest and developments of international significance. This causes national interests of the states to have a role to play in the shaping of international structure. The international structure therefore can be more precisely defined as the interstate distribution of capabilities and interests of the states. These issues and developments are often location specific and attract interests of states of different positions in the structure, and require different levels of capabilities to be organized to enforce a solution or ensure a response.

The idea of the concentration of power in the hands of the victorious Allies quickly confronted the reality that the principal powers supporting the Yalta vision were in fact destined to oppose, contest, and destroy each other – the problem of communist expansion, as George Kennan described in his now classic "X" article (Kennan 1947). Issues of great international interest developed intensively along the East Asian crescent: occupation and reform of Japan and organization of a new state in Korea, Indochina, and China. These led the powers to adjust their understanding of the power requirements and effective force deployment and alignment for a desired international order. These powers also developed innovative institutional arrangements and mechanisms to organize required capabilities into an incorporative network of security forces for maximum influence on the development of these issues.

The newly perceived threat and issues along the East Asian crescent called for capability alignment of a greater scale to counter the concentration of power and the coalition on the other side of the East Asian crescent. These issues redefined the interests of the United States and those of the Soviet Union and the People's Republic of China (PRC) in East Asia and moved them to adjust their strategic posture and association, away from the Yalta vision, through a series of efforts to enforce a post-war settlement on Japan, Korea, Taiwan, and Indochina. The United States shifted its defensive posture in the western Pacific to a more proactive forward posture offshore on the edge of continental East Asia.

The defensive posture, reflecting Roosevelt's strategic thinking on US interests in East Asia at the time of Yalta, was proclaimed as the official US position as late as 1950. But the US forward proactive posture to contain the spread of communism in continental East Asia already started to build up with the Truman Doctrine in 1947. The Truman Doctrine was a US strategic vision and policy guideline during the Cold War. Under this policy guideline, the United States provided direct military and economic support to countries under the threat of Communism. It came to be known after the specific program to support Greece and Turkey announced by President Truman in 1947. In 1948, the US gave up the idea of the UN organizing a new Korean state and moved ahead with the setup of South Korea, with the U.S.-ROC Mutual Defense Treaty signed in 1954. Starting in 1948, the US also gave up on the wartime idea of supporting a united and strong China and reclaimed its commitment to defending the ROC against the PRC. In 1951, the US organized the Allies' Peace Agreement with Japan in San Francisco and the security treaty between the US and Japan in the same year. These ended Japan's status as an imperial power and placed it under the sole occupation of the United States. After the Paris Conference in 1954 that ended French involvement in Indochina, the United States moved ahead with setting up South Vietnam in 1955.

These moves were supported with large-scale military and economic assistance and direct combat operational forces from the United States to these countries in the crescent and to other states in the whole maritime East Asia. These moves effected a shift of the boundaries of US strategic interests and influence in East Asia northwestward up from the original strategic defensive parameter. The domino theory was a popular metaphorical argument in policy circles in Washington during the Cold War that explains or justifies the policy and programs of active engagement and military support with any country, particularly those in the Southeast, to prevent them from falling to Communism. The domino threat was clearly a key factor that motivated the moves. These strategic moves led to the concentration of forces on the East Asian crescent and in maritime East Asia. The capability shift and alignment were clearly not accidental. They were the effects of actions and reactions of the states in search of an equilibrium of structural forces in response to the political vacuum that had arisen and new disturbances.

The same process of proactive and responsive power distribution and strategic concentration also happened in continental East Asia. The Yalta vision envisaged a return of the pre-1904 influence and privilege of Russia to northern East Asia. The defeat of Japan and the establishment of the PRC, however, changed the underlying power structure of such arrangements. The newly established PRC strategically decided to "lean to one side" in international relations, that is, to align itself with the Soviet Union over the United States and United Kingdom. This "leaning to one side" strategy was accompanied by another policy, "starting from scratch," that the PRC would not recognize or accept any international obligations and commitments the ROC or the Chinese empire had signed on to in the name of China.

In 1950, China and the Soviet Union signed the Sino-Soviet Treaty of Friendship, Alliance and Mutual Assistance in which the Soviet Union gave up its use rights of railways and ports in Manchuria, and China accepted the independence of Outer Mongolia. This removed the points of tension between the USSR and the PRC, and a 30-year military alliance was formally established between China and the Soviet Union. This brought the forces of the two states together in continental East Asia and formed a great level of concentration of power corresponding to US-led power incorporation and alignment on maritime East Asia. This power alignment enabled China to engage effectively and strategically on Korea, Taiwan, Indochina – emergent points of force engagement on the East Asian crescent.

ORGANIZATION OF COLLECTIVE FORCES

The distribution and alignment of capabilities was only part of the structuring of IREA. Power would be relevant, effective, and legitimate when such alignments help connect states that have different interests and aims in their interstate activities. This is where classical structural analysis finds it difficult to explain what ultimately drives the distribution of state capabilities (Keohane 1986). Recent literature on international structure and order (Ikenberry 2018; Toje 2018; Goh 2008, 2013) suggests that the normative structure built on institutions and normative practices is what makes the use of a coordinated set of capabilities effective and makes an international order possible and legitimate. What matters here is how interstate relations are organized.

The ways interstate relations were organized in either part of the bipolar structure proved to be quite similar. What emerged in either "camp" was a hierarchical international order led by a hegemonic power at the center of a network of key bilateral alliances and partnerships. The primary purpose of the power grouping was to contain or overcome the power of the other camp. The Soviet Union and China each had a separate set of formal bilateral alliance agreements with countries in continental East Asia. There was significant tension between China and the Soviet Union over leadership in the global "East." In East Asia, though, the Soviet Union did recognize, accept, and, in some way, even encourage China's leadership.

As for the other camp, there is a large body of literature on the nature and character of the US-led East Asian alliance system and the consequent regional security order (Cha 2010; Goh 2008; Yahuda 1996: 1–103). Underlying this international order was a series of bilateral treaty alliances of the United States with countries mostly on the East Asian crescent, and the US hegemonic power and the hierarchical relations between the US and its allies defined and indeed sustained this system now known as the "hub-spoke alliance system." The hub-spoke alliance system in East Asia

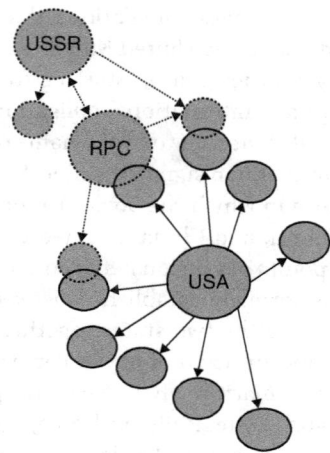

Figure 5.2 Illustration of hub-spoke alliance systems in East Asia in the 1960s

during the Cold War, as illustrated in Figure 5.2, was a soft form of collective security built on a network of asymmetric power structure–based bilateral alliances, with the United States at the dominant position in each of these bilateral arrangements. There was no formal direct connection between and among the junior partners in the bilateral alliances. This was a distinct set of institutional arrangements for international security, in contrast to the practices in Europe at the time where multilateral institutions, NATO and WATO, were formally established for collective security.

Victor Cha (Cha 2010, 2016) detailed the institutional mechanisms underlying this hub-spoke alliance system. Cha uses the hierarchical power structure to explain bilateralism in the US-led hub-and-spoke alliance system during the Cold War. His investigation shows that the hub-and-spoke alliance system is an institutional expression of the power structure underlying interstate relations. This set of institutional arrangements recognized the hegemonic power of the United States. The US sat at the hub position with exclusive domination in each individual set of bilateral alliance relations, and set and enforced the rights and obligations of the states in the hierarchical order. The hub-spoke network connected the capabilities of the states to the platform and formed a collective force countering the one in continental East Asia.

In each case, a collective force formed on the basis of a network of alliances, organized bilaterally by a hegemonic power and sustained with substantive mutual political, security, and economic interests and capabilities of the states and the institutions and normative practices that organized and legitimated the relations. As argued in the literature (Cha 2016; Goh 2007b; Lake 2009; Kupchan 2014; Ikenberry 2014), the structural conditions in a given international setting exert great influence on the form of interstate relations and mechanisms of their organization. In the case of the bipolar structure in East Asia, there is a distinct pattern of distribution of international interests and capabilities. Structurally such a distribution will constantly seek equilibrium. Events, state activities, and actions in the strategic organization of IREA are a response to the power of equilibrium logic. The hegemonic, hierarchical, and hub-spoke network of bilateral alliances and partnerships are effective at securing the interests and enhancing the capabilities of the states in this zero-sum, bifurcated structure.

The process of the distribution of power is one where capabilities are incorporated across borders into a network of forces having a shared purpose in their cooperative activity. It involves a set of institutions and norms that define the rights and obligations of each state in the order. This determines some unique features in the shaping of the bipolar structure and the consequent international order. In the US-led international order and power incorporation in maritime East Asia (MEA), power concentrated on MEA. The collective force was made effective on the East Asian crescent, through a series of US security alliances with power holders on the crescent: the Republic of Korea, Republic of China, and Republic of Vietnam, as well as Thailand, Singapore, Malaysia, the Philippines, and Indonesia.

These institutions were unique in the post-1945 IREA, as this part of the world was experiencing a transformation from an imperial world order to a nation-state system. They were not "designed" on a set of values, but rather evolved from repeated practices in the "powerplay" (Cha 2010) of postwar interstate settlement and order building in East Asia. The hierarchical and hegemonic international order that emerged from the working of this alliance system reflects the interstate power structure's effects on states involved in maritime East Asia and the institutions that supported the power relations. The power structure was imperative for the states to act in certain ways for a cumulative weight against the growing and expanding power of the communist states in continental East Asia.

In continental East Asia, a hierarchical interstate order built on a set of bilateral treaty alliances was also taking shape. Unique to the shaping of this interstate security order was a joint hegemonic dominance of China and the Soviet Union. The Sino-Soviet Treaty of Friendship, Alliance and Mutual Assistance in 1950 defined the "hub" of this alliance system from which China built further "spoke" alliance relations with new states on the East Asian crescent: North Korea, North Vietnam, Laos, and Cambodia. The Soviet-China alliance was established in a standard fashion of international law between two states that incorporated their capabilities into a large collective interstate power.

There is debate over who led or dominated the Sino-Soviet alliance and the Communist hub-spoke alliance network. There were deep-rooted tensions between Moscow and Beijing, and their "comradeship" would soon fall apart in the 1960s. The Soviet-China alliance, however, did provide a basis for an incorporated power concentration in continental East Asia. It formed a hegemonic authority in the large set of bilateral alliance relations of China with states on the East Asian crescent. As Lake points out (Lake 2009, 2017), this type of hegemonic authority is critical for the effectiveness and legitimacy of the power structure for the states holding different positions and roles in the hierarchy. The incorporation of forces in continental East Asia led to a "multi-layered hierarchical order," which Evelyn Goh uses to describe the US-dominated international order in East Asia (Goh 2013).

This other system of bilateral alliances in continental East Asia was a bit more complicated. The actual partnerships or "comradeships," being close like "lips to teeth," had been influencing region-wide strategic interaction and engagement of the two opposite collective forces long before their interstate alliances were formally institutionalized. The Communists in China, Korea, and Indochina worked together in continental East Asia from the 1920s and helped each other to establish the state in their homeland. With Vietnam, much of the "alliance" relations by which China sent military and economic assistance to North Vietnam and conducted its military operations in Vietnam was sanctioned under the normative practices and informal agreements and understandings between the Communist leaderships. The "normative structure" that supported and legitimized the power structure was therefore different in continental East Asia.

The drive for these states to work together, over and beyond the historical difficulties and tensions among them, was overwhelmingly the common cause of Communism International. Their alliance relations operated as comradeships for the international movement of Communism in East Asia. Their alliances did not necessarily require the sanction of a formal treaty. These state actions were largely those of the Communist Parties and armed forces they commanded. Trust in their shared security and mutual expectations of benefits and contributions from their actions had long developed in the years of networking and socialization among the senior leaders of the Chinese, Soviet, Vietnamese, and Korean Communist Parties. The extensive military operational capabilities and operational mechanisms of organizing their Communist cause provided effective institutional and normative support for their new interstate alliances.

The normative structure also legitimized the hierarchical power relations that developed in their long historical interaction and engagement. Both the Soviet Union and China claimed to break away from their imperialist past, though hierarchical relations persisted in the operation of the Communist International and in the working of the Communist hub-stroke alliance network in East Asia. Between China and Korea, and China and Vietnam and beneath their comradeship, the shadow of history was never too far away. They were smoothed over with their shared, higher purpose and ideology at the time.

THE BIPOLAR STRUCTURE IN IREA

The shaping of the new power structure following the collapse of the Japanese empire led to the emergence of a bipolar power structure in East Asia and a hierarchical interstate order on the platform of each block: the US-led hegemonic hierarchical order in maritime East Asia and the Soviet-China dominant hegemonic hierarchical order in continental East Asia. The shaping of the East Asian bipolar structure, as illustrated in Figure 2.1 and Figure 5.2, explains some of the theoretical questions we have on the working of international structures. These questions ask why we have an international structure; how an international structure forms and evolves, and how an international structure influences state behavior and shapes international order. First, an international structure shapes up over the collapse of an existing international order. The collapse of the Japanese empire influenced the United States and the Soviet Union to reassess the risks and opportunities in the emergent power structure and realign states similarly affected by the new power structure into a collective force to counter the perceived force of threat. This implies that the operational logic underlying the structural concentration and incorporation of power drove the associated forces into a bipolar equilibrium.

Second, the socialization of the states and institutionalization of their new power relations is enforced by the hegemonic state in the hierarchical order to ensure the structural effects of the incorporated power. In repeated historical instances in East Asia, an interstate order emerged among states in maritime East Asia and another one in continental East Asia. The network of bilateral power relations on the site of power concentration and incorporation became mostly hierarchical.

Third, the power of states in continental East Asia and that in maritime East Asia are incorporated through a set of institutions and rules of conduct that specify and operationalize the relations to ensure the effect of power and stabilize its bipolar distribution and balance. As a distinct set of social, institutional, and normative dynamics inform the power relations in each international order, the equilibrium between these two opposing collective forces are largely material in nature, referring to the capabilities and interests of states as stipulated in the classical structural analysis of Waltz and Lake. Collective security is achieved through a network of bilateral alliances and partnerships, rather than a multilateral institution.

CORRECTION, DISTURBANCE, AND STRUCTURAL SHIFT

The bipolar structure started to set in from the late 1940s, and the Cold War ended in the early 1990s. There is a debate over whether the Cold War ended in East Asia in 1991 as well (Tang 2014). This is particularly relevant because the tensions in the three defining events: the Korean War, the Taiwan Strait conflict, and the Indochina conflict, have not been resolved. More importantly, it was unclear whether the historical power structure and in particular the part in continental East Asia would collapse.

The bipolar structure, however, had experienced a significant change even before the 1990s. Yahuda, for example, asserts that the Cold War structure was transformed from a bipolar to a tripolar structure in the 1970s (Yahuda 1996: 77–104). Key to the change was the "pole" in continental East Asia where the Sino-Soviet split in the 1960s broke the incorporated collective force in continental East Asia into two, forcing a reconfiguration of power among the states in East Asia. China and the Soviet Union entered into open conflict on their eastern borders in 1969. China and the US normalized their relations in 1971 and China and Japan in 1972. These provided momentum for "alignment" between the United States, PRC, and Japan against the Soviet "hegemonism." The Soviet Union in turn formed a strategic alignment with India in 1971 with the Indo-Soviet Treaty of Peace, Friendship and Cooperation and alignment with Vietnam with the Treaty of Friendship and Cooperation in 1978. China also formed a close partnership with Sihanouk's Cambodia.

In a significant way, these shifts in power and strategic alignment can be seen as effects of the bipolar structure transforming to a tripolar structure, reflecting a "strategic triangle" among the USSR, US, and PRC. This indicates an inability of IREA to be constrained within the bipolar framework. The US-led international order was more effective and influential than that dominated by the Soviet Union-China. The shifts represented one more move of the zone of engagement up northward to the borders of the Soviet Union. The bipolar structure failed to hold up in East Asia, which seemed to be returning to a single hegemonic hierarchical order. Yahuda in the 2019 edition of his *International Politics of the Asia-Pacific* traces the coming of US "unipolarity" in East Asia to the 1990s (Yahuda 2019).

The strategic triangle, as far as East Asia is concerned, shifted the balancing dynamics beyond East Asia and had more to do with the global strategic interplay between the United States and the Soviet Union than reflecting the structural dynamics of IREA. Moreover, this strategic triangle is not the same as tripolarity, certainly not a tripolarity in East Asia. Understanding the evolution of the international structure in East Asia in a larger historical context can help us to think harder about what an international structure is and how it plays out in IREA. International structure is a system condition where the distribution of capabilities of states constantly evolves and tends to result in a particular form of distribution and incorporation of these capabilities at a given time – bipolar, unipolar, multipolar.

The transformations from bipolarity to tripolarity and to unipolarity is a changeover of that form. What drives the transformation is the system condition. We have shown that IREA is such a system where events, developments, actions, and relations are significantly connected in their meaning and logic. We have also shown that the dominant form of manifestation of the international structure in the longer historical experience of IREA has tended to be swinging between a hegemonic hierarchical order and warring states. Seen in this perspective, the bipolar structure is really the dominant form of manifestation of the international structure in IREA in the Cold War period. It reflects the stalemate of the two dominant and coordinated forces to incorporate East Asia in a single hierarchical, hegemonic order.

Beyond the Sino-Soviet split, other developments in IREA have affected the bipolar structure, for example, the rise of a regional economy through region-wide industrial diffusion and integration of production in Japan-led production networks from the 1960s (see discussion in Chapter 7). The economic process brought different parts of East Asia closer to a single market rather than diverging in a binary opposition. The rise of China, the US pivot to Asia, and the strategic hedging of middle and small powers, on the other hand, are more effects of the bipolar structuring. The reclaimed power and influence of the bipolar structure is further complicated by three additional developments. As the bipolar structure has reclaimed itself and exerted its influence in more recent years, the South China Sea has emerged as a theater of strategic engagement and geopolitical interaction between the US and China. Beyond the politics of territorial disputes, there is a full playing out of the structural dynamics. The South China Sea is potentially a platform where continental East Asia will engage with maritime East Asia. This means that the zone of engagement in the bipolar formation will move down southward in the opposite direction of the shift affected by the Sino-Soviet split in the 1970s. This could transform the regional power distribution and return the region to a unipolar order.

The persistence of the reclaiming of a bipolar pattern is also complicated by developments in East Asian regionalism (see discussion in Chapter 8). In particular, China's very bold initiatives – the Belt and Road Initiative (BRI) and Asia Infrastructure Investment Bank (AIIB) – have been received with mixed interpretations. Many see them as an alternative platform for the regional economic order as well as the pluralist value of these initiatives for the region's institutional architecture (Wang 2015; Grieger 2016; Ye 2015). There is a great deal of interest among states in the region in seeing how they can engage with those initiatives and benefiting from being a part of them. Others, though, are cautious about the structural nature of the initiatives and concerned about the return of a hegemonic, hierarchical regional order in East Asia.

From the perspective of the IREA structure, the dynamics that drive BRI and AIIB are not necessarily directed at East Asia or even oriented toward the Asia-Pacific. It is perhaps China's initial concern over the political difficulties on its maritime East Asia front that led it to think "west" of China (Summers 2016; Wang 2016; Fallon 2015). This appears to be pursued as a more effective platform for a new global "division of labor," in the forms and purposes that Wallerstein and North (Wallerstein 1974; North and Thomas 1973) identified in their analyses of Western Europe's global expansion in earlier centuries. In other words, a potential implication of these Chinese initiatives is that they will go beyond the constraints of the bipolar structure in East Asia.

Finally, the persistence of the bipolar structure is further complicated by the strategic interaction between China and the US over how to institutionalize an international order as they envisage it for themselves. The outcome of this strategic interaction will largely depend on how the United States will further organize capacities in the region in response to China's new posture from where its Pivot to Asia left off. The strategic competition between US and China is essentially the effects of a power realignment and reorganization in response to structural disturbances and disequilibrium. The China-US rivalry and competition have put many countries in a very delicate position, caught between the traditional security relations with the US and growing economic and trade interests and relations with China. This anxiety has manifested most vividly with countries on the East Asian crescent extending all the way down to Singapore, where structural pressures are as acute today as they were in the Cold War.

All three of the developments discussed here and the structural disturbances or corrections discussed earlier suggest that the profound changes in IREA have reached a critical point. There is a great level of uncertainty as to whether such changes represent system, systemic, or interaction changes (Gilpin 1981: 40): whether these latest developments are largely the "swinging effects" of the bipolar structure or evidence that the international structure in East Asia is seeking alternative forms to manifest.

A HISTORICAL PATTERN OR A GENERIC STRUCTURE

Our discussion in this chapter has identified a pattern of power distribution and power alignment in post-1945 East Asia. This pattern was shaped by a series of major events and developments in IREA and the building of alliances and partnerships on both sides of the East Asian crescent. This "structuring" process led to the emergence of a concentration of incorporated capabilities of states and a hierarchical, hegemonic interstate order in maritime East Asia and in continental East Asia – a bipolar manifestation of the international structure in IREA. We have also shown that the power relations in a given international order are made effective and legitimate in the context of a specific set of bilateral arrangements through institutional negotiation and socialization. The incorporated or coordinated power is further made relevant and effective in the overall balance of power between continental and maritime East Asia.

The international structure is critical for the development of IREA because it motivated or constrained states to act in a certain way. In the particular form in which it manifested itself in post-1945 East Asia, the region-wide distribution of capabilities and interests of states at a given time influenced their calculation of the interests of states in the events and issues on the East Asian crescent, and the capabilities they needed to enforce a development of the situation. This led to the building of a network of forces in continental East Asia and maritime East Asia and a bipolar distribution of forces across the East Asian crescent. It is unclear whether the bipolar distribution of power at the regional level is a permanent feature of the international structure in East Asia. It is possible, though, to see the Cold War structure as an instance of the tension in the long historical process of structuring and order building in IREA between a hegemonic, hierarchical order and a multistate order.

The discussion of the bipolar structure also helps us better understand some of the critical issues in structuralist analyses of international relations. First, the logic of international structure in IREA suggests that an international structure can be "regional," as a system condition in a definable subsystem of international relations. As such, an international structure can be empirically analyzed rather than just being abstractly debated. Moreover, the working of the international structure also suggests that such a structure is dynamic, constantly searching for an equilibrium in the power distribution. This dynamism has driven the transformation of IREA structure from bipolarity to tripolarity and from unipolarity back to bipolarity in post-1945 East Asia, and between a hegemonic, hierarchical order and a multipolar, galaxy-type order in a greater historical context of the evolution of the structure and institutions of IREA.

Study Questions

1. Do you see an international structure manifested in IREA? Describe a form of that manifestation in the history of IREA.
2. How has the bipolar structure influenced the organization of IREA? Describe the effects of the bipolar structure on IREA.
3. Why are institutions and norms important for the power and effect of the international structure of IREA?
4. Has the bipolar structure changed since the end of the Cold War? Discuss the disturbances and corrective responses to the structural equilibrium in IREA.
5. Is the international structure in IREA transforming from unipolarity to bipolarity or multipolarity? How?

Further Reading

Cha, Victor, 2016. *Powerplay: Origins of the American Alliance System in Asia.* Princeton: Princeton University Press.

Christensen, Thomas, 2011. *Worse Than a Monolith: Alliance Politics and Problems of Coercive Diplomacy in Asia Princeton.* Princeton: Princeton University Press.

Chung, Jae Ho, 2006. *Between Ally and Partner: Korea-China Relations and the United States.* New York: Columbia University Press.

Gaddis, John Lewis, 1987. "Drawing Lines: The Defensive Perimeter Strategy in East Asia, 1947–1951," pp. 72–104 in John Lewis Gaddis, *The Long Peace: Inquiries Into the History of the Cold War.* Oxford: Oxford University Press.

Hasegawa, Tsuyoshi, 2011. *The Cold War in East Asia, 1945–1991.* Stanford: Stanford University Press.

Ikenberry, G. John, 2000. *After Victory: Institutions, Strategic Restraint, and the Rebuilding of Order after Major Wars.* Princeton: Princeton University Press.

Lake, David A., 1984. "Beneath the Commerce of Nations: A Theory of International Economic Structures," *International Studies Quarterly* 28(2):143–170.

Lake, David A., 2009. "Regional Hierarchy: Authority and Local International Order," *Review of International Studies* 35(S1):35–58.

Lake, David A., 2017. "Domination, Authority, and the Forms of Chinese Power," *Chinese Journal of International Politics* 10(4): 357–382.

Rotter, Andrew J., 1987. *The Path to Vietnam: Origins of the American Commitment to Southeast Asia.* Ithaca: Cornell University Press.

Waltz, Kenneth, 1979. *Theory of International Politics.* Reading: Addison-Wesley.

Yahuda, Michael, 1996. *The International Politics of the Asia-Pacific.* London: Routledge.

6 Culture in IREA

In This Chapter...

- Culture in International Relations
- Confucian authority structure
- International policy and behavior, Japanese style
- National identity
- Religion as a political force
- Third-wave democracy
- China's evolving international identity
- The ASEAN way and the Asia-Pacific way
- The normative structure of IREA

Learning Objectives

After studying this chapter, you will be able to
- Understand the context for the problem of culture in IREA in different historical periods and for different countries in IREA
- Use cultural forces and factors as a variable to analyze how culture influences a state's international behavior and policy in IREA
- Explain whether there is an East Asian culture or political tradition that informs the international behavior and policy of the East Asian countries
- Critically analyze how culture in East Asia relates to the shaping of the international structure and order in IREA.

East Asian culture is a uniquely important factor in IREA. Discussions in earlier chapters touched upon the question as to whether culture, political traditions, and norms and identity are an enabling or transformative force in IREA and how they influence the international behavior and policy of individual states and the shaping of IREA. Do the Japanese, for example, conduct their relations with other countries as they do in their interpersonal relations – soft, indirect, and always polite, as the usual perceptions go? For another example, is the way China sees the world and identifies with other states influenced by the political traditions they formed in the past? More specifically, is China practicing a Confucian authority order in IREA? As a group of countries in the region, are East Asian states culturally similar because they share the Confucian culture, "East Asian civilization," or Asian values? Yet another example, can a regional identity be constructed to support ASEAN's effort to engage in IREA as a collective force?

These questions are legitimate and interesting, as the practices and experiences of IREA suggest that there seem to be forces influencing them that are unique to this group of states. They are related to the cultural traits of the peoples of East Asia. These forces affect the quality and character of IREA, war and peace, and development and progress in IREA. European powers encountered different peoples and civilizations when they moved up north into continental East Asia in the nineteenth century. The Americans found the "operational code" of the Japanese and Chinese policymakers intriguing and their policy behavior puzzling as they expanded their influence in post-1945 East Asia. Some kind of cultural codes must have influenced their policy calculation, international behavior, and style of operation.

Moreover, though we are interested in how East Asian culture influences IREA, the patterns of international action and interactions among East Asian states are not consistent across these East Asian states. Either these cultural traditions, practices, and norms are not a decisive factor in their international policy and behavior, or there is a significant diversity or differences in their national culture and political traditions so that they are unable to produce consistent effects.

This chapter will look at the problem of culture in IREA, and whether and how culture influences the shaping of IREA and the international policy and behavior of East Asian states. We are interested in whether there is an East Asian culture that connects these states in IREA. There are two sets of cultural traditions, practices, and norms in IREA. The first are those the nations inherited when the new states were set up in the post-1945 settlement and those that have continued to evolve in the ongoing development of IREA. Japan's cultural values and political tradition in the 1910s, for example, would be different from those in the 2010s. The same goes with every East Asian nation.

The chapter will look at the traditional cultural practices and political values of East Asian states, and how and to what extent these continue to influence their conduct of international relations. We will also investigate changes in their cultural norms and practices, and whether they have continued to form a coherent and consistent force that shapes IREA. Above all, it is of great interest to see whether the effects of East Asian culture pacify or intensify tensions in IREA and contribute to stability and development in East Asia.

CULTURE IN INTERNATIONAL RELATIONS

The first question we are often confronted with on this subject is what culture is in International Relations and, of course, what culture is in IREA. The discipline's interest in the role of culture in International Relations goes back to scholars' curiosities in the 1930s and 1940s, as in the works of Harold Lasswell (1935, 1948). Laswell, like many other behavioral scientists working in the field of politics at the time, was fascinated by the distinct patterns of human behavior as shaped by an individual's personality and psychological character. The dynamics of personality and psychological character are considered a hidden force that influences or even determines the behavior and action of policymakers and politicians and, by extension, the international policy and behavior of nations, particularly in their decisions and actions on war and peace. This led to a strong tradition in the field after World War II that focuses on human actors at the micro level and their behavior pattern and how this shapes international relations.

This tradition developed further in three directions. First, the interest in human nature and character went further to focus on the "cultural character" of decision makers in international policy. Alexander George's essay in 1969 unpacks decision makers' "operational code" that determines their overall political attitude and policy behavior (George 1969). This operational code concerns "philosophical beliefs" and "instrumental beliefs" and explains the "habits" of thinking and reacting by policymakers when facing problems or situations. Policymakers' decision and policy behavior therefore are influenced by their personal beliefs and intellectual habits. This is a critical aspect of culture in international relations. This operational code research program led to the development of a large scholarly tradition on policymakers' thinking and behavior patterns, including Robert Jervis's perception theory and image theory (Jervis 1970, 1976), Irving Janis's group theory (Jervis 1972), and Alexander George's presidential staff theory (George 1980). The cultural nature of this line of inquiry became clearer when these concepts and frameworks were used to explain the behavior and policy of policymakers behind the "bamboo screens" or iron curtains in East Asian countries, Japan and China in particular.

Second, the tradition also focuses on "national character" and its impact on a nation's international policy and behavior. Studies in this area elevate individual personality and behavior to the collective character and identity and the behavior pattern of the nation. Scholars examining such aspects of the tradition investigate how the collective belief system, mindsets, national image, and ethnic identity shape a nation's international policy and behavior (Little & Smith 1988; Zimmerman & Jacobson 1993; Fisher 1997; Schechterman & Slann 1993; Boulding 1959; Kelman 1965). As William Bloom explains, national character is a "particular set of cultural mores and political norms which, through socialization, are passed down from generation to generation within a particular ethnos. Thus, culture by culture, there will be different sets of general ideas and behavioral norms concerned with political methods and structures." "[D]istinctive types of national character," Bloom suggests," lead to distinctive types of foreign policy behavior...[and] nation-states have particular aggregated psychological tendencies which directly influence and motivate their foreign policy decision" (Bloom 1990: 18).

Third, works on political development in developing societies in the 1960s articulated a powerful concept of political culture and influenced generations of scholars to understand and approach the problem of culture in politics. Gabriel Almond, for example, defined political culture as "a particular pattern of orientations to political actions" (Almond 1956: 356). Gabriel Almond and Sidney Verba (1963) proposed the concept of "civic political culture" and showed the different ways political society is organized shape people's attitudes toward the state and authority, and together support a political order. Lucian Pye takes it a step further and sees political culture as "the attitudes, sentiments, and cognitions that inform and govern political behavior in a given society." It is "an ordered subjective realm of politics which gives meaning to the polity, discipline to institutions, social relevance to individual acts" (Pye 1965: 7).

Samuel Huntington, furthermore, explains, in his 1968 work *Political Order in Changing Societies*, that political culture is a distinct set of institutions, norms, and instruments that sustain a political society and hence a political order in the new states. In these pioneering works on the problem of political development in developing societies, political culture relates to a political tradition that incorporates the political attitudes and behaviors of individual members of society and institutions and processes that ensure a political order. This scholarly tradition has taken the problem of culture as a larger issue of the organization of polities across civilizations. It developed further into scholarly interests today in the role of political economy models, civilization, religion, and normative structures in IREA.

These scholarly traditions have come to influence our understanding of IREA. They highlight the importance of cultural factors in the shaping of international policy and the behavior of East Asian states, and in the patterns of war, conflict and peace in IREA. Because much of the post-1945 IREA has been approached within a framework of US engagement and involvement in East Asia and with East Asian countries, cultural factors in those societies' policy behavior have been an important part of the scholarly and policy interest in understanding IREA. A considerable number of works have looked at the historical, ethnic, religious, and cultural conditions for war and conflict in Korea, China, Vietnam, and Southeast Asian countries. A large number of works have been devoted to the Japanese "national character" and the conduct by the Japanese of international policy and negotiation in US engagement with Japan in the early post-1945 decades. A significant amount of scholarly work has investigated the political traditions, social values, and belief systems of political elites and communist bureaucrats in China and how these affect Communist China's international behavior and policy formulation. These issues constituted a great puzzle for US IR researchers and policy analysts during the Cold War.

These cultural focuses developed out of the behavioral revolution in political science that focuses on the micro dynamics of human behavior, and comparative politics that looks at the problem of political development in new states. As such, they somehow weakened the power and integrity of a distinct cultural approach to international relations. They have not developed to the point where a distinct framework on a set of core concepts and assumptions stands out to form a cultural theory or cultural explanations, with the level of effectiveness comparable to that of realism, structuralism, institutionalism, or organization theory. In IREA, "cultural" and "national" are not always easy to separate, particularly when they are perceived from outside. This has contributed to the perennial question of what culture is and particular, what an East Asian culture is. Much of the attention in cultural analyses and explanations is on the ethnic traits of the peoples and how these determine the behavioral pattern of the individuals, groups, and the nation-state. Culturally focused explanations become "soft" knowledge, supplementing the dominant and popular theories in international relations. They usually have weak explanatory power, so much so that the question "does culture matter?" (Harrison & Huntington 2000) was always in the minds of IR theorists.

Interest in and inquiry into the role of culture in IR has continued, though within a broader framework. New trends in cultural explanations see culture as a form of polity organization or constitution, and see culture as more of an ontological problem. From the 1980s, cultural theory, or critical theory, started to have an impact in IR studies. Richard Ashley, in a series of works in the 1980s (Ashley 1984, 1987, 1988), challenged the validity of the modern rationality underlying the dominant IR theories and suggested the cultural and political nature of organization or constitution of international relations. This critical challenge was taken up by two groups of scholars who are interested in understanding the "cultural" nature of the organization or constitution of international relations. One group focuses on the cultural nature of the international system. R. B. J. Walker (Walker 1993) asked us to go beyond the "system" to think about the system's ontological nature and, further, the constructive nature of international relations. These eventually led to the development of constructivist and social theories (Onuf 1989; Kubalkova et al. 1998; Lapid & Kratochwil 1996; Wendt 1987, 1999).

Samuel P. Huntington's 1993 essay "The Clash of Civilizations" influenced the IR culture paradigm to develop in a different direction. Conventional notions of culture, as an alternative to state-centric perspectives, seem insufficient and ineffective as a framework, or a unit of analysis, for explaining international relations. The clash of civilizations, according to Huntington, is at the core of the cultural dynamics that drive nations to tension and conflict and to war and peace. Taking civilization as the unit of analysis here exposes the larger structural and institutional forces underlying cultural dynamics. Civilization here is "a system of homogeneous human activities confined by a set of prevalent rules, habits, and tools developed over a considerably long period of time" (Huang 2002: 218) in organizing the political economic life of a large population. These rules, habits, and mechanisms have stable and predictable effects on human relations and purposes. It is a "way of life" for the larger population. Civilization is not just ethnic traits that influence human behavior, but the way human relations are structured and society is organized. It is "the way of life" of people in a geopolitical and geo economic area. It is more than their linguistic forms, exotic food, arts, folk songs, and architectural styles.

The idea of civilization as a unit of analysis of international relations had been taken up before (Spengler 1926; Toynbee 1934). Historian Arnold J. Toynbee in his *Study of History* explores the rise and fall of about 20 civilizations in world history. For Toynbee, the rise and fall of civilizations shows the historical constraints on the mode of the organization/constitution of human relations and society and how this influences the shaping of different types of "international order."

Civilizational frameworks have also been long utilized by scholars on East Asia (De Bary 1988; Pye 1985; Fairbank et al. 1989; Palais 1991, 1996). Taking cultural traditions in East Asia as part of East Asian civilization, these pioneering works look at the origins and spread of that civilization, the political structure that sustained it, the institutional arrangements and normative practices in the organization of the polity and society, and the connectivity and identity among the Chinese, Japanese, Korean, and Vietnamese peoples. These works laid the foundations for a cultural approach to the problem of the organization of polities in East Asia. They provided substance to the debates in the 1980s and 1990s on Asian values, East Asian modernity, and Asian democracy. These works enriched our understanding of the role of culture in IREA. This, along with the "clash of civilizations" theory, the cultural approaches to international relations, the spread of Third Wave democracy in East Asia, and the East Asian miracle of economic development, has had a significant influence in how we approach the problem of culture in IREA.

These dimensions in the problem of culture in international relations and in IREA are useful for us to understand what culture is precisely in our discussion of the cultural factor in IREA and how cultural forces have changed over time and influenced IREA in different ways. Culture, as discussed here, conveys three different meanings in its relation to IREA. Culture first, for most people, is what the Japanese would refer to as "cultural properties" (文化財), i.e., any tangible forms of interpersonal expression and communication inherited from past eras of human life in a community. These include dancing, painting, architecture, music, religious rituals and ceremonies, writing systems, and so forth. Taking this one step further, culture, in the spirit of "political culture" of Almond, Verba, and Pye, is "a particular pattern of orientation" of a population toward power and authority where "the attitudes, sentiments and cognitions...inform and govern political behavior" (Pye 1965: 7). This orientation manifests in the tangible forms identified in the first category that give meaning to political processes, actions, institutions, and structure.

Culture, taking it yet one more step further in the civilizational, macrohistorical framework, is the "way of life" of a population of significant size and how people organize among themselves in the political economic community for the collective purposes of the larger polity. Culture in these different manifestations influence international relations in diverse ways, and East Asian culture has significantly shaped the organization of IREA.

CONFUCIAN AUTHORITY STRUCTURE

In looking for traditions of political culture in East Asia, we inevitably start with Confucianism and Buddhism, and their influence on East Asia, from continental to maritime East Asia. We are interested particularly in the strands of Chinese political traditions of the Tang Dynasty (618–907) and Ming Dynasty (1368–1644), where the pattern of political structure and the type of supporting institutions and social norms are often referred to as the origins of East Asia civilization as practiced systematically in East Asian states, so much so that even today, when the Chinese look for the original prototypes of their political traditions, they find surviving evidence of these traditions more likely in Korea, closely influenced by the Ming system, in Japan, significantly influenced by the Tang system, in Vietnam, and, of course, in Hong Kong, Taiwan, and Macau, as well as in countries in Southeast Asia.

In this cultural tradition and influence that defines East Asian civilization, however, Buddhism is not really of Chinese or East Asian origin. It spread to East Asia from South Asia, influenced the behavioral norms of individuals, but had a rocky journey toward acceptance as a national religion in East Asian nations. It has certainly never risen to the level of prevalent normative framework that sustains or legitimatizes a particular power structure and the way of life in the large-scale polity in East Asia. One exception was perhaps in Japan before the Meiji Restoration in the mid-nineteenth century. In the Kansei region including Nara and Kyoto, the center of political economic life of Japan at that time, civilization developed under the great influence of sinicized Buddhism from continental East Asia across the East Sea. It served as a powerful spiritual framework that informed the organization and purpose of Japan's increasingly urbanized civic culture.

Underlying the Chinese traditional political culture was essentially Confucianism that provided real institutional and normative substance to East Asian civilization. Confucianism is primarily a set of behavioral norms or "guiding principles" for individuals to act in society. Confucianism is a set of moral standards and social values that developed from the teachings of the Chinese ancient thinker Confucius (551–479BC). Confucianism at one level consists of a set of guiding principles and social norms as expected by society for individuals to follow. "Three Guiding Principles" (三纲) outlines the appropriate manner for individuals to approach others in specific sets of primary social relations: King must guide minister, father must guide son, husband must guide wife, and so forth. "Five Social Norms" (五常) stipulates that one should conduct oneself socially in full appropriateness: be empathic, humble, respectful, righteous, and trustworthy. These are advocated as "heavenly moral principles" (天理). Confucianism advocates a social order based on the ideal behavior of individuals as expected based on their prescribed role in society and their relations with others. Confucianism spread widely throughout continental East Asia, much more fully and systematically practiced in Tang and Ming eras, and then extended its influence beyond to Korea, Japan, and Vietnam.

At the core of the Confucian moral code are the "Three Principles and Five Norms." Confucius crafted these norms and code of conduct in Eastern Zhou (770–255 BC) when the kingdom of the previous dynasty, Shang, had collapsed into feudal warring states. These behavioral guidelines and social norms, along with the rituals, ceremonial music and formations, language, architecture, and arts that conveyed these meanings, were intended to help restore the centralized political structure and social order over these warring states. Much of the norms and rules and associated rituals, ceremony, music, arts, and literature became an important part of Chinese culture and East Asian civilization.

The organizational aspects of Confucianism, however, helped support, sustain, and legitimize a state structure and political order in continental East Asia for thousands of years. A centralized, multilayered system of imperial governance conveyed the authority of Heaven all the way to the family and polities on the edge of the imperial polity with the emperor and scholarly officialdom at the pivotal position of the political structure. This system was fully developed and in effective operation in the Han, Tang, Song, and Ming dynasties and influenced polity organization in other East Asian states at those times.

Lucian Pye summarizes the pattern of political power and authority and their supporting institutions and normative practices in four defining features and conceptualizes them as the cultural dimensions of authority. The Confucian concept of authority stresses that power was supposed to flow inexorably from the morally superior (morality); power was seen as emerging from the relationships between superiors and inferiors (hierarchy); and treating formal government as the legitimate basis for power (legitimacy). In addition, those in power were to use their own exemplary conduct to influence the behavior of others (role model) (Pye 1985: 86–9). These dimensions of authority connect the structure of political power to the institutions and normal practices that sustain the structure and a political order that values mutual dependency, hierarchy, moral legitimacy, and ethical propriety. This model of authority, as Pye observes, is found to be operative in the organization of polity in a whole range of East Asian countries.

There are two primary implications of the Confucian model of authority for IREA. First, the Confucian model institutionalizes and legitimizes a form of polity organization that connects the Mandate of Heaven through the conduct of the emperor to the governance of the polity over a domain through layers of centripetally connected power relations and mechanisms. The Confucian political order is inherently hierarchical, with power flowing from the central power holder to his inferiors in power relations of distinct types.

Moreover, the Confucian model not only enables hierarchy but also legitimizes it by moralizing the absolute power of the emperor as mandated by Heaven and normalizing "all under Heaven" (Zhao 2006, 2011) to act in compliance with the prescribed norms and rules. As individuals are positioned differently in power relations, the Confucian model provides a sense of identity and legitimacy. The tribute system (see discussion in Chapter 3), for example, between China of the Ming and Qing eras and the polities on the outer rim of the Chinese world order was one part of the institutional setup for the power relations and authority structure in continental East Asia (Kang 2010; MacKay 2015; Lee 2017). These two implications, hierarchy and moral legitimacy, are particularly relevant and important for our understanding of and debate over the structure and institutions of international order in East Asia today – whether an international order in East Asia is inherently hierarchical and the precise role of the normative structure in the shaping of an international order in IREA.

INTERNATIONAL POLICY AND BEHAVIOR, JAPANESE STYLE

Among works addressing the influence of culture in contemporary IREA, quite a few focus on Japan: sushi, Zen, national character, personality, soft power – all important signs of Japanese culture that were believed to influence, even determine, Japan's international policy and decision-making behavior in style and substance (Gaenslen 1986; Iriye 1981; Smith 1992; Watanabe 1978). Much of the interest was driven by the puzzles arising from the world's practical dealings with Japan's government officials and operators in diplomacy and business negotiations in the early decades of the Cold War.

Akio Watanabe (1978), for example, explores the Japanese style of foreign policymaking and argues that the Japanese, especially political leaders, are more society/

group oriented than rational individual-oriented people. There is a lack of leadership in the policy process, complicated by strong senior-junior followership, consensus orientation, and diffuseness in policy agencies in the social and organizational environment. They therefore tend to be good at compromising rather than deciding, and Japan's decision-making tends to be accommodating, slow to evolve, secretive, reactive, and passive. According to Watanabe, Japanese cultural behavior follows a pattern of Japanese government officials acting with high-level indecisiveness and weak leadership and tending toward compromise. This is clearly influenced by the Japanese political culture based on group coordination and conflict avoidance and influenced by personality, group dynamics, and intriguing norms of social behavior. This pattern of foreign policy behavior was seen in Japan's international relations in the early postwar decades, but perhaps more broadly in nations across East Asia that the United States found itself having to deal with extensively after World War II. This has resulted in a popular interpretation of Japanese cultural behavior in IR scholarship, which connects the pattern and character of Japan's foreign policy and international behavior to Japanese culture.

Not all scholarly investigations define Japanese culture as such. Using multifaceted dynamics of power and culture to explain Japan's strategic posture in the Pacific War, Akira Iriye sees international relations as "intercultural" as well as "interpower" relations. "A nation is also a culture" (Iriye 1981: vii). All its cultural signifiers, giving meanings to war and other international engagements, informed and motivated the nation's international actions. According to Iriye, Japan and the United States have, over the years before, during, and after World War II, developed a series of similar and, at times, parallel assumptions, or visions, about an international order. These provided a basis for their postwar international cooperation. Japanese culture in Iriye's framework is Japan's vision of the world order and where Japan sits in that order. This explains the inevitable clash between Japan and the United States, leading to the onset of the Pacific War and their subsequent reconciliation.

Here, Japanese culture is dynamic and adaptive. It fundamentally concerns Japan's vision about the international order and its identity with that order. Given the strategic tensions in its identity in the international order since the Meiji Restoration (see discussion in Chapter 3) between East Asia and Europe, this cultural adaptation suggests that Japan found itself to be compatible with an international order led by the United States. This was a shift in Japan's vision and identity in international relations, away from being an imperialist player like European powers to being with the United States for a new world order of international cooperation.

Japan's vision and international identity continued to be shaped by postwar domestic and international developments. The MacArthur Revolution in early post-World War II Japan was intended to reform Japan's state institutions, corporate organization and industrial capital, military, and perhaps the civic culture of Japanese society – the way the Japanese polity was organized. Many reforms were subsequently shaped in different directions as a more urgent Cold War agenda arose that pressed the organization of the state, political economy, and international security of Japan to evolve in a different direction. The Yoshida Doctrine ensured the

1955 system, a conservative political order, would prevail in Japan for much of the Cold War period, with the influence of the progressive forces very much confined if not marginalized.

This conservative political culture, arising partly from the Cold War international politics in East Asia, features the dominance of a state-industrial capital alliance and international political support and security insurance provided by the United States. This was a political order that T. J. Pempel calls "the regime" (Pempel 1998). The regime in Pempel's treatment of the political culture of post-1945 Japan refers to a particular pattern of "the political economy of a nation-state," sustained by a structure of "socioeconomic alliances, political economic institutions, and a public policy profile" (Pempel 1998: 20). This conservative political culture is not simply an operational form of the East Asian political tradition. It has the strong influence of US-led efforts to build a liberal international order in East Asia. This was a region that has been influenced by European imperial interests and institutions in the early decades of the twentieth century and the power and institutions of Communist states spreading out from continental East Asia in the Cold War decades. There occurred the development and rise to predominance of a similar conservative political culture in South Korea, Taiwan, Singapore, the Philippines, Indonesia, and Thailand. The 1955 system of Japan had a much stronger international component that supported the political structure, power relations, and consequent political order that became established in Japan. This conservative political culture relates more to the organization of the polity. The rise and fall of the political economic regime indicates the adaptive nature of Japanese political culture. Some aspects of that culture are not "ethnically" determined but evolved in the "culturing" process" of the political economic community.

As the Cold War ended, the 1955 system experienced a significant challenge. The large-scale expansion of the pattern of rapid economic growth and the development of third wave democratization in East Asia raised important questions about the premises behind the conservative political structure and order. Moving forward to become a "normal state" in the international system, Japan confronted a third Meiji moment in the 1990s. In the first Meiji moment of the mid-nineteenth century, Japan debated between going with Europe or with East Asia in civilizational orientation and the way Japanese state, economy, and society were to be organized. Japan chose "out of Asia to be with Europe" (脱亜入欧). In the second Meiji moment in the mid-twentieth century, Japan, as Iriye has shown, went on to align itself with the United States through a series of arrangements such as those provided under the Yoshida Doctrine and the San Francisco system. In the 1980s, there was great anticipation that Japan would seek greater independence from the United States and pursue its own role and position in the international system on the basis of its significant economic capacity and contributions to global governance.

Prime Minister Yasuhiro Nakasone's vision of internationalization of Japan in the 1980s, though, was unable to go too far in these efforts and was quickly labeled "nationalist." Japan cannot return to its East Asian political roots for becoming a normal state. Developments from the 1990s show that Japan opted to move in a slightly different strategic direction, signaling a different vision of a world order and Japan's international identity with it. Strengthening and updating its strategic alliance with the United States, Japan has fully integrated itself into the US-led liberal international order. Japan upgraded its security alliance with the United States in the mid-1990s and further strengthened it into a more comprehensive and operational strategic alliance in the twenty-first century under the Koizumi and Abe governments. This transformed itself from being a potential threat to being confined in the early postwar decades to being a strong and proactive partner supporting the international order.

It is evident that Japan's international vision and identity have significantly evolved, following or coinciding with the "regime shifts" and reforms in domestic political economy from the 1990s. Scholarship on culture in international relations in the case of Japan focused earlier on ethnicity-informed cultural traditions and how they influenced or determined Japan's foreign policy and international behavior. Increasingly, it has shifted to focus on the national pattern of political economy and how this influences Japan's international policy. Linus Hagström and Karl Gustafsson, in their recent project investigating Japan's changed identity (2015), point to two different sets of explanations of Japan's identity change. One explanation is based on domestic norms and culture, which led to a "pacifist or antimilitarist" Japanese identity mostly during the Cold War years. The second is a Japan-versus-Others explanation that led to a more confident, willing, determined state capable of exerting its influence in international relations. In this analysis, the cultural forces that influenced Japan's vision and identity in international relations can be ethnicity-based cultural traits of the Japanese people as well as material dynamics in the "construction" of Japan's identity in international relations. This in some way validates different understandings of culture and the different mechanisms by which culture informs political structures, institutions, and processes. In either case, culture's influence on a nation's international relations is evident.

Japan's 150 years of experience in search of the most effective and legitimate way of organizing itself and its position in the international system shows that the political culture of a nation is not only about who you are in terms of ethnicity and race, and where you've come from in terms of history and civilization, but also about the nation's purpose and the way this is communicated in its actions. The latter aspect seems to be constantly shaping up in the practice of a nation's self-organization and relation to the larger international environment of security and development. This latter dimension of culture is the "thick culture" of the Japanese nation that continues to influence its international relations and policy.

NATIONAL IDENTITY

The problem of a nation's international identity discussed in the previous section is an important issue in how culture influences IREA. It is part of the large problem of a nation's self-image, collective identity, and shared pattern of political behavior and relations. The question of "who are we as a nation?" is particularly important in modern IREA, which experienced a transformation from imperial systems to the nation-state system. Ethnicity-based national traits served as an important basis for claims on state institutions, political sovereignty, and boundaries of state jurisdiction.

Moreover, the national claim of an "imagined" (Anderson 1983) or nurtured political community challenges the existing state institutions, authority, and jurisdiction. Nationalism is a theory and ideology that nation and state should be institutionally and constitutionally "congruent" (Gellner 1983: 1). It is also a political movement inspired by this theory that seeks such congruence. Nationalism in its original connotation grew out of European experiences of modern state building and was a principle guiding the organization of interstate relations on a national basis, as against the imperial and religious forms of polity. The political movement to transform traditional polities into nation-states provided the material as well as institutional foundations for the rise of the modern international society. Nationalism has been a predominant force influencing the rise of new states and how they relate to each other in IREA and the transformation of the interstate system in East Asia from predominantly imperial forms to that of nation-states.

Nationalism, particularly ethnicity-based nationalism, came to influence the rise of nation-states in IREA in the first half of the twentieth century over the collapsing imperial systems, Chinese, European, and Japanese. The nation-state system was an institutional solution to the problem of imperialist competition in Europe. In East Asia, nation-states rose as the imperial system collapsed. The Chinese world order collapsed along with the tributary arrangements and the Confucian authority structure in the broader East Asia. This affected mostly polities on the East Asian crescent. Contestation over the political culture and identity in Korea, Japan, Hong Kong, Taiwan, Vietnam, and Singapore has always been tense. Such contestation over Taiwan remains unsettled, and the situation there has grown ever more destabilizing for the international order and security in the region.

The collapse of the European colonial system of governance in Southeast Asia led to a more "mutually constitutive" process of the formation of nation and state in maritime East Asia. There is little "congruence" there. As new state institutions and boundaries were largely imposed, significant efforts were concentrated on nurturing the national community by the state. This led to the rise of a different national political structure, order, and identity in, for example, Singapore, Malaysia, and Indonesia. On the other hand, traditional national groups cut apart by the new state boundaries became a factor that continued to generate interstate tension and conflict in IREA (see discussion of this issue in more detail in Chapters 3 and 9). These have all complicated the drive to seek an ethnicity-based national identity in these states during the Cold War and a shared regional identity for ASEAN in the post-Cold War development of multilateralism in the region.

That nation and national identity are largely shaped by politics and the power of the state is also seen in Northeast Asia. World War II and post-1945 settlements in East Asia (see discussion in Chapter 5) brought further developments in the problem of national identity between North and South Korea, the PRC and ROC, and North and South Vietnam. These developments suggest that "nation" can indeed be "nurtured" or even "imagined" rather than being determined only by ethnicity. The political economy and state institutions and organization can be transformative in the shaping of nation and national identity. The state and political economic life can make "nations" out of a nation of shared ethnic, religious, and linguistic ties. It is a fundamental problem in the nation-state system that it takes national traits as given and fixed, and uses that as the basis for political claims and institutional demands. This often leads to tensions and conflict in interstate relations.

The problem of nationalism in East Asia has developed in a slightly different direction in more recent times. Discussions and debates on Japan's efforts to seek an independent international role and identity and increasingly to become a normal state, since the 1980s has been framed as the problem of nationalism (Buruma 1987; Saaler 2016; Matthews 2013; Doak 2006; Hasegawa & Kazuhiko 2008). Chinese reactions to the US bombing of the Chinese embassy in Belgrade in 1999, anti-Japanese demonstrations in Chinese cities in 2012 over Japan's nationalization of the Senkaku Islands, and more signs of China taking more assertive international policy along with the rise of China are critically taken up as the problem of nationalism in China (Gries 2005; Johnston 2017; Gries et al. 2011). It reflects the anxiety of the Chinese people over their national identity, patriotic feelings about the nation, and sentiments over the nation's humiliations in recent history. Much of the politics between the two Koreas and between the PRC and ROC have to do largely with the problem of national identity, and nation and state "incongruence." There is also a whole class of activities in China and Korea over Japan's handling of historical issues associated with Japan's colonial rule and imperial expansion in continental East Asia in the first half of the twentieth century (Hasegawa & Togo 2008; Kingston 2015).

There seems to be a "new kind of nationalism" in East Asia, or East Asian nationalism. This is different from the classical nationalism of the Gelnerian variant, or even different from the nationalism that propelled East Asian states to form in the early part of the last century. East Asian nationalism is a form of national identity–driven political activity and movement. These political activities call for a more assertive and proactive position by the government on critical international issues that affects the nation's identity and international position and status. This new nationalism is increasingly strong in post-Cold War East Asian states. These seem to be an effect of a general logic of how the nation-state operates internationally. People of a nation, be it ethnically based, culturally imaged, or informed on political economy, expect the state to act internationally for the "nation." East Asian states have developed and perhaps "matured" to the point where a strong national identity enables them to articulate "national interests" more effectively. The strong national capabilities they have gained allow the state to act on these inspirations the way they were not able to do previously. Seeing these as the effect of nationalism allows us to see the dynamism with which national identity influences the intrastate and interstate behavior of nation and state.

In sum, nationalism is a mechanism by which a nation's political culture influences its international relations. It is about the effect of the nation's identity: identity among the members of a culturally distinct population as a unit for collective power and influence in the broader international community. National identity can develop on shared ethnic, religious, and linguistic traits or "way of life." East Asian states pose a complicated challenge for our understanding of how national identity influences the international behavior and relations of the state and how this linkage evolves as the nation and the state continue to evolve. East Asian states each had a unique set of historical circumstances under which they emerged as a modern nation-state. This influenced the unique path in which they have evolved from the traditional basis of the nation and state.

RELIGION AS A POLITICAL FORCE

Of the cultural traditions in East Asia, religion has always been suspected of playing an important role in IREA, not only providing a powerful framework for the organization of a polity and a rationale for state institutions, but also as a political force that influences the shaping of political structure and order. Given the European experiences in this regard, there is a strong scholarly tradition that explores how religions relate to state institutions in the building of modern East Asian states. In the shaping of the new independent state of Indonesia in the 1960s, for example, Islamic fundamentalists were one of the key political forces, along with Sukarno-led nationalists, the military, and the Communists, that intended to influence the political orientation of the new state. The idea of an Islamic state of Indonesia, however, quickly faded out under the military-led Suharto regime, established after the military forced out the Communists in 1965.

In the north, Shintoism inspired, moralized, legitimized, or even sanctioned the state power of imperialist institutions and activities in Japan since the Meiji Restoration. Shintoism was very much reduced to a symbol and separated from state institutions and authority in the postwar reforms and new constitution. Daoism was also widely spread in China. But Daoism, of its fundamental nature, is detached from the material world and teaches that the natural order is best without human intervention. It therefore carries no mission for itself to save the world and humankind. It does not seek to influence politics, society, or human life.

For much of East Asia overall, religions of political significance were not home grown but came to the region from different parts of the world. In continental East Asia, for example, state authority and institutions were long established before these religions arrived: Buddhism first from the sixth century from South Asia through the northern corridor; Christianity and Islam later, through trade and missionary activities from South Asia to Indochina and to Southeast Asia; and China's imperial absorption of the Muslim populations in northwest China. The states in China, Korea, Indochina, and Japan made significant efforts to incorporate these religious organizations into the imperial system with administrative and financial support. Buddhism in the early centuries of its coming to China, Korea, Japan, and Indochina is an example.

The states also suppressed, confined, and eliminated "evil" religious forces, mostly Christian and Islamic groups, seeing them as political forces potentially challenging the imperial authority and competing with the state for legitimacy and political influence. In continental East Asia, therefore, religious forces focused on their relationship with the state, seeking a legitimate role for themselves in the already crowded political space and the hierarchical, heavenly mandated political order. They are less inclined to influence the collective identity and political orientation of the nation.

In maritime East Asia, the exogenous nature of the religious influence is much stronger. Confucian Buddhism came from the north to mainland Southeast Asia, being taken as a "sinicized" way of life. There were very weak formal state institutions in those "galactic polities" (Tambiah 1976: 102–31). Theravāda Buddhism came from India and influenced many of the polities in the Indochina Peninsula. Mahāyāna Buddhism, mixed with Confucianism, came from China and had an influence in Vietnam, Singapore, Malaysia, and Indonesia. Christianity and Islam came to influence much of the region from the Indian Ocean to the "East Indies."

None of these religious forces managed to gain influence over the state institutions and constitutional basis of the polity for the new states that emerged there after World War II. This left space for tension among different "ways of life" in and across the states. As religion is often associated with ethnicity, nationality, and civilization in traditional forms of power and authority and the organization of polity in East Asia, the role of religion in IREA is most evident in the contention among different forms of authority over state power and jurisdiction within a country and across state boundaries, leading to a considerable level of communal conflicts and transborder tensions in IREA (see discussions in Chapters 4 and 10).

Tensions generated by religious forces, though, were superseded by Cold War geopolitical and ideological conflicts. Religious and ethnic conflicts, in southern Philippines, southern Thailand, and western Myanmar, as well as in Malaysia, Singapore, and Indonesia, were confined and put down as communist threats. Since the end of the Cold War and in the era of the "clash of civilizations," the challenge came back, partly because the Cold War imperatives in the region are gone; partly because religiously informed tensions and conflict are intensifying in other parts of the world, as seen particularly in the rapid expansion of extremist Islamic forces in Middle East.

The problem of religious forces contending for state power and authority came to life again where the Islamic way of life looks for acceptance as a legitimate way of organizing political economy and society. This realistically and potentially poses a threat to state authority and institutions in many "multination states" (Bertrand & Laliberté 2010) of mixed religious traditions in East Asia, particularly the Philippines, Indonesia, Malaysia, Myanmar, and China. Religion-state tensions add a significant dimension to the dynamism of intrastate and interstate politics in East Asia. The tensions there seem to be on a scale seen in other parts of the world where the "clash of civilizations" drove much of the interstate relations, interaction, and engagement, and, most unfortunately, violence, destruction, and suffering.

THIRD-WAVE DEMOCRACY

One of the key developments in the political culture of contemporary East Asia has been the democratization movement in the 1980s and 1990s. East Asian nations embarked on a grand enterprise of modernization and modern state building in the twentieth century, starting with Japan's Meiji Restoration in the late nineteenth century. Profoundly influenced by socialism and Marxism on the left and liberalism and individualism on the right, both sets of ideals from the West on how to best organize polities under modern conditions, East Asian peoples took efficiency, fairness, and effectiveness as the guiding values in building the modern state as opposed to the hierarchical, communitarian, and centripetal arrangements that underlay East Asian political traditions.

The political developments after World War II led most East Asian states to move into some form of centralized, hierarchical, noncompetitive political order and an authoritarian form of governance in various guises during the Cold War years. The Cold War regime in these East Asian states featured a restricted constitutional order, controlled party politics, and the dominance of a single political force in the political structure and state institutions. This development suggests that the distinct East Asian political culture still seemed to be intact and very much alive, effective, and influential in social, economic, and political activities and organization of the new states.

The Cold War political structure and order that prevailed in East Asian states reflected the values of traditional East Asian culture: hierarchical power relations, centralized state authority, and the family as a political actor and as a model of authority for the state. Moreover, in East Asian cultural explanations of the postwar economic miracle of East Asian countries, communitarianism, state corporatism, and familism are often cited as uniquely contributing to the effective economic organization in the region. All these spurred great debate among scholars, policy analysists, and the general public on Asian values, the East Asian model, Asian modernity, and the conditions and consequence of political modernization in East Asia in the 1980s and 1990s.

The collapse of the Cold War regime in East Asian countries started with China in 1976 when Mao died after 28 years of rule in the PRC; the Philippines in 1986 when Marcos was overthrown after 21 years in office as president; South Korea in 1987 when the military government surrendered state power; Taiwan in 1988 when the martial law of 38 years was lifted; Singapore in 1992 as Lee Kuan Yew stepped down as prime minister after 28 years; Japan in 1992 when LDP lost ruling majority to form a government for the first time in 38 years; Thailand in 1994 as the military retreated from running the government it had dominated since 1932; Malaysia in 2003 when Mahathir stepped down as prime minister after 22 years in office; and Indonesia in 1998 when Suharto resigned as president after 31 years in office. Further development after the collapse went in different directions. A transition to democracy is seen mostly in maritime East Asia, most notably the Philippines, Singapore, Indonesia, Japan, South Korea, and Taiwan.

There are debates as to what drove this wave of political liberalization in East Asia. Modernization theory and new institutionalism argue for the internal logic of modern economic development. The logic explains a competitive political institutional setting is required for economic development or economic development will lead to the institutionalization of a liberal and competitive political order (Lipset 1959; Weber 1947; North 1990). Others see this development in East Asia as part of the global movement toward liberal democracy at the time, the third wave of democratization (Huntington 1991; Diamond & Plattner 1998; Plattner & Chu 2013). Political liberalization seen in such a framework is the effect of the unique logic of political structure, institutions, and order driven by the principles of people's will, citizenship, political participation and representation, and accountability.

The third wave of democratization in East Asia brought about a significant expansion of liberal democracy in East Asia and influenced the overall orientation of East Asian politics and the direction of political change and development in East Asian states. Institutions of liberal democracy include constitution, party politics and political competition, elections and representation, citizenship and political activism, parliamentary politics, and public policy process. These have been established, reformed, consolidated, and made to work. The states that have made the transition to democracy most successfully have been those allies and partners in the US-led Cold War international order in East Asia, largely in maritime East Asia. Their successful democratic transitions significantly enhanced their normative ties and liberal orientation and strengthened the liberal international order in East Asia.

Associated with the institutional revolution, reform, and change has been change in political culture in these states and people's orientation to political action. Critical for the consolidation of the institutional change is change in the supporting political culture. This was noted in the debates in the 1990s over Asian values, Asian democracy, illiberal democracy, and Asian modernity. The real question is whether there is a distinct set of political traditions that inform and govern the organization of politics and government in East Asia; whether such East Asian forms of politics and government work with the institutions and values of liberal democracy; and whether East Asian culture should adapt, change, and reform in response to the political economic conditions in East Asia today. Third wave democratization in East Asia and its outcomes and consequences offer a complex line of evidence to the foregoing questions.

In spite of the early debates over the nature, necessity, and prospects of political change and similar political civil movements and mass revolutions for democratic change, the third wave democratization in East Asia has not successfully secured political change further to the establishment of democratic institutions in continental East Asia. Political elites in China have been shaping the direction of further political change and development. With renewed confidence from the impressive performance of the Chinese model of political economic organization and refreshed interest in seeking institutional insight from its political traditions, the Chinese governing elite seems to be leaning toward being more conciliatory to the traditional structure and supporting institutions. This will have a significant impact on the political culture of China, the development of which was already complicated by China's experiences of Communism under Mao and pragmatism under Deng Xiaoping.

Political culture in East Asian states has become more complicated and multifaceted. Overall, though, we probably can see a more updated, pluralist political culture in maritime East Asian states, including some on the edge of East Asian crescent, South Korea, Taiwan, Vietnam, and Singapore and a more traditional, corporatist political culture in continental East Asia, possibly extending to include states on mainland Southeast Asia. (We will return to discuss this more in Chapter 12.) We have already seen activities and programs in IREA that seem to manifest along the "fault lines" (Huntington 1993: 22) in the emerging normative structure in East Asia.

CHINA'S EVOLVING INTERNATIONAL IDENTITY

This brings us to the problem of the significance of Chinese political culture for IREA, or more precisely the problem of the international identity of China. Chinese traditional culture, the historical and institutional sources of the East Asian political tradition, continued to evolve under the PRC, in a somewhat different direction than in other East Asian states. China's identity in the 1970s projected a sense of being disadvantaged and revolutionary in the hierarchic and binary world political economy and "geo-ideology" and a feeling of being detached and rejected from the traditional East Asian political culture, as embodied then mostly in those former Confucian societies on the East Asian crescent.

Mao's Chinese style of socialist political economy and his Communist international orientation had a great impact on the political cultural character of the PRC. In his 1991 "Peripheries as the Centre" essay on the cultural China or Confucian China (Tu 1991), Tu Weiming depicts cultural China as being overcome by the dynamics and institutions of geopolitical China, and the locus of the strength and influence of the Confucian Chinese culture shifted from the "presumed core area," the Middle Kingdom, to Taiwan, Hong Kong, and Singapore, perhaps along with Japan and South Korea. These "peripheries" of cultural China, with their stunning economic performance and success in meeting the challenge of modernization and Westernization, have risen to redefine and reenergize the Confucian traditions. In this depiction, the Chinese culture operating in the PRC seems to shift away from Confucianism and yet reflect some of its essential elements: collectivism and centripetal dynamics in its radical socialist political economic program. This cultural identity underlay the ambivalent attitude of Communist China toward Confucianism and to the "peripheries" and other states in East Asia in general.

This reversed center-periphery tension over traditional cultural China was soon updated by the profound changes brought on by Deng Xiaoping's reform and opening from 1978. There is vigorous debate as to whether China's reform represented an adoption of the East Asian model of economic development successfully practiced in the early wave of rapid economic development in East Asia (Naughton 2010; Baek 2005; Boltho & Weber 2009). Even with the "Chinese characteristics" added to the label, economic reform and development in the past 40 years in China introduced and established the market economy in the PRC. The opening of the market economy impacted directly some of the core values of the political culture of China at the time, which was a mixture of Marxism-Leninism and Confucian traditions (Tu 1991: 5). These core values concerned attitudes toward money, profit, and purposes and methods in social relations, and in the organization of political economy.

Deng's economic openness and reform have been successful, with the emergence of a very dynamic economic system that continuously propels China to grow, develop, and rise to become a country of significant economic power, military capability, and political influence. At the same time, the Chinese people seem to increasingly feel at a loss over their identity as members of Chinese society. People on both the left and the right challenge the lack of guiding moral principles as well as purpose in what they do. The much-anticipated political liberation has not materialized. Leading political forces look to Chinese history and cultural traditions for inspiration and institutional insights to help them rationalize the organization of the national political economy.

Projecting this to international relations, China also finds a growing challenge in seeking its role and position in the international system. Rapid change in China's interests and capability in international relations moved China from being a champion of the Communist International in the 1950s and a leader of the Third World in the 1960s and 1970s to having a set of "conflicting identities" (Shambaugh 2011; Chan 2014; Johnston 2003) in the 1990s and 2000s. It was unclear whether China favored the status quo, wanted to reform the international system, or aimed to make over the world order. Each of these identities would inform China's relations with a distinct set of countries and international organizations in a different way.

China's international identity seems to have moved away from the ambiguity and contradictions of more recent years. Core to the debate over China's international identity is its relations with the prevalent US-led liberal international order (Ikenberry 2014). In 2005, then-US Deputy Secretary of State Robert Zoellick made a major foreign policy speech, in which he declared, "We now need to encourage China to become a responsible stakeholder in the international system. As a responsible stakeholder, China would be more than just a member – it would work with us to sustain the international system that has enabled its success" (Zoellick 2005: 9). China has made significant efforts in more recent years to develop a "new type of great power relations" with the United States. In the US National Security Strategy of 2018, President Trump labeled China a "revisionist competitor."

It is debatable whether China has become a revisionist competitor; the shaping of China's international identity seems to be not just a choice or strategy by China but also the effects of the squeezing power of the international structure where China's evolving and rapidly expanding international interests and capabilities have encountered the structural and normative imperatives of the ever powerful and influential liberal international order.

In the context of the role of culture in IREA, the cultural character of China, in both behavioral and organizational senses, has experienced significant change and adaptation, along with, and perhaps driven by, significant changes in politics, the economy, and society. This brings a new set of issues to our analysis of how Chinese culture influences IREA and international relations more broadly. These issues are reflected in research and debate on the soft power of China, the tribute relations China pursued in East Asia historically, and the Chinese methods and strategy in the global expansion of its economic and indusial interests and relations.

These issues concern more the organizational dimension of culture, as discussed earlier, i.e., how interstate relations should be organized. In these instances, elements of Chinese culture, mostly related to the historical and traditional culture of China, are resources employed in China's strategy for international power and influence. The setup of Confucius Institutes around the world, for example, is seen as an effective platform on the basis of which China exercises power and expands its influence. This is the effect of the cultural forms of Chinese power, or "soft power" (Nye 2004). Soft power can be seen as a cultural form of political influence in interstate relations – cultural in behavioral, communicational, and organizational senses. The tribute system (Kang 2010; Lee 2017) is also employed as an analytical framework for us to make sense of how China is shaping its relations with East Asian states today. The debate on what the Chinese model means for international relations (McNally 2012; Wan 2013; Norris 2016; Halper 2010) helps us understand the way in which China would like to see how international relations are organized as Chinese political economy internationalizes.

In these instances, how much these cultural constructs or guidelines reflect the original Chinese cultural traditions is less important. The Chinese culture today enables a collective feeling about the world and how China should relate to it. It gives meaning and purpose to what China, or the Chinese, do in the world and, hence, help mobilize or rationalize the Chinese to act in international relations accordingly; it projects a vision or identity of the nation about how nations in the world should be related and for what purposes.

THE ASEAN WAY AND THE ASIA-PACIFIC WAY

Now we come to another important example of how culture influences IREA. We will discuss the ASEAN way in the context of East Asian regionalism in Chapters 7 and 8. Discussion of the ASEAN way here aims to move the discussion in this chapter toward describing how a nation's culture changes and adapts in the practice of international relations, the extent to which an international identity can develop among a group of nation-states, and how the formation of this identity contributes to the strengthening of the collective influence of the states in IREA. There seems to be a reverse of the cause-effect chain as seen in Northeast Asian states in terms of the role of culture in IREA.

The structural configurations and organizing principles of the polity in traditional Southeast Asian states are remarkably similar in power structures, institutional arrangements, and political order, whether they are labeled "galactic," "mandala," or "Indianized." This formed a basis for a shared political culture in Southeast Asia, in contrast to that under the dominant Confucian authority structure and political order in continental East Asia (McCloud 1995). The widely acclaimed "cultural diversity" in Southeast Asia is largely ethnicity-based: ethnic, linguistic, and religious traits that distinguish national groups in the region from each other: Thai, Malaysian, Indonesian, Vietnamese, Cambodian, Singaporean, Laos, Pilipino, or Burmese. Some of them, Singaporean and Malaysian for example, are of new nations based on an ethnic mixture of Chinese, Indian, and Malay and emerged from decades of nation building after the initial state was set up in the 1960s.

In Southeast Asia, though, it is not that these diverse national identities compete for dominance and influence in international relations. The tension among different original "national" identities focused on state power and influence. Rather, the domestic process of national convergence extended further into the political process of the region. In the practice of promoting cooperation among the new states to solve communal conflicts and ensure security against existential threats to the new states, these states developed a set of norms of interstate engagement and a code of conduct. These helped shape a shared "identity" among the states over their otherwise very divisive ethnic differences.

Amitav Acharya, a leading scholar in international relations in Southeast Asia, called the region an "imagined community" (Acharya 2013). Acharya works on the development of a regional identity among ASEAN states. His pioneering work led to the flourishing of research focusing on ideational factors in the development of regional institutions and the constructivist nature of multilateral institution building in ASEAN. In the shaping of the community, ASEAN, a regional identity and a regional culture in international relations, emerged. Investigating "the ASEAN way," Acharya identifies two elements of culture that are relevant to explaining it. The ASEAN way is a mechanism by which ASEAN states relate to one another and approach issues in their relations collectively. This mechanism developed from the processes of interaction and socialization among states in managing their relations. The ASEAN way is an approach of ASEAN states to security cooperation. It is a cultural orientation to interstate engagement that prefers informality, avoidance of excessive institutionalization, nonconfrontation, agreement through consultation and consensus, and "thinking multilaterally but acting bilaterally" (Acharya 1998: 58–69).

ASEAN states have formed a distinct set of stable norms and "habits" with respect to the management of issues of conflict and peace, which Acharya calls "regional security culture." The cooperation revolves around managing the diversity in "culturally determined modes of perception and interaction," (Acharya 1998: 55), i.e., the "traditional cultures" of ASEAN states. Acharya's treatment of "culture" reveals that the states "may develop 'an organized group of learned responses' and 'adjustment of traits' over a period of time through interactions and socialization," in response to conflict and tensions arising from diversity in traditional cultural traits, which are "something preordained, immutable, organic, or entirely subjective" (Acharya 1998: 57). Both the behavioral and organizational dimensions of culture are accounted for in explaining the rise of the ASEAN way. Of course, Acharya also pushes the idea of similar dynamics shaping the ASEAN way in the development of the "Asia-Pacific way" (Acharya 1997). The latter in an important way asks the question of whether an extranational or multinational identity can develop in the larger region of cultural diversity.

THE NORMATIVE STRUCTURE OF IREA

In this chapter, we have examined how culture influences the international policy and behavior of East Asian states and the patterns and developments in IREA. In the eyes of those favoring a cultural explanation, many of the patterns of policy, behavior, and relations in IREA can be seen as culturally influenced. IREA are a distinct set of international relations of global significance and high impact with and among states of non-Western, non-European cultural traditions. Discussions in this chapter have shown that culture influences IREA in three significant ways. Culture is behavioral because it reflects locally nurtured forms of expression of feelings, inspirations, and sentiments of people in a nation. These feelings, inspirations, and sentiments influence and determine, if cultural determinists are right, the decisions of policymakers in international policy and the international character of a nation as a collective actor in the international system.

Culture is also communicational. Cultural constructs, norms, and values give meaning to political actions, structures, processes, and outcomes. Culture as a pattern of political orientation therefore informs, motivates, and justifies the international identity and action of the nation-state in IREA. Culture is also organizational. IREA are influenced by different ways of life, forces, and institutions of religion, political economy, and civilization. States of different "cultural" character will have different levels of organizational homogenization and heterogenization. This has driven much of the dramas of love and hate, cooperation and competition, integration and separation among nation-states in IREA.

These ways in which culture influences IREA are not particularly "East Asian" unless we get a sense of what an East Asian culture is or even whether there is an East Asian culture. Our discussion has shown the origins and spread of East Asian cultural traditions and how they evolved over the twentieth century under different national settings. East Asian political traditions have evolved and adapted in response to various critical challenges of different cultural traditions: to West Europe's ideals of the modern nation-state, communism and socialism, the free market economy, and liberal democracy, as well as to those of other religions and civilizations of global significance.

Today, the political culture in maritime East Asian states has seen more profound changes and adaption toward a capitalist market economy and liberal democracy, while that in continental East Asian states retains or manifests more elements of Confucian authority and associated institutional arrangements and social norms. East Asian political culture bifurcates at the national level. This influences the international policy and strategic relations of these East Asian states in different directions. These developments in national political culture support a bifurcation in the development of political culture, or the normative structure, at the East Asian regional level. This in some way reinforces the bipolar pattern of international structure in IREA and the associated international order.

A normative structure in IREA is the region-level distribution of institutional, normative, and civilizational identities of the states in IREA. As we have shown, countries in IREA are associated loosely in groups. Countries in the same group share the influence of a similar set of the normative forces dominant in their own countries. These two sets of normative forces are distinct in the working of state institutions, the organization of political economy, and societal identification with the East Asian political traditions. They form a normative structure at the regional level. The distribution of international identities of the states resembles, but does not fully correspond to, the Cold War bipolar structure. Much more severe structural tension is seen in countries on the East Asian crescent further extending to Southeast Asia and the South Pacific.

If the international order in IREA is shaped by a stable material structure and normative dynamics, the bifurcation in the normative structure in IREA and the profound shift in the power structure suggest an unstable, fragile international order in the region. Does culture matter in IREA? Many hesitated quite a bit to answer in the affirmative in the Cold War decades. Today, it is much clearer that culture matters in IREA. The real question is what culture matters and how.

Study Questions

1. Discuss specific cases, not covered in this chapter, of indications or evidence that culture influences IREA.
2. Someone has described the Japanese style of foreign policy and international relations as soft, polite, conflict-averse, lacking leadership and decisiveness. Do you agree? Why?
3. Do you think a thin or thick definition of culture is more accurate in explaining IREA?
4. Do you think there is an East Asian culture, traditional or more updated, that unifies East Asian states in terms of their behavioral style, normative orientation, and organizational mode in IREA?
5. What is the East Asian political tradition, or traditional political culture in East Asia states, that scholars often refer to? How is this concept useful in helping us understand the normative structure of IREA?
6. Discuss the characteristics of the normative structure in IREA today.

Further Reading

Acharya, Amitav, 2001. *The Quest for Identity: International Relations of Southeast Asia*. Oxford: Oxford University Press.

Acharya, Amitav, 2013. *The Making of Southeast Asia: International Relations of a Region*. Ithaca: Cornell University Press.

Chay, Jongsuk, 1990. *Culture and International Relations*. New York: Praeger.

Connors, Michael K., 2011, "Asian Values Redux? The International Politics of Rights, Democracy and Culture," pp. 248–266 in Michael K. Connors et al., *The New Global Politics of the Asia Pacific*. London: Routledge.

De Bary, William Theodore, 1988. *East Asian Civilizations: A Dialogue in Five Stages*. London: Harvard University Press.

Fairbank, John, Edwin Reischauer, and Albert Craig, 1989. *East Asia: Tradition & Transformation*. Belmont: Wadsworth.

Fisher, Glen, 1997. *Mindsets: The Role of Culture and Perception in International Relations*. Yarmouth: Intercultural Press.

Flemming, Christianse, and Hedetoft Ulf, 2004. *The Politics of Multiple Belonging: Ethnicity and Nationalism in Europe and East Asia*. Hants: Ashgate.

Fukuzawa, Yukichi, 1875 [2009]. *An Outline of a Theory of Civilization*. New York: Columbia University Press.

Gaenslen, Fritz. 1986. "Culture and Decision-Making in China, Japan, Russia, and the United States," *World Politics* 39:78–103.

Gong, Gerrit W., 1984. *The Standard of "Civilization" in International Society*. Oxford: Clarendon Press.

Huntington, Samuel P., 1996. *The Clash of Civilizations and the Remaking of World Order*. New York: Simon & Schuster.

Kang, David, 2007. "Power, Interests and Identity in East Asia International Relations 1300–1900," pp. 18–49 in Kang, *China's Rising: Peace, Power and Order in East Asia*. New York: Columbia University Press.

Kim, Ji Young, 2015. "Rethinking the Role of Identity Factors: The History Problem and the Japan–South Korea Security Relationship in the Post-Cold War Period," *International Relations of the Asia-Pacific* 15(3), 477–503.

Lapid, Yosef, and Friedrich Kratochwil, 1996. *The Return of Culture and Identity in IR Theory*. Boulder: Lynne Rienner

Li, Rex, 2009. *A Rising China and Security in East Asia: Identity Construction and Security Discourse*. New York: Routledge.

Mozaffari, Mehdi, 2012. *Globalization and Civilizations*. London/New York: Routledge.

Pye, Lucian W., 1985. *Asian Power and Politics: The Cultural Dimensions of Authority*. Harvard: Harvard University Press.

Pye, Lucian, and Sidney Verba, 1969. *Political Culture and Political Development*. Princeton: Princeton University Press.

Sun, Jing, 2013. *Japan and China as Charm Rivals: Soft Power in Regional Diplomacy*. Ann Arbor: University of Michigan Press.

Tu, Weiming, 1991. "Cultural China: The Periphery as the Center," *Daedalus* 120(2):1–32.

Zimmerman, William, and Harold K. Jacobson, 1993. *Behavior, Culture, and Conflict in World Politics*. Ann Arbor: University of Michigan Press.

7 Industrial Development

> **In This Chapter...**
>
> - East Asian growth
> - The lead goose
> - Akamatsu's original model
> - "Four little dragons" and NIEs
> - A theory of East Asian growth
> - The rise of China, economically
> - Debating Smith, Wallerstein, and Kant

> **Learning Objectives**
>
> By the end of this chapter, you will be able to
> - Understand the national systems of industrial production organization in East Asia
> - Understand how industrial diffusion connects national economies and leads to a transborder division of labor for industrial production in East Asia
> - Analyze institutions and mechanisms that have enabled transborder industrial connectivity
> - Understand the national, regional, and global sources of the structure of the East Asian economy
> - Understand the role of Japan and China in the shaping of the regional economic order
> - Understand how the dynamics of the transborder organization of industrial production influence IREA.

Industrial development and trade expansion in East Asia have involved a unique set of dynamics that defined IREA in the second half of the twentieth century and have had a profound impact on world politics and international political economy. Labeled the "East Asian miracle" by the World Bank in the 1990s (World Bank 1993), "waves" of rapid industrialization and long periods of high-speed economic growth since World War II in East Asian countries transformed one East Asian country after another, from among the world's poorest countries into middle-income countries, and ultimately to high-income countries. As Lee Kuan Yew, a principal organizer of this grand transformation in Singapore, has proudly declared, Singapore, for example, transformed itself from the "Third World to First" (Lee 2000).

East Asian growth has added significant capabilities for these countries to pursue their greatly expanded interests and relations in IREA and beyond. Moreover, the way their growth is organized has driven them to seek transborder industrial integration, production networks, and values and supply chains in the region and around the world. This presented a complicating challenge to the prevailing Washington Consensus in the 1990s on how national and international political economy should be organized. This chapter examines these issues and explores how East Asian growth is organized, how such organization has influenced the development of the structure and institutions of industrial production and distribution, and the shaping of the international economic order in East Asia. Here we deal with the power of economic dynamics in the shaping of IREA, having discussed in previous chapters the geopolitical, structural, and cultural forces of the region.

EAST ASIAN GROWTH

A look at the national income levels of the East Asian economies over the past 70 years (Figure 7.1) reveals that East Asian growth has been uneven over time and across economies. Japan, Hong Kong, Taiwan, and Korea are the first-tier economies; their real GDP per capita (RGDPPC) started to rise from the 1950s and exceeded $35,000 in 2016. They all passed the $20,000 threshold by 1997 before the 1997–98 Asian financial crisis. Malaysia, Thailand, China, and Indonesia compose the second-tier group, with RGDPPC above $10,000 but below $25,000 in 2016. Their RGDPPC started to rise in the 1960s and 1970s and passed the $5,000 mark before the 1997–98 Asian financial crisis. The Philippines, Laos, Myanmar, Vietnam,

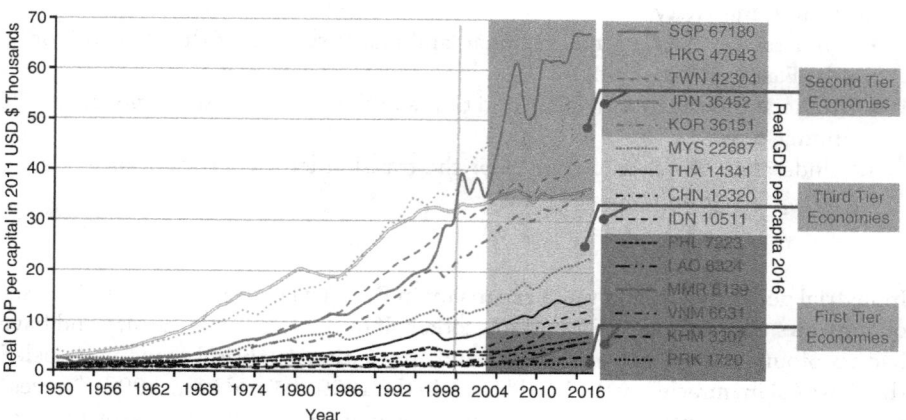

Figure 7.1 East Asian growth: National income level, 1950–2016
Data source: MPD (2018)

Cambodia, and North Korea make up the third-tier group, with a real GDP per capita in 2016 below $8,000, and they are mostly in mainland Southeast Asia, sandwiched between continental and maritime East Asia. If we look at these numbers in the early post-1945 years, Hong Kong ($4,013 in 1950), Malaysia ($2,697), Japan ($2,519), and Singapore ($2,439) were the leading economies in 1950, but their economic growth has moved in different directions since. There is a clear pattern of three waves of rapid economic growth and large-scale social economic change in postwar East Asia.

East Asian growth shows a pattern of consecutive waves of rapid industrialization and prolonged high-speed economic growth in East Asian countries in the second half of the twentieth century. Literature on the East Asian model of economic development (Johnson 1982; Amsden 1989; Wade 1990; Macintyre 1994; Woo-Cumings 1999) has found that East Asian growth was enabled under a set of institutional arrangements that center on the state's organizing responsibilities; export-concentration; separation of domestic and international markets, production, and consumption; and public goods in the international political and economic environment (see World Bank 1993 and Huang 2005 for a detailed discussion). What we are interested in here is how East Asian growth has influenced the behavior and activities of states in IREA and the shaping of the structure and institutions of IREA. There is a structure among the three-tiered groups related to their regional interests, relations, and capabilities in industrial production and distribution. This structure has evolved over time along the waves of their rise in industrial, financial, and trading capabilities. We want to see how the dynamics of national industrial development generated their industrial activities and relations across borders and shaped the economic structure and order in the region.

Behind the significant positive annual rates of GDP growth is how a lead country organized its early industrial development and international expansion under the very unique political economic conditions in the taking-off period, connected national industrial production to external consumption and resources, and created networks of production activities across national boundaries in the region for efficiency and international competitiveness of its products. This pattern of national organization of transborder industrial production was "mimicked" in other East Asian states connected to the networks of production for high-value products. Industrial capital, technology, management skills and knowledge, and parts supplies flowed transnationally. A structure developed in the relations between the lead country and the networked countries. As the production networks further extended, new states were connected and new groupings for different products developed. All these led to new waves of rapid industrial growth and economic development and, ultimately, the rise of an East Asian regional economy.

Industrial production here refers to manufacturing in any sectors that require intensive use of capital, materials, labor, and technology for a product. "Industrial" here is meant not in its narrow sense as a sector in relation to, say, agriculture or service. In an East Asian language context, this is 产业/産業/산업, (of production). Related to this is the product cycle. A product-cycle is the lifespan of a product in stages from development to production, maturity and decline. Raymond Vernon uses the term "product cycle" (Vernon 1966) to explain the changing structure of trade among countries of different growth conditions and, hence, dynamics of national industrial growth in connection with international industrial growth enabled by the logic of comparative advantage. Production network and product cycle are two important concepts that underlie a dominant scholarly theory developed to explain the pattern of East Asian growth, a theory often referred to as the flying geese theory. In this chapter, we will discuss how the flying geese theory explains the leading role of Japan in the waves of industrialization and economic growth in postwar East Asia and the shaping of a set of transborder networks for industrial production and distribution.

We will show how the development of Japanese industrial capital and the way it organized industrial development influenced the industrial and economic development of other East Asian countries; how initially Japan's production forces and relations extended to Korea, Taiwan, Hong Kong, and Singapore, as well as to maritime Southeast Asia and China; how the dynamics of product cycles and production networks drove industrial diffusion, and the spread of industrial capital, technology, and managerial knowledge from one group of countries to another; how this process connected national economies in a transborder network of production and distribution in East Asia; and how all of these helped shape a flying geese pattern of high-speed industrial growth and a hierarchical economic order in East Asia.

THE LEAD GOOSE

The "Japanese miracle" that East Asian watchers refer to is an extraordinary pattern of high-speed industrial development and economic growth for an extensively long period. As shown in Figure. 7.2, Japan's real gross domestic product expanded at an average annual rate of 9.37 percent for the period from 1950 to 1973. If we added the decade of growth of the same magnitude in the 1930s before the war, this makes a 30-year high-speed growth period.

Japan's industrialization and modern economic growth started from the mid-nineteenth century after the Meiji Restoration in 1868. The Meiji Restoration established modern institutions for a centralized state that organized industrial development at the national level. It also established the institutional infrastructure to support industrial manufacturing and construction. The Japan-led, trade-based industrial development with broader transnational integration of growth factors in East Asia started in the late 1920s (Johnson 1983; Gao 1997). This mode of industrial development subsequently influenced the organization of national industrial development in other East Asian countries and the development of transborder production networks in East Asia. Bai Gao's study, for example, details how some of the key organizing principles of Japan's developmentalism emerged from Japan's response to the Great Depression in the 1930s and how they survived in "the ideological framework of Japan's industrial policy

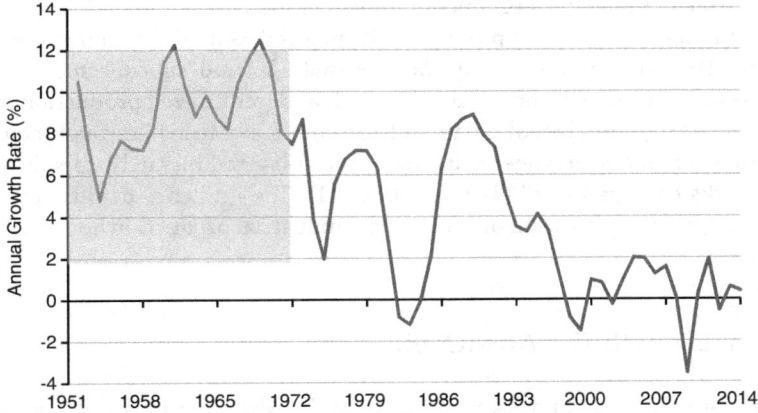

Figure 7.2 Japan's real GDP annual growth and high-speed-growth period (1951–2014, percentage, shaded area)
Data source: PWT9.0 (2017)

and were institutionalized in the governance mechanism of the economy in the post-War Japan." These principles include "the focus on the national economy, the strong production orientation, the restraints on market forces, and the rejection of the profit principle for the successful economic development" (Gao 1997: 299).

At the core of this is the national coordination of production organization. Chalmers Johnson, in his pioneering work on modern Japanese political economy (Johnson 1982), unpacks the institutional complexities and peculiarities of the Japanese state, the "visible hand" that steers this national coordination. This "developmental state" (Johnson 1982: 17) operated through the active role of the very capable and effective economic bureaucracy led by a central state agency. In the case of Japan at that time, the Ministry of International Trade and Industry (MITI) used industrial policy to regulate and influence industrial and business interests and activities to grow in a strategic direction.

Industrial policy is a government-sanctioned policy guideline that informs plans on strategic direction and the focus of the nation's industrial development and governs resource allocation and the regulation of industrial activities of the private sector. The state also utilized intertwined professional, social, and personal relations of state bureaucratic elites, in their intensive engagement with business and social elites, to influence the business behavior of the latter. The state in effect turned the competitive forces of the market and industrial capital into some form of a coordinated project for national trade and economic activities overseas. These state institutions and institutional relations, in Robert Wade's analysis (Wade 1990), governed the market.

This pattern of industrial production organization is also seen in how the firm is organized and how industrial production is financed. Ganesh Trichur, for example, calls our attention to the role of "Japan's multi-layered subcontract system" in Japan's economic miracle and argues that such a "decentralized production system" networked a large number of small and medium-sized firms "through stable and long term cooperative arrangements into a multi-layered hierarchy of subcontracting networks of large firms" (Trichur 2010: 11). The influence of this system was visible in Japan's organization of transborder industrial production and distribution in East Asia.

AKAMATSU'S ORIGINAL MODEL

More critical to the "lead position" of Japan in the waves of industrial development and economic growth in East Asia was Japan's moving up to "the lead country position" in key areas of industrial production in the early twentieth century, replacing Western European industrial powers in the global motion of product cycles. Akamatsu Kaname, for example, noticed in 1935 (Akamatsu 1935) that Nagoya, an emergent industrial center in woolen textiles, "was moving from the stage of import substitution to exporting to international markets" (Korhonen 1994: 94). Akamatsu's statistical analysis (Akamatsu 1962) shows that after several decades of industrial development from the 1870s, Japan led in the production and export of textile yarn, spinning weaving machinery, textile cloth, and machines and tools, far ahead of India and China and certainly the rest of East Asia.

Akamatsu surveyed trade relations and product cycles between Western industrial powers and Asian developing countries in key industries and found a pattern of industrial development in developing countries that went through stages in a similar sequence: from importing from lead countries to import substitution industrialization and to exporting to less developed countries in particular industries. "Industries are diversified and upgraded from consumer goods to capital goods and/or from simple to more sophisticated products" (Kojima 2000: 376). The volume of products of particular types produced in the country changes over time in a reverse V-shaped curve. As illustrated in Figure 7.3, these curves together form a pattern of moving flying geese formations.

"Flying geese" in Akamatsu's original thesis, therefore, is a metaphor for a pattern of the motion of a product cycle in stages of the product's life span. As Akamatsu himself observes, "The wild-geese-flying pattern of industrial development denotes the development after the less-advanced country's economy enters into an international economic relationship with the advanced countries" (Akamatsu 1962: 11). The flying geese pattern here is the working of an underlying logic of industrial development of a nation in the shaping of an international structure of industrial production. It is trade stimulated, product centered, comparative advantage–based national and international industrial development. The flying geese thesis therefore not only describes a sequential movement of a national economy through stages of industrial development, but also a logic of transborder organization of industrial production in the international system. This system relies on international exchange

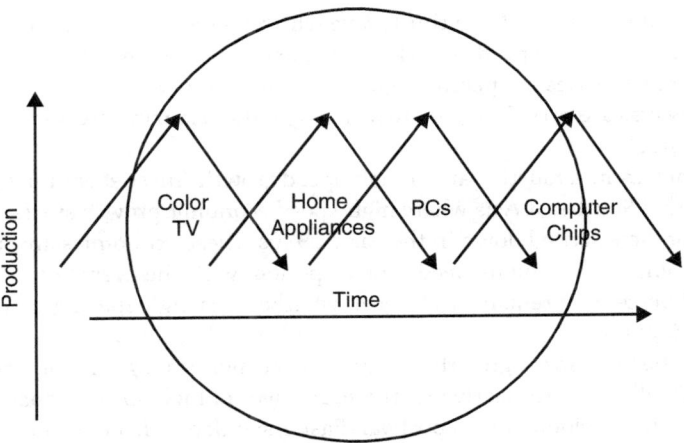

Figure 7.3 Illustration of Akamatsu's flying geese pattern of national industrial development

Based on Akamatsu's discussion (Akamatsu 1962: 11) and using the cases of the rise and fall of industrial production for a particular product in Japan in the 1970s and 1980s

and connectivity to gain industrial competitiveness and efficiency. We will return to this theory later to explain the Japan-led industrial diffusion and transborder production networks in East Asia that emerged following World War II.

"FOUR LITTLE DRAGONS" AND NEWLY INDUSTRIALIZING ECONOMIES

Soon after "Japan as Number 1" (Vogel 1979) was recognized, the world quickly discovered that a group of four countries – South Korea, Taiwan, Hong Kong, and Singapore, the "four little dragons" (Vogel 1993) – was following in the footsteps of Japan and tracing out the same pattern of industrial growth and economic development. The four little dragons are usually considered the second wave of high-speed economic growth in post-1945 East Asia. Their high-speed growth periods started at slightly different times given the varied domestic and international political economic conditions for each, but roughly all in the early 1960s. Their high-speed-growth period ended with the Asian financial crisis in 1997–8. East Asian growth in the second wave, as seen in Table 7.1, lasted about 30 years, with an average real GDP growth rate of 7.6 percent in their respective high-speed-growth period.

Many Southeast Asian nations started their East Asian growth in the early decades along with the four little dragons. But they were later in connecting to East Asian production networks and, as will be shown in what follows, were largely further down in the value and supply chains sustaining the production networks.

They are treated as part of the third wave which includes China. Again, there was about 30 years of high-speed growth, with an average growth rate of 7.7 percent in the separate countries' respective high-speed-growth period. Those in the second and third waves are often referred to as newly industrializing economies (NIEs) in the literature.

There then came a fourth wave of high-speed growth. These economies are mostly in continental Southeast Asia where high-speed economic growth started after geopolitical conflicts settled down in the early 1990s. These economies are currently at the high point of their high-speed-growth period, with the average growth rate so far at 10.8 percent. It remains to be seen whether this high-speed growth will continue for 30 years.

Putting the high-speed growth of East Asian economies together on a timeline, as in Table 7.1, allows us to clearly identify four waves of high-speed industrial growth and economic development in postwar East Asia: Japan from 1950 to the early 1970s, four little dragons from the early 1960s to mid-1990s, major Southeast Asian

Table 7.1 Waves of rapid growth of East Asian economies (1951–2014, percent)

	Postwar Period	Rapid Growth Period	
First wave	5.0	9.1	
Japan	5.0	9.1	1951–1973
Second wave	5.8	7.6	
Hong Kong	6.1	7.7	1962–1996
Korea	7.6	10.6	1963–1996
Taiwan	7.3	9.2	1963–1996
Singapore	9.0	8.5	1966–1997
Third wave	6.2	7.7	
Thailand	6.3	8.6	1959–1996
Malaysia	6.7	7.5	1960–1996
Indonesia	6.0	7.3	1967–1996
China	6.0	7.5	1982–2012
Fourth wave	5.6	10.8	
Vietnam	6.3	8.2	1991–
Myanmar	5.8	14.5	2003–
Cambodia	3.5	8.1	2010–
Laos	6.8	12.4	2015–
Philippines	5.2		
East Asian Growth	6.3	8.9	

Average rate of annual GDP change over previous year. High-speed growth period starts when growth goes above 7.5% and ends when it goes below 7.5%. Data source: PWT9.0 (2017)

countries and China from the 1980s, and continental Southeast Asian states from the 1990s. East Asian growth can therefore be further specified as a pattern of repeated instances of prolonged, high-speed GDP growth at an average annual rate above 7.5 percent in a country's rapid growth period, about 30 years.

A THEORY OF EAST ASIAN GROWTH

A repeated pattern requires an explanation. To the growing curiosity of academics, cultural explanations seemed to gain popularity initially. The four little dragons plus Japan are all societies of traditional Confucian heritage and influence where, according to Vogel, "a Confucian ethic" seemed to be working for their rapid, successful industrial transformation, just like "a Protestant ethic that helped spawn Western capitalism" (Vogel 1993: 86). "The four institutions and cultural practice rooted in the Confucian tradition" – a meritocratic elite, an entrance examination system, the importance of the group, and the goal of self-improvement – helped East Asia make use of their special situational advantages and worldwide opportunities" (Vogel 1993: 101).

Beyond the cultural factors, what mattered also seems to be the shared "situational advantages and worldwide opportunities" for the four plus Japan that connected their industrial activities and relations. The logic of transborder industrial production that drove Akamatsu's flying geese pattern enabled the developing nations to acquire industrial and financial capacities in the process of moving from import to import substitution industrialization and then to export, and from consumer goods to capital goods, a pattern among East Asian nations themselves. Once Japan became a "lead country" itself, it built the same trade relations with "follower countries" in East Asia, just as Western European industrial powers did with Asian nations. This set of relations was aimed at the follower nations as export markets for Japan, at least initially, and collaborative partners for industrial integration and greater manufacturing efficiency.

We can see this in the global structure and regional concentration of Japan's export and foreign direct investment (FDI) over the years. Japan's export to East Asia has been dominant. The East Asian and North American export markets almost leveled off in the 1970s. The East Asian market surpassed the North American market to become the largest export market for Japan from the early 1990s. In the mid-1990s, Japan's FDI outflow to East Asia was 35 percent of its worldwide FDI outflow, already at the same level as its FDI to North America, which was 39 percent.

With respect to Japan's exports and FDI to East Asia, there is a higher concentration of its export to the four countries of the second wave, South Korea, Taiwan, Hong Kong, and Singapore, which averaged 46 percent over the whole period. Its exports to the so-called ASEAN-4, Thailand, Malaysia, Indonesia, and the Philippines, were 21 percent over the high-speed-growth period. However, by 1996, 41 percent of Japan's FDI outflow to East Asia, went to the Northeast Asia 4, while 59 percent went to the Southeast Asia 4. It is evident that Japan's drive for transborder industrial integration and production networks with its FDI brought Northeast and

Southeast together, with an extension of its focus from Northeast Asia to Southeast Asian countries over time.

This East Asia–wide industrial diffusion and regional extension of Japan makes it possible to see these transborder production networks more clearly when NEA-4 and ASEAN-4 are divided into individual countries. Japan's export concentrated on the four little dragons plus China, with each accounting for at least 10 percent of Japan's exports to East Asia. For the same period, Japan's imports from East Asia came from large manufacturing countries of both Southeast and Northeast Asia. Japan's FDI outflow to East Asia over the years concentrated in Southeast Asia, with the top three being Indonesia (22 percent), Thailand (20 percent), and Singapore (15 percent).

Trade and investment reflect a division of labor and a structure in the distribution of industrial, financial, and trading capabilities as well as resources for production and markets for products. Japan-led trade and investment in post-1945 East Asia generated a set of industrial and economic activities in these East Asian economies and propelled the second and third waves of high-speed economic growth in East Asia from the early 1960s to the mid-1990s. Industrial diffusion is a pattern of industrial activities in East Asian growth where industrial capital, technology, management skills, and production networks extend across borders among East Asian countries for the transborder integration of production.

This industrial diffusion is an effect of the logic of industrial production in Japan's miracle industrial growth discussed earlier. According to Akamatsu's original flying geese thesis, once Japan reached the third stage of industrial development, it was able to export its products, particularly to developing countries. The product cycle played out again, this time with Japan as the advanced country and developing countries in East Asia as the follower countries. Bruce Cumings, in his seminal research in 1984 (Cumings 1984), shows that, thanks to their historical, social, and cultural interconnections, East Asian countries became natural and convenient partners in the building of the division of labor through "production networks." As illustrated in Figure 7.4 for a general model, a production network is a particular form of transborder production organization practiced by Japanese firms from the 1960s for the purpose of making product parts in different East Asian countries. This represented a transborder extension of the subcontracting system in industrial organization in Japan itself.

The logic of product cycles also means that Japanese firms would gain, maintain, and eventually lose industrial competitiveness on a strategic product over time. To remain competitive in international markets, Japanese firms, through "industrial upgrading," moved to manufacturing technologically more sophisticated and capital-intensive goods that would require higher industrial, financial, and managerial capabilities of Japan, and the "sunset industries" were shifted to neighboring East Asian countries where competitive labor, land, and resources would make production there more "efficient" and more profitable. This "shift" can mean the transfer of entire production lines but often, more practically, means simply the manufacture of product parts. The Japanese "subcontracted" these industrial activities to their subsidiaries in East Asian countries. Japanese firms set up these subsidiaries massively in ASEAN-4 as well as NEA4 countries starting in the 1960s. The subcontracting

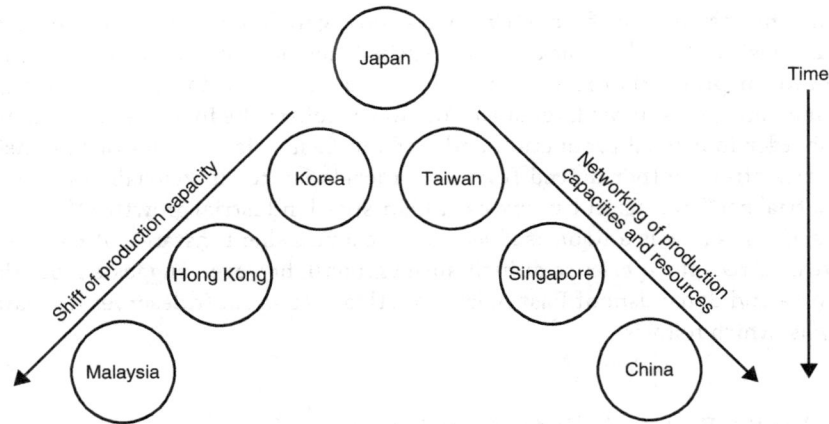

Figure 7.4 Illustration of flying geese model of industrial difusion in East Asia
Production networks for color TV manufacturing in East Asia in the 1980s

system is a key organizational mechanism in Japan's transborder organization of industrial production in East Asia. Kozo Yamamura and Walter Hatch argue that in building Japan-centered production networks in East Asia, Japanese enterprises, replicating the *keiretsu* in Japan, extended the subcontracting system–based production networks to its transborder industrial activities in East Asian countries, which "have made a decisive contribution to the growth of manufacturing industries in Asia" (Yamamura & Hatch 1997: 8).

The Japan-centered production networks in East Asia constituted platforms for Japanese export and international investment. At the same time, they generated intermediate goods that were imported back to Japan. These greatly contributed to the expansion of intraregional trade and industrial integration. A study by IDE-JETRO and WTO in 2011 shows the dominance of Japan in regional production networks, particularly in the high-speed-growth period of these nations. In 1985, for example, supply chains with value added to a product went largely from Malaysia and Indonesia to Japan and from Malaysia to Singapore. In 1990, Korea, Thailand, and Taiwan also rose in the structure, with supplies and value added largely from Japan in the production networks, showing "relocation of Japanese production bases to neighboring countries, triggered by the Plaza Agreement in 1985, was accelerating" (IDE-JETRO & WTO in 2011: 74).

Industrial diffusion from lead countries to follower economies in East Asia provided significant substance and dynamism to subsequent waves of high-speed growth and drove a flying geese pattern of waves of high-speed industrial growth and economic development in East Asia. The analysis of the structure and organization of transborder industrial production here also shows that high-speed growth is not limited to the four little dragons. Japan's export- and investment-led industrial diffusion connected to all East Asian economies, both the four little dragons and ASEAN-4, and more to ASEAN countries. This is a fuller picture of the

Japan-centric structure of industrial forces and organization than the one depicted in Cumings's initial observation. The heavier focus on ASEAN was facilitated by the need for production resources in the initial stage and for manufacturing of intermediate goods in the later stage. The waves reflect the flying geese motion of transborder industrial production and trade in East Asia. One set of East Asian countries after another moved from underdeveloped to "industrializing" and to "industrialized" in consecutive waves of high-speed industrial growth. Of all these waves, China's case is unique as it seems to be an excellent instance of East Asian growth. Its recent experience of high-speed growth, however, suggests more than the force and dynamism of East Asian growth are at work. It deserves a separate analysis, which follows.

THE RISE OF CHINA, ECONOMICALLY

It has been widely debated as to whether the economic rise of China represents an extension of the flying geese pattern or has been driven by the logic of China's own economic growth and industrialization (Naughton 2010; Baek 2005; Boltho & Weber 2009) and whether China fits the pattern of industrial growth and economic development in the way its growth is organized. China's industrial growth and economic development since its reform and opening in 1978 did share some of the characteristics of East Asian growth. As Figure 7.5 shows, China's industrial and economic capability has expanded at an average rate of 7.49 percent for 30 some years from the early 1980s.

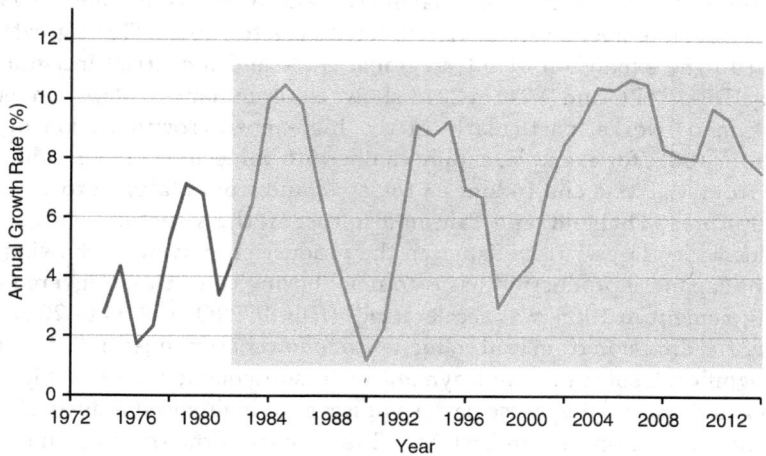

Figure 7.5 China's real GDP annual growth and high-speed-growth period (1982–2014, percentage, shaded area)
Data source: PWT9.0

Moreover, China's industrial and economic growth is also export-led, rising on the same motion of product cycle and constant industrial upgrading. For its products to be competitive in the international market, significant social and institutional resources are engaged by the state for more efficient organization of industrial production. Finally, the state took national economic development, i.e., to become a rich and strong nation, as the primary purpose and focus of the whole nation and state, organized industrial and economic development as a whole-of-nation project, and provided a political structure and an operational environment that focused national resources on industrial competitiveness in the international market. This institutionally stimulated industrial competitiveness was seen in other East Asian economies during their high-speed-growth period.

Two distinct features of China's industrial growth and economic output perhaps separate China from the rest of East Asia and led, in a significant way, to the profound impact that China's economic rise has had on the regional economic structure in East Asia and that of world industrial development and the global economy. The first is the sheer size of the Chinese economy. Using the same high-speed growth rates, the exponential growth of the larger Chinese economy has quickly allowed China, as shown in Figure 7.6, to surpass Japan in 1996 in the size of its economy as measured in real GDP. By 2009, China's economy had grown larger than the other East Asian economies put together. There is a large domestic market associated with this large economy that Japan and the four little dragons did not have. It provides additional dimensions of growth for China's economy. China's industrial growth and economic development extended from the coastal areas to vast inland regions and from labor-intensive sectors to capital-intensive sectors. This has allowed China to

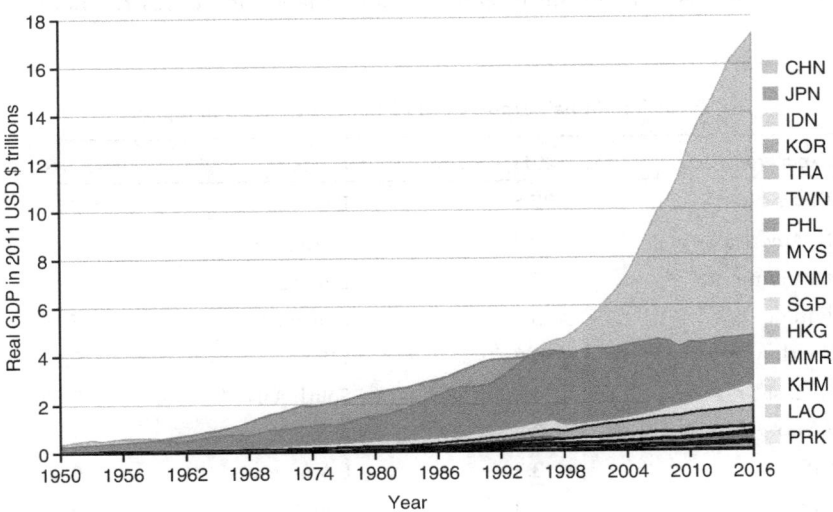

Figure 7.6 Change in weight of national economies in East Asia (1950–2016)
Data source: MPD (2018)

continue to grow and expand at a high speed much longer than the average 30 years that other East Asian economies experienced.

Moreover, international industrial capital played a significant role in China's high-speed growth and the rise of the market economy in China. China's industrial production is deeply connected with the international economic order. FDI was a primary driver of China's rapid growth. The country's growth and expansion engendered a set of powerful integrative dynamics to East Asia, bridging continental East Asia and maritime East Asia, and East Asia and the Asia-Pacific. With a much higher level of interdependence and complementarity with its Northeast Asian neighbors, China's economic rise provides more material substance to Northeast Asia as an effective part of the East Asian structure. These new dynamics of economic interdependence and integration are fundamentally changing the structural character of IREA.

As China moves to the export stage of the flying geese cycle, its economic and trade activities affect the Japan-centered industrial product networks and increasingly the Japan-US–dominated industrial complex and global value chains in East Asia. The aforementioned IDE-JETRO and WTO study shows that by 1995, the Japan-led production networks in East Asia evolved into a structure of Japan-US industrial partnership in global value and supply chains. China then emerged as a "manufacturing giant" (IDE-JETRO & WTO in 2011: 74) and one key end of the supply chain and production networks following Korea, Taiwan, and Singapore. By 2005, China had become the center of production networks exporting finished products to the US and EU.

China's exports to East Asia have grown significantly faster than its exports to other world regions. As shown in Table 7.2, the country's exports to East Asia are almost twice the size of its exports to its second largest export market, North America. There is a significant level of division of labor and industrial networking

Table 7.2 China's exports and FDI outflows to world regions

Export to	2017	FDI in	2016
East Asia	37.5	East Asia	70.30
N. America	22.0	N. America	7.63
Latin America	5.7	Europe	7.63
Europe	5.4	Oceania	5.40
South Asia	4.6	CIS	3.27
M.East	4.4	South Asia	2.67
Africa	3.7	Africa	2.37
CIS	3.2	L America	0.60
Oceania	2.3	Mid. East	0.13

Share of those to a region in China's world total. Data Source: IMF-DOTS (2018)

between China and East Asia. The impact of China's rise on its industrial, financial, and trade capabilities is clearly shown in its overwhelming dominance over Japan and the United States in major economies' exports to East Asia. China has been dominant while Japan and the US have been catching up, contributing to the rise of a true "tripolar" (IDE-JETRO & WTO in 2011: 75) structure of transborder production financing and network building.

China's exports and FDI outflows to East Asia, as shown in Table 7.3, are concentrated largely in Hong Kong and Northeast Asian economies – those in the first and second waves of East Asian growth or Confucian societies. The top East Asian partners for China's exports are Hong Kong, Japan, South Korea, Vietnam, and Taiwan, which account for 80 percent of China's exports to East Asia. Hong Kong accounts for 83 percent of China's FDI outflows. The other top East Asian partners in terms of receiving FDI from China are Singapore, Myanmar, South Korea, and Macau. China has become a manufacturing giant and moved itself up to the export stage in the motion of the flying geese pattern of industrial development in China. It has built tremendous industrial, financial, and trading capabilities and seeks transborder industrial integration in East Asia.

China's transborder industrial expansion is concentrated in industrial areas and sectors where global industrial capital has been less actively engaged. It focuses on infrastructure sectors and industrial parks in developing economies. China's

Table 7.3 China's exports and FDI outflows to East Asian economies

Export to	2017	FDI in	2016
HKG	32.9	HKG	58.5
JPN	16.1	SGP	6.45
ROK	12.0	MMR	1.44
VNM	8.5	ROK	0.97
SGP	5.4	MCA	0.84
TWN	5.1	IDN	0.84
MYS	4.9	THA	0.78
THA	4.5	MYS	0.37
IDN	4.1	JPN	0.15
PHI	3.8	PHI	0.02
MMR	1.1		
KHM	0.6		
PRK	0.4		
LAO	0.2		
BRU	0.1		

Share of those to East Asian economies in China's total to East Asia. Data source: IMF-DOTS (2018)

efforts to build transborder industrial partnerships or production networks take the forms that utilize strengths in the way it organizes industrial growth and economic development. There is a very sophisticated public-private partnership (PPP) for transborder industrial project financing and investment-led development financing. All this has been framed in more recent years in a nationally organized transborder industrial partnership program, the Belt and Road Initiative – an enterprise of China-led bilateral partnerships on transborder industrial projects with countries along the so-called Silk Road Economic Belt and the 21st Century Maritime Silk Road.

This brings us to the fact that China's international industrial and economic interests and relations are as much global as East Asian regional. The impact of China's massive industrial and economic rise on the structure of industrial organization in East Asia can be seen clearly in this feature. The challenge is very similar to that of Japan in the 1970s and 1980s, probably just on a much larger scale. China's exports are 13 percent of the world total in 2016, significantly larger than the second largest exporting nation, the US. However, only 35.7 percent of China's exports go to East Asia, and the rest goes to the rest of the world in almost every country on the planet, with 22 percent going to North America. Regarding FDI, China has become the second largest country in FDI outflow in 2015 in a very short period since it started having significant FDI outflows at the turn of the century. There is clear evidence of rapid expansion of China's FDI outflow to the world.

The global nature of international expansion of China's industrial and economic activities, along with that of Japan's already, has complicated the structural boundary of industrial integration in East Asia. This seems to have a complicating effect on globalization and regionalization, both ironically arising from the economic rise of East Asia and the waves of rapid industrial growth and economic development of the East Asian flying geese.

As the principal nation leading the third wave of East Asian growth, China's industrial growth and international expansion show a similar pattern of product cycle–driven industrial activities. China has moved to the export stage to become an "advance country" in transborder industrial organization and is leading the development of a new global framework for transborder industrial production and distribution. This has had a profound impact on the shaping of the structure and institutions of an international economic order in IREA.

DEBATING SMITH, WALLERSTEIN, AND KANT

The taking off and "flying high" of the East Asian flying geese represents a significant instance of late industrialization and modernization by a group of countries under a set of growth and institutional conditions. It is "late" if we consider the earlier instances: the rise of Western Europe from the sixteenth to nineteenth centuries (North & Thomas 1973; Modelski 1987), climaxing at the formation of the world economic system dominated by the British "industrial, financial and trading superiorities" (Wallerstein 1980: 38); and the rise of the so-called latecomers, Germany, the United States, Russia, and Japan, from the nineteenth century (Gerschenkron

1962; Sylla & Toniolo 1991), to the dominance of the US-led "liberal economic order" in the twentieth century, built on multinational corporations, world economic institutions, and global value and supply chains (Kennedy 1987; Ikenberry 2014).

The economic rise of East Asia in the late twentieth century has sparked debate on some of the principal theories on what enables modern industrial growth, how to organize national economic growth, and how the world economic system is structured. In particular, questions focus on whether backward, developing, or poor countries, particularly those of traditions not based on Western civilization, can move up economically in the hierarchical international structure, how this has been achieved, and the impact of their economic rise and changing position in the world economic system on IREA.

East Asian experiences suggest that backward countries' upward mobility in the world economic system is possible. This very much challenges the logic of the world capitalist system as theorized in Wallerstein's investigation (Wallerstein 1979). It is not only one country by accident. It has been a large group of countries, and a series of repeated instances by East Asian countries. Popular theories such as those of Thorstein Veblen and Alexander Gerschenkron (Veblen 1915; Gerschenkron 1962) consider backwardness as advantages that help make late development possible. Given the historical and institutional conditions of these East Asian countries, one certainly can see their growth and development as a function of the world-capitalist system of which each of these national economies is an integral part.

Regarding what has enabled East Asian growth, or how these East Asian nations managed to take off and fly, much of the scholarly attention and policy analyses focuses on the role of the market and the state, modern institutions, and Confucian values and norms or domestic and international political economic regimes. Questions have been posed, for example, as to whether at a fundamental level East Asian growth has been primarily the effect of the classic laissez-faire Smithian model that relies on the market to drive efficiency in economic activities or that of the East Asian model that relies heavily on the visible hand of the developmental state (Arrighi 2007, 2009). What deserves more attention, though, is the evidence that East Asian growth is the effect of organizing national industrial production and economic growth under a particular set of historical, institutional, and operational conditions within the country and in the international system. It is specifically *East Asian* because these conditions and their coordinated effects on growth participants are unique to these East Asian countries at the time. The logic of industrial development featured in the flying geese theory explains what drives industrial capital to move from being the importing/follower country to that of an exporting/advanced country, and how national industrial capital connects growth factors across borders for more efficient organization of production. All other factors – the state, the market, Confucian values, institutions – are instrumental in making this happen.

There are two aspects to the implications of East Asian growth for IREA and perhaps for international relations in general. First, the economic rise of East Asia has significantly reshaped the world economic structure. An ADB study in 2014 (Figure 12.2) showed that global value chains and product networks of the twenty-first century are structured in three major areas of concentration: China-centered

East Asia, Germany-centered Europe, and the United States. Japan and China have been the world's second and third largest economies for some time, with China looking to overtake the United States as the world's largest economy sooner than expected. East Asia's economic rise has shifted the worldwide distribution of industrial, financial, and trading interests, relations, and capabilities to East Asia. While the new industrial superpowers will seek to build a worldwide division of labor and production networks with follower countries, how East Asian states engage and develop relations with those in the other regions and with those of the earlier waves of modern industrial development, is of great interest to scholars and policy analysts. This topic will be revisited for a fuller discussion in Chapter 12.

Second, given the different waves of East Asian growth, countries in that area have grown into different types of economies with different economic positions in the region. Some moved up to the top of the developed economies, such as Japan and Singapore, while others, such as China, remain in a different stage of modern economic and social development. The scale and focus of their economies differ significantly in terms of industrial sector and global/regional connectivity. Thus, their industrial and development interests and capabilities are different. This affects their approach to further advancing in organizing industrial growth and production networks in East Asia. How this will affect their economic cooperation and competition in East Asia, and even geopolitics among these states, is also of great scholarly and policy interest, a topic we will pick up in Chapter 8.

The last point leads to one key interest in our discussion here: how the growth of trade and economic relations among East Asian countries affects their political relations and shapes IREA in the long term. East Asia has been a theater for geopolitics by great powers (Chapter 4). We have discussed how geopolitical, structural, and cultural dynamics have influenced war and peace in IREA. The economic rise of East Asian states and the growth of regional trade and production relations brought a new set of dynamics to East Asia. This set of new dynamics, national industrial, financial, and trade interests, relations, and capabilities, and interstate collaboration and competition in trade, investment, and development have increasingly shaped the way IREA are organized. Industrial growth and economic development have become a very important part of IREA. While great power geopolitics has been cited as a primary reason for war, conflict, and interstate tensions in East Asia, have these economic dynamics and relations moved IREA to evolve or operate more peacefully and contribute to the good governance of IREA?

This matter has been discussed in many other regions and in explanations of international relations in general. Scholars resort to certain classical theories for an argument. The Kantian peace theory is one such theory. Kantian peace constitutes a theory of the necessary conditions for perpetual peace in a community of nations. Cosmopolitan ties through transnational trade and commerce represent one key set of such conditions. Trade and international commerce are thus considered to have a "pacifying effect" on interstate relations. The theory is attributed to Immanuel Kant in the first wave of globalization driven by Western European industrial growth and global expansion five hundred years ago (Kant 1795) and to liberal economic theorists in the second wave of globalization in the nineteenth and twentieth century such as John Stuart Mill and Joseph Schumpeter. Michael Doyle identifies "cosmopolitan law" as one of the "three definitive articles of the perpetual peace" Kant considered necessary for "the union of republicans" to be peaceful. "The cosmopolitan right to hospitality permits the 'spirit of commerce'," Doyle explains, "sooner or later to take hold of every nation, thus impelling states to promote peace and to try to avert war" (Doyle 1983: 231).

This propensity for peace among nations is nurtured through these cosmopolitan ties that "derive from a cooperative international division of labor and free trade according to comparative advantage" and assure economic interdependence and alliance for security. "International market removes difficult decisions of production and distribution from the direct sphere of state" and "the interdependence of commerce and the connections of state officials help create crosscutting transnational ties that serve as lobbies for mutual accommodation" (Doyle 1983: 232). The pacifying effect of trade, according to Kant, via Doyle, "relied upon international commerce to create ties of mutual advantage that would help make republics pacific" and "the ties of trade, cultural exchange, and political understanding that together both commit existing republics to peace" (Doyle 1983: 350–51).

East Asian growth seems to be an ideal candidate by which to test the Kantian peace theory, except that it is hotly debated as to whether the East Asian countries were "liberal republics" before or after their respective high-speed growth period. If we focus on evidence of the "pacifying effect of trade" on interstate relations, we see conflicting evidence with respect to East Asian growth. Great improvements have been seen in relations among East Asian countries – a reduction in distrust and insecurity and growing openness to transborder commerce among East Asian countries. This helped bring the nations closer to each other and build up higher levels of trust and confidence, for example, between Northeast Asian and Southeast Asian nations, between Japan and other East Asian countries, and between China and its Cold War enemies, and among different sets of ASEAN member states.

On the other hand, the type of industrial growth and economic development achieved in East Asia happened on the basis of a very hierarchical and hegemonic structure dominated by a lead nation's industrial capital. It involved unequal exchange and national competition that have contributed to continual distrust and suspicion between and among states in IREA. Moreover, because of the global nature of East Asian industrial and economic interests and relations, this unequal exchange and international industrial competition also has a global dimension. Other nations have reacted variously to the rise of Japan in the 1970s and 1980s and China in more recent times. The reactions are largely focused on those two countries' trade and investment strategies and, more broadly, on their way of organizing transborder industrial production and distribution. The state, as well as national interests and the national way of political economy, still matters in the organization of transborder industrial activities in a community of nations, something that Kant advised us to ignore some 200 years ago for the perpetual peace of a union of republics.

Study Questions

1. How have economic dynamics emerged to form an important set of conditions that have profoundly influenced IREA?
2. What is the flying geese pattern of industrial development? How does the flying geese theory explain East Asian growth?
3. Discuss the waves of high-speed industrial growth and economic development in the second half of the twentieth century. How do they relate to each other?
4. Why was the Asian financial crisis of 1997–98 a turning point in the waves of East Asian growth?
5. East Asian growth has significantly impacted the regional and global economies. How has it influenced war and peace in IREA?
6. How have the national industrial growth and economic development of Japan and China influenced the structure and institutions of regional economic order in East Asia?

Further Reading

ADB, 2008. *Emerging Asian Regionalism: A Partnership for Shared Prosperity*. Mandaluyong City: Asian Development Bank.

Amsden, Alice H., 1989. *Asia's Next Giant: South Korea and Late Industrialization*. Oxford: Oxford University Press.

Barnard, Mitchell, and John Ravenhill, 1995. "Beyond Product Cycles and Flying Geese: Regionalization, Hierarchy, and the Industrialization of East Asia," *World Politics* 47(2): 171–209.

Cumings, Bruce, 1984, "The Origins & Development of the Northeast Asian Political Economy," *International Organization* 38(1): 1–40.

Ferrarini, Benno, and David Hummels, 2014a. *Production Networks: Implications for Trade, Incomes and Economic Vulnerability*. Cheltenham/Northampton: Edward Elgar.

Ferrarini, Benno, and David Hummels, 2014b. *Asia and Global Production Networks Implications for Trade, Incomes and Economic Vulnerability*. Cheltenham: Asian Development Bank/Edward Elgar.

Grimes, William, 2009. *Currency and Contest in East Asia: The Great Power Politics of Financial Regionalism*. Ithaca: Cornell University Press.

Hatch, Walter, and Kozo Yamamura, 1996. *Asia in Japan's Embrace, Building a Regional Production Alliance*. Cambridge: Cambridge University Press.

Huang, Xiaoming, 2005. *The Rise and Fall of the East Asian Growth System 1951–2000: Institutional Competitiveness and Rapid Economic Growth*. London/New York: Routledge.

Huang, Xiaoming. 2013. *Modern Economic Development in Japan and China: Developmentalism, Capitalism, and the World Economic System*. New York: Palgrave.

Johnson, Chalmers, 1983. *MITI and the Japanese Miracle: The Growth of Industrial Policy, 1925–1975*. Stanford: Stanford University Press.

Kasahara, Shigehisa, 2013. "The Asian Developmental State and the Flying Geese Paradigm," UNCTD Discussion Paper No. 213 UN: UNCTD.

Kojima, Kiyoshi, 2000. The "Flying Geese" Model of Asian Economic Development: Origin, Theoretical Extensions, and Regional Policy Implications," *Journal of Asian Economics* 11: 375–401.

Schröppel, Christian, and Nakajima Mariko, 2003. "The Changing Interpretation of the Flying Geese Model of Economic Development," *Japanstudien* 14(1): 203–236.

Wade, Robert, 1990. *Governing the Market Economic Theory and the Role of Government in East Asian Industrialization*. Princeton: Princeton University Press.

Woo-Cumings, Meredith, 1999. *The Developmental State*. Ithaca: Cornell University Press.

World Bank, 1993. *The East Asian Miracle: Economic Growth and Public Policy*: Oxford: Oxford University Press.

WTO and IDE-JETRO, 2011. *Trade Patterns and Global Values Chains in East Asia: From Trade in Goods to Trade in Tasks*. Geneva: WTO Secretariat.

Yeung, Henry Wai-chung, 2016. *Strategic Coupling: East Asian Industrial Transformation in the New Global Economy*. Ithaca: Cornell University Press.

8 Economic Regionalism

In This Chapter...

- Regionalization and regionalism
- Market forces and institutions as drivers
- Visions of a region
- PBEC, APEC, and Pacific business cooperation
- "Funerals," "weddings," and the noodle bowl
- APT, EAS, and ASEAN centrality
- TPP, RCEP, and BIFURCATION of a region?
- Principal movers and shapers
- Multilateral institutions of economic regionalism

Learning Objectives

By the end of this chapter, you will be able to
- Conduct an institutional analysis of regional economic cooperation and integration
- Understand East Asian regionalism as an intergovernmental and multilateral project for regional economic engagement
- Understand how market forces and institutional dynamics have influenced East Asian regionalism
- Understand the historical trajectory of the forces behind the visions of East Asian regionalism
- Understand the different purposes of the initiatives of East Asian regionalism
- Explain the weaknesses of East Asian regionalism.

The previous chapter discussed the growth of industrial production and economic development and how "market forces" have enabled countries in East Asia to move their industrial activities across borders in the region and organize their industrial production in transborder regional production networks. In this chapter, we will investigate the efforts of nations to organize production and distribution in the region through more formal institutional arrangements, to regulate transborder movements of products, capital, people, and production activities, and to develop an international economic order for growth and development activities in East Asia.

Efforts to build regional economic institutions in East Asia have been a unique set of international activities. These activities are aimed at organizing transborder production and distribution beyond national boundaries in a large regional setting. These activities in the past 30 years are comparable in global significance to those in Europe and North America. They are unique, though, in the way East Asian regionalism has been organized, what it has achieved, and what direction it will take from here. These unique conditions reflect the impact of the global economic structure on the shaping of international institutions in the region. The playing out of these conditions also reveals to a great extent the political nature of multilateral institution building in a predominately nation-state system.

REGIONALIZATION AND REGIONALISM

Regionalism is a theory and the international practice it inspires to organize economic cooperation and integration in a geographical community of states. Regionalization, on the other hand, is a process whereby economic forces seek transborder connectivity, complementarity, and division of labor in production and service provision in a large geoeconomic area. Samuel Kim, one of the leading scholars in IREA, explains the different theoretical and policy expectations of regionalism and regionalization for regional economic cooperation and integration.

For Kim, regionalism is "a normative concept referring to shared values, norms, identity, and aspirations" and to "state-led projects of cooperation that emerge from intergovernmental dialogues and agreement…regional intergovernmental cooperation to manage various problems," while regionalization refers to "non-state-driven – usually market-driven – processes of integration…an ongoing process of economic integration deriving primary motive force from markets, trade, and investment by multinational corporations" (Kim 2004: 40–41). Here regionalism is a normative project by states for intergovernmental cooperation, whereas regionalization is a market-driven process of integration for industrial production and distribution.

This distinction is useful for us to make sense of the contentious development of regional economic institutions in East Asia, and understand the emergent pattern of East Asian regionalism and the scholarly debate over whether a top-down or bottom-up approach in multilateral institutionalism can better explain the balance of influence between market pressures for regional economic integration and cooperation, and institutional pressures in regulating and managing market forces.

East Asian regionalism is a set of intergovernmental efforts and projects to set up rules in a multilateral framework to manage and regulate transborder production and distribution activities in East Asia. It is intergovernmental because these efforts and projects are, to paraphrase a popular line, of the states, by the states, and for the states. While private interests and public goods for the region do have their way of influencing regionalism, it is primarily the dynamics of the national interests as presented and negotiated by governments in a multilateral setting that has significant impact on the process and structure of regionalism.

East Asian regionalism is also largely about rules in trade and production. The so-called rule of origin, for example, concerns how we determine which country a product, or parts of it, comes from or goes to, so that different tariff rates can apply. Rules of development financing, industrial organization, corporate management, and ownership and property rights are another set of important examples of the rules. The working of these rules eventually would lead to a regional economic order for industrial production and distribution. After all, a regional economic order is a set of institutionalized and normalized economic relations and activities of national economic actors in a region. Here a regional economic order can develop in the direction of either an international economic order or an economic order of a regional community, i.e., the direction of economic cooperation or economic integration. It can also develop, as we will show in the case of East Asia, as a mixture of the two. East Asian regionalism has been very ambiguous on this, which might explain what Richard Baldwin (2006) calls the "noodle bowl" of East Asian regionalism.

Moreover, rules are the core of institutions. As Douglass North explains (North 1990), institutions reflect the structure of industrial, financial, and trading capabilities of nations. Regional economic institutions for industrial production and economic activities are dynamic given the rapidly evolving industrial and economic structure in post-1945 East Asia. These projects must be constantly updated, or even new projects added at rather frequent intervals, giving governments of the nations involved more opportunities to inject their national interests. All of these factors contribute to the complexity and the "varieties" of East Asian regionalism (Cho & Park 2014) and repeated "failures" of some projects and their replacement by new ones. These networks or series of projects of regional economic institutions have accumulated over the years and contributed to the noodle bowl pattern.

Finally, East Asian regionalism has been predominantly a multilateral undertaking. Multilateralism in East Asian regionalism is a framework for regulating and managing transborder economic relations that relies on the participation, commitment, and consent of multiple nations of equal vetoing power. This is different from bilateralism. Bilateralism involves two states, and often the stronger nation will have a decisive influence on their relations. The logic of institutionalism suggests that the efficiency and effectiveness of multilateral frameworks tend to be influenced by the number of states involved. Given the intergovernmental nature of the projects and the global dynamics of East Asian growth, East Asian regionalism has involved a large number of countries in and outside East Asia in their early stages of their undertakings, which laid the seeds of tension between different "visions" of the material foundations and scope of an East Asian regional institution, particularly between those of the East Asian focus and those of the Asia-Pacific focus. This feature influenced East Asian regionalism to become an open regionalism.

East Asian regionalism features uniquely open regionalism where not only are memberships not limited to East Asian countries, but also the benefits of agreements are open to nonmembers under the principle of most-favored-nation status for all. Moreover, regional institutions for economic cooperation have their unique political value. As the theory of liberal institutionalism (Keohane 1989; Keohane & Martin 1995) teaches us, countries of small and medium-sized economies look for multilateral institutions as a useful and effective platform for their collective bargaining power in a regional economic order. Countries that cannot achieve a favorable trade agreement bilaterally with economic superpowers can do better through these collective arrangements. This adds another political dimension to East Asian regionalism.

The dominance and complication of national interests and capabilities on the shaping of regional economic institutions has made regional institutional building in East Asia dynamic and competitive. It has constantly looked for better proposals or frameworks that can satisfy the interests of the countries involved. The development of regional economic institutions is therefore piecemeal and progressive and has resulted in more informal, nonbinding, or "soft" arrangements, with the structure and institutions of the ultimate "end" form of an East Asian economic community ever elusive.

MARKET FORCES AND INSTITUTIONS AS DRIVERS

Beyond the intergovernmental nature of East Asian regionalism, we want to understand the large set of dynamics that have driven East Asian regionalism to evolve the way it has. These dynamics are the material and institutional forces that drive the nations to "cooperate to compete." The first of the drivers is certainly the rapid industrial growth and economic development of East Asian countries and the development of a set of regional economic interests and relations. Andrew Hurrell explains the global wave of regionalism (Hurrell 1995). By the end of the 1980s when the new global wave of regionalism was set to spread to East Asia, East Asia had become the area with the third largest concentration of industrial, financial, and trading capabilities and opportunities. As shown in Table 8.1, in 1989 when the Asia-Pacific Economic Cooperation (APEC) had its inaugural gathering, East Asia had 40.2 percent of the world's total GDP and 30.4 percent of merchandise exports. East Asia has emerged as the region with the most dynamic economy, holds a large

Table 8.1 Weight of international economic groupings in East Asia in world economy (%)

Group	Year	GDP	Export
ADB	1966	66	69.7
PBEC	1968	42.2	28.8
APEC	1989	40.9	30.4
APT	1999	16.9	11.4
EAS	2005	30.5	24.5
ASEAN	2008	4.7	6.1
TPP	2008	31	22.7
RCEP	2012	33.9	28.0
AIIB	2014	63.8	66.6

Share in world total of total GDP and export of group's members in year of its formal launch (see more details in online Appendices, Table A.11)

proportion of global wealth and economic activity, and possesses strong and influential industrial, financial, and trading capabilities.

This wealth and economic capability mean opportunities that attract global business and investment. More importantly, East Asian growth is generated through the institutionally manipulated connection of production and consumption in different regions or markets, and corporatist mechanisms of production and distribution organization. This led to the build-up of pressures over time for structural balancing in the world economic system, driving industrial capital in other regional markets to move to East Asia. The major push for trade and investment liberalization in East Asia starting in the 1980s came largely from outside the region.

This major push also occurred at a time when nations around the world were looking for a more effective and efficient way of organizing their national political economy. The tensions built up in the national political economy after decades of the dominance of the state in organizing economic growth and development, since perhaps Roosevelt's New Deal in the United States in the 1930s, and the intensive "race" between capitalism and socialism in the early post-1945 decades. Reaganomics in the United States and Thatcherism in the United Kingdom brought in a powerful economic ideology that privileges markets over the state as the primary force to determine economic activity, relations, and resource allocation. Their rise in the 1980s led to the ascendance of neoliberal political economy in nations of the Anglo-Saxon traditions (Albert 1993; Hall & Soskice 2001) and further the rise to dominance of neoliberalism in the international political economy in the 1990s.

Neoliberalism is an idea and the idea-inspired practice of organizing government and the economy on the principles of markets, competition, and efficiency over state, coordination, and fairness. It was particularly influential in the 1980s and 1990s in international political economy. East Asia became a primary target for the global neoliberal movement as its "model" of economic development was very much at odds with neoliberal principles.

Neoliberal economic dynamics drove global interests to build regional institutions in East Asia. These interests focused initially on the opening of the market in East Asian economies and dismantling of the institutions of state-centric socially and nationally coordinated industrial growth and economic development. This helped shape East Asian regionalism to evolve in a slightly different way than regionalism in Europe and North America, which was accelerating around the same time. The Maastricht Treaty was signed in 1993 to formally establish the European Union (EU), a giant step in the path toward European integration and community building and the establishment of a Europe-wide public authority. The North American Free Trade Agreement (NAFTA) was signed in 1994 to formally establish a free trade area and was a major step toward a North American economic community.

The dominant influence of neoliberalism in international political economy then was also aided by the popularity of new institutionalism in economies and political science at the time (North 1990; Hall & Taylor 1996). New institutionalism has developed largely on Douglass North's theory of efficiency-centered institutional effects on economic growth, which he developed in the 1970s in his original study on the rise of the "Western World" (North & Thomas 1973). New institutionalism holds that efficiency is more broadly based than what classical liberalism focuses on, and parity between social and individual benefits of economic activities of individual actors is possible with institutional interventions. North summarizes his definition of institutions as "the humanly devised constraints that structure political, economic and social interaction" (North 1991: 97). New institutionalism holds that institutions, consisting of rules, norms, and cultural values, influence, if not determine, the decisions and behavior of individual agents under the institutional setting, and institutional design and manipulation can lead to desired behaviors of the agents and bring "efficiency" in national economic activities.

This behaviorist strand of new institutionalism was taken up in the 1980s by Robert Keohane, Joseph Nye, and Lisa Martin (Keohane 1984, 1989; Keohane & Martin 1995; Keohane & Nye 1977) in the discipline of international relations to explore how international institutions can be instrumental in motivating states to cooperate in the anarchic international environment when economic interdependence is increasingly complicating international relations and the conventional geopolitical structure is no longer the only force influencing and motivating states to act. At the core of these varieties of institutionalism is a belief that institutions can influence if not determine the behavior of individual agents. By extension, international institutions influence if not determine the actions of states in international relations and, hence, help structure interstate relations and shape the international order. This thinking of the new institutionalism is quite visible in the growing efforts in the 1990s and 2000s to design and develop regional institutions to regulate and manage transborder economic activities and relations in East Asia where globally significant economic interests, relations, and resources for production and distribution are at stake.

VISIONS OF A REGION

The foregoing discussions draw our attention to the question of the possible final aims of East Asian regionalism, or what types of regional economic order these forces would push East Asian regionalism to achieve. If East Asian regionalism is a largely market-driven process by manufacturers, financiers, and traders to seek political support at intergovernmental levels for national activities and relations in transborder production and distribution, the questions of whether East Asian regionalism is East Asian or Asia-Pacific and whether it is for economic cooperation or economic integration are less critical. Economic cooperation in East Asian regionalism refers to the intentions and efforts of states to institutionalize their transborder economic activities, exchange, and interaction for a multilaterally beneficial economic order, while economic integration refers to the development of a regional market and division of production and the connectivity and complementarity of production interests and capabilities in East Asia for a regional economic community.

Market forces in East Asian economies, in the forms of transborder movement of industrial capital and extension of production networks and value and supply chains, are integrative by nature, and they may initially concentrate in East Asia, but the search for efficiency is not confined to a region. The scope of integrative activities is determined largely by the development of the specific product networks and value and supply chains. Japan's shift from its early focus on East Asia to Asia-Pacific and China's early focus on greater China, which later moved to the global Belt and Road Initiative (BRI) areas, are good examples of this.

If East Asian regionalism is more of an intergovernmental exercise that expects negotiated rules to promote a certain regional economic order for production and distribution in East Asia, then these questions become necessarily important, at the very least, to help guide institutional design and rules negotiation. Tensions between these two sets of visions have influenced East Asian regionalism for decades.

The first set of visions concerns whether the region in question is East Asia, which spans the areas of Asia bordering on the Pacific; or the Asia-Pacific, which covers economies on the Pacific Rim (Figure 8.1). The East Asian vision is informed largely by what is usually referred to as the third pole in the three-region framework of the world economic structure in the 1980s. West Europe, North America, and East Asia emerged with each having a significant concentration of global industrial, financial, and trade interests, activities, and capabilities. Each leaned toward forming a collective body to enhance their security, competitiveness, and further growth. East Asian vision is an ideal framework for organizing economic cooperation and integration in a geoeconomic area consisting of Northeast and Southeast Asia. It is also materially related to the Japan-led spread of East Asian growth, the idea and practice of organizing transborder economic activities and relations, and production networks and supply chains that connect Northeast and Southeast Asia.

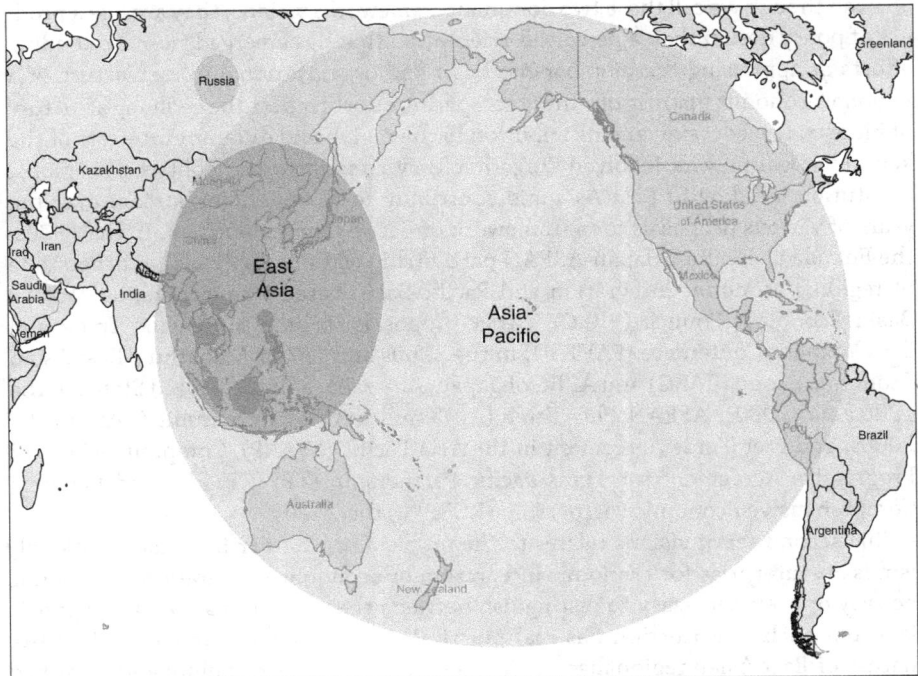

Figure 8.1 Geoeconomic areas of East Asia and the Asia-Pacific

The Asia-Pacific vision, on the other hand, is shaped largely by US global economic interests, relations, and capabilities. These forces moved to connect with the rapidly growing East Asian markets, resources, and industrial, financial, and trade interests and capabilities. It is a framework that engages select economies on the Pacific Rim and connects Pacific America and East Asia. Moreover, Japan's need for a US political partnership in organizing transborder production and distribution contributed to the growth of US-Japan industrial incorporation and the fusion of their industrial interests and capabilities in global value chains and networks of production and distribution. Multinational corporations combined with joint, high-end dominance of US and Japanese firms in global value chains and Japan's dominance in the production networks and supply chains in East Asia brought the dynamics of "horizontal integration" to East Asian regionalism.

Japanese and US firms dominate the high end of global value chains, with superior interests and capacities in industrial capital, technology, and product ownership. Global interests, capabilities, and opportunities in manufacturing and distribution concentrate in East Asia. Horizontal integration at the high end of global value chains provides much substance to the growth of the Japan-US industrial complex and to the framework of Asia-Pacific economic integration. Vertically, however, their relations between different stages of production, between manufacturing and financing, are predominantly those of trade and exchange. The Asia-Pacific version, therefore, carries a mixture of moves toward economic integration and cooperation.

Even though we call these two dominant frameworks visions, they are less a product of policy design than a perceived orientation that has emerged from contending efforts at appraising the membership basis and organizational infrastructure of a regional economic institution. These competing efforts reflect the evolving structure of industrial production and distribution in the region and different interests of the key industrial powers involved. Together they constitute the politics of regional institution building in East Asia and contribute to the unending stream over the years of various proposals for a framework of East Asian regionalism. In the 1970s, the Fukuda vision for a Japan-ASEAN partnership was put forth as the cornerstone of regional economic integration and Pacific-Basin based frameworks, i.e., Pacific Basin Economic Council (PBEC). Other proposals include the Pacific Trade and Development Conference (PAFTAD) in the 1960s and 1970s; Mahathir's East Asian Economic Group (EAEG) and APEC of Japan, Australia, and the United States in the 1980s and 1990s; ASEAN Plus Three (APT) and East Asian Summit (EAS) in the 2000s; and Free Trade Agreement in the Asia-Pacific (FTAAP), Comprehensive and Progressive Agreement for Trans-Pacific Partnership (TPP/CPTPP), and Regional Comprehensive Economic Partnership (RCEP) in the 2010s.

The second set of visions relates to the problem of whether East Asian regionalism is an enterprise for economic integration or economic cooperation. It may not be easy or even necessary to distinguish between these two in East Asian regionalism. But such a distinction has real practical implications for understanding the nature of East Asian regionalism, and assessing its success or failure and what has been achieved. East Asian regionalism is first seen as an international event in regional integration and is often compared to Western Europe (Ravenhill 2001; Yeo 2010; Murray 2010; Webber & Ford 2006), which has enjoyed success in building a European political and economic community. On the other hand, as discussed earlier, East Asian regionalism also entails efforts by nations to build rules and uphold normative practices for economic activities in East Asia through intergovernmental negotiation, agreement, and implementation. It is a pointedly intergovernmental exercise and platform for regulating and managing transborder production and distribution in East Asia.

The idea of East Asian regionalism as a series of steps toward regional integration is clearly influenced by the popular frameworks drawn from the first wave of regional integration in Europe, particularly that of neofunctionalism. In Ernst Haas's and Walter Mattli's discussions (Haas 1964; Mattli 1999), neofunctionalism is a theory of regional integration that explains the complicating effects of nation-state territorialism in regional integration. Sub- and supranational political actors can influence the success of regional integration with the support of functional cooperation among politicians, policymakers, and supranational agencies across state boundaries. Walter Mattli groups integration schemes into two different types. Contractual schemes "confer significant authority to supranational agencies," while the institutional ones are largely "strictly intergovernmental in character and shy away from any institutional elements that weaken or undermine national sovereignty" (Mattli 2012: 1). The success of these schemes in economic integration are determined by the combined effects of political actors and agencies at sub- and supranational levels, as Haas showed in his original discussion of the successful unification of Europe.

This framework is useful for us to see the differences between East Asian and European regionalism. East Asian regionalism seems to have been driven by two different sets of dynamics: national industrial dynamics that seek regional integration for efficiency, and international institutional dynamics for intergovernmental cooperation. The political actor–focused framework will need to be extended further for a fuller understanding of the predominantly intergovernmental nature of East Asian regionalism.

Significant efforts, reflecting the powerful interests involved, have been devoted to integrating production and distribution for efficient growth through various institutional arrangements by firms and other economic actors of different nations in East Asia, as discussed in Chapter 7. These also include the Japan-US industrial complex in global value chains through firm mergers and acquisitions (M&A), joint shareholding and ownership, and complex property rights schemes and formulas. Most major proposals for regional institutions, however, have been primarily for a free trade area (FTA) – intergovernmental cooperation to ensure an open and fair environment for economic exchange. This is a slightly different exercise than industrial integration. APEC's vision, when it was set up in 1989, was to "promote trade and investment liberalization," and this was taken further by TPP and RCEP.

FTAs are based on intergovernmental agreements on rules of transborder economic exchange. In the practice of East Asian regionalism, FTAs have often been expanded to influence the way production and distribution are organized "over the borders." This engagement on the institutions of production organization is crucial for the belief that regional institutions facilitate regional economic integration and clearly reflects the asymmetric structure of international economic power and influence over East Asia. In the early years of East Asian regionalism in the 1980s and 1990s, Japan tended to favor "economic cooperation" for trade dispute resolution and management, evidently to protect its forms of production and distribution organization in Japan and East Asia, while the United States often called for "economic integration" across the Pacific with open and free markets and investment opportunities in East Asia.

Nations' purposes in East Asian regionalism have been very complex and evolved and adapted as power structures shifted. Proposals for building a regional economic community based on production and distribution integration have been put forth for negotiation from time to time. Japan's initial drive from the 1960s for a Pacific Basin–based business community was largely in that direction. In the mid-2000s, when the future direction of East Asian regionalism became uncertain, the idea of an East Asian community was put into action that promised to build a political, economic, and cultural community for East Asia. Even those FTA-named proposals and platforms, such as APEC, TPP, and RCEP, contain elements of a "thick" FTA that deals substantially with "integration" issues: standards in products and services, rules in production organization, and connectivity in different national industrial interests and capacities. Both TPP and RCEP claim to create a twenty-first-century high-quality FTA.

The mixture of elements of economic cooperation and integration in the various regional institutions in East Asia reflects a different structure of ever-evolving national interests and capabilities in transborder production and distribution in East Asia. These differences in national interests and capabilities have further to do with these countries being at different stages of economic development at the time, e.g., developed and developing or industrializing and postindustrial. Countries at these different stages have very different interests, agendas, and capabilities in shaping regional institutions. This can be seen much more clearly in the changing role of China in East Asian regionalism over the past 40 years.

East Asian regionalism in the 1980s and 1990s was dominated by US efforts to connect with the Japan-dominated East Asian organization and networks of production and distribution. The economic rise of China reshaped the structure of production and distribution in East Asia. It is not just the volume of trade and flows of products, parts, materials, capital, and people it generates. It is more importantly the way it organizes production and distribution. As an industrial power with newly gained industrial, financial, and trading interests and capabilities of global significance, China seeks to build its own transborder production and distribution networks and partnerships. China coordinates all these efforts in a national umbrella framework, the BRI. Projects under the BRI are largely transborder industrial projects funded and organized by Chinese enterprises. There is a complex ownership structure in China's industrial capital, and China relies heavily on public-private partnerships (PPPs) for internal corporate financing to assist Chinese enterprises with investing in transborder industrial projects. These projects allow for a significant level of state financing in FDI outflows and in the building of China's transborder network of partnerships for industrial production and distribution.

Moreover, these projects concentrate in the infrastructure sector broadly defined (OECD 2006; ADB 2017). This is conventionally a prominent sector for official development aid (ODA), which refers to intergovernmental financing to support economic development of developing countries, whereas FDI is transborder capital investment in economic projects by industrial capital of another nation. Investment-led development financing embedded in China's BRI projects combines the mechanisms of FDI and ODA through its network of government-sanctioned bilateral industrial partnerships.

China brings quite a bit of the mechanisms of development financing into its FDI. These include an intergovernmental political partnership with the host country; intergovernmental loans and grants, particularly in the early phase of the rise of its industrial capital transborder outflow; and PPP in China in a capital consortium for enterprises to bid on transborder industrial projects. Finally, China itself has been a major recipient of FDI. This contributed significantly to the 40 years of its successful industrial growth and economic development. In organizing China's own outgoing FDI to other countries today, China utilizes many of the mechanisms that effectively attracted and facilitated FDI inflows to China earlier. These include special economic zones, industrial parks, and joint ownership with the host country's industrial capital. These arrangements are often negotiated through the bilateral, intergovernmental political partnership.

China's economic rise, therefore, has not only influenced the material structure of production and distribution but also the institutions and normative practices established over the decades that inform and govern transborder production and distribution in East Asia and beyond. More pointedly, the BRI is China's national framework that enables its industrial capital, through bilateral intergovernmental political partnerships, to engage in transborder industrial projects. It is not a multilateral framework, nor is it focused on or confined to East Asia. The market forces arising out of China's East Asian growth are new forces in the very dynamic process of globalization. It is unclear how China's BRI will relate to the Japan-US indusial partnership that has been dominant in East Asian regionalism. It is clear, though, and increasingly so, that China does not seem to see itself fitting into the role assigned to it in the tripolar structure of the "Asian-US production system" (WTO-JETRO 2011: 76) between East Asia, China, and the United States, with China as a giant assembly factory.

In light of these two sets of visions that have been informing or shaping East Asian regionalism, it is unclear what directions East Asian regionalism will move in going forward. East Asia is increasingly becoming a primary theater for global international economic and industrial competition rather than a region for economic community and integration. Major global industrial and economic powers involved in East Asian regionalism and the market forces these countries represent shape the purpose, scope, and, ultimately, the fate of East Asian regionalism. Let us now take a more in-depth look at how East Asian regionalism has arrived at its current state.

PBEC, APEC, AND PACIFIC BUSINESS COOPERATION

Efforts to "institutionalize" transborder activities for production and distribution in East Asia existed long before major intergovernmental efforts such as APEC or EAS came into play. As shown in earlier discussions, Japan made great efforts to extend its method of organizing industrial growth more broadly to East Asia, even from the interwar years, and more systematically and institutionally from the 1960s. Pacific business cooperation is one key theme running through Japan's ideas and activities to institutionalize transborder industrial organization in the region. Pacific business cooperation is the idea of building a business community among countries across the Pacific Basin.

Two sets of partnerships developed from this. Japan-ASEAN and Japan-US partnerships define the character of the cooperation. As Koyoshi Kojima observed (Kojima 2000), the flying geese dynamics of industrial growth led to the establishment of the PAFTAD in 1968. This annual gathering of mostly scholars from the Pacific Rim countries was intended to be a forum for research and discussion of economic and trade policy in the Pacific.

Around the same time, business leaders from Japan and the United States set up a more formal platform, the PBEC, in 1967, to "promote the mutual cooperation of the business circles in the Pacific countries" (Kosugi 1986: 102). PBEC was designed to build a "business cooperation alliance" across the Pacific among business executives from select countries: Japan, the United States, Australia, New Zealand, and Canada. PBEC is a platform for economic cooperation for the private sector and has remained so today with senior business executives from the Asia-Pacific region.

The intergovernmental dimension emerged earlier on and was taken up further with the establishment of more formal multilateral, intergovernmental platforms to develop regional institutions for organizing transborder production and distribution among member countries. In 1980, with the joint effort of Japan and Australia, government, business, and academic leaders from 15 countries, including the PBEC five, ASEAN five, and South Korea, gathered. The move was spurred largely by the ideas of "Pacific Basin Cooperation" and "Pacific Economic Community" and was favored also by then-Japanese Prime Minister Mosayoshi Ohira.

One key aspect of this move toward more institutionalized forms of Pacific economic cooperation was to bring the intergovernmental dimension into regional business networking and integration. This development was anticipated in neofunctionalism for regional integration, noting the complicating impact of state bureaucrats and sub- and supranational political actors and interest groups on the forms and character of regional integration. Pacific economic cooperation also helped connect the two dominant economies. Japan and the United States, according to an influential study then, "account for 75 percent of total Pacific area GDP" (Kosugi 1986: 115, 106) at the time. Japan's trade with the US exceeded its trade with East Asia by the late 1960s and US trade with the Pacific countries exceeded its trade with Europe in 1978 (*ibid*). This has become an instance of a pattern that the scope of regional institutions reflects a substantial portion of worldwide industrial interests, activities, and capabilities.

PBEC economies, as shown in Table 8.1, represented 42.2 percent of world total GDP and 28.8 percent of world total exports in the period when PBEC was first established in 1968. Moreover, these two groups of economies grew out of very different historical and institutional contexts, as well as a direct conflict between the two in the Pacific War. It required extraordinary political support at the intergovernmental level to nurture mutual interest, trust, and cooperation in organizing production and distribution, as well as moderation on the part of Japan in its focus and partnerships in networking for regional integration. Japan was extra careful about "not pushing through its own logic alone" (Kosugi 1986: 115).

A second aspect of the movement in the Pacific Basin cooperation was to connect Southeast Asia, or "developing East Asia," into this platform and networking. As shown in previous chapters, Japan's efforts at transborder production and distribution were driven primarily by the flying geese dynamics of industrial growth and economic development in East Asia. Internally, at the national level, Japan set up the Japan Export Trade Promotion Organization (JETRO) in 1956, the Export-Import Bank of Japan in 1959 containing the Fund for the Economic Development of Southeast Asia, and the Overseas Technical Cooperation Agency and the Overseas Economic Cooperation Fund in 1961. The Southeast Asia dimension in the development of production and distribution networks and connectivity was promoted and advanced through war reparation arrangements and official development aid programs. Japan established the Ministerial Conference for the Economic Development of Southeast Asian Countries in 1963. This eventually led to the establishment of the Asia Development Bank (ADB) in 1966.

The ADB was given a strong mandate to nurture a development partnership with a growing Asia, "with 31 members that came together to serve a predominantly agricultural region…and focused much of its assistance on food production and rural development" (ADB 2018). The ADB connects industrial capital to Southeast Asia, with both Japan and the United States each having 15.9 percent of the shareholdings and the nonborrowing members coming largely from Western Europe. This reflects Japan's extreme moderation in "pushing its own logic" and its political sensitivity to other parties in the broad membership composition.

Connecting to Southeast Asia is very important for Japan because the region is an important source of raw materials and markets for Japanese products. Much of the flying geese industrial dynamics operate in the development of production networks and value and supply chains between Japan and Southeast Asia countries. This was a politically secure and historically connected part of developing Asia for Japan. The United States was involved in significant strategic and political activities in Southeast Asia, and Southeast Asian nations were important Korean War and Vietnam War allies and partners for the United States, with ASEAN having been just established. Southeast Asia was an effective platform connecting and bridging Japanese and US industrial interests.

In 1977, then-Japanese Prime Minister Takeo Fukuda toured ASEAN countries and made a major policy speech about Japan-Southeast Asian relations – key points of which are now known as the Fukuda Doctrine. Prominently among the points are the "three pillars of Japan's policy with regard to Southeast Asia": "First, Japan, a nation committed to peace, rejects the role of a military power...Second, Japan, as a true friend of the countries of Southeast Asia, ... a "heart-to-heart" understanding with these countries...Third, Japan will be an equal partner of ASEAN and its member countries" (Fukuda 1977). As usual, official policy statements would often require some translation. The Fukuda Doctrine marked the end of Japan's relations with Southeast Asia dominated by Japan's military and imperialist expansion during the Pacific War or even in the larger historical context of the dominance of great powers in Southeast Asia. Japan would provide a positive alternative to promote development and security in the region. A key to that contribution is a partnership for development of the region in alliance with "like-minded outsiders." Both focuses on economic partnership and the political framework for the PBEC were visible.

Connecting Southeast Asia to Pacific economic cooperation brought the development element into ASEAN. The connection also made incorporation of Japanese and US industrial, financial, and trading interests and capabilities practically feasible. More importantly, it helped "reset" East Asian regionalization into Asia-Pacific regionalism, thawing the considerable resistance of ASEAN countries against the proposal by Australia for a formal platform for Pacific Rim economic cooperation. In 1989, 12 countries, 6 ASEAN countries and Japan, US, Australia, South Korea, NZ, and Canada, met to launch APEC, a clear "move forward" from Japan's original focus on East Asia and even from that of the Columbo Plan and ADB, with a wider Pacific focus, bringing production, distribution, and consumption together from the Pacific Rim countries.

"FUNERALS," "WEDDINGS," AND THE NOODLE BOWL

Douglas Webber, a political science professor at NSEAD's Asia Campus in Singapore, published a study in 2001, in which Webber described APEC and ASEAN as "the principal regional organizations in East Asia and Asia-Pacific." Webber observed, though, APEC and ASEAN were "'crisis-stricken', 'becalmed' or 'adrift'," and saw in East Asia "the emergence of a new, as yet embryonic, body, ASEAN Plus Three (APT), and ambitious projects implying closer integration between Northeast and Southeast Asia are being mooted" (Webber 2001: 339). It is not clear whether Webber saw the causes of the problems for APEC and ASEAN as being in the tension between economic integration and cooperation or between the East Asia focus and Asia-Pacific focus. The study, however, did convey a sense of where East Asian regionalism was at as the world entered the twenty-first century and a sense of ambiguity in the direction of further development of East Asian regionalism and the consequent anxiety among the nations over what East Asian regionalism was to achieve and where it would go from there.

The APEC project came into existence in 1989, riding on the global high tide of neoliberal political economy that dominated in key countries such as the United States and the United Kingdom in the 1980s and began to sweep the world in the 1990s. This was also a time for a very subtle political move by Japan to take Pacific Economic Cooperation a step further beyond its initial focus on East Asia. This mixture of intentions and interests of the driver nations planted seeds of tension and ambiguity in what APEC was to achieve and what East Asian regionalism was about.

APEC was set up as a kind of forum for government, business, and academic leaders to meet and discuss ways to "cooperate in economic growth" (APEC 2018). The initial 12-member body was extended, mainly in the 1990s, to include the Greater China Three in 1991: China, Taiwan, and Hong Kong; the Latin America Three: Mexico, Chile, and Peru; Russia and Vietnam in 1998, and Papua New Guinea in 1994. The intergovernmental dimension was significantly strengthened by US President Bill Clinton, who initiated a "summit meeting" of the heads of government of the member economies at the annual forum in the United States in 1993. The summit has since been institutionalized as an annual event within the APEC forum.

Moreover, an APEC secretary was established in Singapore to institutionalize APEC dialogue, exchange, and consultation. Finally, the long-term goals of APEC were also further articulated and formulated as being "to strengthen trade and investment liberalization in the region, and facilitating regional cooperation." These goals were formally and more concretely laid out at the annual 1994 forum in Bogor, Indonesia, which came to be known as the Bogor Goals. Bogor Goals were declared at the APEC Leader Summit in Bogor in 1994. In accordance with these goals, APEC members were committed to achieving free and open trade and investment by 2010 for industrialized economies and by 2020 for developing economies.

The shaping of APEC in the 1990s therefore resulted in the enlargement of East Asian regionalism. This added to the concern of ASEAN countries that they were brought into a large grouping of economies where asymmetry and disparity in national economic interests and capabilities dominated. The framework was evidently aimed more at economic growth than development. Trade and investment liberalization under this economic structure would turn APEC into a platform of economic integration between US superior industrial, financial, and trade capabilities and developing East Asia.

Some countries still embraced the idea of an East Asian community that connected Northeast and Southeast Asia in a developmental partnership. Their voice and interests were very much represented by the idea of an "East Asia FTA" that would include ASEAN 10 and Japan, China, and Korea. Malaysian Prime Minister Mahathir bin Mohamad proposed this idea in 1990 in the name of an East Asian Economic Group (EAEG) and again in 1997 in the name of the East Asia Economic Caucus (EAEC). The idea failed to receive support but elicited strong opposition from the United States, Australia, Japan, and Korea and faded away, eventually becoming a caucus within APEC.

Given the uncertain consequences of trade and investment liberalization, no members wanted to commit themselves to formal institutional constraints. "Annual summit meetings" and "forum" suit most countries and provide enough security as well as flexibility with the level of institutionalization of their interaction, exchange, decision-making, and dispute resolution. The 1990s witnessed the power of the APEC idea and its associated projects and the challenges the nations faced in advancing the idea and projects. APEC brought economic liberalization to the region and deep into each individual country through a series of programs of reform and standardization in the economic structure, administrative organization, currency, monetary, financial, and trade regimes, and macroeconomic policy of national governments. APEC was effective in pursuing its original purpose and agenda, and served the interests of the dominant players.

The 1997–8 financial crisis showed that APEC in its original spirit had inflicted significant "creative damage" to the existing economic and social infrastructure for economic and industrial organization. Regional watchers and national elites started to question the idea of trade and investment liberalization as the basis for regional community building and the role of the United States in this setup (Bowles 2002; Berger 1999). Globally the neoliberal movement of the 1990s met various forms of resistance from around the world. It pushed domestic politics back to the center-left in Europe and North America. But as an institution driven by a specific purpose, APEC had fulfilled its historical role. Institutional inertia has allowed it to continue to operate. But it no longer serves its original purpose and has become increasingly ambivalent in its focus, interests, and ways to move forward.

While APEC is a multilateral and multinational forum for regional cooperation in economic growth, ASEAN is a formal organization established among five Southeast Asian nations in 1967 – Indonesia, Malaysia, the Philippines, Singapore, and Thailand – when they signed the ASEAN Declaration in Bangkok. The founding ASEAN Five were able to form a regional organization among themselves as they responded to some specific challenges in Southeast Asia at the time. Tension and conflict built up among Indonesia, Malaysia, and the Philippines in the mid-1960s over the boundaries of nation and state in Sabah as the formation of Malaysia in 1961 claimed it as part of the new Malaysia. The spread of Communism from continental East Asia to Southeast Asia through war in Indochina and insurgent activities throughout Southeast Asia also posed an immediate threat to the newly established states in Southeast Asia. ASEAN was set up as a formal organization and as a platform for conflict reduction and collective security in the region. While there was general interest in social and economic development, "its core basis," as Amitav Acharya observed, "was the members' common concern with regime survival in the face of domestic and external threats, especially Communist subversion" (Acharya 2003: 379).

ASEAN was formed to provide a multilateral platform in which conflicts of this nature could be avoided or managed. The so-called soft nature of the new setup – "association" rather than "organization," decision-making through consensus, and intergovernmental cooperation rather than supranational integration – was a cautious move by the member states, given that a formal security organization, the Southeast Asia Treaty Organization (SEATO), had already been established and headquartered in Bangkok, with the participation of the US, Australia, and New Zealand. While SEATO was set up mainly to provide collective support for US involvement in the region, ASEAN initially aimed primarily at "internal" conflict management. There was no need for a "contractual" arrangement (Mattli 2012). In retrospect, ASEAN served the interests of those founding nations very well – the original disputes have never resurfaced to spark new tensions and open conflicts.

ASEAN was extended to cover all of whole Southeast Asia with the addition of Brunei in 1984 and Vietnam, Laos, Myanmar, and Cambodia in the 1990s as wars in Indochina winded down. Its role as an organization to promote economic growth and development in Southeast Asia became an increasingly more important focus from the 1980s, as regional economic and development activities picked up apace from the 1970s and ASEAN nations were brought into the framework and process of Pacific economic cooperation. To advance economic integration (within ASEAN itself), ASEAN declared the ASEAN Concord II in 2003 in Bali, Indonesia. It aimed to establish the ASEAN Community by 2020, including an ASEAN economic community. In 2007, a master plan was adopted for the establishment of the ASEAN economic community by 2015. The envisaged ASEAN economic community includes "a single market and production base, a highly competitive economic region, a region of equal economic development and a region integrated into the global economy."

On economic cooperation (with countries in the larger Asia-Pacific region), ASEAN gained great weight in the development of East Asian regionalism. As explained earlier, ASEAN countries were primary partners in Japan-led efforts at transborder development aid production networks in East Asia in the early decades and a core component in the PBEC. ASEAN was also an organized collective body itself with a set of collective interests and capabilities to influence the shaping of regional institutions and an economic community. This was at a time when continental East Asia and South Asia were very much closed and irrelevant to regional economic cooperation and when major economic forces in the region, that of Japan and the United States, and increasingly China, were in a different political position for leading East Asian regionalism. ASEAN's distinct interests evolved amid the tension between the Asia-Pacific framework and East Asian framework. ASEAN wanted to influence the shaping of regional institutions and protect and advance the industrial and economic development of the small, developing economies in the larger regional economic structure.

In practice, ASEAN countries have been at the center of the waves of efforts to build regional economic institutions, connecting them to Japan-dominated Northeast Asia in the 1960s through the 1980s, to the US-dominated Pacific region in the 1980s and 1990s, and, more recently, to a changing East Asia where China increasingly dominates. Institutionally, ASEAN has developed a set of collective interests, favored platforms for advancing these interests, and mechanisms for influencing the shaping of regional economic order. Amitav Acharya summarized the pattern of ASEAN practice in East Asian regionalism in a study published in 1997 as the "ASEAN way"–based "Asia-Pacific way." The Asia-Pacific way, according to Acharya, is an emergent pattern or style of multilateral institution building in the Asia-Pacific, a process informed by the four principles or ideas that derived from the experience of ASEAN development. These include "cooperative security, open regionalism, soft regionalism, and consensus" (Acharya 1997: 320). Acharya suggests that "a least the last two of these are integral features of the 'ASEAN way,'" – a consensual, cautious, and pragmatic "approach to dispute-settlement and regional cooperation developed by the members of ASEAN" (Acharya 1997: 328, see discussions of the ASEAN way in earlier chapters).

This "ASEAN way to Asia-Pacific way" thesis helps us to see the connection between the two processes of regional institution building and the role of ASEAN in them. ASEAN pursues "economic integration" within ASEAN and economic cooperation with countries in the larger East Asia. This split identity of ASEAN with regard to Southeast Asia and East Asia seems to complicate the role it plays in East Asian regionalism. Both the Asia-Pacific way and the ASEAN way are of a form of intergovernmental cooperation. This allowed ASEAN to exercise an influence over developing relations with countries in the larger East Asia region but did not work well for the countries of ASEAN to advance integration and community in ASEAN. The ASEAN way and the Asia-Pacific way are not the institutions for regional integration but institutions for economic cooperation. Moreover, ASEAN is significantly weak in its economic interests and capabilities in the larger East Asian economic structure. It accounts for 4.7 percent of the world's total GDP and 6.1 percent of all global exports in 2008 (Table 8.1). This makes it difficult for ASEAN to move things in East Asia at the intergovernmental level and limits what ASEAN can achieve in either East Asian regionalism or ASEAN community building.

As for the high expectations of East Asia in the 1980s and 1990s to form a single regional organization for economic community, the two major projects, APEC and ASEAN, have not produced the expected outcomes. APEC has caused quite a bit of confusion about the scope and purpose of East Asian regionalism, while ASEAN seemed unable to bring formal institutional influence to bear on the economic behavior of the principal players in East Asian regionalism. By the mid-2000s, there was a great sense of dissatisfaction over the progress of East Asian regionalism, great uncertainty over its future direction, and great anxiety over a fresh alternative to reset East Asian regionalism and strengthen leadership in moving the project forward.

While East Asian regionalism was searching for direction and leadership, countries were actively engaging in bilateral free trade agreements. A study for ADB by Richard Baldwin in 2007 found a massive and messy mushrooming of bilateral FTAs occurring in East Asia. By 2006, 75 FTAs had been signed or were under negotiation between ASEAN and ASEAN states, China, Japan, and Korea (Baldwin 2007: 5–6). The East Asian "noodle bowl syndrome" (Figure 8.2) reflects a global trend whereby nations sought bilateral or even unilateral methods in building a favorable institutional environment in the transborder organization of production and distribution. This trend developed quickly because countries were unable to make progress in multilateral institutions at the global level, for example, in WTO's Uruguay Round negotiations, and at the regional level in East Asia where confusions and uncertainties prevailed.

The noodle bowl syndrome is a pattern of complexity in the large number of multilayered, overlapping FTAs among East Asian countries, metaphorically designated as a sign of problems in East Asian regionalism. It suggests "East Asian regionalism is fragile" (Baldwin 2007: 3). This is a problem because of the significantly higher institutional costs in developing and implementing these agreements and the neutralizing effects of complex and overlapping bilateral FTAs in the shaping of a regional economic order.

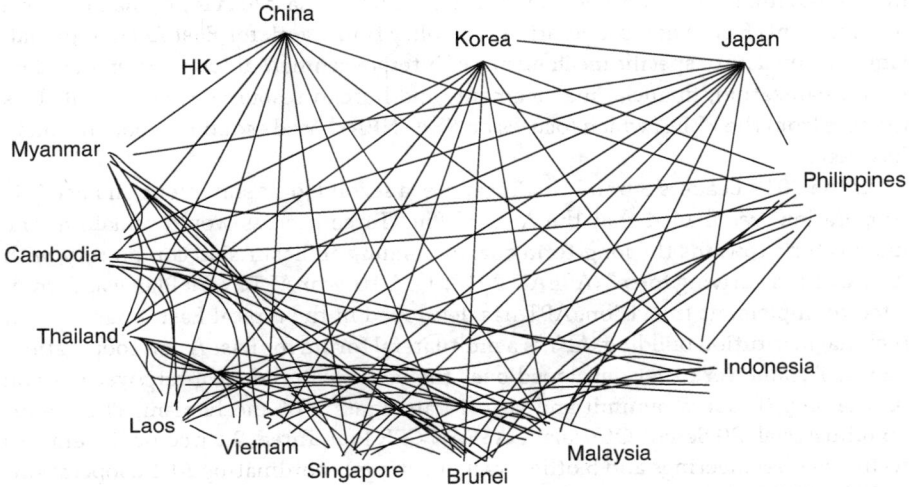

Figure 8.2 Baldwin's depiction of noodle bowl syndrome in East Asian regionalism
Graph Credit: Baldwin (2007: 5)

The noodle bowl syndrome is also seen in East Asian regionalism, in the massive number of proposals and projects, and the messy ways in which they relate to one another for a regional institution for East Asian economic cooperation and community. These proposals and projects feature a weak commitment of nations to formal constraints, ambiguity over the purpose of East Asian regionalism and tension over its scope and membership, and repeated failures to reach agreement on rules and standards for transborder industrial production and distribution – a problem we now turn to for further analysis.

APT, EAS, AND ASEAN CENTRALITY

The mushrooming of bilateral FTAs in East Asia also extended to multilateral institutions in the region. A series of new institutional platforms were proposed and hammered out in intensive intergovernmental interaction and negotiation for a region-wide organization of transborder production and distribution in East Asia. In 1997, leaders of ASEAN states and China, Japan, and ROK met in Malaysia for their first leaders summit. The ASEAN Plus Three (APT) summit was "institutionalized" (ASEAN 2018: 1) in 1999 with a joint declaration on East Asia cooperation. This declaration laid out the objectives of the APT and set up three key working mechanisms to support the framework. These included an East Asian business council on organizing transborder industrial development, Chang Mai initiatives for money and financial cooperation, and the HRD Fund in East Asia for human resource development. East Asian cooperation is a policy framework for East Asian regionalism that consists of specific mechanisms of intergovernmental cooperation in industrial organization, financial management, and human resource development. It is distinct from the PBEC, which focuses on SEA+NEA–based economic cooperation in East Asia.

At the 2018 Leaders Summit in Singapore, a second joint statement on East Asia cooperation "reaffirmed that the ASEAN Plus Three process would remain as the main vehicle towards the long-term goal of building an East Asian community, with ASEAN as the driving force" (ASEAN 2018: 1). A 10-year APT Work Plan was formulated to implement the vision. APT has developed in the typical East Asian style of regional institution building. APT is a multilateral forum for East Asian cooperation. The APT framework that developed over the years featured an intergovernmental partnership (Leaders' summit and vision statements), "65 mechanisms (1 summit, 16 ministerial, 20 Senior Officials, 1 ASEAN CPR Plus Three, 2 Director General, 20 technical level meetings and 5 other track meetings) coordinating APT cooperation" (ASEAN 2018: 1).

Conscious of the political significance of the APT in the larger context of tensions among different nations and subregions in East Asian regionalism, APT countries are cautious not to be seen as an alternative framework for East Asian regionalism. It aims to shape its vision, mechanisms, and institutions in an incremental, evolutionary, and informal fashion and calls the project "ASEAN Plus Three" and includes it as part of ASEAN external relations networks and partnerships, along with three separate ASEAN Plus One projects: ASEAN+China, ASEAN+Japan, and ASEAN+Korea.

In looking for paths forward for a more effective, inclusive, and appropriate institutional framework beyond APEC and ASEAN, ASEAN found itself in the "central" position among various alternatives, and competing or parallel proposals and ideas for a regional economic community. "ASEAN+" is a series of ASEAN-centered processes or networks of regional institution building, including ASEAN+1s (China, Japan, or Korea, as well as India, Russia, EU, Australia, New Zealand), ASEAN+3 (China, Japan and Korea), and ASEAN+6 (China, Japan, Korea, Australia, India, New Zealand). ASEAN centrality is the idea and a policy framework that ASEAN plays a central role in East Asian regionalism through a series of concentric networks of bilateral partnerships with ASEAN at the center. For watchers of East Asian regionalism, this suggests a leadership by ASEAN in moving and shaping East Asian regionalism. For ASEAN itself, it is a policy framework for ASEAN to build its external relations in a "hub-spokes" fashion. Further from there, the principle of ASEAN centrality suggests the importance of the interests and position of ASEAN as a collective body in the shaping of East Asian regionalism and a leadership of ASEAN in advancing East Asian regionalism.

ASEAN centrality motivated ASEAN to take concrete steps to build up an intergovernmental framework for organizing East Asian cooperation, from the basis that the APT process had built up. The East Asian Vision Group (EAVG), of "eminent intellectuals" of the APT states established by APT in 1998, recommended, in its final report in 2001, "the evolution of the annual summit meetings of ASEAN plus Three into the East Asian Summit (EAS)" and envisioned "East Asia as evolving from a region of nations to a *bona fide* regional community" (EAVG 2001: 13). In response, the East Asian Study Group (EASG), composed of government officials of APT states and established also by APT in 2001, concluded that "as a long-term desirable objective of the ASEAN+3, the EAS will serve to strengthen East Asian cooperation," and the ASEAN+3 framework remains the only credible and realistic vehicle to advance the form and substance of regional cooperation in East Asia" (EASG 2002: 13).

Leaders of APT states and India, Australia, and New Zealand met for the first time at the East Asian Summit in Malaysia in 2005. From the very beginning, APT debated which countries should be included in the EAS. At issue was whether EAS should include India, Australia, New Zealand, Russia, or the United States. While ASEAN was interested to have an East Asian focus for the new initiative, it also wanted to have a comfort level among APT states for "the broadest level of acceptance" of this EAS that requires "an evolutionary and step-by-step process" (EASG 2002: 6). The 2010 summit formally invited Russia and the US to join the forum.

The membership issue further reveals the underlying tensions over what the EAS is or how we go about building it. The point of contention is whether the EAS is the conduit or platform for the building of an East Asian community or just one of the multilateral, intergovernmental frameworks for East Asian cooperation. More pointedly, a central issue whether it is the role of APT or EAS to lead the building of an East Asian community and organize East Asian cooperation and whether EAS is a step further from APT in the development of East Asian regionalism or an ASEAN-centered process. These issues have not been resolved and continue to complicate the development of the EAS. The EAS has made little real progress beyond being just a summit and a forum since its creation.

TPP, RCEP, AND BIFURCATION OF A REGION?

The difficulties and complications in forging a pan-East Asian regional economic community also motivated states to seek subregional multilateral grouping for economic cooperation and production networking. Some small states are particularly motivated because they are unable to have their interests recognized in the larger multilateral arrangements or bilateral negotiations where the large economic and industrial powers dominate. These subregional groupings are of nations for trade cooperation, and their scope is smaller than that of either the Asia-Pacific or East Asian region. Some of them progressed to a formal treaty bloc, others remain an elusive idea.

Several subregional trade and industrial groupings were attempted in the 1990s and 2000s, as illustrated in Figure 8.3. An early one was the idea of a greater China

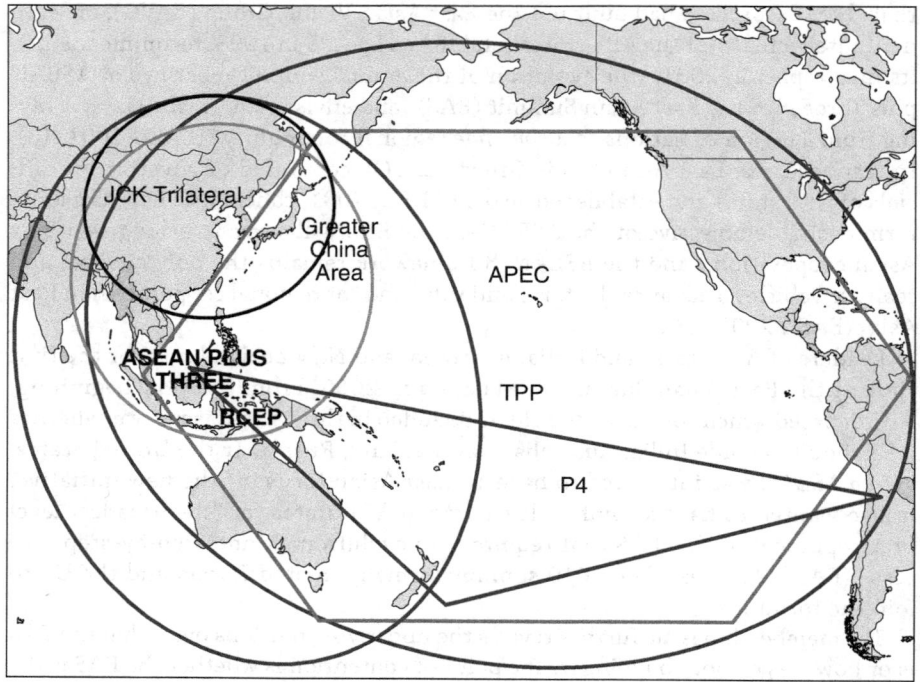

Figure 8.3 In search of a region: a "noodle bowl" of multinational economic institutions in East Asia

area that included China, Hong Kong, and Taiwan. As ties and networks in production and distribution between Taiwan, Hong Kong, and China increased in the 1990s, there was great interest and speculation in the possibility of the area forming multilateral, integrative networks and partnerships in production and distribution in the quite busy space of East Asian regionalism. The idea of a greater China area for industrial integration did not make much progress given the significant political issue between China and Taiwan and the fact that China was preoccupied with the larger Asia-Pacific engagement at that time. The framework that eventually prevailed in the area was a set of bilateral arrangements. China and Hong Kong arranged a Closer Economic Partnership Arrangement (CEPA) in 2003. China and Taiwan reached an agreement on an Economic Cooperation Framework Agreement (ECFA). These are in practice a preferential trade agreement (PTA), not a free trade agreement.

A second subregional trade grouping was among Japan, China, and Korea, or JCK. These three represent the largest economies in East Asia. China and Japan were the second and third largest economies in the world in 2018. These three, as shown in the previous chapter, are the leading "geese" in East Asian growth, with substantive production networks and partnerships, and value and supply chains developed among them. There are always material and political interests to determine whether and how the three countries can join hands for a form of East Asian regionalism.

In 2008, the first summit of leaders of the three countries was held in Fukuoka, and the trilateral summit was "institutionalized" as an annual meeting alongside the ASEAN Plus Three meeting. In 2011, a permanent operating facility, the Trilateral Cooperation Secretariat, was established in Seoul. Progress in institutionalizing JCK cooperation was significantly influenced by the political climate of the time. The idea was effectively pushed by South Korean President Roh Moo-hyun. President Roh had a strong conviction of the leadership role of Korea in East Asia, as a so-called East Asian balancer (Pastreich 2005). The mid-2000s was also a time when Yukio Hatoyama, then Prime Minister of Japan, dominated Japan's political scene, and he is a strong believer in East Asian integration and East Asia as a priority in Japan's foreign policy. The initiative also came at a time when East Asian regionalism was looking for direction, focus, and leadership.

A third subregional grouping was an FTA area between ASEAN and China, Korea, and Japan. China signed the framework agreement for an FTA with ASEAN in 2002. Japan and ASEAN signed their framework agreement in 2003. Korea and ASEAN states signed the framework agreement for an FTA area in 2005. These are all trade grouping agreements with multiple bilateral arrangements under one large web of bilateral frameworks centered around ASEAN.

While the various mega regional frameworks were trying their luck, Singapore, New Zealand, Brunei, and Chile joined hands to form an FTA group, the Trans-Pacific Strategic Partnership (TPSP), in 2005. The four countries are referred to as P4 in subsequent discussions. Given the earlier ineffective experiences of building mega "regional" institutions pushed by large industrial powers, this was a clear, simple, and doable project. Whether it was intended or not, the framework also gave small countries the collective power they needed to advance their interests in larger multinational platforms or in their bilateral relations with major powers. This successful project was quickly and opportunely picked up by others, notably the United States.

TPSP was a simple though comprehensive intergovernmental arrangement for trade facilitation and regulation among the small states in the southern Pacific Rim. The agreement covered rules of origin, intellectual property rights, government procurement, and competition. But it was not a framework intended for economic integration based on integrative industrial dynamics in transborder production and distribution. TPSP removed the political factor of the need for an integrative framework. This need in many other initiatives of East Asia regionalism contained a polarizing requirement in membership and geopolitical and geoeconomic connectivity on projects. On the other hand, TPSP is an arrangement for Pacific economic cooperation among a smaller number of small countries.

The Trans-Pacific Partnership (TPP) was proposed to build on the extension of the P4 project. The emergence of TPP thus has been a "bottom-up" process. It is bottom-up also because it reflects a bit more closely the economic conditions in the area both in terms of an economic community for multilateral institutions and the distribution of economic interests and capacities required for the proposed arrangements to work. To the extent it has evolved so far, including 11 countries now, one can still see this as being relatively smaller in scope and much more doable. The rise of TPP reflects a striking element of shift in regional economic structures and the politics of

East Asian regionalism. This shift indicated that continental East Asia and maritime East Asia may have to be treated separately in building regional economic institutions. The two collectively bring in distinct and different sets of economic interests, activities, and capabilities. Earlier efforts often mismatched the two in their role and position in East Asian regionalism. TPP therefore raised a question about the original visions of a regional institution for East Asia.

The problem of the scope and purpose of East Asian regionalism complicated the TPP project from the very beginning as the United States started to show interest in engaging with this platform. The United States moved beyond a phase of ambiguity over its approach to East Asian regionalism in the mid-2000s. This reflected its initial reactions to APT and EAS. The rolling out of its so-called Pivot to Asia after President Obama took office in 2009 provided a strategic opportunity and an operational framework for Washington to take up leadership in East Asian regionalism.

Obama declared in his Suntory Hall speech (Obama 2009) in Tokyo in 2009 that the United States is "an Asia-Pacific nation" and is at "a moment of renewal in this land of miracles." This renewal entailed a "reengagement" with the Asia-Pacific through multilateral organizations that "can advance the security and prosperity of this region." In 2011, US Secretary of State Hillary Clinton declared in her Pivot to Asia speech (Clinton 2011) that "the United States stands at a pivot point" and called on the government "to lock in a substantially increased investment – diplomatic, economic, strategic, and otherwise – in the Asia-Pacific region" in the next 10 years. As part of this, the US "has moved to fully engage the region's multilateral institutions" and "will participate in the East Asia Summit for the first time and we have worked hard to create and launch a number of 'minilateral' meetings, small groupings of interested states to tackle specific challenges."

There has been debate over the nature and effectiveness of this grand strategy. A more recent assessment by Kurt M. Campbell and Ely Ratner (Campbell & Ratner 2018) reflects on this grand strategy as part of the larger US approach of engagement in East Asia. According to these researchers, the approach has not been effective. But the great enthusiasm reflected in this pivot to Asia for US leadership in multilateral institutions in East Asia drove much of the reset of TPSP to TPP. Much of the controversies in TPP negotiation and engagement involved the challenge of whether and how to include Japan, Vietnam, and China in the grouping. On the surface, the challenge over the membership of Japan, Vietnam, or China arose for different reasons, but in the context of the historical evolution of East Asian regionalism, they all concerned one of the central questions regarding the scope of East Asian regionalism.

Bringing NEA into TPP inevitably drove the TPP project back to where it started – the new project may just end up replicating either APEC or EAS. Great domestic political determination emerged in Japan and Vietnam, who wished to be part of the TPP, while China found the project dubious. Discussions about TPP overwhelmingly framed it as a strategic plan to contain China. TPP negotiations finally settled on having 12 founding members. The TPP agreement was signed in 2016 as a "twenty-first century, high-quality agreement" that sets "new and high standards for trade and investment in the Asia Pacific" and is "an important step toward our ultimate goal of open trade and regional integration across the region" (TPP 2015: 1).

These developments influenced the movement of another group of East Asian economies to form the Regional Comprehensive Economic Partnership (RCEP) that includes ASEAN+6 countries. The RCEP, under negotiation since 2012, was motivated largely by two immediate factors. First, the RCEP is in fact a step forward from the ASEAN Plus processes, not an original plan. The parties to the negotiation process are the same ones that participated in ASEAN Plus Six, except one of the six is India rather than Russia. It is in some way a new attempt at the East Asian vision. Second, the RCEP is clearly influenced by the shaping of the TPP. The ASEAN Plus processes were not able to move forward in the mid-2000s largely over the uncertainties over the direction of the further development of East Asian regionalism. It was uncertain as to whether the new East Asian Summit would include the United States (and Australia and New Zealand) on the one hand, and India and Russia on the other. The launch of the TPP removed that concern.

The RCEP is influenced by the TPP also in the nature and quality of the arrangements being negotiated. Under pressure from the TPP, the RCEP committed to achieving "a modern, comprehensive, high-quality and mutually beneficial economic partnership agreement" (RCEP 2012). In other words, the RCEP and TPP are more than an FTA in a conventional sense. They aim to develop "a workable high-quality template for regional integration" – rather than simply seeking "immediate gains from trade" (Petri et al. 2011: 4). As Peter A. Petri, Michael G. Plummer, and Fan Zhai observed, the TPP "would cover issues ... such as services, investment, competition, and regulatory coherence. These issues are widely seen as crucial for the next wave of economic integration" (Petri et al. 2011: 4).

The RCEP and TPP therefore have inherited a key feature of previous projects of East Asian regionalism. They are projects and frameworks for an FTA area but also platforms for deeper economic integration. The difficulties in the membership of these two illustrate this further. For an FTA area, it surprises no one that Vietnam, Singapore, Chile, Brunei, and New Zealand seek trade liberalization with, for example, the US and Japan. But for economic integration, either to advance the interests and influence of national economies in the area or to build a genuine, coherent single market, do these countries constitute an economic community, or could they potentially?

As summarized in Table 8.2, the problem of the tension in the purpose and scope of the multilateral institutions led to their ineffectiveness in the past, in either developing an FTA area or promoting economic integration. Mixing the purposes without a clearly defined economic rationale or material foundation increases the costs for institutional commitment. As shown in these two cases, a simple commitment to an FTA area would have to come with a more costly commitment to broad economic obligations for an economic community and potentially a single market. On the other hand, the broad economic commitment to regional integration lacks the support of a clearly defined economic community in which parties can absorb the cost and access benefits of their commitment according to their position in the economic community.

Table 8.2 Institutions of East Asian regionalism

EARI projects	YFIL	YOAE	Members at YFIL	Collective GDP in world total at YFIL (%)	Mission/purpose
Asian Development Bank (ADB)	1966	1966	31 countries with global developed economies and Asian developing economies	66	Development aid in Asia
Pacific Basin Economic Council (PBEC)	1968	1968	Australia, Canada, Japan, New Zealand, United States	42	Pacific cooperation
Asia-Pacific Economic Cooperation (APEC)	1989	1989	12 select Asia-Pacific Rim economies	41	Trade and investment liberalization
ASEAN Plus Three (APT)	1999		13, ASEAN members and Japan, Korea and China	17	East Asian cooperation and integration
East Asian Summit (EAS)	2005	2005	16, ASEAN plus six, Japan, China, Korea, Australia, New Zealand, India	31	East Asian political, economic community
ASEAN Community	2008	2015	10 ASEAN countries	5	Political-security, economic, and socio-cultural community
Trans-Pacific Partnership (TPP)	2008	2016	12 select Asia-Pacific countries	31	Modern, comprehensive, high-quality trade agreement
Regional Comprehensive Economic Partnership (RCEP)	2012		16, APT 13 plus India, Australia, New Zealand	34	Modern, comprehensive, high-quality trade agreement
Asian Infrastructure Investment Bank (AIIB)	2014	2015	56, founding prospective members (regional and nonregional)	64	Multilateral development financing

YFIL - Year of formal initiative launch
YOAE - Year of agreement/establishment

Table 8.2 contains a long list of initiatives for East Asian regionalism proposed in the past 30 years. Many of them are still in the stage of "institutionalizing" their efforts to reach an agreement on a regional arrangement, years after their initial launch. Some have never made it past the stage of "sounding the idea," and others died out on the way. Those surviving in the field are intended to do similar things, only with a slightly different configuration of membership. Many countries have conflicting, overlapping memberships to many of these frameworks. This has made their institutional commitment to any of these frameworks politically challenging. These are all signs of the problem of "noodle bowling" in East Asian regionalism.

At a deeper level, the two large multilateral regional frameworks emerged recently out of dissatisfaction over the progress of East Asian regionalism in the early 2000s. Their emergence suggests that political solutions to regional economic cooperation have prevailed and points to the difficulty of organizing many countries of diverse economic interests and capacities in a single institutional framework for an agreed purpose. More uniquely in East Asia, there are also differences among these countries arising from their different levels of economic development and various national systems of organizing production and distribution. Institutionalizing their economic cooperation in the two smaller groups seems to be an expedient way to confront tensions. But the problem of different agendas for economic growth and development among developed and developing Asia remains in East Asian regionalism – a problem that previous regional frameworks, such as APEC and ADB, were designed to deal with.

The political nature of East Asian regionalism was further demonstrated in the subsequent developments with the TPP and RCEP. The US Pivot to Asia gave great momentum for the TPP to take shape. The change in the US's overall approach to the region, with President Trump's more unilateral and bilateral approach to international economic relations, has not led to the derailment of the TPP, as many expected. The TPP nations without the United States updated the original agreement into a new Comprehensive and Progressive Agreement for Trans-Pacific Partnership (CPTPP) in 2018. In the meantime, the RCEP is still under negotiation as of early 2019. The two frameworks seem to have lost much of their momentum initially seen in moving East Asian regionalism forward. There is no longer discussion of whether they are the "pathway" to an ultimate regional arrangement for economic integration or for a pan-Asia-Pacific FTA. Would these two frameworks possibly end up being one of those in the "varieties" of East Asian regionalism and instances of the noodle bowl? Or are they really to be the "building blocks" of a truly East Asian economic community?

PRINCIPAL MOVERS AND SHAPERS

The evolution of East Asian regionalism has shown that the shaping of multilateral institutions for regional economic cooperation is deeply influenced by the interests and capabilities, as well the strategy and methods, of the principal nations in the process. Key to this significant set of enabling and constraining effects is the fact that these nations, Japan, ASEAN nations, China, and the United States, are at different stages of economic development and have grown through the different methods of organizing production and distribution that were most effective and appropriate for them at the historical point of their modern economic development. Japan evolved from a latecomer industrial power into a developed, postindustrial society. The United States is a hegemonic industrial and economic power. China has been building its global industrial power for several decades. Japan, China, and ASEAN countries have been leading the waves of East Asian growth. Some of the ASEAN nations have moved up from a developing to an industrial and to a developed, postindustrial economy. Others remain at the lower ends of the development ladder. These conditions underlie their unique interest and capability in East Asian regionalism and shape their different agendas and strategies in arranging transborder economic cooperation and integration in East Asia.

The first principal mover and shaper in East Asian regionalism is the United States. Discussions on what defines East Asian regionalism attribute the open, soft, and noodle bowl regionalism in East Asia to the tension between external and regional interests and dynamics, an Asia-Pacific and East Asian focus, and, more specifically, the impact of US interests, agenda, and strategy. Takashi Terada, for example, discusses the "inclusion-exclusion logic" in East Asian regionalism that poses a particular dilemma for US policy and strategy in East Asian regionalism (Terada 2011). The inclusion-exclusion logic in East Asian regionalism produces a double-edged effect on the United States: the boundary setting of an East Asian region would exclude the US as an outsider while the development of institutions in East Asia in the twentieth century has involved a significant US contribution and leadership.

The constant anxiety of the United States over being excluded or becoming irrelevant to East Asian regionalism has led the United States to be extremely sensitive to any potential multilateral frameworks that focus exclusively on East Asia and the political and economic interests and intentions behind them. This strategic and historical concern influenced US strategy in approaching East Asian regionalism and has influenced Washington to rely on trusted bilateral alliances, ones with Japan, Singapore, and Australia in particular, and prefer "a network of multiple overlapping institutions" over "a single, more coherent body" (Gannon 2011: 37). This line of US policy and strategy as driven by the inclusive-exclusive logic highlights the global nature of international economic relations and activities. It has profoundly influenced East Asian regionalism and the impact of US interests, agenda, and strategy on the international economic order in East Asia.

Earlier we discussed how Reaganomics and the Washington Consensus in the 1980s and 1990s moved the US to engage with East Asia more actively. Key to this strategic vision was to have a Pacific Rim–based multilateral institutional arrangement. APEC in 1989 was a primary project to structure transborder production and distribution with East Asia and to build global values and supply chains on the basis of the industrial, financial, and trading interests and capabilities of the US and Japan.

Under this framework, there has been significant growth in the industrial alliance between the US and Japan in production networks with East Asia. The latter resulted in a global shift of manufacturing activities and financial and technology

Table 8.3 Weight of major economies' FDI outflows to East Asia (2009–2017) (%)

	2009	2010	2011	2012	2013	2014	2015	2016
US	7.7	8.2	7.7	7.5	7.8	8.2	8.4	7.8
China	88.0	85.0	80.3	78.4	80.5	76.8	75.0	70.3
Japan	32.1	33.7	31.8	32.3	35.5	35.6	34.0	31.0

Data source: IMF-CIDS (2018)
FDI outflows of US, China, and Japan to East Asia as shares of their total of world outflows

Table 8.4 Weight of major economies' exports to East Asia (1980–2017) (%)

	1980	1985	1990	1995	2000	2005	2010	2017
China	54.9	60.6	67.2	57.7	48.5	41.8	36.7	37.5
Japan	26.4	24.5	29.8	42.5	40.4	47.5	54.5	52.8
US	20.6	22.5	26.8	30.0	25.0	23.6	24.6	25.3
Germany	3.9	5.1	6.7	9.9	7.8	8.0	11.2	12.9
World	14.1	14.9	17.6	23.0	21.6	22.7	26.4	28.0

Data Source: IMF-DOTS (2018)
Economies' exports to East Asia as share of their global totals

capabilities and the "substantive economy" of the United States, to East Asia, as seen in Tables 8.3 and 8.4. The substantive economy (实体经济) is the traditional economy in manufacturing and construction as distinct from the financial economy.

The substantive economy usually comprises industrial and enterprise activities in manufacturing, agriculture, and services. It not only produces consumer products but, in doing so, contributes to growth in employment, income, and social welfare, as well as advances in technology, productivity, capital accumulation, and trade relations. This is part of a profound global shift that led to a deep sense in Washington of "global structural imbalance" (Little 2008; Blecker 2012; Ezell & Atkinson 2011; White House 2013). APEC has facilitated trade and investment liberalization and therefore contributed to economic growth and prosperity in East Asia. It has also contributed to the erosion of competitiveness of the substantive economy of the United States and to social and economic tensions arising in US society.

However, the reset adopted in the Pivot to Asia in the early 2010s was partly to address this imbalance. As far as international economic relations are concerned, though, the reset was largely a reinforcement of existing institutions to spur competitors to cooperate and of preferential trade arrangements to enhance US economic competitiveness. This in some way exacerbated the problems in East Asian regionalism and certainly led to a failure to deal with the root problems in US industrial and economic competitiveness. The new international economic policy and strategy of US President Trump, still unfolding, reflects a conservative view deeply rooted in American society and the business community over the US's international economic position and interests, and how to advance them, a reflection of worldview based on classical realism in international relations.

Unlike advocates of liberal institutionalism, Trump sees China, Japan, and Korea as real competitors rather than potential collaborators. He does not believe regional multilateral institutions are effective or useful, but only economic costs and benefits can move China, Japan, and others to the negotiating table to shape an international economic order for the United States. Moreover, dealing with China and Japan is only part of Trump's vision of a global international economic order where regions would not feature as significantly as in the past. Trump's ideal of a world economic order still faces challenges and opposition inside and outside the United States, but the unilateralism mixed with bilateralism that has emerged in his early strategic moves certainly has had a reset effect on East Asian regionalism.

Japan has been a key player in East Asian regionalism. As shown earlier, Japan has been a principal driver of East Asian regionalism, with a very subtle, politically sensible working style that continues to shape its interests, vision, and strategy in East Asian regionalism. Japan's rapid economic growth in the 1950s to 1970s was built on a growth model that combined different growth factors – capital, production, consumption – across national boundaries in a larger economic platform: finance and manufacturing in Japan and markets and consumption outside Japan.

The change in the international economic environment in the 1980s complicated the working of this growth model for Japan. The Plaza Agreement in 1985 was an agreement between the US, France, Germany, the UK, and Japan on the depreciation of the US dollar vis-à-vis the Japanese yen. This arrangement significantly altered Japan's relations with the international economic system and influenced the path of Japan's further development and the shaping of the liberal international order in the 1990s and beyond. Along with the currency arrangement, special trade rules were arranged with the United States, such as voluntary export restraints in the 1980s. The "structural impediments initiatives" that grew out of the debate on globalization and regionalization in 1989/90 were part of the pressures put on Japan to be more open to imports and shift its manufacturing capacity and investment capital to the United States. These contributed to the growth of the industrial alliance for the Pacific framework in East Asian regionalism.

While international arrangements and developments had not supported economic structural reform necessary for Japan at this stage of its development, much of the accumulated capital instead flooded into real estate and finance, rather than being reinvested in the substantive economy. The institutional setting that had facilitated the organization and promotion of its rapid economic growth in the early decades started to fall apart. In this "regime shift" (Pempel 1998), Liberal Democratic Party (LDP) dominance and the state-business alliance for economic growth broke down. The new electoral system, Mixed Member Proportional (MMP), introduced in 1993, institutionalized coalition politics and party politics, which made it very difficult if not impossible to formulate a coherent economic policy and growth strategy. The 1990s became a "lost decade" for Japan – in terms of economic growth – with another lost decade to follow in the 2000s. Japan's normal GDP in 2013 was at the same level as in 1991.

Abenomics was intended to address this, in a quite interesting way, and to revitalize the Japanese economy. The monetary and fiscal components, including a stimulus package and the mechanism of radical quantitative easing, and the expansion of public spending were all designed to "inflate" the economy. These policies reflect a largely Keynesian-inspired, consumption-driven, macroeconomic-policy-based growth strategy. They are easy to implement and quick to take effect. The structural reform part, to increase the birth rate, reduce corporate tax, and introduce competition in the agricultural sector, has taken time to roll out. More importantly, there was a great push for significant institutional reform in the party system and government institutions, particularly in parliamentary organization and structure, to deal with the structural issues in state institutions following the collapse of the LDP dominance in Japanese politics in the early 1990s and to bring back effective leadership in national politics and policy.

The 1990s also marked a significant development in Japan's overall international posture, seeking to upgrade the Japan-US alliance as the core foundation of Japan's international policy and relations. With the further efforts of Prime Minister Junichiro Koizumi and Prime Minister Shinzo Abe in the 2000s and 2010s, Japan has transformed itself into a more active, determined, and confident international actor, and a strong ally and an effective strategic partner with the United States in East Asia. This has enabled Japan to continue to play a leading role in East Asian regionalism, participating in all frameworks proposed, and lead the efforts in the TPP, and the Indo-Pacific initiative. Japan's vision of the region based on a Japan-US strategic and industrial partnership limits Japan's ability to invest in the "East Asian" regional integration that has driven Japan's strategy and activities in East Asia for much of the twentieth century.

China in the 2010s in many ways is like Japan in the 1980s when its rapid economic growth reached a point where the structural conditions that made the rapid economic growth in the past 30 years possible started to lose their effectiveness. China's growth rate fell below 8 percent as it entered the 2010s, indicating an end to its rapid industrial growth and economic development. The growth conditions that supported its model of growth organization and promotion – export driven, FDI led, with domestic consumption long underdeveloped – have changed significantly. China's production capability greatly exceeds what its exports can absorb. It has more capital accumulation that, as in the case of Japan in the 1980s, does not all go toward investments in the substantive economy. A new growth basis is needed.

Deeper structural reforms announced by the ruling Communist Party at its 18th Party Congress in 2012 laid out a long list of initiatives for structural rebalancing and growth strategy adjustment. As a strategy for economic growth, the reform program essentially called for promoting consumption (versus export and investment) as an important source of growth and a more balanced growth for broader economic and social benefits – tax reform to close up income gaps among different income groups, urbanization for urban-rural integration, and further reform in state-market relations for more competition and better regulation, for example. At the policy and strategy levels, preference for structural reform over monetary and fiscal stimulus policy is clear. China tried fiscal and monetary stimulus policies and "quantitative easing" of its own in recent years, but more comprehensive structural reform programs were introduced to deal with the problems at a deeper level. To stimulate domestic consumption, for example, reform programs seek a more even distribution of income so that greater purchasing power would be available to generate growth. Urbanization programs were also designed to ease labor and other cost pressures on growth and enhance the consumption capacity of the wider society.

Like Japan in the 1980s, China is largely a manufacturing superpower. The expansion of domestic consumption itself would not be sufficient or quick enough to absorb excessive capital and production capacity and reduce employment and income pressures. Moreover, China is part of the flying geese industrial diffusion in East Asia. As China rises to the position of an industrial, financial, and trade power itself, its industrial capital will seek to organize its production and distribution across borders in East Asia. China has been the largest recipient of FDI for a long time and has had significant experience in organizing and promoting FDI in other countries.

As in the case of Japan, these dynamics of industrial development will motivate China to look for some forms of division of labor and effective mechanisms in organizing transborder production and distribution. In 2013, China devised a giant initiative, the BRI, to support and enable Chinese enterprises to engage in transborder projects in other countries. It aims to organize transborder industrial production and services. The economic rise of China and the form it takes for transborder industrial production have enabled China to be more effective and influential in East Asian regionalism. It has also added significant new dynamics to East Asian regionalism, affecting the scope and purpose as well as frameworks for East Asian regionalism. Chinese economic interest and relations are global rather than East Asia oriented. Its economic relations with the United States and Japan are increasingly more competitive than complementary.

Finally, there is ASEAN. Southeast Asia was a critical "nod" in the networks of East Asian regionalism. ASEAN emerged as a collective actor in East Asian regionalism while "diversity" among ASEAN states complicated those countries' serious attempts to integrate as a unitary actor. More importantly, their industrial interests and capabilities are relatively limited compared to other major players in East Asian regionalism. This limits ASEAN's ability to influence East Asian regionalism as a collective actor. Partly addressing this, starting in the 1990s, ASEAN has been working on forming a solid, effective regional entity and identity. ASEAN is often cited as one of the unique "instances" of how institutions, ideas, and norms can help develop a collective identity in supporting itself as a regional trade and economic community. But the splitting of a pan-regional framework into several "minilateral" groupings also separates ASEAN states from each other. This continues to make it difficult for the countries of ASEAN to have a collective interest in ASEAN, much less a collective strategy in pursing East Asian regionalism.

This, however, has not prevented ASEAN from developing "bilateral" trade partnerships with countries or groups of countries. Besides the initial three ASEAN+1s, ASEAN also started an FTA with Australia and New Zealand, AANZFTA; and with India, AIFAT, in 2010. There is no evidence that this has been a strategy or vision of ASEAN for a multilateral framework for East Asian regionalism. It has just turned out that way. But it is a pattern of ASEAN-centered bilateral processes in East Asian regionalism. The bilateralism shown here suggests the classic tension between bilateralism and multilateralism in the shaping of a regional economic order. Bilateralism is favored not only by great powers but also by smaller economies, or perhaps a collection of smaller economies.

This mixture of bilateralism and multilateralism also matches with the overall trend in the international system whereby states increasingly fall back on bilateralism or even unilateralism in international political economy. Politics among many countries with diverse interests and capabilities in agreeing on a trade and transborder production arrangement is difficult. For East Asian regionalism, a single regional institution is always only an option rather than the ultimate purpose, as many have advocated. For ASEAN, it is a matter of being realistic and practical in terms of where it can achieve a cooperative economic partnership. The ASEAN organization here is somewhere between a unitary body and a group of nations. Unitary-state-based terms, like bilateral or multilateral, may not be sophisticated enough to capture the nuance of ASEAN's relations with other countries in East Asian regionalism.

This survey of the strategic interests and methods of key players in East Asian regionalism suggests that each major player has a strategy, or there is a pattern in their activities in East Asian regionalism. Each takes a bilateral approach with other parties in East Asian regionalism and has developed a hub-spokes web of partnerships, with itself at the hub. These activities are necessarily focused on or confined to "East Asia." These countries' trade and economic interests and relations, particularly those of Japan, the United States, and China, are global rather than regional, certainly not East Asia directed. Their industrial interests, capabilities, and relations may focus initially on East Asia. They are primarily driven by the logic of industrial growth in a capitalist market system, rather than preconceived notions of the region. They are structurally global. The countries are the leaders of the recent waves of globalization in the world economic system, and cannot and will not confine their industrial activity to East Asia in a closed regional community. This helps explain that market forces, represented by these major players in transborder industrial production and distribution, rather than institutional design for an East Asian economic community, has greater influence on the direction and character of East Asian regionalism – a point we now turn to in the concluding part of this chapter.

MULTILATERAL INSTITUTIONS OF ECONOMIC REGIONALISM

This chapter has discussed the development of regional economic institutions to shed light on the direction and pattern of East Asian regionalism. Behind the intensive forces that drive East Asian regionalism is politics, or, more precisely, international politics. The political nature of East Asian regionalism has a lot to do with what regional institutions are and what they are intended for. This chapter has shown that the institutions discussed in connection with East Asian regionalism fall into two different categories and concern two different aspects of East Asian regionalism. First, institutions are a system of rules that member states agree on for regulating and managing their activities in transborder production and distribution. These are the rules in the agreements the states sign on to.

Second, institutions are patterns of repeated instances of desirable and appropriate actions and activities of states in developing an agreement on the rules in the first category. The former are of institutions in the sense in which new institutionalists, such as Douglass North, use it. These rules are intended to influence the behavior of economic actors in trade and transborder production organization. The latter are more of a process in which the behavior of the states in agenda setting, negotiation, and agreement on the rules repeat and evolve. These behaviors are "institutionalized" to build trust among the states and develop their confidence about their relations and commitment to the rules. Forums, leaders summits, tripartite engagement and consultation with policy, business, and academic elites, and track 1, track 2, and track 1.5 dialogues, represent critical mechanisms for this institutionalization. Institutions in this sense concern forms of East Asian regionalism. These mechanisms of institutionalization, which are prevalent in East Asian regionalism, are sources of the soft and informal regionalism found in East Asia.

In both cases, politics is critical. In the first instance, institutions are effective only when they bring overall benefits to participants. The interests and conditions of the member states vary widely, as in the case of East Asian regionalism. This requires member states to use significant state authority in the national setting to balance and facilitate trade-offs among different interests of national industries, sectors, and enterprises and back up enforcement of multilateral rules. These institutions, therefore, are not simply trade or business rules; they are political solutions to the problem of transborder economic order and the collective action of the states.

Second, rules for a given area of economic relations often form in a larger material and institutional environment. Countries' reactions to institutional change and economic order can come to influence the final shape of the institutions. In a hierarchical and asymmetrical economic structure as in the case of East Asian regionalism, informal mechanisms, such as forums, summits, and multiple and competitive frameworks, platforms, and incremental, piecemeal, ad hoc processes are all part of the building blocks of a final agreement. More often than not, this complex, multilayered political context adds significant transaction costs and calculation burdens in rule making and weakens states' ability to reach an agreement on the final set of rules. This requires even more political capital and leadership of the states to sustain the process.

Third, states have different interests and capacities in relation to East Asia economically. Major industrial powers have significant global trade and industrial interests and relations. Others are largely marginalized in the prevailing structure of industrial production and distribution, and aim to enhance their position given the multilateral constraints and their influence in the negotiation of these constraints. How these different countries are made to commit to the rules of the game and a code of conduct for transborder industrial production and distribution in East Asia is to a large degree a political exercise. The complexities of the situation increase as more states become involved.

That politics influences or even determines the direction and character of regionalism is nothing new and is certainly not exclusive to East Asia. Different experiences of regional institution building in Europe, North America, and East Asia show that politics is particularly heavy-handed in East Asian regionalism. Politics has influenced East Asian regionalism in different ways and overall helped shape the unique character of East Asian regionalism and the emergent international economic order in the region. At a very critical level, there is a quite loose connection or even mismatch between market dynamics and institutional mandate in the development of regional institutions. There is an East Asian focus in the regionalization supported by East Asian growth, but East Asia is not the destination or the purpose of these market forces that are ever searching for a more efficient form of transborder organization. They are global.

Moreover, national interests and capabilities, reflecting predominantly the market forces of these industrial powers rather than a collective East Asian purpose and identity, place greater weight on multilateral enterprises. There are strong state authorities and capabilities to ensure agreement and enforce rules in the interstate space. This fits well with the institutional infrastructure underlying East Asian industrial and economic development where the state tends to coordinate business interests and relations.

Consequently, the prevalence of politics often complicates the picture of the industrial structure and dynamics in the region in the multilateral institutional setup. The industrial rationale that motivates regional institution building in the first place tends to get lost or compromised in the political tensions over the scope and purpose of East Asian regionalism and in the mushrooming of regional institutional frameworks. After all, intergovernmentalism is a core element of East Asian regionalism that not only defines its methods but also structures its purpose.

Study Questions

1. Why are ASEAN-centric institutional processes both bilateral and multilateral?
2. Discuss the varieties of East Asian regionalism and why such varieties exist.
3. Why is the TPP considered by some a significant turning point in the development of East Asian regionalism?
4. Discuss the bottom-up and top-down approaches to regional institution building in East Asia.
5. What is ASEAN centrality and what does it mean for East Asian regionalism?
6. Is East Asian regionalism driven largely by market forces or intergovernmental efforts on behalf of regional economic institutions?
7. What is the noodle bowl syndrome in East Asian regionalism? What caused it?
8. What tensions can you identify between the focuses on East Asia and the Asia-Pacific in East Asian regionalism? How do you explain them?
9. Do soft, open, intergovernmental varieties accurately characterize East Asian regionalism? Discuss one of the forces that helped shape the character of East Asian regionalism.

Further Reading

Acharya, Amitav, 1997. "Ideas, Identity, and Institution-Building: From the 'ASEAN Way' to the 'Asia-Pacific Way'?" *The Pacific Review* 10(3):319–346.

ADB, 2010. *Institutions for Regional Integration, Toward an Asian Economic Community*. Mandaluyong City: Asian Development Bank.

Ba, Alice, 2009. *(Re)Negotiating East and Southeast Asia: Region, Regionalism, and the Association of Southeast Asian Nations*. Stanford: Stanford University Press.

Baldwin, Richard, 2006. "Multilateralizing Regionalism: Spaghetti Bowls as Building Blocks on the Path to Global Free Trade," *The World Economy* 29(11): 1451–1518.

Baldwin, Richard, and Phil Thornton, 2008. *Multilateralizing Regionalism: Challenges for the Global Trading System*. London: Centre for Economic Policy Research.

Beeson, Mark, 2007. *Regionalism and Globalization in East Asia: Politics, Security and Economic Development*. New York: Palgrave Macmillan.

Berger, Mark T., 1999. "APEC and Its Enemies: The Failure of the New Regionalism in the Asia-Pacific," *Third World Quarterly* 20(5): 1013–1030.

Bowles, Paul, 2002. "Asia's Post-Crisis Regionalism: Bringing the State Back in, Keeping the (United) States Out," *Review of International Political Economy* 9(2):244–270.

Cho, Il Hyun, and SeoHyun Park, 2014. "Domestic Legitimacy Politics and Varieties of Regionalism in East Asia," *Review of International Studies* 40(3): 583–606.

Dai, Xinyuan, 2015. "Who Defines the Rules of the Game in East Asia? The Trans-Pacific Partnership and the Strategic Use of International Institutions," *International Relations of the Asia-Pacific* 15 (1): 1–25.

Dent, Christopher M., 2016. *East Asian Regionalism*. London: Routledge.

Ferguson, R. James, 2004. "ASEAN Concord II: Policy Prospects for Participant Regional Development," *Contemporary Southeast Asia* 26(3): 393–416.

Hall, Peter A., and David Soskice, 2001. *Varieties of Capitalism: The Institutional Foundations of Comparative Advantage*. New York: Oxford University Press.

Hall, Peter A., and Rosemary C. R. Taylor, 1996. "Political Science and the Three New Institutionalisms," *Political Studies* 44(5):936–957.

He, Baogang, and Takashi Inoguchi, 2011. "Introduction to Ideas of Asian Regionalism," *Japanese Journal of Political Science* 12(2): 165–177.

Higgott, Richard, and Richard Stubbs, 1995. "Competing Conceptions of Economic Regionalism: APEC vs EAEC in the Asia Pacific," *Review of International Political Economy* 2(3): 516–535.

Katzenstein, Peter J., and Takashi Shiraishi, 2006. *Beyond Japan: The Dynamics of East Asian Regionalism*. Ithaca: Cornell University Press.

Keohane, Robert, 1989. *International Institutions and State Power*. Boulder: Westview Press.

Keohane, Robert, and Lisa L. Martin, 1995. "The Promise of Institutionalist Theory," *International Security* 20(1):39–51.

Kim, Samuel S., 2004. "Regionalization and Regionalism in East Asia." *Journal of East Asian Studies* 4(1): 39–67.

Mattli, Walter, 1999. *The Logic of Regional Integration – Europe and Beyond*. Cambridge: Cambridge University Press.

Murray, Philomena, 2010. "Comparative Regional Integration in the EU and East Asia: Moving Beyond Integration Snobbery," *International Politics* 47(3–4): 308–323.

North, Douglas C., 1990. *Institutions, Institutional Change, and Economic Performance*. Cambridge: Cambridge University Press.

Oga, Toru, 2004. "Rediscovering Asianness: The Role of Institutional Discourses in APEC, 1989–1997," *International Relations of the Asia-Pacific* 4(2): 287–317.

Petri, Peter A., and Michael G. Plummer, 2014. *ASEAN Centrality and the ASEAN-US Economic Relationship*. Honolulu: East-West Center.

Petri, Peter A., Michael G. Plummer, and Fan Zhai, 2011. *The Trans-Pacific Partnership and Asia-Pacific Integration: A Quantitative Analysis*. East West Center Working Paper No. 119. Oct 24. Honolulu: East-West Center.

Ravenhill, John, 2001. *APEC and the Construction of Pacific Rim Regionalism*. Cambridge: Cambridge University Press.

Ravenhill, John, 2002. *APEC and the Construction of Pacific Rim Regionalism*. Cambridge: Cambridge University Press.

Terada, Takashi, 2003. "Constructing an 'East Asian' Concept and Growing Regional Identity: From EAEC to ASEAN+3," *The Pacific Review* 16(2):251–277.

Webber, Douglas, and Bertrand Fort, 2006. *Regional Integration in East Asia and Europe. Convergence or Divergence?* London/New York: Routledge.

Yeo, Lay Hwee, 2010, "Institutional Regionalism Versus Networked Regionalism: Europe and Asia Compared," *International Politics* 47(3): 324–337.

Yeo, Andrew I., 2016. "Overlapping Regionalism in East Asia: Determinants and Potential Effects," *International Relations of the Asia-Pacific* 18(2): 161–191.

Yoo, Tae, 2010. "Power Concentration or Parity? The Conditional Influence of Power Distribution in Regional Economic Integration," *International Relations of the Asia-Pacific*, 47(3): 324–337

9 Cooperative Security

In This Chapter...

- An "after-victory" moment
- China and ASEAN rapprochement
- Concept and theory
- Politics of multilateral engagement
- Institutionalizing an East Asian security order
- East Asian security architecture
- Balance of power or institutions and community?

Learning Objectives

By the end of this chapter, you will be able to
- Understand what is new in the new security concept in post-Cold War East Asia
- Use tools of institutional analysis to analyze the development of institutions of cooperative security in East Asia
- Understand China and ASEAN mutual engagement as a key force driving the multilateral movement toward cooperative security in East Asia
- Understand the competing influence of strategic geopolitics and institutions of cooperative security on the development of the forms and process of international security in post-Cold War East Asia.

Cooperative security is an inspiring term for traditional IR scholars who might think cooperation is impossible as an aim in international security or effective as a means to achieve an international order. If international security refers to a set of measures by states to ensure their safety and survival in the international system, cooperation is meaningful only among states of shared interests against the state of threat to their security. This is illustrated more clearly by the fact that international security as a field of international relations was a special area of inquiry during the Cold War years in the United States on the threat of mutual destruction of US/NATO and USSR/WATO in Europe. The Cold War bipolar structure was an ideal material setting for the idea of international security when the security of a group of states was threatened by another group of states.

In the later years of the Cold War, security conditions were changing. The Soviet Union seemed less likely to launch a nuclear war for territorial gains, while accidental escalation and miscalculation leading to a surprise attack became likely sources of threats to both sides. The concept of "common security" developed among security policymakers and analysts, as "a counter to deterrence" (Dewitt 1994: 1). This concerns measures to build confidence with the Soviet Union and "form an inclusive international security arrangement" (Carter et al. 1992) for tension reduction and conflict resolution. Common security and cooperative security, according to David Dewitt (Dewitt 1994), are notions that "share many common features" and developed out of a similar security experience in Europe and the Asia-Pacific. They essentially refer to a form of international security organization through inclusive, multilateral arrangements for confidence building and threat reduction in a common security community.

This reset on the international security concept and change in the patterns of international security practices also happened in East Asia. As the Cold War ended in East Asia, there was growing interest in scholarly work and policy analysis in the 1990s in this "new security" concept in post-Cold War East Asia. This scholarly interest and policy discussion came with a rich set of proactive international activities and programs to build multilateral institutions for a regional security community. These activities and programs evolved on the premise that East Asian states have common security interests and would work to shape a regional identity and institutions to ensure such an international security order in the region.

This chapter investigates what drove the movement toward cooperative security in post-Cold War East Asia and explores how multilateral institutions and regional identity building have worked in East Asia for an inclusive international security order. In the broader scholarly context, we are interested in how and to what extent this distinct set of dynamics – identity, institutions, and ideas – can influence international security in the region and determine the character of the international security order in East Asia.

AN "AFTER-VICTORY" MOMENT

John Ikenberry, in his 2000 book, *After Victory*, investigates three "great moments of international order building"(Ikenberry 2000: 3) after major wars in modern international history and the strategies of the winning states to create and perpetuate an international order through postwar settlements. In explaining the effectiveness and sustainability of the post-World War II order, Ikenberry argues that the institutional strategy employed by the United States has shaped both the character of the order and its sustaining power. While it is debatable whether the Cold War ended in East Asia when the Soviet Union and the Eastern Bloc collapsed in Europe, there was clearly an "after-victory moment" in IREA: Communism as we knew it was gone. China was reforming and opening up and looked to integrate with the international system, and Communist insurgents in Southeast Asia were largely subdued by the 1990s.

In Chapter 5, we discussed the formation of the bipolar structure in East Asia during the Cold War. Once the Communist threat was gone, a new rationale was needed for the international security order that has prevailed in East Asia and perhaps adjust the way in which international security was organized to accommodate the new reality in IREA, as the United States did in Europe long before the Cold War ended there. Aaron Friedberg (Friedberg 1993) described this new reality as the region evolving into a multipolar structure and argued for the need for international institutions to mitigate power rivalries. While it is debatable whether East Asia had developed international relations as those established in Europe that are capable of managing disputes and settling conflicts (Friedberg 1993; Kang 2003; Acharya 2014a), the rationale for a new international security order in East Asia through multilateral institutions is clear.

"Reordering" must therefore reflect the evolving power structure. But more importantly, as Ikenberry argues, it must focus on building institutions to "solve functional problems or facilitate cooperation" and "lock the states in" an effective network of constraints and incentives on the use of power (Ikenberry 2000: 5). For Evelyn Goh (Goh 2013), at the core of the post-Cold War transformation of the international security order in East Asia was really a renegotiation of the Cold War US hegemonic and hierarchical order, particularly the multilayered institutional and normative arrangements that supported that order. The after-victory moment in East Asia moved scholars, policy analysts, and state actors to look for multilateral institutions as a preferred solution to the "problem of order" (Ikenberry 2014: 11).

The notion of the primacy of institutions and norms in building an international security order in East Asia goes to the heart of liberal institutionalism, which builds on Robert Keohane's theory of international institutions in the 1980s (Keohane 1984, 1989; Axelrod & Keohane 1985; Keohane & Martin 1995; Baldwin 1993). (Also see discussion in Chapter 8). The core problem for the theory is how to ensure that states will cooperate in an anarchic but interdependent world. Keohane observes that the institutions, or "international regimes, created under conditions of American hegemony" facilitate "cooperation even after the erosion of U.S. dominance" (Keohane 1984: 246). International institutions facilitate "post-hegemonic cooperation" because they "provide information and reduce the cost of transactions that are consistent with their injunctions, thus facilitating interstate agreements and their decentralized enforcement" (*ibid.*).

This "institutionalist theory" singles out two key conditions for international institutions to effect cooperative security. These conditions have made the institutionalist movement in East Asia a challenge. First, institutions can facilitate cooperation among "like-minded" states because of their "common interests" (Keohane 1984: 246). In the early years of post-Cold War East Asia, this was not quite clear as the common interests that brought the countries together under the Cold War security order in East Asia had faded away with the collapse of Communism, or at least that is how it was perceived at that time. Common interests would need to be "nurtured." This drove much of the activities in the 1990s and 2000s to reshape the relations, foster dialogue, exchange, interaction, and a common security identity, and develop common interests and norms of practice. All these helped to forge a consensus on obligations, commitments, and a code of conduct for states in an inclusive security order in IREA. In particular, this whole movement centered on engaging with China and other states in continental East Asia and the East Asian crescent, and incorporate them into the new security community.

Second, while Robert Keohane and John J. Mearsheimer debate whether institutions can be effective for cooperation and under what conditions (Mearsheimer 1994; Keohane and Martin 1995), liberal institutionalists like Keohane are quite confident that institutions and norms are more effective, or even primary, in facilitating security cooperation. Their role is prescriptive and transformative in "post-hegemonic cooperation." Their effects are enforced in a decentralized authority environment. In post-Cold War East Asia, the hierarchical and hegemonic security order inherited from the Cold War era prevailed (Ikenberry 2000; Goh 2013). The movement to develop multilateral institutions for an international security order in East Asia had a great propensity to become part of a strategic plan by the leading states to extend and consolidate the effective hierarchical and hegemonic order. On the other hand, with the rise of China, the central role claimed by ASEAN, and the growing interests and capabilities of the middle powers, IREA have also become more "pluralizing" and "multipolarizing." All of these led to an ambivalent nature of the power structure for an international security order in East Asia and pushed the multilateral institutionalist movement to the test in the 2010s.

These two conditions significantly influenced the evolution of the regional security environment, the development of a multilateral institutionalist movement, and the institutions of cooperative security in post-Cold War East Asia. In this context, the rise of China, the role of ASEAN, and the shaping up of the role of middle powers are important. These factors determined how states articulate and nurture a common interest and identity, whether or not multilateralism is really backed up by a more plural power structure. The most significant developments in cooperative security in post-Cold War East Asia have been the rapprochement of China and ASEAN and the problem of whether China is in or out of the institutional framework of a regional security community.

CHINA AND ASEAN RAPPROCHEMENT

Building a new security order in post-Cold War East Asia started with the rapprochement between China and Southeast Asian countries. As shown in Figure 9.1, underlying IREA during much of the Cold War era was the Communist threat from the establishment of Communist states in continental East Asia and their looking to expand over maritime East Asia. Other factors were the spread and antistate activity of Communist movements in Southeast Asian countries. As a political force in national politics, these Communist forces engaged in armed activities, threatening the security and survival of the new states in Southeast Asia. These two forces combined became a principal driver in the formation of ASEAN in 1967. After the real wars over Communism in East Asia had long settled and the Cold War ended in the early 1990s, reorientation of relations between China and ASEAN became necessary for a new regional order in East Asia.

China and ASEAN rapprochement was also important for a certain type of regional security community. This was envisaged to develop through inclusive

Cooperative Security 193

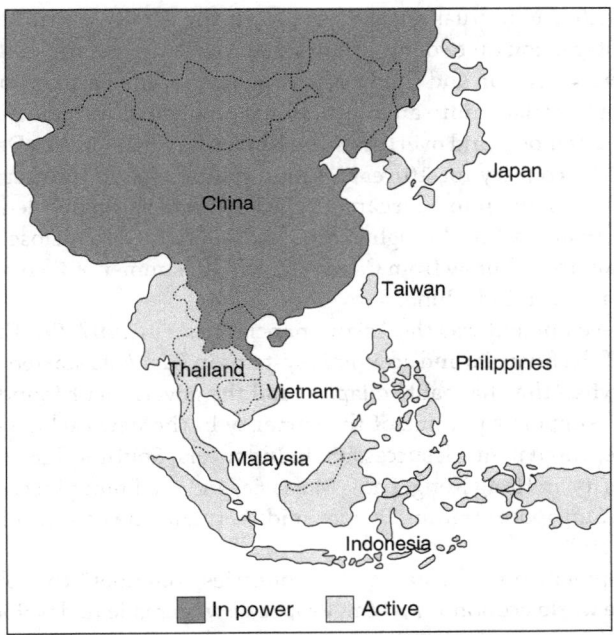

Figure 9.1 Huang's depiction of Communist states in continental East Asia and Communist forces in Southeast Asia, 1950s
Graph credit: Huang (2009: 182)

multilateral institutions and the development of a regional identity. China and ASEAN are critical stakeholders in this process. For ASEAN, "(re)negotiating" a regional security order built on multilateral institutions is essential. Alice Ba (2009) unpacks this process of ASEAN's positioning itself in post-Cold War IREA and explains the double challenge that defines its mode of operating. This double challenge, "internal diversity" and "external disunity," for ASEAN as a unit in IREA prompted ASEAN countries not only to "negotiate" a way to pull themselves together but also to use institutional instruments and platforms to negotiate a wider Asia-Pacific security order for ASEAN. A critical element in negotiating this external unity is to "reach out" to China.

For China, rapprochement with ASEAN reflected a growing recognition of the shifting geopolitical reality in East Asia as the Cold War ended. It opened up space for China to engage with multilateral institutions as a new platform to influence the shaping of the regional security order. As a whole, the countries of ASEAN are geographically and culturally close and rich in historical ties. It is a practical and less risky partner for China's adventure in reestablishing itself in the wider region and in "learning" or "socialization" (Chan 2015: 87) with new forms of international relations such as multilateral institutions.

China and ASEAN mutual engagement from the 1990s was followed by their involuntary interaction on two important issues or developments in IREA. The first was a new wave of tension and conflict over Indochina. The Third Indochina War, as it is known now, escalated into an international problem of war and peace. Vietnam sent troops to Cambodia and overthrew the Khmer Rouge regime in December 1978 and occupied the country for 10 years. China sent troops to northern Vietnam as "punishment" to Vietnam in February 1979. The conflicts further led to Vietnam's tensions with Thailand. This brought China and ASEAN to work closely to put pressure on Vietnam to withdraw from Cambodia and to hammer out a permanent solution to the conflicts in Indochina.

A second development was the Asian financial crisis in 1997–98. The wave of the breakdowns of the financial and economic systems in East Asia started with Thailand in July 1997 when the Thai baht collapsed and the government found itself unable to continue to support the value of the currency in the new exchange regime. The same drama repeated in quick succession in Indonesia, South Korea, and, to a lesser degree of severity, in Hong Kong, Laos, Malaysia, and the Philippines, and further in Japan, China, Singapore, Taiwan, Brunei, and Vietnam. The crisis evolved in escalation well into 1998.

This development brought East Asian countries "together" to feel their shared position in the world economic system. Proposals were made to develop multilateral institutions for a regional financial order and mechanisms to prevent such a crisis from happening again. Among the proposals were the idea of an Asian monetary unit (AMU) and mechanisms of multilateral currency clearance and settlement. The AMU idea, which came from Japan, aroused mixed reactions. The latter further developed into practical projects, a series of bilateral currency clearance arrangements between ASEAN Plus Three (APT) countries, which eventually "multilateralized" into what is now known as the Chiang Mai Initiative, a multilateral arrangement for currency clearance and settlement among East Asian economies. This arrangement allows these countries to organize their trade and economic exchange in their own currencies.

China and ASEAN formal engagement with each other started in 1991 when the Chinese Foreign Minister attended the 24th ASEAN Foreign Minister Meeting in Kuala Lumpur "as a guest of the Malaysian government" (ASEAN 2018). In 1994, China took part in the ASEAN Regional Forum (ARF) annual meeting and became "a consultative dialogue partner" of ASEAN, which was upgraded further to "a full dialogue partner" in 1996. In 1997, the first ASEAN-China Summit, as part of the ASEAN+1 mechanism, was held in Kuala Lumpur between the Chinese president and the leaders of the ASEAN countries. The summit established relations as a partnership of "good neighborliness and mutual trust." This was further upgraded to "a strategic partnership for peace and prosperity" in 2003. Around the same time, a framework agreement for an FTA between ASEAN and China was signed in 2002, and the ACFTA negotiation was concluded in 2010. In 2003, China was the first dialogue partner of ASEAN to sign the Treaty of Amity and Cooperation in Southeast Asia (TAC). In 2012, China established its mission to ASEAN in Jakarta and sent its first resident ambassador to ASEAN.

China-ASEAN rapprochement brought the two main opposing forces in the Cold War structure in East Asia into an "inclusive" multilateral framework for a new security order in the region. While ASEAN was not the only representative of the forces against Communist states and movements, the new China-ASEAN relations helped the fusion of the two principal geopolitical collective forces, those of continental and maritime East Asia. This was the third instance of such a fusion in the history of the shaping of the East Asian structure since the maritime expansion of the Chinese world order before European colonial advance to Northeast Asia and Japanese imperial advance to continental East Asia in the nineteenth and early twentieth centuries. This time, the development was driven more by ASEAN through multilateral institutions.

The development of ASEAN's relations with China is a classic case of how the ASEAN style of multilateral institutionalism operates. To build confidence and trust, remove threats to the security of both, and build an inclusive security community, ASEAN started with small steps at low institutional levels. It built ties through practices of multilateral interaction, exchange and dialogue, and networking in research, consultation, and policy expertise. The level of institutional commitment and compliance gradually increased. A sense of common interest, community, and identity developed. The process of the evolving relationship was open-ended and at least the final outcomes are not predetermined. The end result was the establishment of formal diplomatic relations between ASEAN and China and the integration of the two political forces into the shaping of a regional security community. The gradual, incremental, experimental, and managed process of engaging is, significantly, part of the "ASEAN way" (Acharya 1998) of institutionalization of the new regional security order.

Multilateralism and bilateralism are different methods states use to organize their international relations. There is a persistent tension in these two methods, as we already showed in our discussion of the development of regional economic institutions in Chapter 8. The tension has its unique manifestations in the development of a regional security order. For China, the reset of its relations with Southeast Asia via ASEAN represents a major shift in its thinking about the post-Cold War international order in East Asia and methods for pursuing it. China had experienced various relations with countries in Southeast Asia and did not necessarily see Indochina as part of Southeast Asia. Most importantly, China's relations with Southeast Asian countries had been largely "bilateral." As Gerald Chan observes, "China's bilateral approach towards individual member states of the ASEAN group was born not only out of its general preference for dealing with foreign countries bilaterally but also out of its traditional approach towards solving problems with its neighbors that pre-dates the development of the modern inter-state system" (Chan 2015: 85).

Reorienting with Southeast Asia via ASEAN rather than with individual Southeast Asian countries reflects an intention of China to start fresh in its relations with Southeast Asian countries, accepting ASEAN as its legitimate representative body, to test out a more effective way of advancing relations with Southeast Asian countries, and from there to build a new, favorable security environment. The incremental, piecemeal, experimental approach was also apparent in China's efforts at rapprochement with ASEAN. This worked for China as well as for the ASEAN countries as a strategy in pursuing a post-Cold War new security order in East Asia. It also represents a learning experience for both sides in building cooperative security in East Asia through multilateral institutions.

Moreover, multilateralism here means that China engages with ASEAN as a multilateral organization itself and takes multilateral international organizations as legitimate platforms for interstate interaction and pursuit. It also means China engages with a network of wider, ASEAN-centered, multilateral regional institutions: the ARF, APT, EAS, and ASEAN Defense Ministers Meeting Plus (ADMM+). These constitute a network of bilateral partnerships of ASEAN countries with external partners. In both cases, there is a mixture of multilateral and bilateral elements in their overall international engagement. This, together with preferences for incremental, experimental, and informal processes, suggests a very East Asian approach to cooperative security.

CONCEPT AND THEORY

Cooperative security as a particular form of international security order in East Asia was not only shaped by the practical realities of the post-Cold War security conditions in East Asia but was also influenced by the growing currency of the "new security" concept among academics and policy analysts on East Asian security. The new security concept emerged in IREA in the 1990s and considers the new conditions for regional security – a wider range of different forms of security threats – that require different methods, particularly multilateral institutional arrangements and processes, to meet the challenge and the participation and contributions of different actors to the international security order.

Scholarship and policy debate used concepts of common security, comprehensive security, security community, and multilateral institutions for regional security in the Asia-Pacific (Acharya 1997, 2001a, 2003; Alagappa 1998, 2003; Evans 2004; Suh & Katzenstein 2004) to refer to the new conditions and new methods. Cooperative security, for example, refers to an international security situation where a wider range of security issues pose a threat to both or all states in a security community that requires multilateral cooperation among the states to remedy and mitigate the security threat. Comprehensive security, for another example, refers to a security situation where security issues pose a threat not only to the state but to the people, individuals, and their economic, social, environmental security, and wellbeing that requires the action of states, international organizations, and civil society groups to ensure an international security order.

At a deeper level, the post-Cold War developments suggest a profound shift in the thinking of scholars and policy analysts regarding the nature of international security in post-Cold War East Asia. Questions were raised over what causes threats to international security, security of whom, and security by whom. This shift prompted a reset in the practice of states in the region in approaching and addressing security matters. This shift was clearly articulated by some of our leading thinkers on this issue. Amitav Acharya and Muthiah Alagappa (Alagappa 1998, 2003; Acharya 1995, 1999, 2001a), for example, have significantly influenced the shaping of the whole paradigm of analyzing and explaining the new security conditions in the Asia-Pacific and ways to mitigate threats.

The idea of "new security" is built on a particular reading of the new post-Cold War international framework in the Asia-Pacific. First, the end of the Cold War suggested the diminishing threat of Communism to ASEAN from the North. Without security threats and with no clearly identifiable enemies, the conventional security arrangements and strategy lost their justification and left security interests and relations of nations open to redefinition. Second, as an overall approach to regional security, it is important to develop a sense of community in which countries can identify with each other for their common security interests and develop effective institutional mechanisms to ensure the development of common interests and "instrumental and normative" effects (Alagappa 2003) on countries' behavior and policy.

The new security theory and practice is new as it moves beyond "traditional" security. Threats to international security include nonconventional threats (to human security, economic security, environment security versus national/state security); threats that affect the security and survival of two binary opponents or all states (rather than just those that threaten others); and accidental/escalation of defensive reactions (rather than offensive territorial aggression using weapons of mass destruction). As the hard core Cold War security issues increasingly faded, a new security order would be built with content and methods different from those in the Cold War. These ultimately must be comprehensive, inclusive, and cooperative.

POLITICS OF MULTILATERAL ENGAGEMENT

With all the intentions, agenda, and working styles of East Asian multilateral institutionalism discussed earlier, the ARF was one of the first "order-building" projects to develop in East Asia. It was an early ASEAN-centric multilateral process and a first practical form of multilateral Track I dialogue for East Asian security. It is a "dialogue and consultation" forum set up as a mechanism for ASEAN's dialogue and consultation with its dialogue partners, including Australia, Canada, China, the EU, India, Japan, Korea, New Zealand, Russia, and the US, on political and security matters in the Asia-Pacific. The ASEAN Ministerial Meeting in 1993 in Singapore agreed to establish the ARF "to foster the habit of constructive dialogue and consultation on political and security issues of common interest and concern ..." and "to make significant contributions to efforts towards confidence-building and preventive diplomacy in the Asia-Pacific region" (ARF 1994).

The ARF has developed in a typical "ASEAN way." It is a multilateral platform for intergovernmental or "Track I" dialogue and consultation on security in East Asia. Though it was set up as a platform for ASEAN to facilitate dialogue with its external partners, it treats all states of ASEAN as equal participants in the forum. It is designed for the Asian-Pacific but includes dialogue partners from around the world that have significant interests and influence in security matters in the region. Moreover, soft mechanisms, such as ministerial meetings, expert seminars, workshops, roundtables, intersessional meetings, expert group meetings, training programs, are the main platforms for developing "a more predictable and constructive pattern of relations." They were aimed at collectively developing an institutional framework for regional security order in a three-stage process: agreeing and acting on measures for confidence building, preventive diplomacy, and eventual establishment of a multilateral capacity for conflict resolution.

The informal method to institutionalize a set of formal relations on East Asian security matters met its first challenge when it set to define the scope of networking. Political and security matters involved the interests and concerns of various political entities, some of which are not internationally recognized states. Even if they have significant security interests and influence, their participation and representation are not possible politically for the "intergovernmental" platform. At the beginning of the ARF, this was the problem with the memberships of Taiwan and North Korea, which had large stakes on the security issues in the region.

Moreover, unlike ASEAN-centric multilateral processes for regional economic institutions that often evolve multiple track dialogues, there is another process paralleling the development of the ARF in the shaping of the post-Cold War regional security order in East Asia. In 1993, strategic studies centers, notably among them the ASEAN Institutes of Strategic and International Studies (ASEAN ISIS), Japan Institute of International Affairs (JIIA), Pacific Forum/CSIS (Honolulu), and the Seoul Forum for International Affairs (SFIA), of 10 countries in the Asia-Pacific, including Australia, Canada, Indonesia, Japan, South Korea, Malaysia, the Philippines, Singapore, Thailand, and the US, agreed to establish a Council for Security Cooperation in the Asia Pacific (CSCAP) to "provide a more structural regional process of a *non-governmental nature* ... to contribute to the efforts towards regional confidence building and enhancing regional security through dialogues, consultation and cooperation" (CSCAP 1993).

CSCAP is a "Track II" mechanism for scholars and policy analysts from leading think tanks in East Asian countries to discuss and study security issues in the region in a nonstate capacity and make recommendations for action to intergovernmental processes, largely the ARF. Participants are individual scholars and policy analysts organized into a member committee of the country and participate in study groups on specific issues. CSCAP has participation from the Democratic People's Republic of Korea (DPRK, or North Korea) as a full member committee and from the Republic of China (Taiwan) as "other participants" at the study group level.

That multilateral institutionalism on East Asian security evolved in parallel mechanisms reinforces one distinct feature of East Asian multilateral institutionalism – the role of Track II dialogue in institutionalizing cooperative security and nurturing national engagement on regional security issues through their think tanks, research centers, and policy-oriented academics. Track II dialogue is a nongovernmental mechanism, as distinct from Track I dialogue, which is between government officials of the involved countries. There is also Track 1.5 dialogue, which represents a mixture of Track I officials and Track II nonofficial participants, or government officials participate in an unofficial capacity. Track II dialogue emerged as one of the key mechanisms in the working of multilateral institutionalism in East Asian security where issues are discussed and opinions are exchanged between states through academics, policy analysts, and practitioners from the countries. Track II dialogue is also an important mechanism in the public policy sector of the country that incorporates scholarship, policy analysis, and government agenda formulation for effective national influence on multilateral processes and the shaping of a regional security order.

The developments also dealt with the problem of the power structure that influences the working of East Asian multilateral institutions. Compromises and flexible arrangements are made for the process to be able to proceed. These multilateral institutional processes and mechanisms developed and are organized by relatively weak states, ASEAN, in the hierarchical and hegemonic power structure in East Asia. This shows the collective power of small states in the multilateral institutional setting and the enormous influence of the interstate structure on multilateral institutions. This challenge became even more overwhelming as major forces informed by the shifting regional power structure were better organized to take on multilateral institutionalism as their own multilateral strategic option when East Asia entered the 2010s.

INSTITUTIONALIZING AN EAST ASIAN SECURITY ORDER

The East Asian security landscape showed signs of significant change as the region entered the 2010s. After years of debate on the rise of China, states in East Asia finally started to feel the real scale and magnitude of the impact of China's rapidly growing interests and capabilities with respect to East Asian security. A view now prevails that with its growing interests and capabilities, China is moving to be more assertive, "stride for achievement," on regional security issues, apparently abandoning the earlier posture of "keeping a low profile" or what Avery Goldstein calls "neo-Bismarckianism" in China's grand strategy (Yan 2014; Glaser 2015; Goldstein 2003).

On the other hand, as President Obama took office, the United States took its engagement with East Asia to a higher level, committing significant political capital and resources to secure an international security order in East Asia, in the Pivot to Asia strategy. This implied a strategic shift for more substantive and effective engagement with East Asia. In both cases, multilateral institutionalism is finally taken up as a useful platform for such engagement by Washington and Beijing. For both the United States and China, multilateral institutions work alongside, on top of, and complementary to other forms of engagement, for example, bilateral alliances and strategic partnerships. This multilateral institutionalism, however, is led by or centered around China or the United States. Each is looking to engage through multilateral institutions to shape a regional security order for its interests primarily and those of their partners.

The US made great efforts to revitalize and consolidate the alliance system, adding more substantive functions and content in the alliance relations and shifting more resources and operational capabilities to East Asia. It also took a more active approach to regional institutions and multilateral processes. Efforts to combine elements of both bilateral and multilateral frameworks in the US strategic posture in East Asia came when it decided to join the EAS in 2011, 6 years after its establishment. The US took a proactive, engaging, and leadership role in the working of ASEAN-centric regional institutions and processes.

On regional security institutions and processes, the United States has invested a great deal of political capital in the working of the Shangri-La Dialogue. The Shangri-La Dialogue is a Track I intergovernmental forum with multitrack dialogues, held annually at the Shangri-La Hotel in Singapore. This is a mechanism established by an influential think tank based in London, International Institute for Strategic Studies (IISS). It is very similar to the ARF, in terms of the way it intends to facilitate "institutionalization of defense or military interactions" (Capie & Taylor 2010), as well as its membership as an intergovernmental forum on East Asian security. The dialogue, however, focuses on defense issues with the participation of defense ministers, chiefs of defense forces, and chiefs of defense operations and intelligence, as well as scholars, journalists, and policy analysts. It is not an ASEAN-centric mechanism. Under the US Pivot-to-Asia initiative, the US has taken on a more proactive role in Shangri-La Dialogue from 2011 and seen it as a proper mechanism or platform for the multilateral institutional engagement part of its pivot to Asia.

China in the meantime made great efforts to enhance its role and influence in the ASEAN-centric regional institutions. It actively participated in APT and played a significant role in the movement to establish the EAS in the 2010s. It took a more proactive approach to APEC and led the development of a roadmap for a FTAAP at the 2014 APEC summit. All seemed to be aimed at influencing the direction of East Asian regionalism, based on the idea that the region would eventually move toward a single institution or organization for an East Asian community. On security institutions and processes, China has led a full-scale engagement with the AFR, CSCAP, and the Shangri-La Dialogue, and clearly seen them as useful platforms for China to communicate its strategic interests, security concerns, and policy priorities in the region and to engage with states of traditional sources of security threat to China in the Asia-Pacific.

For China, however, these constitute only part of its broad and rapidly expanding range of security interests and projects. There are security threats that are ethnic and religious in nature in and around Central Asia connecting Russia and China, posing a threat to the security of the Chinese state, particularly in the northwestern region. Tensions and conflict on the Korean Peninsula threaten to escalate into a real war that would seriously impact China and the regional security order. In the southwest border area adjacent to India, the traditional roots of the problem with India over the area seemed to intensify tensions and security concerns. Territorial disputes with Japan in the East China Sea and over the Diaoyutai Islands became another source of increasing tensions and security concerns in the 2010s. Finally, while PRC's relations with Taiwan and Hong Kong were largely insulated from the structural shift in the region, they could become a significant source of tension and security challenge for China as the geopolitical conditions in the region continue to evolve and shift.

There is a long list of critical pockets of security concerns largely around Chinese borders. Many of them are of the classic type of security threats in East Asia that affect territorial integrity, state security, and "regime survival" (Fravel 2005: 53) of China. While various strategies exist to deal with these security threats, China applied ideas of multilateral institutionalism in some of these issue areas, hoping to "institutionalize" interstate interactions for a security order in the given geopolitical setting. In 1996, the heads of the Shanghai Five, China, Russia, Kazakhstan, Kyrgyzstan, and Tajikistan, met in Shanghai and agreed to the Treaty on Deepening Military Trust in Border Regions. The practice of summitry repeated annually until 2001 when the Shanghai Five plus One, Uzbekistan, declared the establishment of the Shanghai Cooperation Organization (SCO), a formal treaty organization that emerged directly from the Shanghai Five mechanism.

The SCO was originally designed to deal with security issues in the region as a mechanism for confidence building, preventive diplomacy, and, more specifically, as a multilateral convention for combating "three evil forces": terrorism, separatism, and extremism (SCO 2001a, 2001b) in central Asia. In 2018, SCO became a full-scale international organization with eight member states extending to South Asia to include India and Pakistan, four observer states, and six dialogue partners, further extending to South Asia and Middle East, and covers a full range of issue areas, politics and security, economic and trade, and social and cultural development.

Six Party Talks (SPT) is another mechanism in multilateral institutionalism on East Asian security. It emerged from intensive diplomatic interaction among the six countries for a diplomatic solution to the security tensions over the development of North Korea's nuclear weapons program. SPT was a series of frequent meetings from 2003 to 2009, hosted by China in Beijing, among senior officials of South Korea, North Korea, China, United States, Japan, and Russia to negotiate a solution to the tension and crisis over North Korea nuclear issues. The formation of the mechanism was considered by some as a top-down formation of a multilateral institution.

There was great scholarly speculation as to whether SPT is an instance of multilateral institutionalism and whether it is a working model of building regional institutions for security in East Asia. SPT has been largely a multilateral response to a specific international security crisis. Tension escalated quickly into conflict in a pattern of multilateral interaction. Further developments and deep currents in geopolitics on Korean nuclear issues and the larger problem of security order on the Korean Peninsula, however, have complicated its further development. The mechanism has not institutionalized further to be a more formal multilateral institution for regional security in East Asia as many had hoped it would become.

SCO and SPT can be seen as mechanisms of multilateral engagement by China for security order in a particular "region" or on a specific issue. These China-"centric" regional institutions raised a question regarding the definition of the region, Asia-Pacific, East Asia, or Asia. This has been an issue for ASEAN-centric regional institutionalism. Alongside the development of SCO has also been a China-led project to build a multilateral dialogue and consultative mechanism for security matters in broad Asia.

In 1999, the foreign ministers of 15 member states that "at least, have a part of its territory geographically located in Asia" (CICA 2004: 2) met for the first time in Almaty, Kazakhstan, for the Conference on Interaction and Confidence-Building Measures in Asia (CICA). CICA has since established a biannual intergovernmental forum for developing and implementing confidence-building measures on political and security matters in Asia, following a model of institutionalization of interstate interaction on political and security matters in East Asia, very similar to that of ARF. At the CICA Summit in 2014 when China took over chairmanship, Chinese President Xi Jinping declared "Asian security for Asians and by Asians" and set the agenda for CICA to lead the shaping of security architecture in Asia.

To further strengthen China's leadership in building multilateral institutions for the regional security order, particularly in response to the increasing influence of the Shangri-La Dialogue, China also reorganized an existing Track II mechanism of its own, the Xiangshan Forum, and upgraded it from a Track II mechanism organized under the China Association of Military Science to a Track 1 platform with multi-track mechanisms for Asia-Pacific security dialogue. The forum aims to be a "high-level security and defense forum in the Asia-Pacific with significant international influence" (BXF 2018). The forum invites delegates, international organizations, experts, and scholars from countries around the world to the annual gathering.

These US-centric and China-centric multilateral frameworks and mechanisms for cooperative security in East Asia, along with the ASEAN-centric ones, bring to the fore the question of whether these regional institutions and mechanisms are designed for the building of a security community in the region, however one defines it – East Asia, the Asia-Pacific, or Asia. The geopolitical scope of the security community seemed to be consistently contended and contested. This suggests a complexity in building multilateral institutions for security in East Asia under the prevailing political, security, and technological conditions.

Moreover, these sets of multilateral frameworks and mechanisms are advanced by states with significant stakes and capabilities in East Asian security – the US, ASEAN, China, and others – as useful platforms for their strategic engagement on security issues in the region. We have seen different national/group perspectives or visions on a regional security architecture. The development and functioning of multilateral institutionalism were complicated or compromised by a never clearly defined notion of community and its security priorities, and the hierarchical power structure underlying IREA. Both aspects added to the mutual embeddedness of multilateral institutionalism and interstate power distribution, and undermined the power of multilateral institutions to constrain the actions of states, particularly powerful states, for cooperative security in post-Cold War East Asia.

EAST ASIAN SECURITY ARCHITECTURE

Central to cooperative security in East Asia is building confidence and trust, as well as common interests and a shared vision, on regional security issues through inclusive, multilateral institutional mechanisms and processes. This will ultimately lead to a regional security order. As we showed earlier through a sample of the developments in the past 30 years, multilateral institutionalism has brought powerful and different visions to the platforms. It is unclear how these different visions can transform to support a coherent international security order in East Asia as envisaged in the theory of cooperation security in East Asia.

In more recent years, the notion of an East Asian security architecture became a popular topic at these multilateral forums and roundtables, and in consultation papers on East Asian security. If an East Asian security "landscape" refers to the overall character of the security conditions in East Asia, an East Asian security "architecture" prescribes a set of structural relations, institutional arrangements, and a set of mechanisms in interstate interaction for an international security order. The US-centric network of bilateral alliances and multilateral partnerships, an ASEAN-centric network of bilateral and multilateral partnerships and processes, and a China-centric network of bilateral and multilateral partnerships are versions of the East Asian security architecture. The intense interest in clarifying or articulating the dominant East Asian architecture reflects the anxiety among some countries over the indeterminate nature of a cooperative security order in East Asia. This became evident when the China factor entered the picture.

As China embarked on a full-scale engagement in multilateral institutions, it started to look intensively into the precise nature of the regional security architecture debate. This reflects China's enthusiasm as well as frustration with the Asia-Pacific approach to the regional security order unfolding in the 2000s. China has focused on shaping the East Asian security architecture in its multilateral engagement with ASEAN and ASEAN-centered regional institutions, the SPT, SCO, and CICA. As these projects continually expanded, China, as represented by its political leaders and scholars and policy analysts associated with China, proposed its own "new security concept." China's advocacy of a "new security concept" came in the late 1990s.

In its 1998 Defense White Paper, China first made a case for a new security concept and what this new security concept would entail. This new security concept broadened security to include military, political, economic, social, and development issues, apart from the narrow Cold War concept of security heavily focused on military security (IOSCC 1998). This is to a great extent in line with Alagappa's call for a broader view on security in post-Cold War East Asia (Alagappa 1998). The call for mutual trust, mutual benefit, equality, and coordination in the new security concept for a regional security order in the Asia-Pacific suggests that it was largely China's new security concept that served as the rationale behind China's move toward multilateral engagement in the Asia-Pacific.

In 2014 at the CICA, Chinese President Xi Jinping moved the new security concept to the forefront of the multilateral forum and proposed a "New Asian Security Concept" as China's preferred framework for the East Asian regional security architecture. Built on the emphasis on multilateral institutionalism in the original "new security" concept, this framework is "Asian." "It is for the people of Asia to run the affairs of Asia, solve the problems of Asia and uphold the security of Asia," as Xi declared (Xi 2014). China's advocacy of the "new Asian security" concept brings politics to focus in the debate on East Asian security architecture and the tension between structure and institutions to a higher level in the shaping of the international security order in the region.

China has all the reasons and clearly has over the years ventured to accept multilateral institutionalism as an important platform for advancing its vision and interests on regional security. But for China, like the United States, multilateralism is probably only one form of engagement for international security. Bilateralism and even unilateralism are legitimate frameworks for China. And like the United States and ASEAN, China has a wide range of bilateral partnerships to support its multilateral institutional engagement. A hub-spokes system seems to work for each major mover and shaper in IREA. As China's capacity grows, its areas of security interest and concern expand, and China-led multilateral institutions increase, it will encounter a regional security order built on ASEAN-centric multilateral institutions, and the US-dominated hierarchical power structure embedded in its hub-spokes alliance system. The bilateral structural framework or multilateral institutional framework seems inadequate for explaining the dynamism of the shaping of the East Asian security order.

A growing body of scholarship on the postwar liberal international order, and the East Asian security order in particular, led by the works of G. John Ikenberry, Evelyn Goh, and others (Ikenberry 2014; Goh 2013; Toje 2018), appears to reflect a serious effort to deal with the problem. In the debate over the challenge of the rise of China, leading scholars and policy analysts have focused great attention on the challenge posed by the rise of China. The rise of China has significantly influenced the power structure underlying the international system, brought the profound shift in the global distribution of international interests and capabilities. The rise of China is also seen as a challenge to the international institutions and norms that have evolved to support the liberal international order and US-led hierarchical and hegemonic order in East Asia in particular.

For Ikenberry, the structural and normative dynamics are not separate or mutually exclusive in the shaping of an international order. Using his vast knowledge on "the order building projects of the Westphalian system and the liberal ascendency" (Ikenberry 2014: 84), Ikenberry makes a convincing case that an effective international order is supported by a power structure where a dominant state has "material capabilities to coerce and entice other states into the order" and a "normative consensus" to provide legitimacy to the distribution and exercise of power and justification for the distribution and allocation of obligations and benefits in the collective action, and the provision of "functional benefits and services" (Ikenberry 2014: 84). Power structures and institutions and norms are integral to the working of an international order, at least for the post-1945 US-led liberal international order.

The close intertwinedness and mutual dependence between a hierarchical power structure and supporting institutions and norms is further exposed in Evelyn Goh's investigation of the US-led hierarchical and hegemonic East Asian order. Goh argues that "hegemonic power is based on both coercion and consent, and hegemony is crucially underpinned by shared norms and values. Thus, hegemons must constantly legitimize their unequal power to other states." International order, according to Goh, "is a pattern or arrangement that sustains the primary goals of a society of states. It must involve limits on behavior, the management of conflict, and the accommodation of change without undermining the common goals and values of society ... and the effect of the normative structure of regional society." Goh further sees the post-Cold War reshaping of the regional order in East Asia as a transformation of the order where the institutions and norms are "renegotiated" for the hegemonic hierarchical order to continue.

China's interest in the East Asian security architecture reflects in the first instance its own vision about an East Asian security order and its interest in the structural and institutional foundations or requirements of that. The debate on the East Asian security architecture in the later years of the post-Cold War movement on cooperative security reflects the possibility, or perhaps the reality, of different visions over an East Asian security order. These different visions are backed up and made effective by real national interests and capacities. Whether these different visions can be reconciled and incorporated into an inclusive vision for all in the region, through multilateral institutional processes and mechanisms, remains an open question at the end of the 2010s.

BALANCE OF POWER OR INSTITUTIONS AND COMMUNITY?

This brings us to the very basic question for this chapter – whether institutions, identities, and ideas constitute significant forces driving the multilateral institutionalist movement and shaping the international security order in East Asia. The foregoing discussions showed that multilateral institutional processes are complicated by the interests and capabilities of the principal nations. The issue is at the heart of the debate over cooperative security, the new security concept and methods, and whether an international security order is determined primarily by material forces and interests or international institutions, norms, and identity.

Analysts of East Asian security have long pointed to the two different security orders and, potentially, the tension between them. G. John Ikenberry and Jitsuo Tsuchiyama note, for example, two alternative security orders, "an order based on balance is one where the power of the leading state is counterbalanced by other states," and "a community-based security order is one where binding security institutions and shared political interests and values exist to shape and limit how power can be exercised." They insist that the "prevailing security order in the Asia-Pacific region at the time is a mixture of bilateral alliances, multilateral dialogues, and ad hoc diplomacy ... and is somewhere between a balance-of-power and community based system" (Ikenberry & Tsuchiyama 2002: 72, 90).

Muthiah Alagappa (1998, 2003), as discussed early in the development of the new security concept, endeavors to broaden the notion of security to reflect the changing conditions in the postcolonial era. This new concept of security brings the large social context, national and international, into the problem of "political survival of Asian states" (1998: vii). Alagappa further argues that there is a stable regional security order in East Asia, and this security order is shaped by various different dynamics, "hegemony, balance of power (including alliance), concert, global and regional multilateral institutions, bilateralism, and self-help – all play key role." For Alagappa, these "pathways" to a regional security order are integral forces from different "functional" area that together shape the regional security order.

This mixture of bilateral alliance systems and multilateral dialogues and informal diplomacy is part of a larger debate on bilateralism or multilateralism as the primary organizing framework in IREA. Kent E. Calder and Francis Fukuyama discuss this dilemma in their discussion of the "contours" in the East Asian security architecture (Calder & Fukuyama 2008: 34). William T. Tow and Brendan Taylor believe both bilateralism through the US alliance system and multilateralism in ASEAN-centric regional institutions are an active framework for an East Asian security order. Bilateral and multilateral approaches, they argue, "can work alongside each other" on the basis of "complementarity and overlaps, even convergence between the bilateral and multilateral modes of international security cooperation" (Tow & Taylor 2013: 5). Bilateralism and multilateralism are not alternative, mutually exclusive modes of security cooperation, bilateralism is not a "stepping stone to multilateralism," and multilateralism is not "ultimately for enhanced bilateral interaction" (Tow & Taylor 2013: 5). For them, both forces are effective, even complementary, for an East Asian security order.

The challenges come, first, from those who believe the power structure, particularly the power structure that helped shape the existing security order in the region, still matters the most in the shaping of the new regional security order (Krauss & Pempel 2004; Calder & Fukuyama 2008; Green & Gill 2009). Krauss and Pempel, for example, focused on the "bilateral and relatively exclusive" US-Japan alliance to transform, in the rapidly changing geopolitical conditions in post-Cold War East Asia, into multilateral institutions and asserted that the relationship should go "beyond bilateralism" and perhaps embrace multilateral institutions (Krauss & Pempel 2004: 2).

Kent Calder and Francis Fukuyama and colleagues (2008) recognized the importance of both the US-led hub-spokes alliance system, the US-Japanese alliance in particular, and East Asian multilateralism in the shaping of the East Asian regional architecture but seemed to be ambiguous in US strategic choice. While there is a need to go "beyond the hub and spokes," Calder and Fukuyama have some questions as well as advice on how to close up the "East Asia organization gap" (Calder & Fukuyama 2008: 1). Michael Green and Bates Gill in another study (Green & Gill 2009) also see multilateral institutionalism as being problematic as a national strategy for countries with large stakes and influence in East Asia, where cooperation and competition coexist. Moreover, multilateralism is also seen as more of a method of cooperation in "functional areas": trade and finance, regional governance, and non-traditional security.

Amitav Acharya, however, sees the new security order in post-Cold War East Asia as a different type of security order. Acharya's writings in the 1990s on multilateral institutions in East Asia (Acharya 2003) articulated a regional security order in Southeast Asia as facilitated or shaped through "multilateral security dialogue and regional community formation." The regional security order was achieved through the working of ASEAN (Acharya & Tan 2005: 37) rather than the US-dominated, hub-spoke system of bilateral alliances. Acharya proposed that "the ASEAN way" (Acharya 1997) can be a model for shaping the post-Cold War regional security order in the Asia-Pacific. Here the ASEAN model of regional security order is seen as an *alternative* to the one built on a balance of power and bilateral alliance for the wider East Asia in the post-Cold War era. A security order, as Acharya envisaged, emerges in the process of building a community of sovereign nations for their common security.

Seeing the East Asia security order as being shaped by two contending sets of dynamics, we have a better understanding of the problem of international security in post-Cold War East Asia, the means and ways of East Asian security, and the prospects of cooperative security in East Asia. The debate on which set of dynamics has a greater influence on the shaping of regional security order and what the East Asian security architecture entails reveals contending sets of national interests and forces seeking to influence the East Asian security order with a unique set of methods, strategies, and frameworks. It will take time for multilateral institutionalism to institutionalize interstate interaction to the point of establishing a security community, if we ever get there without being pushed aside by geopolitical forces and their structural dynamism.

Study Questions

1. Discuss the balance of power and institutions/community as two different forces shaping the international security order in East Asia.
2. What is meant by East Asian security landscape, architecture, and order?
3. What is multilateral institutionalism for East Asian regional security?
4. How do you see the geopolitical scope of an East Asian security community? Is East Asia, Asia-Pacific, Asia, or Indo-Pacific a better or just different term? Why?
5. Discuss and compare ASEAN-, US-, and China-centric frameworks of multilateral institutionalism for regional security.
6. Has multilateral internationalism been successful for East Asian security? Is cooperative security a useful, effective framework for organizing international security in East Asia?

Further Reading

Acharya, Amitav, 1998. "Culture, Security, Multilateralism: The 'ASEAN Way' and Regional Order," *Journal of Contemporary Security Policy* 19(1): 55–84.

Acharya, Amitav, 2001a. *Constructing a Security Community in Southeast Asia*. London: Routledge.

Acharya, Amitav, and Alastair Iain Johnston. 2007. *Crafting Cooperation: Regional International Institutions in Comparative Perspective*. Leiden: Cambridge University Press.

Alagappa, Muthiah, 1998. *Asian Security Practice: Material and Ideational Influences*. Stanford: Stanford University Press.

Alagappa, Muthiah, 2003. *Asian Security Order: Instrumental and Normative Features*. Stanford: Stanford University Press.

Calder, Kent E., and Francis Fukuyama, 2008. *East Asia Multilateralism*. Baltimore: The Johns Hopkins University Press.

Chang, Jun Yan, 2016. "Essence of Security Communities: Explaining ASEAN," *International Relations of the Asia-Pacific* 16(3) 335–369.

Dewitt, David, 1994. "Common, Comprehensive, and Cooperative Security," *The Pacific Review* 7(1): 1–15.

Green, Michael J., and Bates Gill, 2009. *Asia's New Multilateralism: Cooperation, Competition, and the Search for Community*. New York: Columbia University Press.

Hemmer, Christopher, and Peter J. Katzenstein, 2002. "Why Is There No NATO in Asia? Collective Identity, Regionalism, and the Origins of Multilateralism," *International Organization* 56(3): 575–607.

Hong, Ki-Joon, 2015. "Institutional Multilateralism in Northeast Asia: A Path Emergence Theory Perspective," *North Korean Review* 11(1): 24–41.

Ikenberry, G. John, and Takashi Inoguchi. 2007. *The Uses of Institutions: The U.S., Japan, and Governance in East Asia*. New York: Palgrave Macmillan.

Ikenberry, G. John, and Jitsuo Tsuchiyama, 2002. "Between Balance of Power and Community: The Future of Multilateral Security Cooperation in the Asia Pacific," *International Relations of the Asia Pacific* 1(2): 69–94.

Keohane, Robert, and Lisa L. Martin, 1995. "The Promise of Institutionalist Theory," *International Security* 20(1): 39–51..

Krauss, Ellis S., and T. J. Pempel, 2004. *Beyond Bilateralism: U.S.-Japan Relations in Asia and the Pacific*. Stanford: Stanford University Press

Mearsheimer, John J., 1994. "The False Promise of International Institutions," *International Security* 19(3): 5–49.

Suh, J.J., and Peter J. Katzenstein, 2004. *Rethinking Security in East Asia: Identity, Power, and Efficiency*. Stanford: Stanford University Press.

Tow, William T., and Brendan Taylor, 2013. *Bilateralism, Multilateralism and Asia-Pacific Security*. London: Routledge.

10 Transnational Challenge

In This Chapter...

- Transnational issues
- Ethnicity, religion, and the nation-state
- Rights movement and transnational activism
- Environmental security
- International institutions of transborder governance
- States and interstate politics

Learning Objectives

By the end of this chapter, you will be able to
- Understand the unique set of forces in East Asia that transcend nation-state boundaries and influence IREA
- Understand that threats to the security of persons, groups, the environment, and the state and nation have been a major issue in IREA
- Use nontraditional security frameworks to analyze security challenges in IREA today
- Understand the role of nonstate agencies as well as that of the state in meeting transnational challenges
- Understand how international institutions form or evolve for regional governance on transnational issues.

East Asia is popularly known as a region where conventional forms of international relations have fully played out since World War II: geopolitics and wars, bipolar structure of interstate relations, and state-led economic development and competition in international commerce and business. Increasingly, though, IREA are faced with more nontraditional security and human development issues that transcend nation-state boundaries and authorities. Many of these issues are very "East Asian" in terms of their root causes, how they affect IREA, and the types of responses required in meeting these challenges.

This chapter will discuss these different types of transnational challenges in East Asia and the ambiguous role of the state in East Asia where state boundaries and interests tend to be barriers to the transnational interests. State responsibilities and capabilities are required for an effective response to transnational tensions, conflicts, and crises. We will discuss some of the critical cases to see how these challenges are met and through what mechanisms and arrangements. The chapter will consider some of the issues that influence the emergence of more effective mechanisms and arrangements for regional governance. But first we want to clarify the notion of "transnational" in our discussion as this is useful for us to understand the nature of the problem we discuss here.

TRANSNATIONAL ISSUES

Transnational issues are unique in the contemporary international system where nation-states are generally accepted as the primary and sovereign unit of polity organization. Transnational challenges are more acute in East Asia as the nation-state system has had a painful experience with establishing itself in post-1945 East Asia. As discussed in earlier chapters, most states in East Asia were being newly set up politically, with the boundaries of their authority being either unclearly defined or contentious.

Transnational, transborder, transboundary, and nontraditional are sometimes used interchangeably, but they mean slightly different things here. A core aspect that connects these terms is that they all indicate that the causal chains of human interests, activities, and relations extend across boundaries of political authority of different sovereign states. "Transborder" or "transboundary" is probably a more precise word for the same meaning here, as it connotes that a coherent set of human interests, activities, and relations fall within the political boundaries of different states that have conflicting, overlapping, or no jurisdiction over them. "Transnational," on the other hand, is often used when the issue is discussed in the discipline of international relations where national and state boundaries are considered "congruent" under the current nation-state system (see background discussion on this in Chapter 4). In reality, national boundaries are not "congruent" with the state boundaries has become an import factor that drive transnational challenges in East Asia.

Transnational challenge here is a slightly different concept from transnational activism, which refers to transborder activities that advocate for state responsibility and obligation in meeting these transnational challenges and engage in a nongovernmental capacity on behalf of certain people and issues on which no state has exclusive statutory jurisdiction. Transnational activism is "transnational" in organizing advocacy and engagement to pressure the states ultimately to act on transnational issues. Transnational challenges we discuss here are about these people and issues themselves. It involves a unique set of issues and dynamics that significantly impact on states' action and interaction and the development of national and multilateral institutions and mechanisms for regional governance.

That transnational issues are taken up as a major challenge in the study of international relations can be traced to the works of Robert Keohane and Joseph Nye in the 1970s (Keohane & Nye 1971, 1977). In their initial work, Keohane and Nye identify a growing influence of "transnational relations" on the state-centric international system. Transnational relations are "contacts, coalitions, and interactions across state boundaries that are not controlled by the central foreign policy organs of governments" and see "the reciprocal effects between transnational relations and the interstate system as centrally important to the understanding of contemporary world politics" (Keohane & Nye 1971: xi). While using "non-state actors" as a framework to sort out what these transnational relations are, they incorporate into the definition of transnational relations a broad range of interests, activities, and relations. These include multinational corporations, transnational organizations, and nonstate actors. The central problem they identify then is still valid in international relations today – how these transnational dynamics and interests influence the state's action and policy and interstate interactions.

Research on these political and economic transnational forces has further developed to focus on specific sets of transborder issues and dynamics. One of these forces is ethnicity-, religion-, or civilization-based "communal conflicts." Communal conflicts in IREA are tensions and conflicts over state-ethnic relations in the multination state and, increasingly, those over political economy and resources in local communities. In East Asia, these communal conflicts are often over resources and state benefits claimed by people of the same ethnic, religious groups across state boundaries. With the constraining effect of the Cold War structure easing, these transnational interests, activities, and relations have become more intensive.

A second stream of the forces driving the development and influence of transnational relations are those under the general category of "nontraditional security" challenges. There is no clear consensus as to what counts as a nontraditional security issue. There is a trend, though, toward making the list comprehensive, reflecting the growing security concerns over threats that are not "state centric and military oriented" (Caballero-Anthony 2016: 5) or violence not by the state in a military form that threatens the security of the state. Mely Caballero-Anthony explains nontraditional security as "a product of the time and place" that reflects the severity of the challenge in post-Cold War East Asia. Nontraditional security is not non-state-centric. This is reflected in its primary concern with human security rather than state security. The latter involves the problem of territorial integrity and regime survival. Human security broadens the traditional concept of international security and focuses on international threats to individual people: their physical, economic, and social security. This "reconceptualizing security" (Caballero-Anthony 2016: 5) is a key element in the shift away from the Cold War security paradigm in East Asia. Nontraditional security issues therefore include threats to economic, environmental, food, energy, water, health, and communal security, and tend to be seen as issues of comprehensive security, with a large list of security issues involved.

A third stream of developments in the transnational challenge in East Asia is interstate tensions and conflicts over national solidarity activities and movements across state boundaries that challenge the security and even legitimacy of the existing state. This seems to be an old or unsolved problem from the early Cold War decades where new states and the interstate system in East Asia emerged at the same time (see discussion in Chapter 4). The tensions and conflicts in the early 1960s over the establishment of Malaysia in Sabah and Sarawak, for example, led directly to the rise of ASEAN. In more recent times, the issue of similar historical roots reemerged in Mindanao, though reflecting a different religious and ethnic challenge to the Philippine state.

In mainland Southeast Asia, the insurgence of Malay groups in southern Thailand connecting with Malaysia has for decades been in a state of low-intensity violence that escalated into often conflict with Thai government forces from time to time. Up further north, tensions and violence between the Buddhist state of Rakhine and the Rohingya Islamic groups in Myanmar escalated into a series of humanitarian crises. This forced huge outflows of refugees from Rakhine to Bangladesh, Malaysia, and Indonesia and caused a triple security crisis: security of the Rohingya people, security of the neighboring countries, and security of the Rakhine state/Myanmar state.

Further north, in far western regions of China, different ethnic, religious, and national populations were incorporated into the state structure of the PRC: Uyghurs in Xinjiang and Tibetans in Xizang. As in the cases mentioned earlier, these populations are often parts of the larger national groups extending across borders. Tensions between the state and ethnic groups around China's border areas, the Koreans and Mongolians in the north, various small groups in the south connecting Indochina, and Uyghurs, Muslims, and Tibetans in the west, have been dealt with in different levels of settlement. Tensions in the western regions, though, reached a new high level and presented a security challenge to the people in these areas, the Chinese state, and states across the borders.

All these cases of transnational challenge share some common features. They all involve national groups across state boundaries where parts of the group in one state appeal for their rights and position in and with another state based on ethnic, religious, communal, and historical ties to the large national, ethnic, religious, or civilizational group across the borders. These interests and activities and the state's response can take violent forms that often threaten the security of the state, the security and wellbeing of the ethnic and religious, communal groups, and the security and wellbeing of the states whose populations are "nationally" connected. Moreover, these issues are motivated by the fact that the national community exists across jurisdictions of different states. These states have different and often conflicting interests and considerations in managing tensions and security threats. This often leads to high expectations of a more neutral public authority, nongovernmental or international organizations, for example, to intervene and help bring resolution to conflicts.

These features define transnational challenges in East Asia in general. The core problem of a transnational challenge is the mismatch between the transborder nature of the interests, activities, and relations of peoples and issues and the state structure and institutions set up in the interstate system. This, as Mohammed Ayoob argues (Ayoob 1995), is a particular security problem in "postcolonial" states in East Asia where the tensions between the state and transborder ethnic, religious, and communal forces in state building cause security problems for the state and people.

As such, we define transnational challenge in IREA in three categories: (1) tensions and conflicts over resources and natural conditions, such as water, land, forests, raw materials, and access to them because of conflicting, overlapping, or no clearly defined state jurisdiction, e.g., "unlawful, illegal" activities in a shared water way among states or on the high seas; (2) tensions and conflicts arising from ethnic, religious, or civilizational differences that cannot be addressed within state and interstate institutions; and (3) issues associated with the prevailing models of economic growth and political organization in East Asia where labor conditions, women's rights and positions, movements of people, human rights in politics and society, and balanced development constitute a distinct set of problems.

These issues not only transcend nation-state authorities and boundaries. Many of these issues see state authority and institutions, and the nation-state system itself, as part of the problem. Their remedy therefore often requires innovative international cooperation and intervention. These issues revolve around the unique conditions in politics, the economy, and society in East Asian states and affect the security of the state, people under its jurisdiction, and, in many cases, the security of the particular way they organize politics, the economy, and society.

ETHNICITY, RELIGION, AND THE NATION-STATE

Let us start with the first set of cases – the category of those driven by tensions between the state and its national constituencies – and explore how this set of challenges continues to be a source of interstate and intrastate tensions and conflicts and threatens the security of states and peoples and regional governance in IREA. We will also discuss how these issues complicate the interests and abilities of the state to respond with a positive solution and point out some of the nonstate mechanisms and processes that have emerged to meet the challenges.

Mindanao in Southern Philippines

The first case is Mindanao in the southern Philippines where Muslim populations dominate and were incorporated as the Autonomous Region of Muslim Mindanao in the Philippines, which is largely a Roman Catholic country. The tension between the state and the Muslim communities have deep historical roots to the time when Islam spread eastward in the Malay Archipelago to Sulu and Mindanao through today's Brunei and Sarah from the fourteenth and fifteenth centuries. Postcolonial state building in Southeast Asia saw the formation of Malaysia and Indonesia. ASEAN was formed initially as a collective response to the dispute over the territorial demarcation of the new states that claim jurisdiction over different parts of the Islamic populations.

While the tensions over the establishment of the jurisdiction of different states over different parts of the Muslim communities were dissolved through the ASEAN framework, the tension from the Muslim communities with the Philippine state continued, and violent conflict in the region started from the 1960s. In 1971, the Moro National Liberation Front was established to promote a separate political jurisdiction of Muslim communities in Mindanao, and political and insurgent activities have been a feature of life there ever since. The Philippine government has used military operations and martial law in the region to combat the insurgent activities and engaged in negotiations with the MNLF for a political solution.

The MNLF's position on the goal of the movement evolved over time from seeking independence to semi-autonomy. In 1984, a "splinter group" of the MNLF, the Mindanao Islamic Liberation Front, was established to push the cause further. In 1989, the government and MNLF agreed to establish the Autonomous Region in Muslim Mindanao within the Philippines constitutional structure, with the regional government to have a full range of executive, legislative, tax, and budget powers, with Sharia law the ruling authority, but committed to the notion that the region "shall remain an integral and inseparable part of the national territory of the Republic" (COP 2011: III-1). In 2011, the MIFL also moved to accept autonomy rather than independence in the region.

The Islamic insurgents and separatist movement in Mindanao took a significant turn in 2017 when the city of Marawi in the forefront of the Autonomous Region in Muslim Mindanao was attacked and besieged by armed, ISIS related militant groups. The Duterte government, with the assistance of other countries in the region, declared martial law and launched full-scale military operations to fight the "terrorists" and "liberated" the city. Thousands of people were killed and hundreds and thousands forced to evacuate the city, which was largely destroyed after months of armed conflict and urban fighting.

Muslim communities in Southern Thailand

A very similar case also occurred in southern Thailand, where Malay Muslim populations dominate in some states while the majority religious ethnic group in Thailand is Confucian Buddhist. The state has used both political and military means to incorporate the Muslim ethnic group into the Thai state. The Malay Muslims are part of the civilizational population of the Sultanate of Pattani that has spread into the "three border provinces" as well as Songkhla Province and Kelantan in northwestern Malaysia. The majority population of the "three border provinces" in the southern tip of Thailand connecting Malaysia is Malay Muslim.

The Sultanate was conquered by Thailand in the eighteenth century, and the 3.5 provinces have been part of Thailand ever since. Separatist insurgency started there after World War II, with "low-intensity violence" sustained there between militant insurgents and government counterinsurgent forces. Separatist groups attack police, schools, and other government buildings and facilities. Violence escalated rapidly in the new twenty-first century and added an element of militant jihadism to local ethnically inspired separatist activities. The violent insurgency and state counterinsurgency campaigns created a serious security threat to the people in the region, both Malay Muslim and Buddhist, for the Thai state and the people of Malaysia.

Muslim insurgence in the Philippines has been organized as a political movement aimed at achieving a separate political status for Muslim communities. Southern Thailand insurgency, however, has historically been a reaction to the state's "Thaification" policy from the 1930s and 1940s. This policy entailed the forced assimilation of Patani people and other ethnic groups into the Thai nation. In 1947, the Patani People's Movement was formed to seek autonomy for the Patani people.

Nationalist movements of Malay insurgence, the Patani National Liberation Front from 1959 and the Patani United Liberation Organization from 1968, were established, seeking to use organized violence to achieve independent statehood. These movements have not achieved what was achieved in the Philippines, and the separatist movements seem to have lost their way in the new century.

Rohingya in Northwest Myanmar

The Rohingya refugee crisis in more recent years bears some significant resemblance to the cases discussed earlier in terms of the root causes and the relations involved. Myanmar is one of the two East Asian states, the other being Indonesia, that have had a federal state system and a typical "multination state" (Bertrand & Liebert 2010). "National groups" in the postcolonial or postimperial polity all wished to claim statehood, but many have been incorporated into a single state structure and been pressured to assimilate into the majority nation. A multination state is a polity type with several "national" groups at its constitutional foundation. In East Asia, these types of states often have one distinct majority ethnic, religious, or civilizational group at the national and local levels.

This structure of the polity builds on the transnational nature of the national minority group and is a source of constant tension in interstate and intrastate ethnic relations. There are, as Bertrand and Liebert note, "parallel processes" of state building and nation building in the multination state often "poses a fundamental challenge to the idea of the homogenous nation state … each state represents a single, relatively cohesive nation" (Bertrand & Liebert 2010: 2). In the case of Myanmar, the federal state has seven "regions" that have the Burmese as the majority population (in central Myanmar) and seven "states" where a national minority population (non-Burmese) is the majority population in the local polity (in eastern and western Myanmar).

While the Myanmar state has engaged a Filipino- or Thai-style campaign, political and military methods combined to deal with the problem of the political status of "minority ethnic populations" in the local state, the Rohingya conflict took on a distinct form. Rohingya is a Muslim minority group in the northern area of Rakhine state bordering Bangladesh in the north where Muslims historically came via South Asia to Southeast Asia. Communal conflicts have been going on for decades, where the Rohingya people want to be recognized as a legitimate ethnic people there and the majority people in the local state are Buddhist, known as the Rakhine, and they resent the presence and expansion of Muslims in the state.

Neither the Myanmar government nor Rakhine state recognized "Rohingya" as a legitimate ethnic group and have prevented the Rohingya people from gaining full citizenship. "The tension is deepened by religious differences that have at times erupted into conflict" (CFR 2018) between Muslim groups and Buddhist nationalists. Notable among the crises are the one in 2015, which resulted in a mass migration of Rohingya people out of Myanmar, and the one in 2017, which saw violent skirmishes between the militant group, the Arakan Rohingya Salvation Army, and the government's antiterrorist forces. The "dissimilative" and discriminative approach of the state toward the Rohingya people and the violence in the state forced the Rohingya people to flee the country to Bangladesh, Malaysia, Thailand, and Indonesia, deepening the crisis into a transnational humanitarian one.

The refugee crisis is a syndrome of a larger and deep-rooted historical problem: multinational claims for a position in the state in the modern nation-state building of Myanmar. Unlike Muslim groups in Mindanao or Patani, the transborder Muslim groups in western Myanmar and northern Rakhine state were not asking to separate from Myanmar but rather for being accepted and assimilated into Myanmar. The federal political structure has a different majority group dominating in each state at each level, and the nationalist approach of the state and federal government resulted in a very discriminative political environment for the Rohingya. This is a multifaceted security problem for the Rohingya people, who form a minority group in the federal state, in Rakhine state, and are refugees to the neighboring countries affected by the massive influx of refugees from Myanmar.

Uyghur Muslims in Southern Xinjiang

A fourth case of an ethnicity-/religion-based transnational challenge is that of the Uyghur Muslims in southern Xinjiang in China. This area borders Central Asian states where historically Turkic Muslim populations dominated. Xinjiang was Islamized from the tenth century with nomadic Buddhist Mongols dominating in northern Xinjiang and Turkic Muslims in southern Xinjiang. As the land changed hands over a thousand years of history, the boundaries of state authorities also shifted or changed. The Chinese state, from the Qing Empire onward, subdued Turkic Muslims in southern Xinjiang, conquered Buddhist Mongols in northern Xinjiang, defeated Soviet-backed Uyghur separatist attempts in the 1930s and 1940s to form the First and Second East Turkistan Republic, and eventually turned Xinjiang into a province of China and, in 1955 under the PRC, into the Xinjiang Uyghur Autonomous Region. The majority population in the south are Uyghur Muslims, while the majority population in the north are Han Chinese.

Dru Gladney (1998) frames the problem of ethnic tensions largely as one of ethnic-state relations in China. The lower level of development of the Uyghur Muslims in the south relative to the Han Chinese in northern Xinjiang and the dynamics of the market economy increased social and economic gaps among the different ethnic groups, which flamed ethnic tensions. Violent clashes erupted from time to time between different ethnic groups in Xinjiang. With the September 11 attacks in 2001 and the US global war on terror, a new element was added to the problem of Uyghur Muslim relations with the Han Chinese and fundamentally with the political structure of the PRC. The ethnic and religious tensions already present below the surface has erupted into open conflict and violence, and the state has authorized a harsh crackdown on any Islam-inspired ethnic or religious activities.

The aforementioned cases show a pattern of transnational challenges and their effects on interstate and intrastate relations in IREA. Transborder ethnic and religious minority groups in the state they physically and institutionally reside in face various difficulties in determining their relations with the state. The majority ethnic group in the state provides the national basis and rationale on which the state exercises its power and authority. The transboundary nature of ethnicity- and religion-based political activities leads to a pattern of state-ethnic relations and interactions, as well as interstate relations and interactions. There is a threat to the security and wellbeing of individuals from the different ethnic groups involved and the security and legitimacy of the state.

As this set of transnational challenges has shown, the root causes of the transnational challenge go back in history to when these East Asian states established their modern form on a mixed national basis. Often with the strong nationalist conventions and state-centric institutional setup in these East Asian states, the tensions between ethnic and religious groups and between the groups and the state seem incapable of resolution within the current nation-state-based international system. The pattern of this set of transnational challenges also echoes some of the debates on nontraditional security issues in East Asia, such as "security for whom," "security from what," and "security by whom" (Caballero-Anthony 2016: 7, 9, 20–35). These transnational challenges in East Asia remind us of the unique East Asian political and national conditions and the complex mixture of traditional and nontraditional security elements in transnational challenges.

RIGHTS MOVEMENT AND TRANSNATIONAL ACTIVISM

A second set of transnational challenges also center around the problem of the forms of political organization of the polity in East Asian states. These challenges concern one aspect of nontraditional security issues. They relate to the security and wellbeing of individuals. Pushed further, though, human security, as defined by the United Nations Development Programme, is about security concerns in the "daily life" of individuals: job security, income security, health security, environmental security, security from crime (UNDP 1994: 3).

Moreover, human security issues, particularly in East Asia, are significantly related to the process of industrial development and the way it is organized. Most East Asian states were established after World War II. They engaged in large-scale and rapid industrialization in their organizing model (see additional discussion of this topic in Chapter 7). In this model of industrial growth, the growth interests and priorities of the state and industrial capital dominate. Lower labor costs, transaction costs, investment costs, and organizational costs enabled international competitiveness of products and business.

As economic growth continues with progressive industrial upgrading, these costs rise. The social structure under the institutional setting of the growth model would be able to continue to "suppress" the rising demands of individuals – labor, women, and the environment. These individuals were generally weak in the overall political structure, and the social and cultural system. They are often organized as a group in a particular sector, industry, or profession to seek the state's recognition of their contribution and entitlements in law and regulations, and influence in government policy on issues. Political and social movements have been an important form of collective action for individuals to gain their rights and entitlements as human beings living in a modern state. For some issues, such as environmental security, representative advocacy is necessary for effective results.

Moreover, the problem of human living conditions under the political economic system and social and cultural traditions in East Asia has been increasingly an international issue. The distinct patterns of labor conditions, women's rights, and environmental wellbeing are easily identified in an international comparative context. The political economic development of traditional East Asian societies is an important part of international movements and political economic change of the twentieth century. What makes these nontraditional security issues a transnational challenge is also the fact that these issues are globally connected and transcend national boundaries. Transnational activism and civil society groups emerged as active players that bring to bear successful experience in advancing human security and the wellbeing of these groups of individuals in developed societies and the standards and normative practices in these areas to the political process in East Asian states. They form a larger transnational movement for these groups of individuals for effective advocacy outcomes.

Labor rights movements

Labor rights movements in East Asia arose and intensified their activity in different East Asian countries at a similar stage of their industrial and economic development – mostly toward an advanced stage of industrial development in the given country: Japan in the 1950s and 1960s, Singapore, Korea, and Taiwan in the 1980s and 1990s, and China from the 2000s. In each country, the development of industrial relations in response took a slightly different form. In Singapore and Japan, for example, the state organized an employer-employee partnership in setting wages and other labor conditions and legal protections for labor. In Japan, for example, negotiations in response to a series of labor strikes in the 1960s led to the strengthening of the practice of "life-long employment" in Japanese firms. The establishment of the National Wage Council in 1972 in Singapore set up a tripartite mechanism among the government, trade unions, and employers to review and set rates for wage growth every year. The tripartite partnership evolved into a popular institutional arrangement for issue governance on labor conditions and industrial relations in East Asian countries.

Labor rights movements were much better and more effectively organized in South Korea. The involved organizations staged large-scale strikes and protests against the government in the 1980s and 1990s in South Korea and became an important part of the larger political movement for democratization in the country. This tradition of labor activism continues to be an important force that influences politics in Korea today. China has become a major site of tension over labor conditions and labor rights activities since the turn of the century. Various strategies seen in other East Asian countries have been devised to confront the problem.

While in each of these cases industrial relations and labor conditions are a complex national political issue or a problem of significant local complexity, there is a strong transnational dimension. Industrial growth and economic development in East Asia are uniquely known as an international process informed particularly by the region's state-centric development model. Its investment capital and production networks and export markets are international, global, and East Asia regional (see discussion in Chapter 7). These capital formations and networks are in part motivated by different national standards and requirements for labor compensation and influence labor conditions and rights standards under national settings.

Because the problems of labor conditions are transnational and the political structure there largely favors this type of growth model, the forms and actors who bring to bear political pressure and collective action for change in the state institutions and policy on labor rights and conditions are remarkably transnational. In discussing how agency for change comes more effectively from outside the political structure, Sabrina Zajak sees "transnational labor-rights activism" (Zajak 2017b: 2) groups and international organizations as an important layer in the global multi-level mobilization for "global regulatory modifications and a change in local practices" (Zajak 2017a: 125) in East Asian states. This is clearly seen in the development of labor conditions and rights movements in China.

Gender inequality

Labor rights issues in East Asian states often include the problem of child labor and that of the structures, institutions, and practices against women. Gender discrimination in labor conditions and rights, though, is part of the larger problem of women's status in society in East Asian states. Women's status in society is particularly a challenge for modern state building in East Asia because of the traditional social structure and cultural norms (see discussions in Chapter 6). Women are traditionally not expected to participate in social, economic, and political life on their own, and institutionally they are dependent on the household head, who is male, for their identity and livelihood.

Social, economic, and political changes resulting from efforts to build the modern state in East Asian countries for much of the twentieth century have changed the situation in various ways and to various extents. These changes also added new dimensions to the problem. Women are forced to participate in economic activities under still very discriminatory conditions in the workplace. A major World Bank report found in 2012 a relatively high female labor force participation rate in East Asia – "roughly 70 percent of women in East Asia and the Pacific participate in economic activities, higher than any other region," a higher participation of women "in the management and ownership of firms than in other developing regions," and a significant reduction in gender inequality in education and health (World Bank 2012: 1).

Social and political movements and advocacy for gender equality in East Asian societies are transnational or "crossing borders" (Wiesner-Hanks 2011: 357). The idea that all women in different countries face the same challenge of inequality in national societies and actively seek political, economic, and social rights spread to East Asian countries in the dual process of modern state building and globalization, remarkably through the work of international organizations and transnational women's rights networks and groups. Mina Roces and Louise Edwards in their collaborative project describe in detail women's movements in Asia and the role of international feminist movements, organizations, and activist groups in breaking up national boundaries in promoting women's rights in East Asian countries.

Linda Etchart (2015: 703–4) identifies three waves of transnational feminist activism in the twentieth century and their different international foci and content in rights development. The first wave occurred in the late nineteenth century and the first half of the twentieth century, with largely an Atlantic focus on women's suffrage; the movement in the second stage, in the 1960s and 1970s, extended to the Third World in their efforts at modern state building, finally, the third stage started in the 1980s with the increasingly fast pace of globalization. Transnational women's activism and movements in East Asia are a particular response to the early waves and aimed to engage more effectively with local political, social, economic, and cultural conditions.

The evolution of women's rights movements in East Asian countries reflects the development of transnational feminist activism. The early waves of transnational feminist activism focused on the universal rights of women in politics, economics, society, and education. Transnational feminist activity extended from working through the dynamics and mechanisms of the worldwide projects of modern state building in the 1960s and 1970s and globalization from the 1980s. Various women's rights alliances and networks in East Asian countries are a manifestation of the real essence of transnational feminist movements where women act transnationally to exercise power and influence and spearhead political, economic, and social processes for change. The United Nations Decade for Women of 1976–1985 and the series of four *United Nations Conferences on Women* (UNCW) between 1975 and 1995 demonstrated the important role of international organizations in transnational movements for women. The 1995 UNCW in Beijing was an instance of a high-impact event that generated debate on the issue and provided a platform for action on promoting gender equality in East Asia.

Women's rights activists in East Asian countries found a challenge in what Shelley Cavalieri considers the victim-agent problem (Cavalier 2011) in transnational women's activism and movement. The victim-agent problem in transnational women's activism and movements reflects different considerations in the nature of the woman question. Women are seen by some activist groups as victims of political, social, cultural, and economic structures and conditions, and they are encouraged to challenge the roles and positions society imposes on them. Others encourage women to defend their jobs and positions but to seek greater protection and state support of their rights.

The two dominant paradigms arise largely from their different assumptions of the woman question. As Mina Roces contends, "For large parts of the twentieth century, Asian women activists disliked the word 'feminism' because it was associated with 'Western feminism' that was caricatured as aggressively individualistic, anti-male, anti-children, and therefore anti-family… and alien and inapplicable to the 'Asian' context" (Roces 2010: 1). Women's activists in East Asia have practiced their own "Asian feminism" appropriate and relevant to the conditions in each "national" context.

ENVIRONMENTAL SECURITY

Another issue area in transnational challenge in this category is that of environmental security. The transnational challenge of environmental security in East Asia is associated more closely with the rapid and large-scale industrialization that East Asian countries have collectively experienced than the problem of global climate change. This has not only helped generate unique forms and content of transnational activism and movements on environmental security in East Asia but also influenced the character of the transnational environmental movement. Robert D. Kaplan, in his 1994 *Atlantic Monthly* essay on "The Coming Anarchy," cited "environmental degradation" as a national security issue, which led to an interesting debate in the field about environmental problems and national security (Kaplan 1990; Deudney 1990; Levy 1995). Scholarship on this topic, though, has evolved into a rapidly growing new field of nontraditional security studies. One primary message from Kaplan's original "Coming Anarchy" argument, that environmental security should be a primary transnational challenge in many East Asian countries, is still relevant and influential.

Rapid industrialization and economic development and the way it is organized and the global shifting of manufacturing to East Asian countries (Chapter 7) led to significant levels of environment degradation in these countries, particularly at the peak stage of production and manufacturing in countries' industrial development. This has also been accompanied by growing communal and transnational competition and conflict over resources and materials. The market-driven business model of industrial sectors has focused little attention on the environment effects of business growth and development. The government's growth-focused policy and programs, on the other hand, exacerbated the security threat to people in these countries.

Simon Avenell conducted an interesting study to investigate how transnational environmental activism developed in Japan and Korea in the 1960s and 1970s from being "a domestic phenomenon of local mobilizations against pollution and development" and "expanded into a new array of transnational initiatives, many with a specific focus on pollution in the countries of East Asia" (Avenell 2017a: 1). Transnational environmental activism in East Asia connects sources and effects of threats to the environment across national boundaries as they are related to transborder networked industrial activities in East Asian countries. A transnational movement developed in Korea and Japan in the 1970s, for example, to "stop the relocation of a polluting mercurochrome plant from Japan to South Korea." The development of transnational activism on this issue involves transforming of Japanese domestic activism from focusing on victims of the Japanese state and industry to transnational activists that see the pollution problem in a broader perspective beyond the Japanese nation-state.

Along similar lines, Fengshi Wu and Bo Wen (2014) investigate the development of transnational environmental activism in Japan, Korea, Taiwan, and China. It is a transnational phenomenon in which "the dynamics of environmental movements is not only shaped by the trajectory of industrialization and state–market structures, but also, if not more importantly, by the overall political development and the process of democratization" (Wu & Wen 2014: 105). The differences in the "key features of political culture and progress" of these countries explain the divergence in the forms of environmental activism in these countries, the different roles of "NGO-centered policy advocacy and mass-based protests," and the different levels of effectiveness of environmental activism in East Asian countries. While nongovernmental organizations (NGOs) have contributed substantially to the rise of public environmental awareness in East Asian societies, their role in the actual national policy and political process on environmental issues is circumscribed and certainly much more limited in China.

In a study within the same project on environment and society in East Asia, Piya Pangsapa (2014) looked at the development of environmental activism in mainland Southeast Asia and showed the complexity of environmental problems in the larger context of East Asia-wide industrialization and economic development and the challenge for environmental activists on local environmental issues "to develop a perspective that is less state centric and more focused on regional relations and processes" (Pangsapa 2014:39) and engage local knowledge and community interests in advocacy. Regional environmental actors, with a strong sense of ecological citizenship and environmental justice, play an important role in bringing justice to the environment. Environmental activism brings regional and local dynamics together to pressure the state to make changes in national policy and institutions.

Environmental problems in East Asia, particularly industrial pollution, have been a primary issue area for environmental activism and movements in these countries and across the region. This has been increasingly a transnational challenge because environment degradation is closely related to industrial development and the way it is structured in East Asian countries. The model of industrial and economic growth that prevails in the region connects these East Asian countries in production networks and transborder value and supply chains. It also poses a transnational challenge because pressures for government to act in policy and regulation and for industrial corporations to change their practices arise from the transnational complexity of manufacturing organization in East Asia and transnationally organized collective action to influence national governments and industrial sectors. It is the dual-track dynamism of moving away from and beyond the nation-state-centric framework and building transnational political pressures on the state and national corporations that defines the development and character of transnational environmental activism and the politics of environmental security in East Asia.

East Asian development has advanced to a new stage where the regional economy is heavily influenced by a much stronger, more outward looking Chinese industrial capital and capacity. A significant part of the internationalization of Chinese industrial and economic activities is connected to East Asia and the world. Chinese investment and efforts to build networks of industrial and development projects in East Asian countries, more recently in the large platform of the BRI initiative, focuses largely on the infrastructure sector in the form of industrial parks and special economic zones. While this helps spur further industrial growth and economic development in both China and the host countries, it inevitably engenders the same problem of the social and economic consequences of industrial capital–led development that early industrialized countries experienced: labor conditions, environmental problems, effects on traditional forms of economic life, community interests, and established interests of local industries and people in the host country.

Some interesting themes have emerged from our discussion of transnational challenges in labor rights, women's rights, and environmental security. These issues are transnational because of the transnational nature of industrial growth and economic development in East Asian countries. There is also a pattern of tensions in East Asian transnational activism in framing actors as victims of the state, industrial capital, social structures, and cultural traditions, and as agents of their causes for rights and justice; and therefore tension arises between pursuing international standards and norms and engaging local knowledge, and political economic and cultural conditions. These patterns reflect the challenge for transnational activism to support and influence modern political and economic development in East Asia.

INTERNATIONAL INSTITUTIONS OF TRANSBORDER GOVERNANCE

The third set of transnational challenges relates to many of the issues in the first two sets in terms of the causes and issue areas, such as environmental problems and communal conflicts over resources. But these transnational issues cause harmful effects across the borders or in areas with no clearly agreed exclusive jurisdiction of the state: activities on shared waterways among several states, crime against persons in international waters, forced transborder migrants, and so forth. These activities affect the interests of states and people in different ways. Because they tend to cause tension and conflict between nation-states, these issues will ultimately require states to cooperate to find a collective resolution to conflicts.

This is where international institutions develop in particular functional issue areas beyond and above the sovereign state, a mechanism that neofunctionalism on regional integration has noted long before (Mitrany 1948; Haas 1964; and see discussion in Chapter 8). In East Asia, there is a lack of international institutions in regulating these issues, though industrial and economic activities are interconnected and integrative in the region. Transborder security issues are pervasive in the region in relation to water, food, health, natural disasters, energy, climate, and migration. We discuss two cases of transborder security issues and show how international institutions evolved for a multilateral solution to the problems.

Governance of international waters

The first case is the development of the Mekong River Police Patrol regime. The Mekong River is a waterway running through mainland Southeast Asia from China in the north to Vietnam in the south, bordering Myanmar, Laos, Thailand, and Cambodia in between. The waterway is a lifeline for countries bordering on the river and a primary trade route for shipping products and materials across borders and is also a site for drug trafficking, armed robbery, hijacking, and other crimes. The notorious Golden Triangle for opium traffic and human smuggling is in the border area on the river between China, Myanmar, Thailand, and Laos.

Mekong is a "transboundary river" that runs across the boundaries of at least one country, and parts of it therefore fall under separate jurisdictions of the surrounding states. It is also a boundary river that runs between two states, so the river's water is "international water" that falls outside the jurisdiction of those states. The increase in transborder crimes on the river poses the challenge of whose responsibility it is and who has the authority to provide security for people and property on and around the river. In the early 1990s, the wars on mainland Southeast Asia winded down and narcotics growth and trade in the Golden Triangle area rose quickly as a security problem for the "subregion." In 1993, China, Laos, Myanmar, and Thailand, facilitated by the United Nations International Drug Control Program (UNDCP), signed a Memorandum of Understanding on Drug Control in the Greater Mekong Subregion for transborder cooperation in law enforcement in fighting narcotics in the region. One key mechanism implemented was to set up a series of border liaison offices (BLOs) at "recognized border crossings" along the Mekong River from 2000.

These BLOs are coordinating offices for national law enforcement agencies "on each side of the national border" and act as "a centralized clearing house for information received from the vicinity of border areas" (UNODC 2010: 4). By 2009, there were 70 BLOs in the greater Mekong subregion. In 2003, joint BLO patrols on the Mekong River started. In 2009, BLO functions extended to cover "migrant smuggling, environmental and wildlife crimes" with the support of UN and national agencies. In the wake of the 2011 armed attacks on Chinese ships on the river in the Golden Triangle area that killed 13 crew members in execution style, China has taken a more proactive approach and organized a "long-term mechanism" of Joint Police Armed Patrol in the river by China, Laos, Myanmar, and Thailand, with a true law enforcement mandate and genuine capabilities.

This is a classic case of a nontraditional or, more precisely, transnational security issue in East Asia. It involves the shaping of a security order in an area where national interests, capacities, and jurisdictions are coordinated for regional governance. In this case, cooperation at the "subregional" level is enabled by efforts at multiple levels: by international organizations such UNODC and national agencies on either side of the border operating in the BLO that has "jurisdiction" and operational mandate and capabilities over transboundary issues and activities. This mechanism is effective in areas beyond the boundaries of the nation-state and sanctioned by both supranational and national authorities; the mechanism transforms a transnational issue into an international framework of area governance.

Regional institutions for climate change regulation

Another issue concerns the transborder effects of harmful climate conditions originating in one country on the health of people across borders in other countries. This is the case of the Southeast Asian haze that affects people in Brunei, Indonesia, Malaysia, Singapore, and, to a lesser degree, the Philippines and Thailand. Slash-and-burn is a traditional method in agriculture in Southeast Asia. This is true particularly in Sumatra and Kalimantan in Indonesia, where slash-and-burn is an effective and economical method of land cultivation and clearing. Among other damaging effects, the haze caused by the smoke from fires creates harmful climate conditions, and often the haze appears over countries that have nothing to do with the fires. Over the past 10 years, there have been eight major haze crises in Southeast Asia that caused health problems and disruptions in travel.

At the core of international tensions over the haze has been the question of who is responsible for the disaster, whether it is a natural disaster or manmade disaster, and how the states should respond to the problem. In debating the cause of the haze problem, researchers and political analysts have concentrated on this farming practice, agribusiness, and land use (Varkkey 2016: 3) and the business model of land development in Sumatra and Kalimantan, Indonesia (Varkkey 2016; Islam et al. 2016). Indonesia sees this as largely an internal matter of a sovereign nation and has been reluctant to sign onto a multilateral solution to the problem. Indonesia was the last country to sign, in 2013, the 2002 ASEAN agreement on combating haze pollution.

On the other hand, frustrated by the meager process in an ASEAN collective solution to the problem, Singapore, the country that is most significantly affected by this, took up the problem as a domestic problem and enacted a law, the Transboundary Haze Pollution Act in 2014, that is "extraterritorial" (Mohan 2017: 2) and "imposes both civil and criminal liability on errant companies domiciled or operating overseas but which cause or contribute to haze pollution in Singapore."

As a transborder security issue, the Southeast Asian haze spurred intensive regional efforts to combat the problem. ASEAN held a Workshop on Transboundary Pollution and Haze in ASEAN Countries in 1992, forged an agreement on the Cooperation Plan and Haze Technical Task Force in 1995 that organizes the ASEAN Ministerial Meeting on Haze, the Regional Haze Action Plan in 1995, the Regional Haze Action Plan in 1997 that set up an operational mechanism for haze monitoring by the ASEAN Specialized Meteorological Centre, the Hanoi Plan of Action, and the ASEAN Peatland Management Initiative in 2002.

All these efforts led incrementally to a legally binding ASEAN agreement on combating haze pollution. Moe Thuzar sees these region-wide efforts as having "had limited success in managing the problem" (Thuzar 2016: 19), perhaps partly because of the ASEAN way of regional institutions, partly because of "the political nature of regional responses," and the reality that ASEAN countries are "more responsive to their domestic priorities over collective regional interests." To make responses to the transnational challenge more effective, the states that are most affected resort to bilateral and unilateral negotiation and bargaining. In particular, Singapore and Indonesia, and Malaysia and Indonesia agreed to cooperate in peatland management to support the operation of the ASEAN environmental framework, along with assistance from international organizations and NGOs.

The case of the Southeast Asian haze shows some unique features or patterns of institutional development. Mechanisms and frameworks have developed gradually and the binding power of multilateral arrangements for regional governance on transborder security issues has strengthened incrementally, very much in line with the ASEAN way. The process is largely intergovernmental and multilateral in shaping a transborder security order for multilateral governance on climate conditions. This is intergovernmental between and among the states that are affected by the issue. These states relate to the problem in different ways, which makes a regional multilateral solution hard to come by. It involves inputs of bilateral and even unilateral efforts for states to develop consensus, compromise and tradeoff, and input of national capabilities to influence state actions across borders. It shows the pluralist nature of regional governance where interests and capabilities at multiple levels, national, regional, subregional, and international, converge for an effective outcome of multilateral arrangement.

These are yet more instances of transnational challenges in this category in IREA. The two cases discussed in this section are representative of the long list of similar cases across East Asia in this very critical area of transnational challenge. The two cases, though, are substantive in demonstrating key features of transnational challenges and the complexity of the national and regional context in which these transnational challenges arise and the responses of the states and nonstate actors evolve.

STATES AND INTERSTATE POLITICS

In this chapter, we have discussed various aspects of transnational challenge. We have covered a significant amount of what would be categorized as "nontraditional security issues," but it is not all about nontraditional security issues. Nontraditional security issues, in a significant way, concern security threats to individuals rather than to states, nations, territories, or communities. In actual practice, at least in East Asia, as we have shown, it is difficult to separate them. More often, it is the threat to a state, nation, or ethnic, religious, economic, social, or cultural community that generates much of the transnational, transborder, transboundary dynamics and tension. Moreover, effective responses or solutions to these problems often involve a combined effort at different levels that evolve over a period: regional, subregional, international, and, overwhelmingly, national. Therefore, "transnational" or transborder and transboundary capture the essence of the set of security issues.

Furthermore, "nontraditional security issue" concerns the distinct forms in which security threats manifest and defines security in an all-encompassing fashion that includes almost all functional issue areas in international relations. This broad framework allows the extension of traditional security concepts and methods to broad functional issues and unnecessarily "securitizes" (Buzan et al. 1998) these issue areas. Security in this definition loses its distinct value as a subfield in international relations and is ineffective at providing useful knowledge to support finding a solution to the challenge.

More importantly, the defining debate on the security of whom, by whom, and for whom seems to have an unintended effect of confusing agent and victim, individual actor and group actor, and cause and effect of the security threats and concealing the real problem underlying transnational issues in East Asia: the state or the nation-state. Our discussion has shown that it is the indeterminacy of state and nation that causes "transnational challenges" to be transnational in the first place. This indeterminacy involves the problem of the boundaries of the nation-state, its jurisdiction, identity, the scope of communal political economy, and the parallel evolution of the nation and the state. All of these factors make a national and international response a complex challenge for all actors involved. In the end, regional efforts toward a resolution to transnational issues and toward regional governance often come down to pressuring the state to act in support of regional governance on the issue.

The transnational challenges in East Asia as discussed in this chapter exhibit some unique features. First, these issues challenge state authority and structures because they are the cause of transnational security issues, or the issues fall outside state jurisdiction. Moreover, they are transnational because the causes and effects of challenges to human security are distributed across state boundaries. This creates significant difficulties in cause removal, damage compensation, and threat control and prevention.

Furthermore, these issues are transnational also because they require a significant level of transnational activism by a mixture of mobilized and networked international and local activities and nongovernmental advocacy groups. Finally, they are also transnational because a more practical and, perhaps, effective form of response to these challenges is provided, or expected to provide, by multilateral mechanisms and multilevel partnerships above and beyond the sovereign state.

Study Questions

1. Why are transnational challenges particularly acute in East Asia?
2. A significant paradigmatic shift in security analysis has occurred in post-Cold War IREA. What is this shift? What are the implications of the shift for the region's approach to transnational issues?
3. How do the regime types of East Asian states impact the development and resolution of transnational issues in East Asia?
4. How does the East Asian model of industrial growth and economic development influence the character of transnational challenges in East Asia?
5. Discuss the role of international organizations, rights movements, and nongovernmental activists in meeting the transnational challenge in East Asia.
6. Discuss specific examples of the transnational challenge not covered in this chapter and debate some of the issues and themes discussed in the chapter.
7. Does the transnational challenge in East Asia indicate a level of deficiency of the existing nation-state-centric institutions in East Asia? How?

Further Reading

Avenell, Simon, 2017b. *Transnational Japan in the Global Environmental Movement*. Honolulu: University of Hawaii Press.

Ayoob, Mohammed, 1995. *The Third World Security Predicament: State Making, Regional Conflict, and the International System*. Boulder: Lynne Rienner.

Baksh, Rawhide, and Wendy Harcourt, 2015. *The Oxford Handbook of Transnational Feminist Movements*. Oxford: Oxford University Press.

Baldwin, David, 1997. "The Concept of Security," *Review of International Studies* 23: 5–26.

Buzan, Barry, Ole Wæver, and Jaap de Wilde, 1998. *Security: A New Framework for Analysis*. Boulder: Lynne Rienner.

Cavalier, Shelley, 2011. "Between Victim and Agent: A Third-Way Feminist Account of Trafficking for Sex Work," *Indiana Law Journal* 86(4): 1410–1458.

CFR, 2018. *The Rohingya Crisis*. New York: Council on Foreign Relations.

Davison, Remy, 2011, "Actors Beyond Borders? Transnational Actors in the Asia Pacific," pp. 225–248 in Michael K. Connors, et al., *The New Global Politics of the Asia Pacific*. London: Routledge.

Deudney, Daniel, 1990. "The Case Against Linking Environmental Degradation and National Security," *Millennium* 19(3): 461–476.

Emmers, Ralf, 2013. *Resource Management and Contested Territories in East Asia*. Basingstoke: Palgrave Macmillan.

Emmers, Ralf, Mely Caballero-Anthony, and Amitav Acharya, 2006. *Studying Non-traditional Security in Asia: Trends and Issues*. London/New York: Marshall Cavendish Academic.

Haas, Ernst B., 1964. *Beyond the Nation-State: Functionalism and International Organization*. Stanford: Stanford University Press.

Hameiri, Shahar, 2015. "Governing Transboundary Pollution: Southeast Asia's Haze from Part II – Case Studies," pp. 77–124 in Shahar Hameiri, Lee Jones *Governing Borderless Threats*. Cambridge: Cambridge University Press.

Harris, Paul G., 2014. *Graeme Lang, Routledge Handbook of Environment and Society in Asia*. London: Routledge.

Harris, Paul G., and Graeme Lang, 2014. *Routledge Handbook of Environment and Society in Asia*. London: Routledge.

Lee, Geun, 2002. "Environmental Security in East Asia: The Regional Environmental Security Complex Approach," *Asian Perspective* 26(2):77–99.

Lim, Kyunghan, 2015, "Non-traditional Maritime Security Threats in Northeast Asia: Implications for Regional Cooperation," *Journal of International and Area Studies* 22(2): 135–146.

Mitrany, David, 1948. "The Functional Approach to World Organization," *International Affairs* 24 (3): 350–363

Narine, Shaun, 2007. "Economic Security and Regional Cooperation in the Asia-Pacific: Evaluating the Economics-Security Nexus," pp. 195–219 in

Amitav Acharya and Evelyn Goh, *Reassessing Security Cooperation in the Asia Pacific*. Cambridge: MIT Press.

Roces, Mina, and Louise Edwards, 2010. *Women's Movements in Asia: Feminisms and Transnational Activism*. London: Routledge.

Thakur, Ramesh, 2001. "Threats Without Enemies, Security Without Borders: Environmental Security in East Asia," *Journal of East Asian Studies* 1(2): 161–189.

Umegaki, Michio, Lynn Thiesmeyer, and Atsushi Watabe, 2009. *Human Insecurity in East Asia*. Tokyo: United Nations University Press.

USODC, 2010. *Border Liaison Offices in Southeast Asia 1999–2009*. Vienna: United Nations Office for Drug Control.

Wiesner-Hanks, Merry E., 2011. "Crossing borders in Transnational Gender History," *Journal of Global History*, 6(3): 357–379.

World Bank, 2012. *Toward Gender Equality in East Asia and the Pacific*. Key Finding. Washington, DC: World Bank Group.

Zajak, Sabrina, 2017a. "Rethinking Pathways of Transnational Activism," *Global Society* 31(1): 125–143.

Zajak, Sabrina, 2017b. "Transnational Activism," *Global Society* 31(1): 125–143.

Zha, Wen, 2017. "Trans-Border Ethnic Groups and Interstate Relations Within ASEAN: A Case Study on Malaysia and Thailand's Southern Conflict," *International Relations of the Asia-Pacific* 17(2): 301–327.

11 Domestic Structures

> **In This Chapter...**
>
> - The "second image" problem
> - Three types of domestic structures
> - Regime types and IREA
> - International policy of the developmental state
> - Liberal states, pacific community, and democratic peace
> - Social ideas, economic interests, and national identities
> - When Duterte became president
> - Mechanisms of domestic and international linkage
>
> **Learning Objectives**
>
> By the end of this chapter, you will be able to
> - Understand the general features of internal structures of East Asian states as they are relevant to IREA
> - Use the framework of domestic-international linkage to analyze the sources of influence on IREA
> - Understand how social and economic interests in a country influence the country's preferences in international policy and relations
> - Explain why national identity and domestic contestation over it is a unique factor influencing IREA
> - Understand that the way in which a polity is organized in a state influences its policy preferences and international behavior in IREA.

Understanding the causal link between the structures and dynamics of national politics and society on the one hand, and the international behavior and policy of a country and, hence, war, peace, and development in international relations on the other, is a perennial problem for IR scholars and the discipline. This is particularly so for IREA.

From discussions in previous chapters, we have seen many instances of how national politics and society influence issues and developments in IREA and the complexity and extraordinariness of the impacting power of the economic interests, social preferences, and state institutions of a nation. Here we are particularly interested in whether domestic politics, and social, economic, and normative preferences and identities of East Asian states significantly influence, if not determine, the patterns and dynamism of IREA, and how these forces, interests, and behavioral patterns at the national level translate into policy orientations and interaction patterns in IREA. Such knowledge is useful for our understanding of IREA and our explanation of war and peace, development and underdevelopment in East Asia. We would be ineffective if we confined their causes to the structures and dynamics to the international and global levels.

This chapter discusses what these national structures and dynamics are, how they influence outcomes and developments in IREA, how the perennial problem of domestic-international linkage manifests in IREA, and how we use this framework to explain IREA in the context of the larger issue of the boundary and connection between domestic and international politics.

THE "SECOND IMAGE" PROBLEM

The problem that national structures and dynamics influence and complicate international development and outcomes has been part of the literature on the location of the causal structures and forces in the international system. Kenneth Waltz, in his pioneering work *Man, the State, and War* (1959), "stratifies" the international system into three levels: the individual, the state, and the international, with a profound conviction that the forces at the state level, or the dynamics of "the internal structure of states" (Waltz 1959: 82), explain war and peace among states. Waltz calls the forces at the state level the "second image of international relations" (Waltz 1959: 122).

Waltz, however, did not really believe that the second image is valid and did not call for a "reverse" (Gourevitch 1978). Waltz can't really reconcile, for example, the policy preferences of the liberals in the United States and United Kingdom and the character of the international outcomes arising from the actions of these states in the early part of the twentieth century, which were not all that "liberal." This, we all know, led Waltz to prefer the third image, international anarchy and structure, in building up his major contribution to the post-1945 development of international relations theory and to the rise to dominance of the international structure theory. The structural theory is generally dismissive of the second image in explaining foreign policy and international outcomes.

Evidence of the forces of the second image influencing IREA, however, has been abundant and persistent. In explaining war and peace in IREA (Chapter 3), for example, we are consistently led to investigate the impact of the constitutional dynamics of nation-states and the different types of regimes on the state's actions in war and peace. In explaining international development outcomes in East Asia, and the development of regional economic integration and institutions in particular (Chapters 6 and 7), we are unable to understand the unique pattern and character of East Asian regionalism unless we understand how national political economy is organized in these states. In explaining the increasingly more nontraditional security challenges in IREA and the ineffectiveness of the current interstate institutions and mechanisms in coping with the challenges (Chapters 8 and 9), we have seen the resilience of the forces of states' internal structures. And of course, regarding the "cultural dynamics" in East Asia discussed in Chapter 6, much has to do with the social structures, mechanisms of social organization, and the national identity and preferences of the national states.

Beyond IREA, the second image analysis has still occupied an important position in IR scholarship. Some of the themes in Waltz's original second image thesis are taken up for further exploration and debate, updated with contemporary developments. One stream of the scholarship on the topic looks at whether liberal states tend more toward peace, an idea that goes even farther back, to Immanuel Kant in the eighteenth century and his "perpetual peace thesis" (Doyle 1983, 1986). These "liberal" states are specified as "democratic" states in the further development of the research program and the "democratic peace" theory that focuses specifically on whether there is a connection between democratic states and international peace. This is, of course, part of a broad debate on "regime types and conflict involvement of states" (Maoz & Abdolali 1989: 3). A key organizing proposition treated in Waltz's original thesis, this is systematically investigated in an analytical and empirical fashion significantly influenced by the Correlations of War Project, led by David Singer from the 1960s (Gurr 1974; Gochman & Maoz 1984; Maoz & Abdolali 1989; Singer & Small 1972).

With all the explorations, controversies, and debates in the research program, the literature on the issue validates the theoretical and methodological importance of the second image problem. It also provides a useful framework for seeing what "internal structures" we are looking at in these second image analyses and how we identify, measure, and analyze the causal link between the internal structures of states and actions, outcomes, and developments in IREA.

THREE TYPES OF DOMESTIC STRUCTURES

The long list of different national structures and dynamics can be grouped into three general categories, or three different types of internal structures, considering the different analytical frameworks scholars use in their investigations. The first set consists of the types of state or *regime types*. The second image problem was originally raised over how different types of states, good or bad, republican or imperial, democratic and nondemocratic states, relate to the behavioral propensity of the state in war or peace. Realism's fundamental assumption of the state as a unitary actor influences the notion that different states act differently in international relations. Scholarly interest in whether and how different types of states lead to their war- or peace-prone behavior has dominated the research paradigm on the internal structures of the state.

Increasingly, though, scholars are driven to look inside the state to see how it is internally organized. The question is why we have different types of states in the first place. Researching social, pluralist, and, indeed, liberal theories of how states are internally organized and how the national interest and purpose in international relations form internally has become an important trend. It focuses on the formation of *"social preferences"* (Moravcsik 1997: 513) of the state in international politics, the social structures behind them, and, more specifically, on social groups and classes and their interests, ideas and relations. These have a bearing on state institutions, policy preferences, and international behavior and identity.

This is particularly relevant to investigations of IREA where the particular way a national political economy is organized and the contested process of modern nation-state building posed a significant challenge for understanding not only what meaning the types of states have in East Asian countries but also, and perhaps more importantly, how these different states have come about and how their interests and relations bear on the state's international behavior with respect to war, peace, and development.

The third type of internal structure has to do with the *institutions of national politics* of the state. This relates somewhat to the first category, regime types, but they are more of a locally institutionalized way of how politics, politicians, and policy operate in the state. This set of internal structures entails, for example, whether the country has a presidential or parliamentary system, whether there are regular, competitive elections and, hence, frequent change in political leadership, how politicians, state bureaucracy, and public policy are institutionally related, and where causal chains lie in international policy formulation. This set of internal structures influences and impacts one country's international policy preferences and relations with other countries. The way they influence these preferences and relations is unique and specific to the internal conditions of states. We now turn to a discussion of these different regime types in specific cases to show how regime type, social preferences, and institutions of national politics of the state matter in IREA.

REGIME TYPES AND IREA

Regime type refers to the political structure and organization of a polity. Regime type theory is about whether and how a state's regime type makes a difference in its international policy orientation and behavioral preference. One key intention behind Waltz's original second image thesis is to see whether being a "good or bad" state matters in war and peace and, if so, whether there are things we can do to remove defects from bad states to reduce the probability of war or at least to more effectively explain war (Waltz 1959: 80–158). The issue is really regime type where regime here concerns how the governing authority is organized in a polity. The underlying theme that bad, defective states are likely to resort to war led to the development of a massive research paradigm on the relationship between liberal states and war. Regime type theory hypothesizes that different regime types matter in a state's propensity to seek peace or economic development. Research inspired by this theory focuses on proving that liberal states tend more toward peace, and democracies are likely to succeed in economic development.

The development of regime type theory and the research programs it inspires is also aided by another influential stream of scholarship on the role of different regime types in modern economic development. Seymour Lipset proposed in his original Lipset thesis that democracy is likely to work better as a nation's economy and society arrive at some stage of development (Lipset 1959). This thesis stood against the large background of the overwhelmingly dominant modernization theory and policy frameworks in the 1950s and 1960s that see the defects in states in the developing world as the primary obstacle to economic development and call for "getting the regime type right" first to pave the way to modern economic development. Adding weight to the debate, Samuel Huntington, in one of his early works on states of non-Western culture and civilization (Huntington 1968), argues that political priorities in "developing societies" are different, so state institutions required for organizing state authority would also be different.

INTERNATIONAL POLICY OF THE DEVELOPMENTAL STATE

One influential type of state in East Asia, as shown in earlier chapters, has been the developmental state. There seems to be a great theoretical and mythological interest in seeing how the developmental state influences the state's international activities, relations, and policy, which is not typically covered in developmental state literature. In discussing the developmental state as an instance of internal structures, we take the developmental state as a typical and prevalent form of state in industrializing East Asia. Developmental state is a type of state that operates under a whole-of-nation framework of organizing national industrial and economic development and features a tripartite organizational structure based on a state-industrial capital-bureaucracy alliance and collaboration. Development states are found to be particularly active and influential in East Asian countries with their rapid industrial growth and modern economic development. The term is well established in the scholarship on East Asian development and political economy (Johnson 1983; Woo-Cumings 1999), reflecting a widespread pattern of the organization of polities in East Asian countries in modern industrial development in the twentieth century.

Political development in East Asia since the end of the Cold War has been moving on. Japan, Singapore, South Korea, and Taiwan have passed their "developmental" stage to become more of a postindustrial society. This reflects in the way the state is organized in these societies today. On the other hand, China seems to have moved further into an advanced stage of industrial development, taking the "whole-of-nation" approach to its development enterprise globally. This also influences the way the state and political economy are organized in many countries in continental East Asia and mainland Southeast Asia. Whether East Asian states are still strictly developmental states today is a matter of debate, but the notion that the state is the chief organizer of national political economy remains valid. The institutions required for this practice are getting stronger in some states than in others. Our focus on the developmental state here therefore recognizes the complexity of the experiences and developments in state organization in East Asian countries and allows us to conduct a focused analysis of how this pattern of state organization influences IREA.

Distinct features in the internal organization of the developmental state are vividly described by Chalmers Johnson in his pioneering work from 1983 *MITI and Japan's Miracle*. At the core of the organization of Japan's developmental state, according to Johnson, is a "skewed triangular relationship" (Johnson 1983: 50) of cooperation and engagement among the "central institutions" defining the developmental state:

"the bureaucracy, the LDP (ruling politicians), and the larger Japanese business." An iron triangle is a three-way relationship of cooperation and engagement among the state's bureaucracy, ruling politicians, and business elites. This form of governing authority sustained the developmental state in Japan and that of many other East Asian countries.

These institutions and relations constitute the institutional infrastructure for a set of social and economic interests. Ruling politicians set state priorities and mobilize bureaucrats to engage with the business community and implement the state's industrial policy and strategic direction, with the private sector managing competition and ensuring compliance. Bureaucratic elites, for their own career development, engage with both ruling politicians and business elites for professional achievements. Business elites, often senior leaders in large and strategically important corporations, seek privileged access to resources and policy preferences for the development of their business and industry through deep engagement with bureaucratic and political elites.

In this triangular relationship, state bureaucrats play a dominant role, according to Johnson. More importantly, this multilayered, multidimensional relationship of cooperation and mutual engagement is enabled in the social and organizational structure and professional dynamics. Johnson discusses how the parliamentary system, for example, works. The LDP dominates the legislative process; senior bureaucrats seek positions in the LDP and in large business corporations after retiring from the bureaucracy; and factions, or social political professional networks, develop through marriage or personal financial ties, for example, where members of such networks are connected by a common birthplace, university, or other institution (Johnson 1983: 55). These enable elite to move and connect with others across institutions, dovetail their group interests, and influence policy. The triangular relations form a self-contained process of policy formulation, implementation, and engagement that keeps out "peripheral interests" or nondevelopmental interests, or squeezes them into the formal institutional process for public policy where the LDP actually dominates.

Johnson examines the internal structure of the developmental state in Japan to explain the effectiveness and efficiency in the organization of high-speed industrial development in Japan. This internal structure, as Waltz would advise, influences the country's international policy preference and the way it advances its national interests and relations on international issues. Social dynamics influence national interests and purposes, and the social organizations and networks shape the methods, strategy, and even style of international policy. These in turn become sources of tension and cooperation in international relations.

In Japan's case, this internal structure served as an important foundation for Japan's overall international policy orientation in the early decades of the Cold War, as seen in the earlier discussion on the Yoshida Doctrine. In the early chapters on the flying geese, we also discussed how the national institutions of industrial development organization and the subcontract system in particular were extended to Japan's efforts to build transborder production networks in East Asia in the 1970s and 1980s. T. J. Pempel observes a "regime shift" in the 1990s (Pempel 1998), where the iron triangle collapsed. This change in the institutional infrastructure of the governing authority brought about a reorientation of its overall international policy from the 1990s.

While the structure and institutions of the developmental state have long faded away in Japan and there is great debate as to whether China has followed the East Asian model or is of the developmental state, the real spirit of the developmental state is alive and well, and the institutions of state dominance and party-state-industrial capital collaboration and mutual engagement are only getting stronger in China. In the Chinese version of the developmental state, ruling politicians are made much more powerful by the institutional setup of the Communist Party of China. Recently, the CPC has been seen to not simply want to "control" the state but to see itself as the primary institution of the state. The business community and industrial capital of various ownership types are further incorporated in the state structure, along with other social groups and institutions.

The internal structure of the state in China, with a more dominant role of the CPC and a much deeper incorporation of social groups and institutions, shows the effect of forging a multilayered, multidimensional relationship of cooperation and mutual engagement among "central institutions" for national industrial development. The strengthening of the developmental state is reflected in its international policy and program. China is prepared to take on the challenge of global industrial development, in trade relations, in international organizations, and in the development and expansion of transnational production networks and partnerships. Its BRI initiative intensively reflects how the internal structures of the state influence the content and orientation of its international policy and methods of organizing transborder industrial development. The public-private partnership in China enables Chinese enterprises to go abroad and the state to seek bilateral political partnership with countries in supporting Chinese enterprises to take part in transborder industrial projects in other countries.

The way the internal structures of the developmental state evolve and exert their influence reflects the sway of the unique set of political economic conditions of East Asian states at the time. It is not all that convincing, as Johnson warned (Johnson 1983: 8), to see it as culturally driven. It is the effect of the interaction and mutual engagement of the primary institutions of national political economy. Douglass North identified this logic in his explanation of institutions, institutional change, and economic performance (North 1991). Using internal structures of the state to explain its international policy choices and behavior, as we showed in the case of the developmental state in East Asia, has its advantage as a general model of analyzing international relations.

LIBERAL STATES, PACIFIC COMMUNITY, AND DEMOCRATIC PEACE

Regime type theory further developed in the 1990s from an earlier focus on states in the developing world during the Cold War to focus on liberal states. The rise of liberal theory brings research back to the original themes of not only Waltz's second image thesis, but further to Kant's perpetual peace theory, thanks to works by Michael W. Doyle (Doyle 1983, 1986). Research has overwhelmingly focused on democratic peace. There is some degree of ambiguity in the boundaries between liberal peace theory and democratic peace theory (Rosato 2003; Doyle 2005) and how each uses the regime type to explain the cause of war and conflict or lack thereof. The original meaning of "liberal" and "going to war" is contested somewhat in the intensive debate over the validity and sufficiency of the evidence for the causal link between democratic regimes and the state's involvement in war.

This becomes clearer when the theory looks for evidence in East Asia. It is difficult to apply democratic peace theory to IREA and test it, perhaps because the theory was largely formulated in connection with liberal states, and East Asian states were considered largely nonliberal (Kivimaki 2001; Goldsmith 2006, 2007; Acharya 2010; Lind 2011; Johnston 2012; Tang 2012;). Ben Goldsmith observes that the literature has "not found support for democratic peace in Asia" (Goldsmith 2014: 60). Instead, in his search for causes to the "long peace" in post-1945 East Asia, Goldsmith finds strong evidence of a conflict-reducing effect of "economic interdependence" in Asia and believes this satisfies "liberal expectations" (Goldsmith 2007; Souva & Prins 2007), going all the way back to the "definite articles" of Kant's perpetual peace proposal. Confirmation of the "strong intra-Asian effect of trade interdependence" is perhaps part of the large research program (Kivimäki 2014; Tønnesson 2015) on the causes of the long East Asian peace and developmental peace where economic development provides motivating and constraining conditions for peace in the region.

The empirical challenges to democratic peace theory in East Asia also raise some theoretical questions. In the "defining articles" of Kant's perpetual peace proposal for a federation of free republican states with the rights of world citizens to universal hospitality (Kant 1795), "republic" as a regime type was distinctly liberal at the time when forms of state organization in Europe experienced a profound shift from traditional, imperial, and absolutist configuration to a popularist, contractually framed, sovereign state. A federation of free republican states contrasts with those tied up and standing for the traditional forms of state authority configuration in different parts of Europe then.

Moreover, beyond the liberal regime type, other liberal conditions must exist or be constructed so that these states can be freely associated, connected, and interacting under the condition of universal hospitality that facilitates transborder commerce and trade. The resultant economic and social connectivity and interdependence in the federal community and the formal and informal institutions arising to ensure it are strong insurance for perpetual peace in the federal community. In a way, the long peace in East Asia is precisely the working out of this liberal logic.

Furthermore, Kant's liberal theory seems to naturally concern more the European peace in the eighteenth century. More recent scholarship looks at peace and stability in East Asia within a longer historical and broader international framework (Kang 2007, 2010; Goh 2007b; 2013) and suggests that peace and stability in East Asia are much larger historical phenomena and points to the particular hierarchical, hegemonic political structure as the set of structural conditions for the long East Asian peace. David Kang singles out the China-centric world order and its institutions and norms, primarily the tribute system, in managing interaction and exchange between nations, which "resulted in a clear hierarchy and lasting peace" (Kang 2010: 2) and the stability of that world order. Evelyn Goh also uses these types of structural conditions, a hierarchical system, to explain the security order and stability in East Asia during the Cold War. "The relative stability of the US position at the top of the regional hierarchy" is a central force "constituting Asian stability and order" (Goh 2007b: 120), and, as in the Chinese case in Kang's account, working through a set of institutions and norms for "hierarchical assurance and hierarchical deference," primarily the hub-spoke alliance system.

In both cases, the hegemonic hierarchical structure and the institutions and practices that come with it recall something opposite to Kant's liberal world order. What matters for us here on the problem of the relations between regime type and war/peace is how the state is organized and, as Kant insists, how these states are associated and how cross-border economic and social activities are treated. Instances of war and peace and the conditions leading to them in East Asia provide good insight into the validity and scope of the problem pursued in the Kantian theory. This spurs us to consider further some of the basic assumptions underlying Kantian theory and the democratic peace theory, which in turn would allow us to answer the question more effectively as to whether regime types matter in IREA and, if so, how.

SOCIAL IDEAS, ECONOMIC INTERESTS, AND NATIONAL IDENTITIES

The developmental state and its supporting structures and institutions concern largely the type of state. There are other forces in the internal structures of the state that influence state policy preference and behavior in international relations. In reformulating "liberal international relations theory in a nonideological and nonutopian form," Andrew Moravcsik argues that "societal ideas, interests, and institutions influence state behavior by shaping state preferences, that is, the fundamental social purposes underlying the strategic calculations of governments. ... The configuration of *state preferences* matters most in world politics" (Moravcsik 1997: 513).

The social preference theory of world politics, as formulated by Moravcsik, uses social ideas, interests, and institutions to explain the state's preference and state behavior in international politics. It is a pluralist theory of state actions in international relations. In particular, Moravcsik identifies three sets of mechanisms that transform social ideas, interests, and identities into state preference: (a) social identities that shape "domestic public order" that legitimizes state institutions in "geographical borders, political decision-making processes, and socioeconomic regulation"; (b) "economic interests" of social groups and organizations that define the purpose and interest of the state in international relations; and (c) "domestic institutions and practices" that "aggregate those demands, transforming them into state policy" (Moravcsik 1997: 525–533).

This framework introduces social forces into the "internal structures" of states. Indeed, social ideas and identity, and society's economic interests influence indirectly or get "translated" into state preferences through domestic institutions and practices. These forces often work intertwinedly to have an impact on the preferences and behaviors of East Asian states. Sheila Smith, for example, shows how shifts in domestic interests – the collapse of the governing coalition, changing attitudes of the business community, and public opinion – led to changes in Japan's policy toward China "from reconciliation to reciprocity" (Smith 2015: 25).

In another example, for Il Hyun Cho and SeoHyun Park, there is a close link between domestic legitimacy politics in Korea and Japan, and their preferences for particular types of East Asian regional institutions and the varieties in East Asian regionalism. Cho and Park argue that "South Korea and Japanese political leaders, at different time periods, proposed their own alternative region-making initiatives appealing to domestically contested views on how best to seek autonomy from the region's Great Powers as a way to enhance their political standing domestically and regionally" (Cho & Park 2014: 583).

Similar links, or translating mechanisms, are also found in Taylor Favel's explanation of China's approach to territorial disputes. Favel argues convincingly that internal political pressures arising from state-ethnic relations led the state to take a more concessional position and prefer a cooperative strategy on territorial disputes in the border areas where non-Chinese ethnic groups are the majority. This supports the argument of Moravcsik that national identity politics affects the state's position on the "geographical borders" of "domestic public order" (Moravcsik 1997: 525).

A final case of the linkage concerns the impact of domestic economic interests on the trade policy of Southeast Asian states. Helen Nesadurai makes the case that the institutional forms in which policy elites conduct trade cooperation has a bearing on state trade policy. "Protectionist trade policies" are adopted in Southeast Asian countries "in the midst of official liberalization rhetoric" (Nesadurai 2012: 315) in the region. The "high level of ambivalence, incorporating elements of trade liberalization and trade protectionism" in Southeast Asian states, is caused by the "collective agency" of the states that allow them "to intervene in the global economy through interstate cooperation so that politically valuable domestic economic arrangements, even if uncompetitive, can be sustained" (Nesadurai 2012: 322).

In another study, Yoon Ah Oh (2018) examines interstate bargaining between China and Southeast Asian countries on China's infrastructure development projects to build high-speed railways in these countries. The study shows how the differences between China and Southeast Asian countries in "strategic development priorities" and the different levels of matching in the project's economic benefits and risks arising from the unique set of economic interests and conditions of the host country give significant bargaining power to the host country. These dynamics influence the outcome of their negotiations on project arrangements, which would otherwise be determined primarily by the hierarchical power relations between China and Southeast Asian countries.

A unique set of mechanisms in East Asian states links social ideas, economic interests, and identity to state preferences and behavior in IREA. The state's policy preferences and behavior influenced by this mixture of domestic forces lead to a persistent pattern of policy direction and behavioral orientation in IREA and, from time to time, to ambiguous, contradictory, and irrational international policy outcomes in IREA.

WHEN DUTERTE BECAME PRESIDENT

Changes in the political leadership of a state are increasingly being seen to lead to instant shifts in a country's position on a critical issue, development, or project in IREA. This adds a significant challenge to the analysis of the international policy and behavior of the countries and in the future development of the issue, problem, or project. In May 2016, for example, Rodrigo Duterte was elected president of the Philippines for a six-year term, taking over from President Benigno Aquino III. President Aquino had led the challenge to China's territorial claims in the South China Sea and taken an arbitration case to the International Court of Justice (ICJ) over the legality of the territorial claims in the South China Sea, particularly those of China. The ICJ was expected to rule in a month's time. President Duterte took a very different stand on the issue and, even though the court ruled in favor of the Philippines, the overall movement to confront China on this issue seemed to lose momentum without the Philippines' leading role.

In December 2016, President Park Geun-hye of South Korea was impeached by the country's National Assembly on political corruption charges. There had been significant tension among key political forces, between the progressive and conservative forces in South Korea, over the country's position in the highly charged geopolitics of Northeast Asia and its approach to dealing with the nuclear threat from North Korea. Both issues concern Seoul's relations with the United States, China, and Japan. Presidential politics leading to the impeachment sent confusing and contradictory signals to concerned parties to the Korea nuclear issue and Korea-centered geopolitics in Northeast Asia. The new president, Moon Jae-in, with his new Sunshine Policy or New North Policy, quickly helped to push the nuclear issue, the geopolitics issue, and the issue of inter-Korea relations to move in a different direction and in a very coordinated fashion.

The change in political leadership, in the presidency in both cases, is an instance of the "political cycle" in the working of the formal political institutions. Political cycles here refer to periodical changes in the head of government leading to unpredictable developments in the state's international policy and behavior and the consequent change in issues, relations, or projects in IREA. Both countries have a presidential system with only one term of five to six years for the presidency. The system emerged from the third wave of democratization movement in East Asia in the 1980s. Conventional scholarship on the impact of political cycles focuses largely on how the election schedule influences public policy debate and choices (Quandt 1986; Martinez 2009). What we are interested in here is how political cycles in states in IREA influence the development of issues in IREA. This is about how political institutions operate in these states, especially those states where interests and stakes as well as willingness and capabilities to act on issues are critical. It is critical also for a good understanding of those dynamics that are practically influential but relatively less noted in IREA analyses of the internal structures of the state.

The problem of political cycles, however, goes beyond the procedures and schedule of national political institutions. It often involves more profound changes in the political leadership of a country that influences IREA. Changes may occur not only in terms of who holds political office but also in the overall ideology and vision of key decision makers, which brings significant new content and perspective to issues in a state's international policy. In 2017, for example, President Donald Trump of the United States took office and immediately withdrew from the Trans-Pacific Partnership (TPP) agreement, which the previous administration had just signed a year prior. President Trump backed away from many multilateral efforts in the Asia-Pacific (and around the world) and opted for a more bilateral approach to regional economic, trade, and security issues (see discussion on this in Chapters 6 and 7). The US Pivot to Asia, a signature project by Trump's predecessor, seemed to have lost steam quickly. This fundamental shift in the US approach to the region generated a significant reshuffling, realignment, and reconfiguration in geopolitics and geo-economics in IREA and a reinvestment of political capital by states in IREA.

Also in 2017, the Chinese Communist Party confirmed a second term for Xi Jinping as the Secretary General of the Party, President of the state, and Chairman of the Central Military Commission. It also announced an ambitious program of moving the nation in the direction of becoming an internationally competitive state, industrial power, and military power and a whole set of reforms in state institutions to enable this program. This new strategic direction brings in new frameworks, mechanisms, and capabilities in China's engagement on regional issues. These added to a move by China to go beyond the dominant multilateral institutional and normative practices that have developed in recent decades in IREA.

There are debates over whether the change in the US position and approach to regional issues was inevitable. Many think that President Trump's rise to power was incidental. In the Chinese case, there has been a substantial level of uncertainty and anxiety among China watchers over the direction of China's politics and policy under the leadership of President Xi, leading to the major shift in recent years. In both cases, it is the political cycle of the state that crystallizes the intense and profound struggle going on among the principal political forces in the country. The shift in both cases reflects the outcome of the contest over the configuration of state preferences. There is perhaps a genuine political logic that drives the process. A good understanding of the logic and the fundamental forces in national politics and policy and their institutional manifestations would help us to gain more confidence in preparing for the type of political program and policy that will rise to the top political office and, from there, influence issues and developments in IREA.

MECHANISMS OF DOMESTIC AND INTERNATIONAL LINKAGE

James Rosenau reminded us decades ago of the importance of the linkage between national and international systems of politics for our understanding of foreign policy and international behavior of states (Rosenau 1969). Such a linkage is "any recurrent sequence of behavior that originate in one system and is reacted to in another" (Rosenau 1969: 45). Decades on, evidence of the linkage and its effects is abundant. The question for us here today in IREA is how political forces and structures at the national level influence IREA and precisely by what mechanisms.

We started this chapter with an underlying assumption that the international interests, policy, and behavior of the state have a significant influence on the shaping of interstate relations, issue developments, and policy outcomes in IREA; and the interests, preferences and behavior of the state evolve through an internal system of political organization, configuration, and articulation. This system is often nationally unique, functionally sophisticated and complex, and analytically not always easy to explain. The second image problem is about the challenge in understanding political forces at the national level or, more precisely, the domestic structures of the state.

There are various types of "internal structure of states" that influence state preference and behavior, and impact IREA in different ways: the developmental states, liberal states, democratic states, national identity, economic interests and interest groups, institutions and processes of policy formulation and implementation, political cycles, and so forth. While different mechanisms operate in different types of internal structure and translate them into state preferences and behavior in IREA, content in these issue areas shows some features of the linkage across the board in East Asian countries.

There is some complication on the pattern of how regime types influence IREA, partly because of the theoretical and methodological assumptions behind individual research programs. The unique character of both East Asian regime types and IREA adds significantly to this complication. Insights on the influence of national identity, social interests, and domestic institutions and processes are clear and convincing. There is an overwhelming importance of the way political economy is organized in East Asian states in the link between the national dynamics and outcomes, patterns, and developments in IREA. This shows the strongest evidence of not only the linkage but also the mechanisms by which the effects of domestic structures are transmitted to IREA. In analyzing all of these, we have discussed some key theoretical traditions in approaching the problem of domestic-international linkage. Our discussion has demonstrated that the second image does matter in IREA. Discussions following this line of inquiry strengthen our ability to explain or even forecast issues and developments in IREA.

Study Questions

1. What is the second image problem in international relations? How does this manifest in IREA?
2. Discuss different types of internal structure of East Asian states and why they are a legitimate and effective variable in explaining IREA.
3. Do East Asian states have a common regime type? What are the theoretical and methodological implications of your answer for a second image analysis of IREA?
4. What is "liberal" in the liberal theory of international politics as Michael Doyle or Andrew Moravcsik explain?
5. How do instances of war and peace in East Asia and the conditions leading to them help us understand the problem of the link between regime type and the level of a state's conflict involvement in IREA?
6. Discuss some examples (not covered in the chapter) of how national identity, economic interests, social preferences, or state institutions and processes influence IREA?

Further Reading

Acharya, Amitav, 2010. "Democracy or Death? Will Democratization Bring Greater Regional Instability to East Asia?" *Pacific Review* 23(3): 335–358.

Atanassova-Cornelis, Elena, 2013. "Shifting Domestic Politics and Security Policy in Japan and Taiwan: The Search for a Balancing Strategy Between China and the US," *Asia-Pacific Review* 20(1): 55–78.

Baviera, Aileen S. P., 2012. "The Influence of Domestic Politics on Philippine Foreign Policy: The Case of Philippines-China Relations Since 2004," RSIS Working Paper 241.

Cho, Il Hyun, and Seo-hyun Park, 2014. "Domestic Legitimacy Politics and Varieties of Regionalism in East Asia," *Review of International Studies* 40(3): 583–606.

Chung, Chien-peng, 2004. *Domestic Politics, International Bargaining and China's Territorial Disputes*. London: Routledge.

Collignon, Richard, and Chikako Usui, 2001. "The Resilience of Japan's Iron Triangle," *Asian Survey* 41(5): 865–895.

Doyle, Michael, 2005. "Three Pillars of the Liberal Peace," *American Political Science Review* 99(3): 463–466.

Fravel, M. Taylor, 2005, "Regime Insecurity and International Cooperation Explaining China's Compromises in Territorial Disputes," *International Security* 30(2): 46–83.

Gochman, Charles S., and Zeev Maoz, 1984. "Militarized Interstate Disputes, 1816–1976." *Journal of Conflict Resolution* 29(4): 585–615.

Goldsmith, Benjamin E., 2007. "A Liberal Peace in Asia?" *Journal of Peace Research* 44(1): 5–27.

Gourevitch, Peter, 1978. "The Second Image Reversed: The International Sources of Domestic Politics," *International Organization* 32(4): 881–912.

Gurr, Ted R., 1974. "Persistence and Change in Political Systems, 1800–1971." *American Political Science Review* 68(4): 1482–1504.

Huntington, Samuel, 1968. *Political Order in Changing Societies*. Yale: Yale University Press.

Kant, Immanuel, 1795 [1927]. "Perpetual Peace: A Philosophical Proposal," pp. 19–59 in Helen O'Brien (Translator), *Kant's Perpetual Peace: A Philosophical Proposal*. London: Sweet & Maxwell.

Kivimäki, Timo, 2014. *The Long Peace of East Asia*. London: Routledge.

Lind, Jennifer, 2011. "Democratization and Stability in East Asia," *International Studies Quarterly* 55(2): 409–436.

Lipset, Seymour Martin, 1959. "Social Requisites of Democracy: Economic Development and Political Legitimacy," *The American Political Science Review* 53(1): 69–105.

Maoz, Zeev, and Nasrin Abdolali, 1989. "Regime Types and International Conflict, 1816–1976," *The Journal of Conflict Resolution* 33(1): 3–35.

Martinez, Leonardo, 2009. "A Theory of Political Cycles," *Journal of Economic Theory* 144: 1166–1186.

Moravcsik, Andrew, 1997. "Taking Preferences Seriously: A Liberal Theory of International Politics," *International Organization* 51(4): 513–553.

Nesadurai, Helen E. S., 2012, "Trade Policy in SEA: Politics, Domestic Interests and the Forging of New Accommodations in the Regional and Global Economy," pp. 315–330 in Richard Robison, *Routledge Handbook of Southeast Asian Politics*. London: Routledge.

Putnam, Robert D., 1988. "Diplomacy and Domestic Politics: The Logic of Two-Level Games," *International Organization* 42(3): 427–460.

Quandt, William B., 1986. "The Electoral Cycle and the Conduct of Foreign Policy," *Political Science Quarterly* 101(5): 825–837.

Rosato, Sebastian, 2003. "The Flawed Logic of Democratic Peace Theory," *The American Political Science Review* 97(4): 585–602.

Singer, J. David, 1961. "The Level-of-Analysis Problem in International Relations," *World Politics* 14(1): 77–92.

Smith, Sheila A., 2015. Intimate Rivals, Japanese Domestic Politics and a Rising China. New York: Columbia University Press.

Souva, Mark, and Brandon Prins, 2007. "The Liberal Peace Revisited: The Role of Democracy, Dependence, and Development in Militarized Interstate Dispute Initiation, 1950–1999," *International Interactions* 32(2): 183–200.

Tang, Chih-Mao, 2012. "Southeast Asian Peace Revisited: A Capitalist Trajectory," *International Relations of the Asia-Pacific* 12(3): 389–417.

Tellis, Ashley J., and Michael Wills, 2007. *Domestic Political Change and Grand Strategy in Asia*, Seattle/Washington, DC: National Bureau of Asian Research.

Tønnesson, Stein, 2015. "Explaining East Asia's Developmental Peace: The Dividends of Economic Growth," *Global Asia* 10(4): 7–13.

Waltz, Kenneth N., 1959. *Man, the State, and War: A Theoretical Analysis*. New York: Columbia University Press.

Woo-Cumings, Meredith, 1999. *The Developmental State*. Ithaca: Cornell University Press.

12 East Asia in the World

In This Chapter...

- East Asia as a civilization
- International society and East Asia
- Triple transformations
- Industrial revolution, East Asian style
- Democratic transitions
- Civilizational identity of the region
- Three challenges
- Agent, structure, and East Asia as a platform

Learning Objectives

By the end of this chapter, you will be able to
- Develop a better understanding of the issues in IREA in a global context
- Understand the contributions of East Asian states to the shaping of the global international system
- Understand the impact of the global expansion of international society on the modern development of IREA
- Understand the significance of the transformations of East Asia for IREA and its relations with the world
- Use the structure-agent framework to analyze the changing relationship of East Asia with the rest of the world.

We now arrive at the last issue on this subject: how East Asia relates to the world system of international relations. This is an important topic for understanding IREA in the larger global context. As we saw in our discussions in earlier chapters, there is a tendency for scholars of IREA to focus primarily on how global forces of great power politics, world economic structures, social institutions, norms, and values have influenced and shaped IREA. There exists a weak recognition of how East Asia has changed in the twentieth century and how a changed East Asia has impacted the world system of international relations and the way it operates.

This pattern has a lot to do with how global material, institutional, and ideational forces have moved across regions and nations in the world of the time. It would be interesting to see how much this changed over the twentieth century and how East Asia in the early twenty-first century interacts with the world economy and shapes the global movement of products, wealth and capital, technology, and people.

If these forces and their distribution in the international system is the basis upon which international society develops and global governance forms, insights on this aspect of IREA will help us understand how the structures, institutions, and norms of international society are connected with those in IREA.

This also matters for the problem of the "unit of analysis" in studying IREA. We have investigated the structures and institutions of IREA, and even those of East Asian states, to understand the pattern and dynamism of IREA. Knowledge on this aspect of IREA can help us more fully understand the larger context in which structural, institutional, and normative dynamics in IREA operate. After all, IREA involve international relations with East Asian nations, among East Asian nations, and by East Asian nations.

This chapter starts with a focused discussion of the problem of East Asia's position in the world system of international relations, and the instances and circumstances in which the problem of East Asia in the modern international system first arose. We then discuss three profound transformations of East Asia itself that have not only strengthened its capabilities to impact and influence but also complicated the forms of its global impact and influence. Finally, we discuss how this or, more broadly, the historical interaction of East Asia and the world has contributed to the shaping of the structure, institutions, and norms of global society and the directions and focuses of this contribution in the future.

EAST ASIA AS A CIVILIZATION

Our discussions so far have largely focused on the "internal" structures, institutions, and normative dynamics of East Asia and how they together add up to a coherent and effective framework for analyzing IREA. IREA as a unit of analysis of international relations can also be looked at in the "external" relations of East Asia. This is the problem of East Asia as a unit of international activity and interaction.

The notion of East Asia is significantly shaped by the practice of international relations, from the "Far East" in the nineteenth century, to "East Asia" in the first half of twentieth century, and to the "Asia-Pacific" in the second half of the twentieth and early twenty-first centuries. This is seen by many as effects of great powers coming to compete in the region. We can also see the material interests and capabilities of East Asian nations as well as how the opportunities they represented effected a shift of the forces of international political economy to East Asia.

Different streams of scholarship have never failed to remind us of "East Asia at the center" (Reischauer & Fairbank 1960; Pye 1985; Mancal 1984; Arrighi 2009; Kang 2010), though they disagreed about the scope and content of an East Asian civilization. East Asian civilization connotes a mode of political economic organization in East Asia and the initial communal conditions, ethnic, religious, racial, linguistic, geographic, and so forth, for its institutionalization. The notion was at the center of a major research program in the 1960s, led by Edwin Reischauer and John Fairbank at the Center for East Asian Research at Harvard University. While there are different focuses on Japan, China, Korea, and Southeast Asia, the overall framing in the scholarly tradition on a singular East Asia is seen through discussions on East Asia's interaction with Western civilization.

This research program articulated a set of institutions and cultural practices that are believed to have sustained East Asian civilization. In achieving this, the literature also traces the shifting boundaries of the civilization in its expansion to the Muslim world to the west, the Mongol and Russian worlds to the north, and the Hindu and Muslim world to the south. Primarily, though, this scholarly tradition defines the East Asian tradition in its interaction with European civilization in the latter's global expansion to East Asia from the sixteenth century. While the "West impacts-East Asia responds" framework may have introduced "Western-centric distortions" (Cohen 2010: 3) to our understanding of East Asia, the literature does help advance the concept of East Asia as a unit of political economic organization and a set of ethnicity-/religion-based cultural relations and behavioral patterns.

In this concept of "East Asia," we see the dynamics of economic and political life in a domain that transcended ethnic and religious variations, and motived and enabled peoples to organize society and polity in a distinct way. The Confucian structure (see earlier discussion in Chapter 6) and its support institutions, social norms, and cultural values, as Lucian Pye and John Fairbank showed (Pye 1985; Fairbank 1968), emerged as a dominant form of polity in continental East Asia, where federal, feudal, and anarchic forms arose to intervene from time to time.

This form of polity, modeled after family organization in terms of structure, differentiated memberships and roles, and lines of legitimacy, responsibility, and authority, would be labeled traditional, imperial, or absolutist in different scholarly frameworks. It operates on the foundation of a hierarchical economic and social structure, i.e., an unequal but socially reinforced distribution of interests and capabilities of individuals and their groups and, consequently, of benefits, resources, and authority in society. It is enabled and supported by a set of institutions for organizing production and distribution, regulating relationships among people and their groups, and managing its relations with other polities; and by a set of social norms and values that motivate and constrain people, rationalize their actions, and legitimize the overall structure of their relations.

This form of polity was transplanted to, or adopted by, many other polities in areas of today's Korea, Japan, Taiwan, Indochina, and Southeast Asia, in various forms and to various extents. The East Asian civilization spread through the pendulum shifts of the boundaries of the empire in continental East Asia and through outflows of products, people, and contents of human knowledge, information, and communication from continental East Asia to maritime East Asia. This is the East Asian civilization that Fairbank, Reischauer, Pye, and others discovered and the European powers encountered when they moved directly to engage in continental East Asia in a massive imperialist expansion and competition there in the nineteenth century.

Since then, there has been profound change in the states active and influential in IREA. This shaped IREA to develop in a different direction. The first was the rise of Japan and its swift adoption of Western institutions of state organization, industrial development, and the normal practices and even fashion of high society in Europe. Then the European powers and Japan lost out to the United States and China in East Asia at the end of World War II. The United States successfully took over the areas left behind by the retreating European powers and organized an effective coalition of forces around maritime East Asia to force the collapse of the Communist alliance in continental East Asia in the 1970s.

In the meantime, the internal dynamics of East Asia drove the East Asian model of economic development to flourish while political liberalization in the 1980s and 1990s brought different modes of politics and state organization in East Asia. These dynamics of political and economic development have "pluralized" East Asia and the way region-wide political economy is organized. Debate intensified over the Asian model, Asian values, East Asia and the Asia-Pacific, and the future directions of East Asian regionalism. The economic rise of China in more recent years, in the form of the Chinese model, drove its strategic operational programs and the mechanisms and networks of industrial growth and expansion to roll out in East Asia and in the world. All these led East Asia watchers to wonder whether "East Asia" has come to a point of reclaiming its form of political economic organization and renegotiating its boundaries, and whether East Asia remains an effective site of a distinct civilization.

INTERNATIONAL SOCIETY AND EAST ASIA

With the ascendance of US international power and influence to world dominance after 1945 came the rise of the "American social science of international relations" or the "realism revolution" (Hoffman 1977). This American social science focuses primarily on the power of states, the way it is distributed in the international system, how a special form of distribution disciplines states and helps create an order in international relations, and the scientific methods of analysis, interpretation, and explanation of international politics. Hans Morgenthau (1948) and Kenneth Waltz (1979) were leading thinkers in the shaping of this American social science.

This, however, brought some sense of anxiety among scholars in the "old Europe" who were used to perceiving the world in the intellectual and scholarly traditions arising from their exploration of the traditional world order in Europe in the preceding several centuries. These intellectual and scholarly traditions focus on classical realism, diplomacy, international law and norms, and history. Scholars traced the traditions to Hugo Grotius, who developed the idea of governing the society of states through international law – rules and arrangements mutually agreed upon and enforced by states (Grotius 1646). His advice influenced the establishment of the Peace of Westphalia in 1648 and the birth of the modern system of international relations.

In the 1950s and 1960s, the British Committee on the Theory of International Politics, led by principal scholars of international politics at the time in Britain, Herbert Butterfield, Martin Wight, Hedley Bull, and Adam Watson, convened to theorize the intellectual traditions. Works produced under its auspices greatly shaped the development of what was later called the English School of international relations. Influential works of the English School, those by Hedley Bull and Adam Watson (Bull 1977; Bull & Watson 1985; Watson 1992) in particular, explored the shaping of the international order in modern Europe and the rise and global expansion of international society. The English school is a major, influential intellectual and scholarly tradition that arose out of the European research community, with a principal focus on the institutions and normative dynamics of international society in modern Europe and its global expansion.

This is where the problem is first treated of how East Asia sits in the international system or, at least analytically, how East Asian states fit into the expanded European international society. Gerrit Gong, one of the key researchers along this line, details, in his major contribution to this strand of the English School (Gong 1984), how well non-European nations, mainly China, Japan, and Thailand of East Asia in his case studies that also include Turkey, adopted the institutions and practices of international law and diplomacy in the mid-nineteenth and early twentieth century. The "standard of civilization" in Gong's investigation is largely the institutions and practices of international law and diplomacy for the settlement of international conflicts. Those institutions and practices were associated largely with the rise of the international order in modern Europe. Gong finds, among other things, that Japan adopted the standard much better and more smoothly than China.

Pursuing this line of inquiry further, Yongjin Zhang (1991) explains the difficulties in China's entry into international society and the dilemma China faced in adopting the code of conduct and the institutions and norms of the Westphalia system in settling disputes with incoming European powers through international treaties. The substantive institutional setup that sustained the Chinese world order found itself having to accept the treaty-port system that emerged out of the working of international law and the treaties China signed with European powers (see discussion in Chapter 3).

While trying to ascertain whether "European international society" expanded to become a global international society or its global expansion is part of the growth of global/world society, the English School is challenged to clarify and articulate further the organizing institutions and norms of international society. Barry Busan, for example, argues that the English School's institutions are "more fundamental" (Buzan 2004: 167) than the institutions of the liberal institutionalism of Robert Keohane and Stephen Krasner (see discussions in Chapter 8). They are master or constitutive arrangements of international society. The list of "primary institutions of international society" (Buzan 2004: 184, Table 2) overwhelmingly focuses on the master institutions of "Westphalia international society," which include "sovereignty, territoriality, diplomacy, balance of power, equality of people, inequality of people, trade, nationalism." Busan, though, does arrive at a list of "contemporary international institutions," however hierarchically nested, that includes primary institutions (master and derivative) and secondary institutions for functionality of international society.

This general framework connects the English School to the liberal institutionalism of Keohane and Krasner (Keohane 1984; Krasner 1981, 1982) and to the world society and global governance scholarship (Clark 1999, 2007; Hurrell 2008; Hurrell & Woods 1999). The latter are both concerned with globalizing processes and dynamics in contemporary international relations and the role of international institutions and norms in the shaping of global governance and world society. East Asia, having undergone profound changes itself since 1945, features prominently in the subsequent scholarly discussion and policy debate over the implications of the profound globalizing processes and dynamics. Busan and Zhang, bringing English School scholars and East Asian specialists together, investigate the particular characteristics of the primary institutions of an East Asian "regional international society" (Busan & Zhang 2014: 212). In that overall "West-global core" framework, they find that "there is almost no coherent way of differentiating East Asia from the West-Global core, ... and East Asia remains closely bound both to the basic Westphalian primary institutions plus nationalism and to the global economy" (Busan & Zhang 2014: 212).

The English School problematizes East Asia's relationship with the world as a problem of non-Western nations that wish to "enter" the globally expanded Westphalian international society. In doing so, it makes a significant contribution to the development of the idea of international society and develops the forms and substance of the primary international institutions and practices that "constitute" international society. It also contributes to the idea of region as a unit in the international system, i.e., East Asia as a regional international society. It is unclear, though, whether this historical process of non-Western nations entering international society was really an early instance of "clash of civilizations," civilization in the sense of the way an international political economy is organized across national boundaries.

Even on the idea of East Asia as a unit in the international system, it has been less successful, particularly when it comes to contemporary IREA. East Asia has enormously transformed since the nineteenth century. This in itself brings significant challenges to reconciling the international society framework and IREA. Even in Busan and Zhang's heroic attempt at this, it is not clear whether we are looking for "international social structures" or "primary institutions" (Busan & Zhang 2014: 1–4) in assessing whether there is an East Asian regional international society and how distinct such a society might be in relation to the Western-global international society. The significant change in East Asia is reflected intensively in the three transformations we turn to now.

TRIPLE TRANSFORMATIONS

Samuel S. Kim, an influential scholar on IREA at Columbia University during the Cold War and early post-Cold War years, contributed a "three-transformations" conception (Kim 2008) in his interpretation of the historical evolution of IREA. Kim essentially identified *three sets of international structures and orders* in East Asian international history: the Chinese tribute system, the Japanese imperial system, and the Cold War system, presumably the US hegemonic hierarchical system. The focus on international structures in East Asia, though, has since developed further to explore how these international structures translated into international institutions and, hence, shaped the international order in East Asia at the time. As we have shown in discussions in various chapters, scholars are working hard to understand the distinction as well as connection between international structures, institutions, and orders in framing the East Asian system and identifying its constitutive substance.

More importantly, while Kim tried to identify the changing dynamics of the East Asian system, his analytical framing focused largely on the geopolitical dynamics, which generations of IREA scholars then were known to be excellent at analyzing. There have been substantive political economic changes in East Asian countries and in the region as a whole since Japan's Meiji Restoration in the mid-nineteenth century. These changes contributed significantly to the transformations of the East Asian system. We categorize the political economic changes into three sets of East Asian transformations in the economic, political, and social organization of IREA. They are sometimes referred to as a "miracle" because of the unconventional way they evolved, because of the unusual outcomes of global significance, and often because of the controversial consequences for what East Asia is and how IREA work. These deserve a fuller and more systematic exploration for our understanding of East Asia in the world.

INDUSTRIAL REVOLUTION, EAST ASIAN STYLE

There is a large body of literature on the original East Asian miracle (World Bank 1993). Essentially, East Asian states acquired, over the relatively short span of several decades in the second half of the twentieth century, a globally significant ability to produce and provide for the livelihoods of their national populations, for people in the region and indeed in the world. It is an "industrial" revolution in the broad sense of an organization of the substantive economy. "Industrial," in the Japanese, Korean, or Chinese language context, means 产业/産業/산업 or "of production sectors," as in "industrial policy"(产业政策/産業政策/산업정책). East Asian countries gained such an ability in an unusual way, with respect to speed, scale, and organizing regime.

This has resulted, as Figure 12.1 shows, in a tremendous increase in national wealth, industrial capital, and manufacturing capacity and in the countries' collective share in the world totals of wealth creation and transborder movement of wealth and goods to other countries. If we go with Waltz's definition and measurement of international structure (Waltz 1979; Lake 1984), this historical change in the global distribution of capabilities and interests of states reflects a profound shift in the structure of the international system where East Asia has become a primary area of origin of these economic interests and capabilities.

Moreover, this shift helped shape a pattern of global distribution. An ADB study, as shown in Figure 12.2, for example, finds that in the global distribution of the capabilities in adding value to products and services through networked global value and supply chains, there are three core areas of concentration of these capabilities worldwide: China in East Asia, the United States in North America, and Germany in Western Europe.

This structural change, however, is not only material. Along with the movement of products, capital, organizing arrangements, and people from East Asia came methods of organizing production, investment, and trade (see background discussion of this in Chapters 6 and 7). These "methods" manifest in various forms at different stages of industrial growth and development: the developmental state, Japan,

254 *International Relations of East Asia*

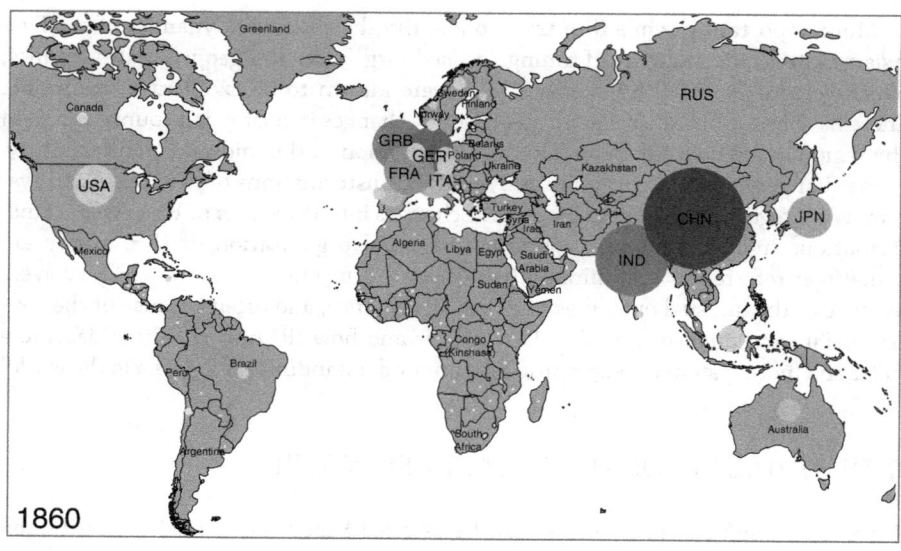

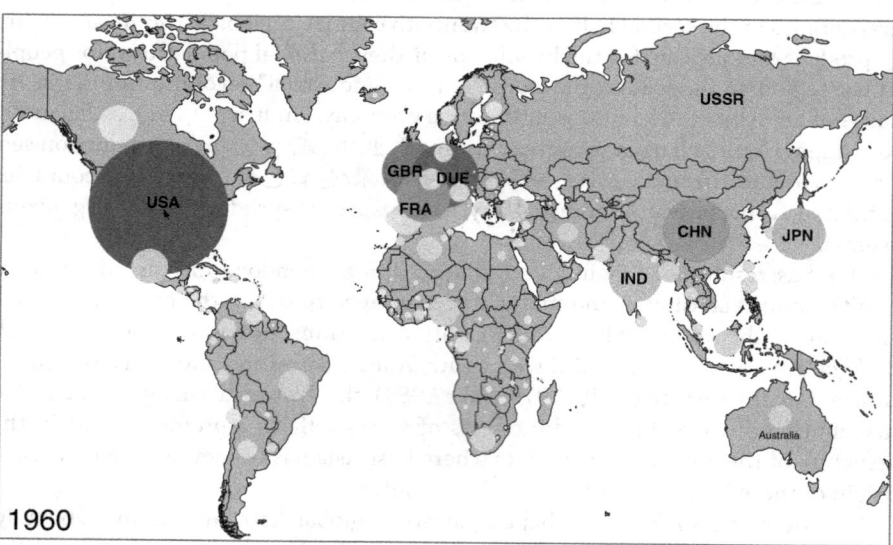

Figure 12.1 Structural shift in global distribution of national wealth and economic capabilities (1860s–2010s)

Real GDP of states geoeconomically located with size measured in 2011 USD

Data source: PWT9.0 (2017), MDP (2018)

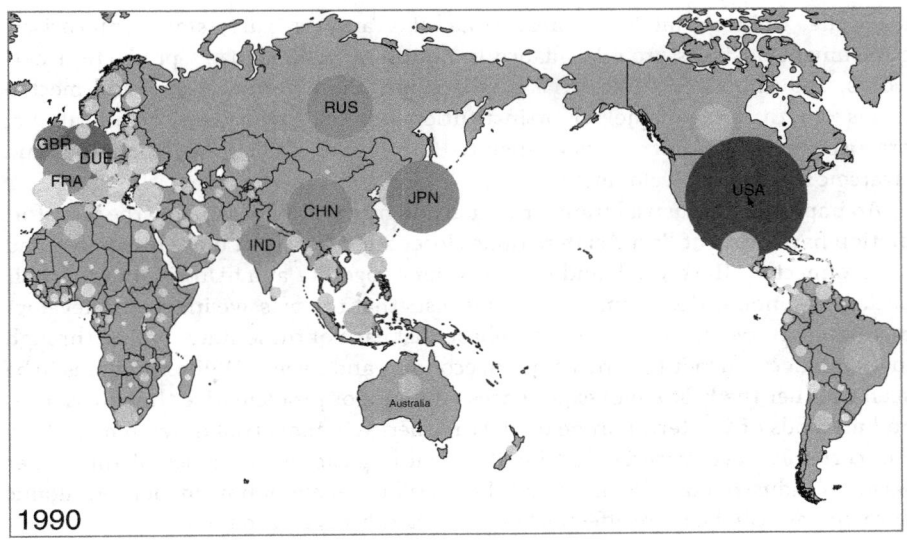
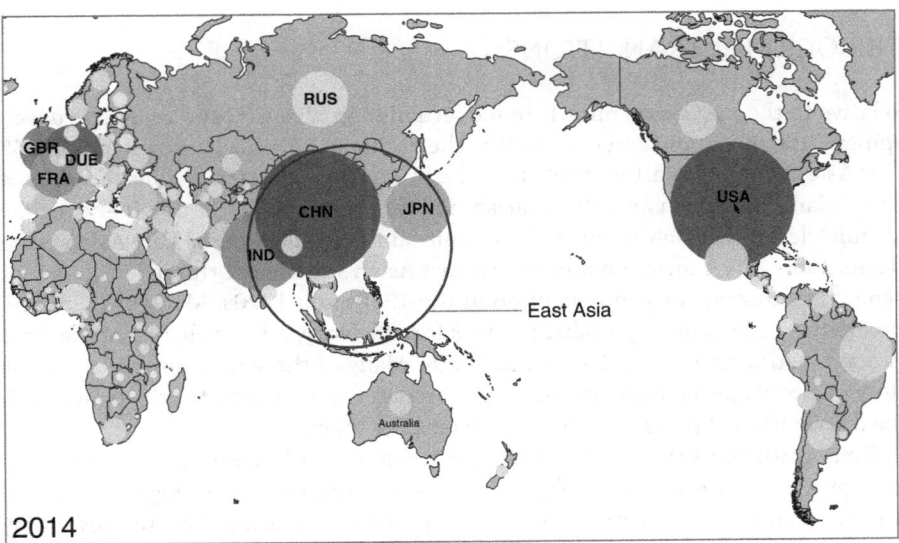

Figure 12.1 (Continued)

Inc., the Chinese model, Korean *chaebol*, Taiwan's party-state enterprises, government-business growth alliance in Southeast Asia, Japan's production networks, and China's BRI industrial partnerships. These various forms and mechanisms constitute a unique set of institutional arrangements and organizational practices in these countries that generated the very dynamic growth activities and strategic industrial development.

An impressive industrial transformation and methods of organizing the transformation have brought East Asian nations closer and the region more integrated and interconnected. The growth and methods came together at a historic stage of their national economic development. This suggests that the massive industrial development seen in the region can be just a phase that each of these states will go through in their longer journey toward a modern economy and society. While it remains to be seen whether the East Asian experiences vindicate or problematize the experiences and methods of Western Europe or North America in industrial development, they will certainly have material and institutional impacts on countries of the earlier waves of industrial development and those still in search of how modern economic development can be more effectively and efficiently organized today.

DEMOCRATIC TRANSITIONS

Relative to the East Asian miracle in modern industrialization and economic development, the forms and extent as well as the nature of political change in post-1945 East Asia are more a matter of debate. Third wave democratic transitions of a class of East Asian states from an authoritarian, military, or single-party dominant regime are miracles in themselves and no less significant than the original East Asian miracle. As Table 12.1 shows, 7 out of the 16 East Asian states went through the wave of democratic movement and revolution in the 1980s and 1990s. Many of them also experienced substantive pluralist reforms for efficiency, effectiveness, and fairness of state institutions in the 1990s and 2000s. Many of the states are still under the sway of two major political and ideological forces for dominance in the polity, with the distribution of power shifting in different directions.

Democratic transitions in the 1980s and 1990s in East Asia were part of a century-long process and experience of political change. Peoples in the region strove to become modern states with a "rich country and strong army" and to move away from traditional East Asian political structure, institutions, and order. This stream of activities, movements, and programs for political change, was framed and motivated by the ideas and values of liberal democracy, which became the most popular, influential, and widely accepted guidelines for political change in the 1980s and 1990s. This political change has essentially "pluralized" the political structure in East Asian states, which was then still very much in effect with respect to the principles of the hierarchical power structure for discipline, compliance, and performance. The latest developments on the ground show that the tensions between

Table 12.1 Political change in East Asian states from 1980s

	Democratic movement	Pluralist reform	Political contention and reverse
Brunei			
Cambodia		1990s	2010s
China	1989	2010s	2010s
East Timor			
Indonesia	1998	2010s	
N Korea			
S Korea	1987	1990s	2010s
Japan		1990s	
Laos			
Myanmar	1990	2010s	2010s
Malaysia		1990s	2010s
Philippines	1987		Ongoing
Singapore		1990s	
Taiwan	1990	1990s	Ongoing
Thailand	1997	2010s	2010s
Vietnam		1990s	Ongoing

liberal and conservative forces have not really been resolved in East Asian states since the democratic transition of the 1980s and 1990s.

The World Bank's Worldwide Governance Indicators measure governance quality and performance of states and their change over the years from the mid-1990s to the mid-2010s. Governance is defined in the index system as consisting of "the traditions and institutions by which authority in a country is exercised" (World Bank 2018), and the quality of governance in a state at a given time is indicated by an index value ranging from –2.5 (weak) to 2.5 (strong). This set of indicators can be used for our discussion of what has changed in East Asian states in terms of political development and how much has changed. We use this to separate one type of states (scores above zero, denoting liberal, pluralist, competitive) from the other type (those with scores below zero, denoting centripetal, hierarchical, corporatist, and traditional). As shown in Table 12.2, of the 16 East Asian countries, 8 had scores below zero in 1997 and one more was added to this category in 2017. From 1997 to 2017, liberal and pluralist states became more liberal and pluralist, while conservative and traditional states became more conservative and traditional.

Table 12.2 Governance quality of East Asian states

	Voice and accountability		Stability and no violence		Government effectiveness		Regulatory quality		Rule of law		Control of corruption		Overall	
	1996	2017	1996	2017	1996	2017	1996	2017	1996	2017	1996	2017	1996	2017
Brunei	−0.65	−0.95	1.24	1.19	0.93	1.14	1.35	0.72	0.82	0.65	0.48	0.71	0.69	0.58
Cambodia	−0.75	−1.16	−1.10	0.17	−0.72	−0.66	−0.23	−0.50	−1.19	−1.06	−1.02	−1.29	−0.84	−0.75
China	−1.36	−1.50	−0.10	−0.25	−0.35	0.42	−0.27	−0.15	−0.55	−0.26	−0.27	−0.27	−0.48	−0.34
East Timor	−1.72	0.34		0.03		−1.00		−0.74	−1.57	−1.17		−0.54	−0.55	−0.51
Indonesia	−0.92	0.13	−1.13	−0.51	−0.71	0.04	−0.05	−0.11	−0.49	−0.35	−0.86	−0.25	−0.69	−0.17
N Korea	−1.92	−2.20	−0.50	−0.48	−1.89	−1.69	−2.28	−2.34	−1.15	−1.71	−1.28	−1.48	−1.51	−1.65
S Korea	0.67	0.74	0.57	0.29	0.47	1.08	0.45	1.11	0.80	1.16	0.38	0.48	0.56	0.81
Japan	1.07	1.01	1.16	1.12	0.91	1.62	0.77	1.37	1.35	1.57	1.19	1.52	1.08	1.37
Laos PDR	−1.13	−1.75	0.37	0.43	−0.64	−0.36	−1.04	−0.72	−1.05	−0.88	−0.72	−0.94	−0.70	−0.70
Myanmar	−1.89	−0.87	−1.26	−1.08	−1.21	−1.05	−1.68	−0.83	−1.58	−0.95	−1.50	−0.56	−1.52	−0.89
Malaysia	−0.18	−0.40	0.57	0.16	0.54	0.84	0.78	0.68	0.52	0.41	0.38	0.03	0.44	0.29
Philippines	0.26	0.08	−0.48	−1.24	−0.31	−0.06	0.02	0.02	0.07	−0.41	−0.36	−0.48	−0.13	−0.35
Singapore	0.14	−0.17	1.12	1.59	1.99	2.21	2.18	2.12	1.24	1.82	2.11	2.13	1.46	1.62
Taiwan	0.67	1.01	1.06	0.89	0.55	1.27	0.87	1.37	0.76	1.14	0.58	0.96	0.75	1.11
Thailand	0.31	−1.05	0.47	−0.76	0.18	0.38	0.06	0.14	0.54	0.04	−0.36	−0.39	0.20	−0.27
Vietnam	−1.09	−1.40	0.53	0.31	−0.58	0.00	−0.60	−0.40	−0.48	0.07	−0.49	−0.58	−0.45	−0.33

CIVILIZATIONAL IDENTITY OF THE REGION

While significant change occurred in political structure, institutions, and order in post-1945 East Asian states, change is also visible at the regional level. In early chapters, we discussed East Asian intellectual and scholarly traditions and debates that treat East Asia as a whole on the basis of shared cultural values, social structures, and civilizational qualities, and in particular the dominance and influence of the Confucian tradition in continental East Asia over the region, particularly over the Muslim world in southern and western East Asia and Christianity from European colonial movements in East Asia.

Cultural values, normative rules, and civilizational identities, though, change and evolve over time, reflecting the changing political economy of society and the ensuing material and institutional changes. Confucianism was "overthrown" and "condemned" at the origin and center of its practice, continental East Asia, in the twentieth century, and the tradition was very much marginalized in the wave of modern economic, social, and political change in those Confucian societies, as Weimin Tu pointed out many years ago (Tu 1991, see discussion in Chapter 5).

Industrialization and economic development bring industrial capital into the political structure and seriously "dilute" the power and authority of the state and the state-dominated political order. Political change of a liberal democratic type has significantly reshaped the political structure and institutions in East Asian countries, away from the traditional East Asian way of politics and governance. Huntington's clash of civilizations thesis focused primarily on the contest between Christianity and Islam (Huntington 1993, 1996). But the tension between the Confucian way of life and Christianity and Islam in East Asia have been historically there and seems to have grown more prominent in recent years in the struggles over international institutions, the territory, state jurisdiction, and international rights of national, ethnic, and religious groups, and the purposes and norms of global governance.

We have seen profound cultural and social change in East Asia. Moreover, the way this change has evolved across the region suggests that an understanding of East Asian values and normative identities based on a single trait of East Asian people, whether their ethnic, religious, linguistic, or even social character and qualities, is insufficient to capture the real change and the emergent distribution of cultural values and civilizational identities in East Asia. Political culture, insofar as it is relevant and influential in interstate relations, is a set of shared values of a population about how society, the economy, and politics should be organized and the pattern of the behavioral propensity of individuals to participate in their organization. We can see East Asian nations as having been dominated by Confucian political traditions before modern times, as discussed in Chapter 6. These political traditions can be summarized as a unique set of normative values and behavioral guidelines for organizing politics, society, and the economy. These political traditions value and legitimize a hierarchical social structure and relations built on gender, age, social-class differentiation; the state's overwhelming role and responsibility in organizing the economy and providing public goods; and the state-centric political organization of society over pluralist competition and representation.

These political traditions, often debated within the framework of the East Asian model, Asian values, Confucianism, developmental state, Asian democracy, and so forth, faced a significant challenge in the twentieth century from all ideological directions, but more intensively from liberal institutionalism from the 1980s. Significant change in social, economic, and political structures brought on by the first two miracles allows us to hypothesize that the normative values of the peoples of East Asian countries have changed. The question is whether such change has resulted in a large-scale shift in the overall political culture and values that can provide a unifying normative support for the region-wide political economic order and its collective identity and position in the international system.

To see how much political culture has shifted away from the political traditions in East Asia, we use the World Values Survey data for an empirical assessment. The World Value Survey has been an influential research project that surveys the cultural values of peoples of different countries in the world over the past 30 years. Its latest Sixth Wave Survey in 2011–2014 includes most East Asian countries covered here (Japan, South Korea, China, Taiwan, Thailand, Philippines, Malaysia, and Singapore).

We select three sets of indicators to measure the distribution of the values of individuals across the region and the national populations on (a) social organization (v49–v54, v160), in their attitude toward male-/seniority-privileged social norms and practices; (b) economic organization (v96–99), in their attitude toward the institutions and normative practices of state ownership, state provision, income equality (vs. market, competition, efficiency incentivizing); and (c) political organization (v25–29, v85–89, v96–99, v108, v112–118, v127–130), in their attitude toward government agencies, political parties, civil society organizations and activities, different state types, and political advocacy and agency. From these three sets of indicators we identity their attitudes as being more traditional Confucianism or liberal institutionalism. For a benchmark analysis, we also include those of the US and world averages for comparison, as well as Northeast Asia and Southeast Asia because the two subregions may have different levels of influence on East Asian political traditions.

Table 12.3 shows an interesting pattern of how much East Asian countries have shifted from the presumed East Asian traditional values. East Asia overall is split between those for East Asian traditional values and norms (48 percent) and those for values and norms of liberal institutionalism (47.3 percent). Southeast Asian countries are more on the traditional values (52.7 percent versus 47.4 percent) than Northeast countries (45.6 percent versus 45.7 percent). In comparison to the US, East Asia is still very much on the side of East Asian traditional values (10 percent difference). On individual issue areas, East Asian people are solidly on the side of the values and norms of liberal institutionalism in the social and economic order (51.1 percent versus 42.8 percent; 54.5 percent versus 42.5 percent) but is still some distance from the US (62.5 percent versus 36.3; 67.1 percent versus 30.2 percent).

On political organization, East Asian people are much stronger on East Asian values and norms while the US is split (52.2 percent and 45.8 percent). Clearly values and norms have significantly shifted in East Asia, moving away from East Asian traditions, particularly in social and economic organization. This change has also driven the shaping up of a bifurcated political order between the conservative and

Table 12.3 Value distribution in East Asian countries (%) (2011–2014)

	Overall		Society		Economy		Politics	
NEA	45.6	45.4	39.8	48.9	40.8	53.0	56.4	34.2
SEA	52.2	47.5	51.2	48.6	44.0	56.0	61.3	37.9
EA	48.0	47.3	42.8	51.1	42.4	54.5	58.8	36.3
World	50.4	45.3	47.9	48.3	45.9	50.4	57.2	37.4
US	39.6	58.5	36.3	62.5	30.2	67.1	52.2	45.8

NEA: Northeast Asia: Japan, China, South Korea, Taiwan
SEA: Southeast Asia: Malaysia, Philippines, Thailand, Singapore
EA: East Asia: Average across the individual countries
% of respondents for East Asian traditional values
% of respondents for values and norms of liberal institutionalism
Data source: WVS6, World Values Survey (2018)

the liberal in political organization in these countries, and perhaps at the East Asian regional level as well. It is not a pattern of linear and unitary development, as many expected, but a unique pattern of political change.

THREE CHALLENGES

Today's East Asia is different from the East Asia of 150 years ago, when Japan's Meiji Restoration launched Japan on its long and turbulent journey of modern development. Modern IREA have taken shape in a context of economic, political, and cultural development of East Asian societies in the twentieth century and influenced people to see East Asia as an area structured by a coherent set of geopolitical and political economic interests and dynamics and organized in a unique set of social institutions, cultural traditions, and normative values. Though different East Asian nations and peoples developed their own sets of interests, relations, and arrangements with the world, there is a clear level of coherence and connectivity in these different interests and relations in East Asia, and these would continue to influence not only the interstate relations of these nations themselves but also their relations with the world. These "miracle transformations" and their material and institutional consequences discussed earlier will be critical in the further development of East Asia's relations with the world.

First, modern development in East Asia has significantly increased the material capabilities of East Asian countries and their geopolitical and economic interests. These interests and capabilities extend globally. If the international system is built on the material interests and capabilities of nations as well as the relations and institutions that serve to protect and further advance them, these East Asian interests and capabilities have significantly reshaped the structure of the international system and will continue to do so. Moreover, these interests and capabilities will drive efforts to ensure international institutions to recognize the changing international structure and protect and further advance the countries' interests and relations. The further evolution of East Asia's relations with the world will continue to intensify the tension between the shifting structure and the prevalent institutions and normative practices in the international order. This is a classic problem of international order transformation. In the case of East Asia, this has been going on since the East Asian economic miracle in the 1980s or even earlier and has been driven by a leading East Asian country of a different time.

Second, the increasing influence of East Asian society, political economy, and politics on the world system has also come at a time when globalization, driven by new-generation technologies, platforms, and mechanisms, is helping push products, capital, and services to move across borders. More importantly, the process decentralizes the global flow of materials, people, and information because the sources that drive the movements are global, and they "exchange" across borders instantly on a global scale. The new globalization enables fundamentally different ways of organizing production and distribution, the economy, society, and politics. East Asian countries are leaders in bringing new business models, platforms and mechanisms of production, and media for exchange and distribution into our lives. Ironically, this poses a formidable challenge to some of the institutions and norms of the state-centric international system.

Third, challenges to public policy at the national level are increasingly global: environmental issues, energy resources, natural disasters, nontraditional security issues, and human development. At the core of these issues is the problem of resource allocation and public policy priorities at the global level. New material forces and dynamics complicate the shaping of global society. The problem of international society has long been debated in connection with the institutions and normative practices needed for global governance. East Asian countries will clearly have an influence in the shaping of global civil society where threat assessment and resource allocation must be done in a global rather than international framework. With the experiences stemming from East Asia's past encounter with the international system, and the significant material interests and capabilities they have accumulated in their waves of industrial growth and economic development over the twentieth century, how East Asian countries manage and conduct their relations with the world will have a critical impact on the unfolding of what Gilpin calls "systems change" in world politics (Gilpin 1981; Ikenberry 2014b).

AGENT, STRUCTURE, AND EAST ASIA AS A PLATFORM

In 1987, Alexander Wendt published an article on the problem of agent and structure in international relations and called the reader's attention to the "mutually constitutive" role of both the agent and structure in the shaping of international relations (Wendt 1987). This is against a backdrop of the discipline at the time being dominated by two schools of thought. Classical realism, as represented by Han Morgenthau (1948), focuses on the nation-state as the primary unit of action in pursuit of power and interests and exercise of national capabilities and strategy in world politics. Structural realism, as envisaged by Ken Waltz (Waltz 1979), sees the international structure, the system-wide distribution of capabilities of states, as the primary source of power that motivates or constrains states to act in the anarchic international system. Wendt's structuration theory suggests that the state and the international structure both influence the development and contribute to the organization of international society and that, in doing so, they shape one another.

Structuration theory notes the importance of the socialization process of "mutual constitution" and largely leaves the question of what the structure is and who the agent is in the shadow of the Westphalian framework of international society. It has been a tradition in international relations scholarship to treat East Asia and its relations with the world as an agent-structure problem. Moreover, in treating East Asia as an agent, the literature focuses primarily on key nation-states in East Asia, Japan, China, ASEAN, and so forth. In such an analytical framework, it is a challenge to understand and assess the impact of East Asia on world politics and its role in the shaping of the international system. While there is great interest in academia and policy circles in this line of analysis, such interest is easily obscured by debates on whether East Asia is a unitary actor in world politics and international relations.

East Asia in IREA is not an actor or agent in the sense Morgenthau, Waltz, or Wendt uses the term. East Asia is more a platform as in computer science, where interstate interaction, engagement, and penetration take place and where the interests, capabilities, and actions of the states are systematically connected and help form an international structure, international institutions, and an international order founded on platform. In this text, we have discussed the emergence and evolution of the international structure in modern IREA. This structure has been shifting largely between unipolar and bipolar distributions of interests and capabilities. We have also discussed the profound economic, social, and political transformation of East Asian states in the twentieth century that have shaped and will continue to shape the international structure in IREA.

We have further discussed the way the political economic development of East Asian states is organized, the institutions, normative practices, and cultural traditions that have developed and exerted an influence on their organization, and how and to what extent the effects of this normative structure have manifested at the regional level. In discussing the material, institutional, and normative dynamics in IREA, we have examined the shaping of the international order in modern East Asia. What is important in the problem of East Asia and the world are the structural, institutional, and civilizational dynamics of IREA. East Asia is a platform where material interests and capabilities of states are concentrated. This affects national interests and relations of states in IREA. The concentration of power and capabilities in East Asia clearly reflects a shift in the global international structure. Moreover, the ways political economy is organized in East Asia serve as examples of how international political economy is organized and its possible institutional instruments, mechanisms, and arrangements. The experiences of IREA, their structural character and transformation, institutional and normative development, and the ways in which war, peace, and development have played out in IREA offer great insights into how structural, institutional, and normative dynamics affect one another and how the consequent shaping of the international order at the regional and global levels will play out in the years and decades to come.

Study Questions

1. Discuss how the English School's notions of international society and primary institutions influence the frameworks we use to analyze East Asia's relations with the world.
2. Has East Asia transformed itself over the twentieth century? In what ways? How have East Asian transformations influenced the development of cultural values and normative identities of East Asian peoples and societies?
3. Robert Gilpin proposes three types of international political change. Do you think current changes and developments in the international system amount to a "systems change," "systemic change," or "interaction change"? What role do East Asian states play in the shaping or reshaping of the global international order and the governance of global society?
4. What do IREA mean for us in our understanding of international relations in general?

Further Reading

Arrighi, Giovanni, 2009. *Adam Smith in Beijing: Lineages of the 21st Century*. New York: Verso.

Bull, Hedley, and Adam Watson, 1985. *The Expansion of International Society*. Oxford: Oxford University Press.

Busan, Barry, and Yongjin Zhang, 2014. *Contesting International Society in East Asia*. Cambridge: Cambridge University Press.

Buzan, Barry, 2004. *From International to World Society? English School Theory ad Social Structure of International Society.* Cambridge: Cambridge University Press.

Cohen, Warren I. 2000. *East Asia at the Center: Four Thousand Years of Engagement with the World*. New York: Columbia University Press.

Lee, John S. 2016. "The Fragile Foundations of the 'Asian Century'," *The Journal of East Asian Affairs* 30(1): 41–66.

Mahbubani, Kishore. 2008. *The New Asian Hemisphere: The Irresistible Shift of Global Power to the East*. New York: Public Affairs.

Morgenthau, Hans J., 1948. *Politics among Nations: The Struggle for Power and Peace*. New York: Alfred A. Knopf.

Pye, Lucian W., 1985. *Asian Power and Politics: The Cultural Dimensions of Authority*. New York: Harvard University Press.

Reischauer, Edwin O., and John K. Fairbank, 1960. *East Asia: The Great Tradition*. Boston: Houghton Mifflin.

Ringmar, Erik, 2012. "Performing International Systems: Two East-Asian Alternatives to the Westphalian Order," *International Organization* 66(1): 1–25.

Smith, R. B. 2007. *Changing Visions of East Asia, 1943–93: Transformations and Continuities*. Oxon: Routledge.

Waltz, Kenneth, 1979. *Theory of International Politics*. Reading: Addison-Wesley.

Wanandi, Jusuf, and Tadashi Yamamoto 2008. "East Asian Regionalism and Global Governance," in *East Asia at a Crossroads*. Tokyo: Japan Center for International Exchange.

13 Conclusion: Futures of IREA

> In This Chapter...
> - Key dynamics of IREA
> - Three key areas to watch for future IREA

The chapters in this text are designed to show how structural, institutional dynamics change and how they influence the shaping and transformation of the international order in IREA. As introduced in Chapter 1 and discussed in more detail in Chapter 2, the framework we employed to explain IREA looks at the importance of the structural shift in the distribution of power and capabilities of states in IREA. These shifts are propelled by the rise and fall of powers with significant influence on IREA and enabled through a set of institutional arrangements and normative practices. These institutional arrangements and normative practices legitimize the emergent power relations, and they together shape a set of stable and effective authority relations among the states. This set of authority relations manifest in a form of international order in IREA.

Previous chapters discussed the transformation of the international order in IREA over the past 150 years and how the structural shifts and institutional and normative changes related to the transformations. Individual chapters also showed how this dynamism works in a specific functional area of IREA, and how these critical forces shaped an international order in the functional area. In this final chapter, we summarize key aspects of the dynamism as it has driven the evolution of modern IREA and discuss the direction of future IREA development. After all, what we have learned about IREA here will give us a greater sense of the structure and pattern inherent in IREA and a higher level of confidence about the direction of IREA in the years and decades to come.

KEY DYNAMICS OF IREA

The first aspect of the dynamism that drives IREA is great power politics in East Asia. While it is true that at different times, different great powers were involved in IREA, it is still great power geopolitics that has been shaping and driving IREA from day one. Great power politics concerns primarily the interests and capabilities of states and their international distribution. *Realpolitik* among "warring states" has waxed and waned for a thousand years in continental East Asia. Then, in more recent times, the main battles in the region were waged by the European powers, who directly confronted China and the Chinese world order, and led to the emergence of new great powers in IREA – Japan, Russia, and the United States.

Japan emerged as the new hegemonic power in East Asia in the first half of the twentieth century, but the short-lived hegemonic order crashed with the rise of US power and influence in East Asia in the Pacific War. Then great power politics in East Asia changed from among USSR, China, and the US during the Cold War to among the US, China, and Japan after the Cold War, with China and the United States increasingly leading a binary rivalry. Great powers are holders of significant material forces, chief organizers of force alignment for strategic engagement in a region, and principal enforcers of an international order. Collaboration and competition among great powers set in motion the movement and alignment of forces in the power structure and generate and enforce strategic alliances and partnerships. They are the core of the structural dynamics in IREA. The future of the international structure in East Asia will be significant and be determined by the power and capabilities of the United States and China and their allies and partners.

The second aspect of the dynamism that drives IREA is the industrial growth and economic development of East Asian states in the twentieth century and economic cooperation and competition among states in IREA. Post-World War II East Asian growth has brought with it a significant set of new dynamics and substantive activities in IREA. It not only brought about great improvements in the social and economic life of East Asian peoples but also a significant rise in the economic capabilities and influence of East Asian states in regional and global economic cooperation and competition.

In particular, the way East Asian nations organize industrial growth and economic development has an intensely national focus on the transborder coordination of industrial development and a greater focus on the substantive economy – manufacturing and infrastructure building. This East Asian growth has extended the economic interests and organizational relations of East Asian states to the region and to the world. It has made East Asian regionalism a dynamic, though ambiguous, project and will continue to have a complicating influence on the existing international economic order. The future impact of East Asian growth, led by the leading industrial powers arising as a result of East Asian growth, will focus on technology, product cycles, global value and supply chains, forms of business organization, and the international institutions that underlay the international economic order of the twentieth century. In these areas, the leading industrial powers in East Asia are shaping the institutions and normative practices of the international economic order in East Asia and in the world.

The third aspect of the dynamism that drives IREA is East Asian culture, identity, and civilization. East Asian nations are uniquely related to each other and to the historical roots of East Asian culture, civilization, and polity. These cultural, civilizational, and political traditions have evolved in various forms in modern times. Institutionally, these traditions have transformed into the system of nation-states, with the great influence of other civilizations, particularly those of European and American modes of national organization of society, economy, and politics. A distinct set of normative forces in a state influences how the nation identifies with other countries in IREA. We have shown, in Chapter 6 in particular, that countries in IREA can be categorized loosely in two groups as dictated by the dominant institutional, normative, and civilizational identities of these states. This has reinforced the bifurcation of the distribution of these identities at the regional level, with one set of normative forces closely related to traditional East Asian political structure, values, and identities and the other more in line with those of the US-led liberal international order in East Asia.

With the increasingly close connection between domestic structures and IREA, this unique normative structure of IREA will have important implications for the international order in broader East Asia. East Asian nations not only have failed to build a region-wide political and economic community, they have also failed to hold up a coherent East Asian culture, identity, and civilization as a normative framework to guide their purpose and conduct in IREA. This is not uniquely "East Asian" in the world of increasingly close interdependence as well as tension between forces of globalization, regionalization, nationalism, and transnational challenges. But it is uniquely "East Asian" because East Asian culture, identity, and civilization were among the most prominently established in human history when modern IREA started to develop from the nineteenth century.

These three key sets of dynamics together have been driving IREA, shaping the international order in East Asia and enabling its transformation through a series of significant international orders in the region. This current state of IREA seems to open up different possibilities of future development: an international order of multilateral institutionalism based on a bipolar structure, an international order of hierarchical arrangements by a sole hegemonic power, or an international order with a mixture of them all.

These dynamics have also influenced the shaping of the platforms, institutions, and mechanisms in which IREA have been pursued, from institutions and arrangements in empire building to strategic engagement and competition for a hierarchical and hegemonic order, from multilateral institutions and norms for discipline and regulation on state action and interaction to measures and mechanisms of confidence building and interstate socialization in the development of common interest and purpose for a community of IREA. These dynamics also incorporate domestic interests and structures into IREA, and regional interests and structures into the global system of international relations.

THREE KEY AREAS TO WATCH FOR FUTURE IREA

With all these aspects of the dynamism of structure, institutions, and international order in IREA so connected, how do we go about identifying the possible direction of IREA's future development? The first issue area to watch is the Korean Peninsula: whether there will be a settlement of the 70-year-old Korean War and what postwar security and geopolitical arrangements can be agreed to in Northeast Asia. This is not just about the issue of North Korea's nuclear weapons and the danger they pose to other parties. It is about the international security order in East Asia, the balance of power, and institutional arrangements and processes for achieving that balance.

As part of any possible settlement, a form of a unified Korea may be attempted, at least by the two Koreas themselves. This will have a great impact on the long-term development of the large corridor that connects the greater area of Korea, the

Russian Pacific region, Mongolia, and China's *Dongbei*. The direction in which the situation on the Korean Peninsula develops will also be significant for the shaping of the international security order in East Asia as a whole. The Korea issue is an instance of how the Cold War bipolar strategic conflicts are settled and transformed. This will have implications for the continued tension between Beijing and Taipei across the Taiwan Strait and the strategic position of Indochina states for the region's geopolitics. Moreover, the developments on the Korean Peninsula will also have significant implications for force deployment and alliance arrangements in the wider region: e.g., the US alliance with Japan, South Korea, and ASEAN states; and the balance of power of the US and China in Northeast Asia, Southeast Asia, and beyond.

The second issue area to watch is how the world engages with China's BRI and, more broadly, the global movement of China's economic interests and forces. This is about more than just the political significance of this initiative for China. The BRI is a large-scale network of bilateral partnerships for transborder manufacturing and construction projects. Will the initiative focus on East Asia in a way that will affect the regional economic order there? Or is the initiative global in focus, so that it will inevitably crowd the very competitive space of the global political economic order? More specifically, how does the "hub-spoke" partnership system for transborder industrial organization fare with the existing liberal international economic order that features multilateral institutionalism, multilateral corporations, and hierarchical transborder global value/supply chains and production networks? How will China's BRI influence the established institutions and practices in development aid and foreign direct investment?

A third issue area to watch is how the tensions between Japan and China evolve, not so much over territorial disputes or historical problems but over the institutions and values of the international order, and their interests and identity as a leading East Asian state. Japan and China have been two major powers of geopolitical, economic, and normative influence in IREA from within the region itself. Their distinct ways of organizing national society, industrial development, and fitting themselves into international society have made a great impact on the shaping of the material structure, institutions, and international order in IREA and the collective identity of East Asia in global international relations. While Japan and China have developed comparable national capabilities in industrial production and economic development, and risen up to positions of great power and influence in geopolitics and geoeconomy, their historical experiences of rising to their respective positions have shaped their different paths and different sets of relations with the existing international order. This different position in the normative structure of the international system will continue to complicate their roles in IREA and the shaping of the international order in East Asia – and indeed that of the global international order.

East Asia is a second region in the world, with Europe being the first, where a cluster of nations have engaged successfully in industrial development and modern state building and developed interstate relations and influence on a global scale. The structure, institutions, and normative practices that developed in IREA are largely the effects of the establishment, implementation, and function of the nation-state-centric international system in East Asia in the twentieth century. Their experiences have raised complicated questions regarding the legitimacy and effectiveness of the nation-state system.

Large-scale dynamics have been driving East Asia to become a stand-alone political, economic, and cultural community. But twentieth-century IREA have also been driven significantly by the key nations of global interest, capability, and influence, and their efforts to engage with the global international relations in their own way. This in some way is not that different from the pattern that seemed to be in the first wave of the European experience. But the ambiguity of East Asia as a collective entity, with its mixture of national and civilizational elements, suggests that East Asian states' engagement with one another and with the broader international system will be fraught with complications in the years and decades to come. Ultimately, the national boundary, as everywhere else, is the "fault line" in IREA.

Bibliography

Acharya, Amitav, 1991. "Association of Southeast Asian Nations: Security Community or Défense Community?" *Pacific Affairs* 64(2): 159–178.

Acharya, Amitav, 1995. "A Regional Security Community in Southeast Asia?" *Journal of Strategic Studies* 18(3): 175–200.

Acharya, Amitav, 1997. "Ideas, Identity, and Institution-Building: From the 'ASEAN Way' to the 'Asia-Pacific Way'?" *The Pacific Review* 10(3): 319–346.

Acharya, Amitav, 1998. "Culture, Security, Multilateralism: The 'ASEAN Way' and Regional Order," *Journal of Contemporary Security Policy* 19(1): 55–84.

Acharya, Amitav, 1999. "A Concert of Asia?" *Survival* 41(3): 84–101.

Acharya, Amitav, 2001a. *Constructing a Security Community in Southeast Asia*. London: Routledge.

Acharya, Amitav, 2001b. *The Quest for Identity: International Relations of Southeast Asia*. Oxford: Oxford University Press.

Acharya, Amitav, 2003a. *Regionalism and Multilateralism*. Singapore: Eastern Universities Press.

Acharya, Amitav, 2003b. "Will Asia's Past Be Its Future?" *International Security* 28(3): 149–164.

Acharya, Amitav, 2010. "Democracy or Death? Will Democratization Bring Greater Regional Instability to East Asia?" *Pacific Review* 23(3): 335–358.

Acharya, Amitav, 2013. *The Making of Southeast Asia, International Relations of a Region*. Ithaca: Cornell University Press.

Acharya, Amitav, 2014a, "Power Shift or Paradigm Shift? China's Rise and Asia's Emerging Security Order," *International Studies Quarterly* 58(1): 158–173.

Acharya, Amitav, 2014b. "International Relations Theory and the 'Rise of Asia'," pp. 120–140 in Saadia Pekkanen, John Ravenhill, and Rosemary Foot, *The Oxford Handbook of the International Relations of Asia*. Oxford: Oxford University Press.

Acharya, Amitav, and Barry Buzan, 2007. "Why Is There No Non-Western International Relations Theory? An Introduction," *International Relations of the Asia-Pacific* 7(3): 287–312.

Acharya, Amitav, and Barry Buzan, 2010. *Non-Western International Relations Theory: Perspectives On and Beyond Asia*. London: Routledge.

Acharya, Amitav, and Barry Buzan, 2017. "Why Is There No Non-Western International Relations Theory? Ten Years On," *International Relations of the Asia-Pacific* 17(3): 341–370.

Acharya, Amitav, and Alastair I. Johnston, 2007. *Crafting Cooperation. Regional International Institutions in Comparative Perspective*. Cambridge: Cambridge University Press.

Acharya, Amitav, and See Seng Tan, 2005. "Betwixt Balance and Community: America, ASEAN, and the Security of Southeast Asia," *International Relations of the Asia-Pacific* 5(2): 37–59.

Acheson, Dean, 1950. "National Press Club Speech," January 12, 1950. Washington, DC: Truman Library.

ADB, 2008. *Emerging Asian Regionalism: A Partnership for Shared Prosperity*. Mandaluyong City: Asian Development Bank.

ADB, 2010. *Institutions for Regional Integration, Toward an Asian Economic Community*. Mandaluyong City: Asian Development Bank.

ADB, 2017. *Meeting Asia's Infrastructure Needs*. Mandaluyong City: Asian Development Bank.

ADB, 2018. *ADB History*. Mandaluyong City: Asian Development Bank.

AFR, 1994. "Chairman's Statement of the First Foreign Ministers Meeting of the ASEAN Regional Forum," 25 July 1994. Bangkok, Asian Regional Forum, ASEAN Secretariat.

Akamatsu, Kaname, 1935. "Waga kuni yomo kogyohin no susei. [The Trend of Foreign Trade in Manufactured Woolen Goods in Japan]." *Shogyo Keizai Ronso Higher Commercial School of Nagoya* 13(July): 129–212.

Akamatsu, Kaname, 1962. "Historical Pattern of Economic Growth in Developing Countries," *The Developing Economies* 1: 3–25.

Alagappa, Muthiah, 1998. *Asian Security Practice: Material and Ideational Influences*. Stanford: Stanford University Press.

Alagappa, Muthiah, 2003. *Asian Security Order: Instrumental and Normative Features*. Stanford: Stanford University Press.

Alagappa, Muthiah, 2014. "International Peace in Asia: Will It Endure?" *Asian Forum*, 19 December.

Albert, Michel, 1993. *Capitalism vs. Capitalism: How America's Obsession with Individual Achievement and Short-Term Profit Has Led It to the Brink of Collapse*. New York: Four Walls Eight Windows.

Almond, Gabriel A., 1956. "Comparative Political Systems," *The Journal of Politics* 18(3): 391–409.

Almond, Gabriel, and Sidney Verba, 1963. *The Civic Culture: Political Attitudes and Democracy in Five Nations*. Princeton: Princeton University Press.

Amsden, Alice H., 1989. *Asia's Next Giant: South Korea and Late Industrialization*. New York: Oxford University Press.

Anderson, Benedict, 1983. *Imagined Communities: Reflections on the Origin and Spread of Nationalism*. London: Verso.

Ang, Cheng Guan, 2018. *Southeast Asia's Cold War: An Interpretive History*. Honolulu: University of Hawaii Press.

APEC, 2018. *APEC Mission Statement*. Singapore: Asia-Pacific Economic Cooperation Secretariat.

Arase, David, 2016. *China's Rise and Changing Order in East Asia*. Basingstoke: Palgrave.

ARF, 1994. *Chairman's Statement: The First Meeting of The ASEAN Regional Forum*. Bangkok, 25 July, 1994.

Armstrong, Charles K., Gilbert Rozman, and Samuel S. Kim, 2005. *Korea at the Center: Dynamics of Regionalism in Northeast Asia: Dynamics of Regionalism in Northeast Asia*. London: Routledge.

Arrighi, Giovanni, 2007. "States, Markets, and Capitalism, East and West," *Positions: East Asia Cultures Critique* 15(2): 251–284.

Arrighi, Giovanni, 2009. *Adam Smith in Beijing: Lineages of the 21st Century*. London: Verso.

Arrighi, Giovanni, and Jessica Drangel, 1986. "The Stratification of the World-economy," *Review* 10(1): 9–74.

ASEAN, 2018a. *Overview of ASEAN Plus Three Cooperation*. Jakarta: ASEAN Secretariat.

ASEAN, 2018b. *Overview of ASEAN-China Dialogue Relations*. Jakarta: ASEAN Secretary.

Ashley, Richard K., 1984. "The Poverty of Neorealism," *International Organization* 38: 225–286.

Ashley, Richard K., 1987. "The Geopolitics of Geopolitical Space: Toward a Critical Social Theory Of International Politics," *Alternatives* 12: 403–434.

Ashley, Richard K., 1988. "Untying the Sovereign State: A Double Reading of the Anarchy Problematique," *Journal of International Studies* 17: 227–262.

Avenell, Simon, 2017a. "Transnational Environmental Activism and Japan's Second Modernity," *The Asia-Pacific Journal/Japan Focus* 15(14): 2.

Avenell, Simon, 2017b. *Transnational Japan in the Global Environmental Movement*. Honolulu: University of Hawaii Press.

Axelrod, Robert, and Robert Keohane, 1985. "Achieving Cooperation Under Anarchy: Strategies and Institutions," *World Politics* 38: 226–254.

Ayoob, Mohammed, 1991. "The Security Problematic of the Third World," *World Politics* 43(2): 257–283.

Ayoob, Mohammed, 1995. *The Third World Security Predicament: State Making, Regional Conflict, and the International System.* Boulder: Lynne Rienner.

Ba, Alice, 2009. *(Re)Negotiating East and Southeast Asia.* Stanford: Stanford University Press.

Baek, Seung-Wook, 2005. "Does China Follow 'the East Asian Development Model'?" *Journal of Contemporary Asia* 35(4): 485–498.

Baldwin, David, 1993. *Neorealism and Neoliberalism.* New York: Columbia University Press.

Baldwin, David, 1997. "The Concept of Security," *Review of International Studies* 23: 5–26.

Baldwin, Richard, 2006. "Multilateralizing Regionalism: Spaghetti Bowls as Building Blocks on the Path to Global Free Trade," *The World Economy* 29(11): 1451–1518.

Baldwin, Richard E., 2007. *Managing the Noodle Bowl: The Fragility of East Asian Regionalism.* ADB Working Papers Series on Regional Economic Integration, No. 7. Manila: Asian Development Bank.

Baldwin, Richard, and Phil Thornton, 2008. *Multilateralizing Regionalism: Challenges for the Global Trading System.* London: Centre for Economic Policy Research.

Barnard, Mitchell, and John Ravenhill, 1995. "Beyond Product Cycles and Flying Geese," *World Politics* 47(2): 171–209.

Beasley, William G., 1987. *Japanese Imperialism, 1894–1945.* Oxford: Oxford University Press.

Beeson, Mark, 2018. "Multilateralism in East Asia: Less than the Sum of Its Parts?" *Global Summitry* 2(1): 54–70.

Berger, Mark T., 1999. "APEC and Its Enemies: The Failure of the New Regionalism in the Asia-Pacific," *Third World Quarterly* 20(5): 1013–1030.

Bertrand, Jacques, and André Laliberté, 2010. *Multination State in Asia.* Cambridge: Cambridge University Press.

Blecker, Robert A., 2012. "Global Imbalances and the U.S. Trade Deficit," pp. 187–217 in Barry Z. Cynamon, Steven Fazzari, Mark Setterfield, *After the Great Recession The Struggle for Economic Recovery and Growth.* Cambridge: Cambridge University Press.

Bloom, William, 1990. *Personal Identity, National Identity and International Relations.* Cambridge: Cambridge University Press.

Bolt, Jutta, Robert Inklaar, Herman de Jong, and Jan Luiten van Zanden, 2018. *Maddison Project Database 2018.* Groningen: Groningen Growth and Development Centre, University of Groningen.

Boltho, Andrea, and Maria Weber, 2009. "Did China Follow the East Asian Development Model?" *The European Journal of Comparative Economics* 6(2): 267–286.

Boulding, Kenneth E., 1959. "National Images and International Systems," *Journal of Conflict Resolution* 3: 120–131.

Bowles, Paul, 2002. "Asia's Post-Crisis Regionalism: Bringing the State Back in, Keeping the (United) States Out," *Review of International Political Economy* 9(2): 244–270.

Brooks, Stephen, and William Wolfforth, 2016. "The Rise and Fall of the Great Powers in the Twenty-First Century," *International Security* 40(3): 7–53.

Bull, Hedley, 1977. *The Anarchical Society: A Study of Order in World Politics.* New York: Columbia University Press.

Bull, Hedley, and Adam Watson, 1985. *The Expansion of International Society.* Oxford: Oxford University Press.

Buruma, Ian, 1987. "A New Japanese Nationalism," *New York Times*, April 12.

Busan, Barry, and Yongjin Zhang, 2014. *Contesting International Society in East Asia.* Cambridge: Cambridge University Press.

Buzan, Barry, 2004a. "The Primary Institutions of International Society" pp. 161–204 in *From International to World Society? English School Theory ad Social Structure of International Society.* Cambridge: Cambridge University Press.

Buzan, Barry, 2004b. *From International to World Society? English School Theory and Social Structure of International Society*. Cambridge: Cambridge University Press.

Buzan, Barry, 2010. "China in International Society: Is 'Peaceful Rise' Possible?" *The Chinese Journal of International Politics* 3: 5–36.

Buzan, Barry, 2014. "The Logic and Contradictions of 'Peaceful Rise/Development' as China's Grand Strategy," *Chinese Journal of International Politics* 7(4): 381–420.

Buzan, Barry, Ole Wæver, and Jaap de Wilde, 1998. *Security: A New Framework for Analysis*. Boulder: Lynne Rienner.

BXF, 2018. *About Beijing Xiangshan Forum*. Beijing: Xiangshan Forum Secretary.

Caballero-Anthony, Mely, 2014. "Understanding ASEAN's Centrality: Bases and Prospects in an Evolving Regional Architecture," *The Pacific Review* 27(4): 563–584.

Caballero-Anthony, Mely, 2016. *An Introduction to Nontraditional Security*. Los Angeles: Sage.

Campbell, Kurt M., and Ely Ratner, 2018. "The China Reckoning: How Beijing Defied American Expectations," in Wang Jisi, J. Stapleton Roy, Aaron Friedberg, Thomas Christensen and Patricia Kim, Joseph S. Nye, Jr., Eric Li, Kurt M. Campbell, in response, "Did America Get China Wrong? The Engagement Debate," *Foreign Affairs*, March/April, and June/July.

Capie, David, and Brendan Taylor, 2010. "The Shangri-La Dialogue and the Institutionalization of Defense Diplomacy in Asia," *The Pacific Review* 23: 359–376.

Carter, Ashton B., William J. Perry, and John D. Steinbruner, 1992. *A New Concept of Cooperative Security*. Washington, DC: Brookings Institution Press.

Cavalier, Shelley, 2011. "Between Victim and Agent: A Third-Way Feminist Account of Trafficking for Sex Work," *Indiana Law Journal* 86(4): 1410–1458.

CFR, 2018. *The Rohingya Crisis*. New York: Council on Foreign Relations.

Cha, Victor D., 2010. "Powerplay: Origins of the U.S. Alliance System in Asia," *International Security* 34(3): 158–196.

Cha, Victor, 2016. *Powerplay: Origins of the American Alliance System in Asia*. Princeton: Princeton University Press.

Chan, Gerald, 2014. "Capturing China's International Identity: Social Evolution and Its Missing Links," *The Chinese Journal of International Politics* 7(2): 261–281.

Chan, Gerald, 2015. "China Eyes ASEAN: Evolving Multilateralism," *Journal of Asian Security and International Affairs* 2(1): 75–91.

Chan, Stephen, and Cerwyn Moore, 2009. "Non-Western Approaches to International Relations," Vol. IV, in Stephen Chan and Cerwyn Moore, *Approaches to International Relations*. Los Angeles/London: Sage.

Chay, Jongsuk, 1990. *Culture and International Relations*. New York: Praeger.

Cheng, Chwee Kuik, 2008. "China's Evolving Multilateralism in Asia: The Aussenpolitik and Innenpolitik Explanations," pp. 109–142 in Kent E. Calder and Francis Fukuyama, *East Asian Multilateralism: Prospects for Regional Stability*. Baltimore: Johns Hopkins University Press.

Cho, Il Hyun, and SeoHyun Park, 2014. "Domestic Legitimacy Politics and Varieties of Regionalism in East Asia," *Review of International Studies* 40(3): 583–606.

Chong, Ja Ian, 2014. *External Intervention and the Politics of State Formation: China, Indonesia, and Thailand, 1893–1952*. Cambridge: Cambridge University Press.

Choucri, Nazli, and Robert C. North, 1975. *Nations in Conflict: National Growth and International Violence*. New York: Freeman.

Chu, Shulong, and Lin Xinzhu, 2008. "The Six Party Talks: A Chinese Perspective," *Asian Perspective* 32(4): 29–43.

CICA, 2004. "CICA Rules of Procedures." Conference on Interaction and Confidence Building Measures in Asia, Beijing.

Clark, Ian, 1999. *Globalization and International Relations Theory*. Oxford: Oxford University Press.

Clark, Ian, 2005. *Legitimacy in International Society*. Oxford: Oxford University Press.

Clark, Ian, 2007. *International Legitimacy and World Society*. Oxford: Oxford University Press.

Clark, Ian, 2014. "International Society and China: The Power of Norms and the Norms of Power," *Chinese Journal of International Politics* 7(3): 315–340.

Clinton, Hillary, 2011. "America's Pacific Century," *Foreign Policy*, October 11.

Cohen, Warren I., 2000. *East Asia at the Center: Four Thousand Years of Engagement with the World*. New York: Columbia University Press.

Cohen, Paul, 2010. *Discovering History in China: American Historical Writing on the Recent Chinese Past*. New York: Columbia University Press.

Collignon, Richard, and Chikako Usui, 2001. "The Resilience of Japan's Iron Triangle," *Asian Survey* 41(5): 865–895.

Cooley, Alexander, and Hendrik Spruyt, 2009. *Contracting States: Sovereign Transfers in International Relations*. Princeton: Princeton University Press.

COP 9054, 2011. *Republic Act 9054. Republic of the Philippines*. Manila: Congress of the Philippines.

Cox, Alvin D., 1988, "The Pacific War," pp. 315–376 in Peter Duus, *The Cambridge History of Japan: The Twentieth Century*. Cambridge: Cambridge University Press.

CSCAP, 1993. *The Kuala Lumpur Statement, 8 June 1993*. Kuala Lumpur: Council for Security Cooperation in the Asia Pacific.

Cumings, Bruce, 1981. *Origins of the Korean War, Vol. 1: Liberation and the Emergence of Separate Regimes, 1945–1947*. Princeton: Princeton University Press.

Cumings, Bruce, 1984. "The Origins & Development of the Northeast Asian Political Economy," *International Organization* 38(1): 1–40.

Cumings, Bruce, 1990. *Origins of the Korean War, Vol. 2. The Roaring of the Cataract, 1947–1950*. Princeton: Princeton University Press.

Cumings, Bruce, 2010. *The Korean War: A History Modern History*. New York: Modern Library.

Davidann, Jon, 2003. "Citadels of Civilization: U.S. and Japanese Visions of World Order in the Interwar Period," pp. 21–43 in Richard Jensen, Jon Davidann, and Yoneyuki Sugita, *Trans-Pacific Relations: America, Europe, and Asia in the Twentieth Century*. New York: Praeger.

Davidson, Robert Harold, 1969. *The Far East Agreements of the Yalta Conference of February 4–11, 1945, and the Sino-Soviet Agreements of August, 1945*. Dissertation, Portland State University.

Day, Tony, 2002. *Fluid Iron: State Formation in Southeast Asia*. Honolulu: University of Hawaii Press.

De Bary, William Theodore, 1988. *East Asian Civilizations: A Dialogue in Five Stages*. Harvard: Harvard University Press.

Dent, Christopher M., 2008. *China, Japan and Regional Leadership in East Asia*. Cheltenham: Edward Elgar.

Dent, Christopher M., 2016. *East Asian Regionalism*. London: Routledge.

Deudney, Daniel, 1990. "The Case Against Linking Environmental Degradation and National Security," *Millennium* 19(3): 461–476.

Dewitt, David, 1994. "Common, Comprehensive, and Cooperative Security," *The Pacific Review* 7(1): 1–15.

Diamond, Larry Jay, Marc F. Plattner 1998. *Democracy in East Asia*. Johns Hopkins University Press.

Diamond, Larry Jay, Marc F. Plattner, Yunhan Chu, 2013. *Democracy in East Asia: A New Century*. Johns Hopkins University Press.

Doak, Kevin M., 2006. *A History of Nationalism in Modern Japan: Placing the People*. Boston: BRILL.

Doyle, Michael W., 1983. "Kant, Liberal Legacies, and Foreign Affairs," *Philosophy & Public Affairs* 12(3): 205–235, and (4): 323–353.

Doyle, Michael W., 1986. "Liberalism and World Politics," *American Political Science Review* 80(4): 1151–1169.

Doyle, Michael, 2005. "Three Pillars of the Liberal Peace Three Pillars of the Liberal Peace," *American Political Science Review* 99(3): 463–466.

EASG, 2002. *Final Report of the East Asia Study Group*, ASEAN+3. Jakarta: ASEAN Secretary.

EAVG, 2001. *Towards an East Asian Community: Region of Peace, Prosperity, and Progress*, ASEAN+3. Jakarta: ASEAN Secretary.

Eisenstadt, Shmuel, 1987. *European Civilization in a Comparative Perspective*. Oxford: Oxford University Press.

Eisenstadt, Shmuel, 1997. *Japanese Civilization: A Comparative View*. Chicago: University of Chicago Press.

Emmers, Ralf, 2009. *Geopolitics and Maritime Territorial Disputes*. London: Routledge.

Etchart, Linda, 2015a. "Demilitarizing the Global: Women's Peace Movements and Transnational Networks," pp. 703–722 in Rawwida Baksh and Wendy Harcourt, *The Oxford Handbook of Transnational Feminist Movements*. Oxford: Oxford University Press.

Etchart, Linda, 2015b. "Demilitarizing the Global: Women's Peace Movements and Transnational Networks," pp. 1–25 in Rawwida Baksh and Wendy Harcourt, *The Oxford Handbook of Transnational Feminist Movements*. New York: Oxford University Press.

Evans, Paul M, 2004. "Human Security and East Asia: In the Beginning," *Journal of East Asian Studies* 4(2): 263–284.

Ezell, Stephen J., and Robert D. Atkinson, 2011. *The Case for a National Manufacturing Strategy*. Washington, DC: Information Technology & Innovation Foundation.

Fairbank, John K., 1953. *Trade and Diplomacy on the China Coast: The Opening of Treaty Ports, 1842–1854*. Harvard: Harvard University Press.

Fairbank, John K., 1965. *East Asia: The Modern Transformation*. Boston: Houghton Mifflin.

Fairbank, John K., 1968. *The Chinese World Order*. Harvard: Harvard University Press.

Fairbank, John, Edwin Reischauer, and Albert Craig, 1989. *East Asia: Tradition & Transformation*. Belmont: Wadsworth.

Fallon, Theresa, 2015. "The New Silk Road," *American Foreign Policy Interests* 37(3): 140–147.

Feenstra, Robert C., Robert Inklaar, and Marcel P. Timmer, 2015. "The Next Generation of the Penn World Table," *American Economic Review* 105(10): 3150–3182.

Ferrarini, Benno, and David Hummels, 2014. *Asia and Global Production Networks*. Cheltenham: Edgar and ADB.

Fisher, Glen, 1997. *Mindsets: The Role of Culture and Perception in International Relations*. Yarmouth: Intercultural Press.

Fravel, M. Taylor, 2005. "Regime Insecurity and International Cooperation: Explaining China's Compromises in Territorial Disputes," *International Security* 30(2): 46–83.

Fravel, M. Taylor, 2009. *Strong Borders, Secure Nation Cooperation and Conflict in China's Territorial Disputes*. Princeton: Princeton University Press.

Friedberg, Aaron L., 1993. "Ripe for Rivalry: Prospects for Peace in a Multipolar Asia," *International Security* 18(3): 5–33.

Friedberg, Aaron L., 2011. *A Contest for Supremacy: China, America, and the Struggle for Mastery in Asia*. London: Norton.

Fukuda, Takeo, 1977. "Speech by Prime Minister Takeo Fukuda" Manila, August 18, 1977. At Tanaka Akihiko, *Database of Japanese Politics and International Relations*, National Graduate Institute for Policy Studies. Tokyo: University of Tokyo.

Fukuzawa, Yukichi, 1875 [2009]. *An Outline of a Theory of Civilization*. New York: Columbia University Press.

Fukuzawa, Yukichi, 1885. "Datsu-A Ron" ("Off Asia"), *Jiji Shinpō*, March 16.

Gaddis, John Lewis, 1987. "Drawing Lines: The Defensive Perimeter Strategy in East Asia, 1947–1951," pp. 72–104 in John Lewis Gaddis, *The Long Peace*. Oxford: Oxford University Press.

Gaenslen, Fritz, 1986. "Culture and Decision-Making in China, Japan, Russia, and the United States," *World Politics* 39: 78–103.

Gannon, James, 2011. "Engaging in Asia: The Evolving US Approach to Regional Community Building," pp. 15–41 in Mark Borthwick and Tadashi Yamamoto (eds),

A Pacific Nation: Perspectives on the US Role in an East Asian Community. Tokyo/ New York: Japan Center for International Exchange.

Gao, Bai, 1997. *Economic Ideology and Japanese Industrial Policy: Developmentalism from 1931 to 1965.* Cambridge: Cambridge University Press.

Geertz, Clifford, 1973. "Thick Description: Toward an Interpretive Theory of Culture," pp. 3–30 in *The Interpretation of Cultures: Selected Essays.* New York: Basic Books.

Gellner, Ernest, 1983. *Nations and Nationalism.* Basil: Blackwell.

George, Alexander, 1969. "The Operational Code: A Neglected Approach to the Study of Political Leaders and Decision-Making," *International Studies Quarterly* 13: 190–222.

George, Alexander, 1980. *Presidential Decision-Making in Foreign Policy: The Effective Use of Information and Advice.* Boulder: Westview Press.

Gerschenkron, Alexander, 1962. *Economic Backwardness in Historical Perspective.* Cambridge: Harvard University Press.

Gilpin, Robert, 1981. *War and Change in World Politics.* Cambridge: Cambridge University Press.

Gladney, Dru C., 1998. *Making Majorities: Constituting the Nation in Japan, Korea, China, Malaysia, Fiji, Turkey, and the United States.* Stanford: Stanford University Press.

Glaser, Charles L., 2015. "A U.S.-China Grand Bargain? The Hard Choice Between Military Competition and Accommodation," *International Security* 39(4): 49–90.

Gochman, Charles S., and Zeev Maoz, 1984. "Militarized Interstate Disputes, 1816–1976," *Journal of Conflict Resolution* 29(4): 585–615.

Goh, Evelyn, 2005. *Meeting the China Challenge: The U.S. in Southeast Asian Regional Security Strategies.* Washington, DC: East-West Center.

Goh, Evelyn, 2006. *Understanding 'Hedging' in Asia-Pacific Security* PacNet 43, August 31. Pacific Forum CSIS. Honolulu: Hawaii.

Goh, Evelyn, 2007a. "Great Powers and Hierarchical Order in Southeast Asia: Analyzing Regional Security Strategies," *International Security* 32(3): 113–157.

Goh, Evelyn, 2007b. "Hegemony, Hierarchy and Order," pp. 101–121 in William Tow, *Security Politics in the Asia-Pacific: A Regional-Global Nexus?* Cambridge: Cambridge University Press.

Goh, Evelyn, 2008. "Hierarchy and the Role of the United States in the East Asian Security Order," *International Relations of the Asia-Pacific* 8(3): 355–377.

Goh, Evelyn, 2013. *The Struggle for Order: Hegemony, Hierarchy, and Transition in Post-Cold War East Asia.* Oxford: Oxford University Press.

Goh, Evelyn, 2017. *Rising China's Influence in Developing Asia.* Oxford: Oxford University Press.

Goldsmith, Benjamin E., 2006. "A Universal Proposition? Region, Conflict, War, and the Robustness of the Liberal Peace," *European Journal of International Relations* 12(4): 533–563.

Goldsmith, Benjamin E., 2007. "A Liberal Peace in Asia?" *Journal of Peace Research* 44(1): 5–27.

Goldsmith, Benjamin E., 2014. "Domestic political institutions and the initiation of international conflict in East Asia: some evidence for an Asian democratic peace," *International Relations of the Asia-Pacific* 14(1): 59–90.

Goldstein, Avery, 2003. "An Emerging China's Emerging Grand Strategy: A Neo-Bismarckian Turn?" pp. 57–96 in G. John Ikenberry and Michael Mastanduno, eds., *International Relations Theory and the Asia-Pacific.* New York: Columbia University Press.

Gong, Gerrit W., 1984. *The Standard of "Civilization" in International Society.* Oxford: Clarendon Press.

Gourevitch, Peter, 1978. "The Second Image Reversed: The International Sources of Domestic Politics," *International Organization* 32(4): 881–912.

Green, Michael J., 2017. *More than Providence: Grand Strategy and American Power in* the *Asia Pacific Since 1783*. New York: Columbia University Press.

Green, Michael J., and Bates Gill, 2009. *Asia's New Multilateralism: Cooperation, Competition, and the Search for Community*. New York: Columbia University Press.

Grieger, Gisela, 2016. *One Belt, One Road (OBOR): China's Regional Integration Initiative*. Luxembourg: European Parliament Research Service.

Gries, Peter Hays, 2005. *China's New Nationalism: Pride, Politics, and Diplomacy*. Berkeley: University of California Press.

Gries, Peter Hays, Qingmin Zhang, H. Michael Crowson, and Huajian Cai, 2011. "Patriotism, Nationalism and China's US Policy: Structures and Consequences of Chinese National Identity," *The China Quarterly* 205: 1–17.

Grotius, Hugo, 1646. *On the Law of War and Peace*, translated by Francis W. Kelsey, Oxford University Press [1925].

Gurr, Ted R., 1974. "Persistence and Change in Political Systems, 1800–1971." *American Political Science Review* 68 (4): 1482–1504.

Gurr, Ted Robert, 1993. "Why Minorities Rebel: A Global Analysis of Communal Mobilization and Conflict Since 1945," *International Political Science Review* 14(2): 161–201.

Gurr, Ted Robert, 1994. "Peoples Against States: Ethnopolitical Conflict and the Changing World System," *International Studies Quarterly* 38(3): 347–377.

Haas, Ernst, 1964. *Beyond the Nation-State: Functionalism and International Organization*. Stanford: Stanford University Press.

Hack, Karl, and Geoff Wade, 2009. "The Origins of the Southeast Asian Cold War," *Journal of Southeast Asian Studies* 40(3): 441–448.

Hagström, Linus, and Karl Gustafsson, 2015. "Japan and Identity Change: Why It Matters in International Relations," *The Pacific Review* 28(1): 1–22.

Hall, Peter A., and David Soskice, 2001. *Varieties of Capitalism: The Institutional Foundations of Comparative Advantage*. New York: Oxford University Press.

Hall, Peter A., and Rosemary C. R. Taylor, 1996. "Political Science and the Three New Institutionalisms," *Political Studies* 44(5): 936–957.

Halper, Stefan, 2010. *The Beijing Consensus: How China's Authoritarian Model Will Dominate the Twenty-First Century*. London: Basic Books.

Harris, Paul G., and Graeme Lang, 2014. *Routledge Handbook of Environment and Society in Asia*. London: Routledge.

Harrison, Lawrence E., and Samuel P. Huntington, 2000. *Culture Matters: How Values Shape Human Progress*. New York: Basic Books.

Hasegawa, Tsuyoshi, and Kazuhiko Togo, 2008. *East Asia's Haunted Present: Historical Memories and the Resurgence of Nationalism*. New York: Praeger.

Hata, Ikuhiko, 1988. "The Japanese Colonial Empire, 1895–1945," pp. 271–314 in Peter Duus, *The Cambridge History of Japan: The Twentieth Century*. Cambridge: Cambridge University Press.

Hatch, Walter, and Kozo Yamamura, 1996. *Asia in Japans Embrace, Building a Regional Production Alliance*. Cambridge: Cambridge University Press.

He, Baogang, and Takashi Inoguchi, 2011. "Introduction to Ideas of Asian Regionalism," *Japanese Journal of Political Science* 12(2): 165–177.

Hemmer, Christopher, and Peter J. Katzenstein, 2002. "Why Is There No NATO in Asia?" *International Organization* 56(3): 575–607.

Higgott, Richard, and Richard Stubbs, 1995. "Competing Conceptions of Economic Regionalism: APEC vs EAEC in the Asia Pacific," *Review of International Political Economy* 2(3): 516–535.

Hoffmann, Stanley, 1977. "An American Social Science: International Relations," *Daedalus* 6(3): 41–60.

Holsti, K. J., 1985. *The Dividing Discipline: Hegemony and Diversity in International Theory*. Boston: Allen & Unwin.

Hong, Ki-Joon, 2015. "Institutional Multilateralism in Northeast Asia: A Path Emergence Theory Perspective," *North Korean Review* 11(1): 24–41.

Hook, Glenn D., Julie Gilson, Christopher W. Hughes, and Hugo Dobson, 2001. *Japan's International Relations: Politics, Economics and Security*. London: Routledge.

Hook, Glenn D., Julie Gilson, Christopher W. Hughes, and Hugo Dobson, 2011. *Japan's International Relations: Politics, Economics and Security*. London: Routledge.

Hosoya, Chihiro, 1974. "Characteristics of the Foreign Policy Decision-Making System in Japan," *World Politics* 26(3): 353–369.

HSJ, 2018. *Historical Statistics of Japan, Statistics Bureau*. Tokyo: Japanese Government.

Huang, Xiaoming, 2001. "The Zen Master's Story and an Anatomy of International Relations Theory," pp. 222–243 in Stephen Chan and Peter Mandaville, *The Zen of International Relations*. London: Palgrave.

Huang, Xiaoming, 2002. "Culture, Institutions and Globalization: What Is 'Chinese' About Chinese Civilization?" pp. 218–241 in Mehdi Mozaffari, *Globalization and Civilizations*. London/New York: Routledge.

Huang, Xiaoming, 2005. *The Rise and Fall of the East Asian Growth System 1951–2000: Institutional Competitiveness and Rapid Economic Growth*. London/New York: Routledge.

Huang, Xiaoming, 2007a. "Do Asian Values Matter – For an East Asian Community?" *Politics & Policy* 35 (1): 154–161.

Huang, Xiaoming, 2007b. "The Invisible Hand: Modern Studies of International Relations in Japan, China, and Korea," *Journal of International Relations and Development* 10(2): 168–203.

Huang, Xiaoming, 2009. *Politics in Pacific Asia*. New York/London: Palgrave.

Huang, Xiaoming, 2010a. "Crafting the Modern State: Religion, Family and Military in Japan, China and Korea," pp. 21–50 in Mehdi Amineh, *State, Society and International Relations in Asia: Reality and Challenges*. Amsterdam: University of Amsterdam Press.

Huang, Xiaoming, 2010b. "Culture, Civilization and International Relations," pp. 49–72 in Wang Jianwei, 国际关系学 (*International Relations*). Beijing: 中国人民大学出版社[China Renmin University Press].

Huang, Xiaoming, 2013. *Modern Economic Development in Japan and China: Developmentalism, Capitalism, and the World Economic System*. New York: Palgrave.

Huang, Xiaoming, Robert G. Patman, 2013. *China and the International System Becoming a World Power*. London and New York: Routledge.

Hund, Markus, 2003. "ASEAN Plus Three: Towards a New Age of Pan-East Asian Regionalism? A Skeptic's Appraisal," *The Pacific Review* 16(3): 383–417.

Huntington, Samuel P., 1968. *Political Order in Changing Societies*. Yale: Yale University Press.

Huntington, Samuel P. 1991. *The Third Wave: Democratization in the Late Twentieth Century*. Norman: University of Oklahoma Press.

Huntington, Samuel P., 1993. "The Clash of Civilizations?" *Foreign Affairs* 72: 22–49.

Huntington, Samuel P., 1996. *The Clash of Civilizations and the Remaking of World Order*. New York: Simon & Schuster.

Hurrell, Andrew, 1995. "Explaining the Resurgence of Regionalism in World Politics," *Review of International Studies* 21: 549–569.

Hurrell, Andrew, 2008. *On Global Order: Power, Values, and the Constitution of International Society*. Oxford: Oxford University Press.

Hurrell, Andrew, and Ngaire Woods, 1999. *Inequality, Globalization and World Politics*. Oxford: Oxford University Press.

Huxley, Tim, 1996. "Southeast Asia in the Study of International Relations: The Rise and Decline of a Region," *The Pacific Review* 9(2): 199–228.

IDE-JETRO and WTO, 2011. *Trade Patterns and Global Value Chains in East Asia: From Trade in Goods to Trade in Tasks*. Geneva: World Trade Organization Secretariat.

Ikenberry, G. John, 2000. *After Victory: Institutions, Strategic Restraint, and the Rebuilding of Order After Major Wars*. Princeton: Princeton University Press.

Ikenberry, G. John, 2014a. *Power, Order, and Change in World Politics*. Cambridge: Cambridge University Press.

Ikenberry, G. John, 2014b. "The Logic of Order: Westphalia, Liberalism, and the Evolution of International Order in the Modern Era," pp. 83–106 in G. John Ikenberry, *Power, Order, and Change in World Politics*. Cambridge University Press.

Ikenberry, G. John, 2018. "A New Order of Things? China, America, and the Struggle over World Order," pp. 33–53 in Asle Toje, *Will China's Rise Be Peaceful? The Rise of a Great Power in Theory, History, Politics, and the Future*. Oxford: Oxford University Press.

Ikenberry, G. John, and Jitsuo Tsuchiyama, 2002. "Between Balance of Power and Community: The Future of Multilateral Security Cooperation in the Asia Pacific," *International Relations of the Asia Pacific* 1(2): 69–94.

IMF-CDIS, 2018. *Coordinated Direct Investment Surveys*. Washington, DC: International Monetary Fund.

IMF-DOTS, 2018. *Direction of Trade Statistics*. Washington, DC: International Monetary Fund.

Inoguchi, Takashi, 2007. "Are There Any Theories of International Relations in Japan," *International Relations of the Asia-Pacific* 7(3): 369–390.

Inoguchi, Takashi, and Paul Bacon, 2001. "The Study of International Relations in Japan: Towards a More International Discipline," *International Relations of the Asia-Pacific* 1: 1–20.

IOSCC, 1998. *China's National Defense 1998*. Beijing: Information Office of the State Council of China.

IRAP, 2017. "Why Is There No Non-Western International Relations Theory? Ten Years On," *International Relations of the Asia-Pacific* 17(3): 341–370.

IRAP, 2018. "Theorizing China's Rise in and Beyond International Relations," Special Issue, *International Relations of the Asia-Pacific* 18(3): 289–311.

Iriye, Akira, 1981. *Power and Culture: The Japanese-American War 1941–1945*. Cambridge: Harvard University Press.

Iriye, Akira, 1997. *Japan and the Wider World: From the Mid-Nineteenth Century to the Present*. London: Longman.

Islam, Md Saidul, Yap Hui Pei, and Shrutika Mangharam, 2016. "Trans-Boundary Haze Pollution in Southeast Asia: Sustainability Through Plural Environmental Governance," *Sustainability* 201(8): 498–513.

Jager, Sheila Miyoshi, 2014. *Brothers at War: The Unending Conflict in Korea*. London: Norton.

Janis, Irving L., 1972. *Victims of Groupthink: A Psychological Study of Foreign-Policy Decisions and Fiascos*. Boston: Houghton Mifflin.

Jayakumar, S., Tommy Koh, and Robert Beckman, 2014. *The South China Sea Disputes and Law of the Sea*. Cheltenham: Edward Edgar.

Jervis, Robert, 1970. *The Logic of Image of International Relations*. Princeton: Princeton University Press.

Jervis, Robert, 1976. *Perception and Misperception in International Politics*. Princeton: Princeton University Press.

JETRO, 2018. *Japanese Trade and Investment Statistics*. Tokyo: Japan External Trade Organization.

Johnson, Chalmers, 1982. *MITI and the Japanese Miracle: The Growth of Industrial Policy, 1925–1975*. Stanford: Stanford University Press.

Johnston, Alastair I., 2003. "Is China a Status Quo Power?," *International Security* 27(4): 5–56.

Johnston, Alastair I., 2012. "What (If Anything) Does East Asia Tell Us About International Relations Theory?" *Annual Review of Political Science* 15: 53–78.

Johnston, Alastair I., 2017. "Is Chinese Nationalism Rising? Evidence from Beijing," *International Security* 41(3): 7–43.

Kang, David C., 2003. "Getting Asia Wrong: The Need for New Analytical Frameworks," *International Security* 24(1): 57–85.

Kang, David, C., 2007. *China Rising: Peace, Power, and Order in East Asia*. New York: Columbia University Press.

Kang, David C., 2010. *East Asia Before the West: Five Centuries of Trade and Tribute.* New York: Columbia University Press.

Kant, Immanuel, 1623. "Perpetual Peace: A Philosophical Sketch," pp. 93–115 in Hans S. Reiss and H. B. Nisbet. *Kant: Political Writings.* Cambridge: Cambridge University Press.

Kant, Immanuel, 1795 [1927]. "Perpetual Peace: A Philosophical Proposal," pp 19–59 in Helen O'Brien (Translator), *Kant's Perpetual Peace: A Philosophical Proposal.* London: Sweet & Maxwell.

Kant, Immanuel, 1795 [1949]. "Perpetual Peace. A Philosophical Sketch," in Carl J. Friedrich, *The Philosophy of Kant.* New York: Modem Library.

Kaplan, Robert D., 1990. "The Coming Anarchy," *The Atlantic Monthly*, February.

Kasahara, Shigehisa, 2013. "The Asian Developmental State and the Flying Geese Paradigm," UNCTAD Discussion Paper No. 213. Geneva: UNCTAD.

Kelman, Herbert, 1965. *International Behavior: A Social-Psychological Analysis.* New York: Holt, Rinehart & Winston.

Kennan, George F. "X," 1947. "The Sources of Soviet Conduct," *Foreign Affairs*, July.

Kennedy, Paul M., 1987. *The Rise and Fall of the Great Powers.* New York: Random House.

Keohane, Robert, 1984. *After Hegemony: Cooperation and Discord in World Political Economy.* Princeton: Princeton University Press.

Keohane, Robert, 1986. *Neorealism and Its Critics.* New York: Columbia University Press.

Keohane, Robert, 1989. *International Institutions and State Power.* Boulder: Westview Press.

Keohane, Robert, and Lisa L. Martin, 1995. "The Promise of Institutionalist Theory," *International Security* 20(1): 39–51.

Keohane, Robert O., and Joseph S. Nye, 1971. *Transnational Relations and World Politics.* Cambridge: Harvard University Press.

Keohane, Robert O., and Joseph S. Nye, 1977. *Power and Interdependence: World Politics in Transition.* Boston: Little, Brown.

Kim, Samuel S., 2000. *Korea's Globalization.* Cambridge: Cambridge University Press.

Kim, Samuel, 2003. *The International Relations of Northeast Asia.* Lanham: Rowman & Littlefield.

Kim, Samuel S., 2004a. "Regionalization and Regionalism in East Asia," *Journal of East Asian Studies* 4(1): 39–67.

Kim, Samuel S., 2004b. *Inter-Korean Relations, Problems and Prospects.* Gordonsville: Palgrave.

Kim, Samuel S., 2006. *The Two Koreas and the Great Powers.* Cambridge: Cambridge University Press.

Kim, Samuel, 2008. "The Evolving Asian System: Three Transformations," pp. 35–56 in David Shambaugh and Michael Yahuda, *International Relations of Asia.* Lanham: Rowman & Littlefield.

Kingsbury, Damien, 2005. *South-East Asia: A Political Profile.* Oxford: Oxford University Press.

Kingston, Jeff, 2015. *Asian Nationalisms Reconsidered.* London: Routledge.

Kivimaki, Timo, 2001. "The Long Peace of ASEAN," *Journal of Peace Research* 38(1): 5–25.

Kivimäki, Timo, 2014. *The Long Peace of East Asia.* London: Routledge.

Kojima, Kiyoshi, 2000. "The 'Flying Geese' Model of Asian Economic Development: Origin, Theoretical Extensions, and Regional Policy Implications," *Journal of Asian Economics* 11: 375–401.

Koo, Min Gyo, 2010. *Island Disputes and Maritime Regime Building in East Asia: Between a Rock and a Hard Place.* London: Routledge.

Korhonen, Pekka, 1994. "Theory of the Flying Geese Pattern of Development and Its Interpretations," *Journal of Peace Research* 31(1): 93–108.

Kosugi, Ryoji, 1986. "Japan's Role in the Coming Pacific Era," in Richard B. Finn, *U.S.-Japan Relations: Learning from Competition.* New Brunswick: Transaction Publishers.

Krasner, Stephen D., 1976. "State Power and the Structure of International Trade," *World Politics* 28: 317–347.

Krasner, Stephen D., 1981. "Transforming International Regimes: What the Third World Wants and Why," *International Studies Quarterly* 25 (1): 119–148.

Krasner, Stephen D., 1982. "Structural Causes and Regime Consequences: Regimes as Intervening Variables," *International Organization* 36(2): 185–205.

Krauss, Ellis S., and T. J. Pempel, 2004. *Beyond Bilateralism: U.S.-Japan Relations in Asia and the Pacific*. Stanford: Stanford University Press.

Kubalkova, Vendulka, Nicholas Onuf, and Paul Kowert, 1998. *International Relations in a Constructed World*. Armonk: M.E. Sharpe.

Kumar, Krishan, 2013. "Empires and Nations: Convergence or Divergence?" pp. 279–300 in George Steinmetz, *Sociology and Empire*. Durham: Duke University Press.

Kumar, Krishan, 2017. *Visions of Empire: How Five Imperial Regimes Shaped the World*. Princeton: Princeton University Press.

Kupchan, Charles A., 2014. "Unpacking Hegemony: The Social Foundations of Hierarchical Order," pp. 19–60 in G. John Ikenberry, *Power, Order, and Change in World Politics*. Cambridge: Cambridge University Press.

Lake, David A., 1984. "Beneath the Commerce of Nations: A Theory of International Economic Structures," *International Studies Quarterly* 28(2): 143–170.

Lake, David A., 2009a. "Regional Hierarchy: Authority and Local International Order," *Review of International Studies* 35(S1): 35–58.

Lake, David A., 2009b. *Hierarchy in International Relations*. Ithaca: Cornell University Press.

Lake, David A., 2017. "Domination, Authority, and the Forms of Chinese Power," *The Chinese Journal of International Politics* 10(4): 357–382.

Lapid, Yosef, and Friedrich Kratochwil, 1996. *The Return of Culture and Identity in IR Theory*. Boulder: Lynne Rienner.

Lasswell, Harold D., 1935. *World Politics and Personal Insecurity*. New York: Whittlesey.

Lasswell, Harold D., 1948. *Power and Personality*. New York: Norton.

Lawrence, Mark Atwood, 2010. *The Vietnam War: A Concise International History*. Oxford: Oxford University Press.

Lee, Kuan Yew, 2000. *From Third World to First: The Singapore Story – 1965–2000*. New York: Harper.

Lee, Geun, 2002. "Environmental Security in East Asia: the Regional Environmental Security Complex Approach," *Asian Perspective* 26(2): 77–99.

Lee, Ji-Young, 2017. "Understand the Tribute System," pp. 27–55 in *China's Hegemony: Four Hundred Years of East Asian Domination*. New York: Columbia University Press.

Leifer, Michael, 1999. "The ASEAN Process: A Category Mistake," *The Pacific Review* 12(1): 25–38.

Lemke, Douglas, and Ronald L. Tammen, 2003. "Power Transition Theory and the Rise of China," *International Interactions* 29(4): 269–271.

Levy, Marc A., 1995. "Is the Environment a National Security Issue?" *International Security* 20(2): 35–62.

Lieberman, Victor, 2003. *Strange Parallels: Southeast Asia in Global Context, c. 800–1830, Vol. 1: Integration on the Mainland*. Cambridge: Cambridge University Press.

Lind, Jennifer, 2011. "Democratization and Stability in East Asia," *International Studies Quarterly* 55(2): 409–436.

Lipset, Seymour Martin, 1959. "Social Requisites of Democracy: Economic Development and Political Legitimacy," *American Political Science Review* 53(1): 69–105.

Little, Jane Sneddon, 2008. *Global Imbalances and the Evolving: World Economy*. Boston: Federal Reserve Bank of Boston.

Little, Richard, and Steve Smith, 1988. *Belief Systems and International Relations*. Oxford: Blackwell.

Logevall, Fredrik, 2001. *Choosing War: The Lost Chance for Peace and the Escalation of War in Vietnam*. Berkeley: University of California Press.

Macintyre, Andrew, 1994. *Business and Government in Industrializing Asia*. Sydney: Allen & Unwin.

MacKay, Joseph, 2015. "Rethinking the IR Theory of Empire in Late Imperial China," *International Relation of the Asia Pacific* 15(1): 53–79.

Maliniak, Daniel, Susan Peterson, Ryan Powers, and Michael J. Tierney, 2018. "Is International Relations a Global Discipline? Hegemony, Insularity, and Diversity in the Field," *Security Studies* 27(3): 448–484.

Mancall, Mark, 1984. *China at the Center: 300 Years of Foreign Policy*. London: The Free Press.

Maoz, Zeev, and Nasrin Abdolali, 1989. "Regime Types and International Conflict, 1816–1976," *The Journal of Conflict Resolution* 33(1): 3–35.

Martinez, Leonardo, 2009. "A Theory of Political Cycles," *Journal of Economic Theory* 144: 1166–1186.

Matthews, Eugene A., 2013. "Japan's New Nationalism," *Foreign Affairs*, November/December.

Mattli, Walter, 1999. *The Logic of Regional Integration – Europe and Beyond*. Cambridge: Cambridge University Press.

Mattli, Walter, 2012. "Comparative Regional Integration: Theoretical Developments," pp. 1–19 in Erik Jones, Anand Menon, and Stephen Weatherill, *The Oxford Handbook of the European Union*. New York: Oxford University Press.

McCloud, Donald G., 1995. *Southeast Asia: Tradition and Modernity in the Contemporary World*. Boulder: Westview Press.

McNally, Christopher A., 2012. "Sino-Capitalism: China's Reemergence and the International Political Economy," *World Politics* 64(4): 741–776.

Mearsheimer, John J., 1994. "The False Promise of International Institutions," *International Security* 19(3): 5–49.

Mearsheimer, John, 2001. *The Tragedy of Great Power Politics*. London: Norton.

Mearsheimer, John J., 2014. "Can China Rise Peacefully?" *The National Interest*, October 25.

Mitrany, David, 1948. "The Functional Approach to World Organization," *International Affairs* 24(3): 350–363.

Modelski, George, 1987. *Long Cycles in World Politics*. London: Macmillan.

Mohan, Mahdev, 2017. "A Domestic Solution for Cross Border Human Rights Harm: Singapore's Haze Pollution Law," *Business and Human Rights Journal* 5: 1–9. Research Collection School of Law, Singapore Management University.

Moore, Aaron, 2013. *Constructing East Asia: Technology, Ideology, and Empire in Japan's Wartime Era 1931–1945*. Stanford: Stanford University Press.

Moravcsik, Andrew, 1997. "Taking Preferences Seriously: A Liberal Theory of International Politics," *International Organization* 51(4): 513–153.

Morgenthau, Hans J., 1948. *Politics Among Nations: The Struggle for Power and Peace*. New York: Alfred A. Knopf.

MPD, 2018. *Maddison Project Database 2018*. Groningen: Groningen Growth and Development Centre, University of Groningen.

Murray, Philomena, 2010. "Comparative Regional Integration in the EU and East Asia: Moving Beyond Integration Snobbery," *International Politics* 47(3–4): 308–323.

Myers, Ramon Hawley, and Mark R. Peattie, 1984. *The Japanese Colonial Empire, 1895–1945*. Princeton: Princeton University Press.

National Diet Library, 2003a. *Cairo Communiqué, December 1, 1943*. Tokyo: National Diet Library, Japanese Government.

National Diet Library, 2003b. *Potsdam Declaration, July 26, 1945*. Tokyo: National Diet Library, Japanese Government.

Naughton, Barry, 2010. "China's Distinctive System: Can It Be a Model for Others?" *Journal of Contemporary China* 19(65): 437–460.

Nesadurai, Helen E. S., 2012. "Trade Policy in SEA: Politics, Domestic Interests and the Forging of New Accommodations in the Regional and Global Economy," pp. 315—330 in Richard Robison, *Routledge Handbook of Southeast Asian Politics*. London: Routledge.

Nexon, Daniel, 2009. *The Struggle for Power in Early Modern Europe: Religious Conflict, Dynastic Empires, and International Change.* Princeton: Princeton University Press.

Nguyen, Hong Thao, and Ramses Amer, 2011. "Coastal States in the South China Sea and Submissions on the Outer Limits of the Continental Shelf," *Ocean Development & International Law* 42(3): 245–263.

Nixon, Richard M., 1969. "Vietnamization Speech," November 3. Transcript of Televised Speech, pp. 1–13 in Karlyn Kohrs Campbell (2014), *The Great Silent Majority: Nixon's 1969 Speech on Vietnamization.* Collage Station: Texas A&M University Press.

Norris, William J., 2016. *Chinese Economic Statecraft: Commercial Actors, Grand Strategy, and State Control.* Ithaca: Cornell University Press.

North, Douglass C., 1990. *Institutions, Institutional Change, and Economic Performance.* Cambridge: Cambridge University Press.

North, Douglass C., 1991. "Institutions," *The Journal of Economic Perspectives* 5(1): 97–112.

North, Douglass, and Robert Paul Thomas, 1973. *The Rise of the Western World: A New Economic History.* Cambridge: Cambridge University Press.

Nye, Joseph S., 2004. *Soft Power: The Means to Success in World Politics.* New York: Public Affairs.

Obama, Barack, 2009. *Remarks by President Barack Obama at Suntory Hall.* President Obama White House Achieves. https://obamawhitehouse.archives.gov/the-press-office/remarks-president-barack-obama-suntory-hall

OECD, 2006. *Infrastructure to (2030), Telecom, and Water, Land and Electricity.* Paris: Organization of Economic Cooperation and Development.

Oga, Toru, 2004. "Rediscovering Asianness: The Role of Institutional Discourses in APEC, 1989–1997," *International Relations of the Asia-Pacific* 4(2): 287–317.

Oh, Yoon Ah, 2018. "Power Asymmetry and Threat Points: Negotiating China's Infrastructure Development in Southeast Asia," *Review of International Political Economy* 25(4): 530–552.

Olson, Mancur, 1982. *The Rise and Decline of Nations: Economic Growth, Stagflation, and Social Rigidities.* Yale: Yale University Press.

Onuf, Nicholas, 1989. *World of Our Making.* Columbia: University of South Carolina Press.

Organski, A. F. K., 1958. *World Politics.* Columbia: New York.

Palais, James B., 1991. *Politics and Policy in Traditional Korea.* Cambridge: Harvard University Asia Center.

Palais, James B., 1996 [2014]. *Confucian Statecraft and Korean Institutions: Yu Hyongwon and the Late Choson Dynasty.* Washington, DC: University of Washington Press.

Pangsapa, Piya, 2014. "Environmental Justice and Civil Society: Case Studies from Southeast Asia," pp. 36–52, Paul G. Harris and Graeme Lang, *Routledge Handbook of Environment and Society in Asia.* London: Routledge.

Park, Seo-Hyun, 2017. *Sovereignty and Status in East Asian International Relations.* Cambridge: Cambridge University Press.

Pastreich, Emanuel, 2005. "The Balancer: Roh Moo-hyun's Vision of Korean Politics and the Future of Northeast Asia," *The Asia-Pacific Journal Japan Focus* 3(8): 1–14.

Peattie, Mark R., 1988. "Continental Expansion, 1905–1941," pp. 217–270 in Peter Duus, *The Cambridge History of Japan: The Twentieth Century.* Cambridge: Cambridge University Press.

Pekkanen, Saadia, John Ravenhill, and Rosemary Foot, 2014. *The Oxford Handbook of the International Relations of Asia.* Oxford: Oxford University Press.

Pempel, T. J., 1998. *Regime Shift: Comparative Dynamics of the Japanese Political Economy.* Ithaca: Cornell University Press.

Petri, Peter A., and Michael G. Plummer, 2014. *ASEAN Centrality and the ASEAN-US Economic Relationship.* Honolulu: East-West Center.

Petri, Peter A., and Michael G. Plummer, Fan Zhai, 2011. *The Trans-Pacific Partnership* and *Asia-Pacific Integration: A Quantitative Analysis*. East West Centre Working Paper No. 119, Oct 24. Honolulu: East-West Center.

PWT9.0, 2017. *The Database: Penn World Table version 9.0*. Groningen: Groningen Growth and Development Center, University of Groningen.

Pye, Lucian W., 1965. "Political Culture and Political Development," pp. 3–26 in Lucian Pye and Sidney Verba, *Political Culture and Political Development*. Princeton: Princeton University Press.

Pye, Lucian W., 1985. *Asian Power and Politics: The Cultural Dimensions of Authority*. Cambridge: Harvard University Press.

Pye, Lucian W., 1992. *The Spirit of Chinese Politics*. Cambridge: Harvard University Press.

Qin, Yaqing, 2007. "Why Is There No Chinese International Relations Theory?" *International Relations of the Asia-Pacific* 7(3): 317–340.

Qin, Yaqing, 2011. "Development of International Relations Theory in China: Progress Through Debates," *International Relations of the Asia-Pacific* 11(2): 231–257.

Qin, Yaqing, 2016. "A Relational Theory of World Politics," *International Studies Review* 18(1): 33–47.

Qin, Yaqing, 2018. *A Relational Theory of World Politics*. Cambridge: Cambridge University Press.

Quandt, William B., 1986. "The Electoral Cycle and the Conduct of Foreign Policy," *Political Science Quarterly* 101(5): 825–837.

Ravenhill, John, 2001. *APEC and the Construction of Pacific Rim Regionalism*. Cambridge: Cambridge University Press.

RCEP, 2012. *Guiding Principles and Objectives for Negotiating the Regional Comprehensive Economic Partnership*. Jakarta: ASEAN Secretary.

Reilly, Benjamin, 2002. "Internal Conflict and Regional Security in Asia and the Pacific," *Pacifica Review* 14(1): 7–21.

Reischauer, Edwin O. and John K. Fairbank, 1960. *East Asia the Great Tradition*. Boston: Houghton Mifflin.

Ringmar, Erik, 2012. "Performing International Systems: Two East-Asian Alternatives to the Westphalian Order," *International Organization* 66(1): 1–25.

Roces, Mina, 2010. "Asian Feminism: Women's Movements from the Asian Perspective," pp. 1–20 in Mina Roces and Louise Edwards, *Women's Movements in Asia: Feminisms and Transnational Activism*. London: Routledge.

Roces, Mina, and Louise Edwards, 2010. *Women's Movements in Asia: Feminisms and Transnational Activism*. London: Routledge.

Root, Hilton L., 2013. "Does China Challenge the Global Legitimacy of Liberalism?" pp. 197–216 in Hilton L. Root, *Dynamics Among Nations: The Evolution of Legitimacy and Development in Modern States*. Cambridge: MIT Press.

Rosato, Sebastian, 2003. "The Flawed Logic of Democratic Peace Theory," *The American Political Science Review* 97(4): 585–602.

Rösch, Felix, and Atsuko Watanabe, 2018. *Modern Japanese Political Thought and International Relations*. London: Rowman & Littlefield.

Rosenau, James, 1961. *Public Opinion and Foreign Policy*. New York: Random House.

Rosenau, James N., 1969. *Linkage Politics: Essays on the Convergence of National and International Systems*. New York: Woodrow Wilson School of Public and International Affairs, Center of International Studies, Free Press.

Rosenau, James N., 1990. *Turbulence in World Politics: A Theory of Change and Continuity*. Princeton: Princeton University Press.

Saaler, Sven, 2016. "Nationalism and History in Contemporary Japan," *The Asia-Pacific Journal Japan Focus* 14(20): 1–17.

Schechterman, Bernard, and Martin Slann, 1993. *The Ethnic Dimension in International Relations*. Westport: Praeger.

Schmid, Andre, 2002. *Korea Between Empires*. New York: Columbia University Press.

Schröppel, Christian, and Nakajima Mariko, 2003. "The Changing Interpretation of the Flying Geese Model of Economic

Development," *Japanstudien* 14(1): 203–236.

Schweller, Randall L., and Xiaoyu Pu, 2011. "After Unipolarity: China's Visions of International Order in an Era of U.S. Decline," *International Security* 36(1): 41–72.

SCO, 2001a. *The Shanghai Convention on Combating Terrorism, Separatism and Extremism*. Beijing: Shanghai Cooperation Organization.

SCO, 2001b. *Statement by the Heads of Government of the Member States of the SCO*. Beijing: Shanghai Cooperation Organization.

Shambaugh, David, 2011. "Coping with a Conflicted China," *The Washington Quarterly* 34(1): 7–27.

Shambaugh, David, 2018. "Is China a Global Power?" pp. 212–229 in Asle Toje, *Will China's Rise Be Peaceful? The Rise of a Great Power in Theory, History, Politics, and the Future*. New York: Oxford University Press.

Shambaugh, David, and Ren Xiao, 2012. "China: The Conflicted Rising Power," pp. 1–30 in Henry R. Nau and Deepa Ollapally, *Worldviews of Aspiring Powers: Domestic Foreign Policy Debates in China, India, Iran, Japan and Russia*. New York: Oxford University Press.

Shih, Chih-yu (石之瑜), 2010. "国际关系研究的亚洲地方性学派"国际政治科学 (*Quarterly Journal of International Politics*) 23(3): 51–73.

Shih, Chih-yu, 2013. "China Rise Syndromes? Drafting National Schools of International Relations in Asia," *Intercultural Communication Studies* XXII(1): 9–25.

Shimizu, Kosuke, Josuke Ikeda, Tomoya Kamino, and Shiro Sato, 2008. *Is There a Japanese IR? Seeking an Academic Bridge Through Japan's History of International Relations*, Afrasian Centre for Peace and Development Studies, Research Series 5. Kyoto: Ryukoku University.

Shin, Gi-Wook, 2006. *Ethnic Nationalism in Korea: Genealogy, Politics, and Legacy*. Stanford: Stanford University Press.

Shin, Gi-wook, and Michael Robinson, 1999. *Colonial Modernity in Korea*. Cambridge: Harvard University Asia Center.

Singer, J. David, 1961. "The Level-of-Analysis Problem in International Relations," *World Politics* 14(1): 77–92.

Singer, J. David. and Melvin Small, 1972. *The Wages of War, 1816-1963*. New York: John Wiley & Sons.

Smith, Robert J., 1992. "The Cultural Context of the Japanese Political Economy," pp. 13–31 in S. Kumon and H. Rosovsky, *The Political Economy of Japan*, Vol 3. Stanford: Stanford University Press.

Smith, Sheila A., 2015. "Diplomacy and Domestic Interests," pp. 17–56 in *Intimate Rivals: Japanese Domestic Politics and a Rising China*. New York: Columbia University Press.

Snyder, Scott, 2009. *From Nuclear Talks to Regional Institutions: Challenges and Prospects for Security Multilateralism in Northeast Asia*. San Francisco: The Asia Foundation.

Souva, Mark, and Brandon Prins, 2007. "The Liberal Peace Revisited: The Role of Democracy, Dependence, and Development in Militarized Interstate Dispute Initiation, 1950–1999," *International Interactions* 32(2): 183–200.

Spengler, Oswald, 1926. *The Decline of the West*, Alfred A. Knopf.

Spruyt, Hendrik, 1994. *The Sovereign State and Its Competitors: An Analysis of Systems Change*. Princeton: Princeton University Press.

Stubbs, Richard, 2001. "ASEAN Plus Three: Emerging East Asian Regionalism?" *Asian Survey* 42(3): 440–455.

Suh, J. J., and Peter J. Katzenstein, 2004. *Rethinking Security in East Asia: Identity, Power, and Efficiency*. Stanford: Stanford University Press.

Sullivan, Michael P., 2015. *The Vietnam War: A Study in the Making of American Policy*. Lexington: University Press of Kentucky.

Summers, Tim, 2016. "China's 'New Silk Roads': Sub-National Regions and Networks of Global Political Economy," *Third World Quarterly* 37(9): 1628–1643.

Suzuki, Shogo, 2009. *Civilization and Empire: China and Japan's Encounter with European International Society*. London: Routledge.

Sylla, Richard and Gianni Toniolo, 1991. *The Nineteenth Century: Patterns of European Industrialization*. New York: Routledge.

Tambiah, Stanley J., 1976. *World Conqueror and World Renouncer: A Study of Buddhism and Polity in Thailand against a Historical Background*. Cambridge: Cambridge University Press.

Tang, Chih-Mao, 2012. "Southeast Asian Peace Revisited: A Capitalist Trajectory," *International Relations of the Asia-Pacific* 12(3): 389–417.

Tang, James T. H., 2014. "Has the Cold War Returned to East Asia?" *Cold War History* 14(4): 647–656.

Tellis, Ashley J., and Michael Wills, 2007. *Domestic Political Change and Grand Strategy in Asia*. Seattle/Washington, DC: National Bureau of Asian Research.

Terada, Takashi, 2003. "Constructing an 'East Asian' Concept and Growing Regional Identity: From EAEC to ASEAN+3," *The Pacific Review* 16(2): 251–277.

Terada, Takashi, 2011. "The United States and East Asian Regionalism: Inclusion-Exclusion Logic and the Role of Japan," pp. 134–156 in Mark Borthwick and Tadashi Yamamoto, *A Pacific Nation: Perspectives on the US Role in an East Asia Community*. Tokyo: Japan Center for International Exchange.

Thuzar, Moe, 2016. "ASEAN's Transboundary Issues: A Hazy Lining to Regional Solutions?" *The IIAS Newsletter* 73(Spring): 19. Leiden: International Institute of Asian Studies.

Tickner, Arlene B., and Ole Wæver, 2009. *International Relations Scholarship Around the World*. London: Routledge.

Tilly, Charles, 1990. *Coercion, Capital, and European States, AD 990–Coercion Capital and European States, AD 990–1990*. Cambridge: Basil Blackwell.

Toje, Asle, 2018. *Will China's Rise Be Peaceful? The Rise of a Great Power in Theory, History, Politics, and the Future*. New York: Oxford University Press.

Tønnesson, Stein, 2015. "Explaining East Asia's Developmental Peace: The Dividends of Economic Growth," *Global Asia* 10(4): 7–13.

Tønnesson, Stein, 2017. *Explaining the East Asian Peace*. Copenhagen: NIAS Press.

Tow, William T., and Brendan Taylor, 2013. *Bilateralism, Multilateralism and Asia-Pacific Security*. London: Routledge.

Toynbee, Arnold J., 1934. *The Geneses of Civilizations*. New York: Oxford University Press.

TPP, 2015. *Summary of the Trans-Pacific Partnership*. https://ustr.gov/about-us/policy-offices/press-office/press-releases/2015/october/summary-trans-pacific-partnership

Trichur, Ganesh K., 2010. "East Asian Regional Dynamics in the 21st Century World System," pp. 3–25 in *The Rise of Asia the Transformation of the World-System*. London: Routledge.

Tsuzuki, Chushichi, 2000. *The Pursuit of Power in Modern Japan 1825–1995*. Oxford: Oxford University Press.

Tu, Weiming, 1991. "Cultural China: The Periphery as the Center," *Daedalus* 120(2): 1–32.

Tucker, Nancy B., 2008. *Dangerous Strait: The U.S.-Taiwan-China Crisis*. New York: Columbia University Press.

Tunsjø, Øystein, 2017. *Strategic Adjustment and the Rise of China: Power and Politics in East Asia*. New York: Cornell University Press.

UNCTAD-FDI, 2018. *UNCTAD Stats-Foreign Direct Investment*. Geneva: UN Conference on Trade and Development.

UNDP, 1994. *Human Development Report*. New York: United Nations Development Program.

UNODC, 2010. *Border Liaison Offices in Southeast Asia 1999–2009*. Vienna: United Nations Office for Drug Control.

Varkkey, Helena, 2016. "The Politics of Fires and Haze in Southeast Asia," p. 27 in *The Oxford Research Encyclopedia: Politics*. New York: Oxford University Press.

Veblen, Thorstein, 1915 [1990]. *Imperial Germany and the Industrial Revolution*. New Brunswick: Transaction Publishers.

Vernon, Raymond, 1966. "International Investment and International Trade in the Product Cycle," *Quarterly Journal of Economics* 80(2): 190–207.

Vogel, Ezra F., 1975. *Modern Japanese Organization and Decision-Making*. Berkeley: University of California Press.

Vogel, Ezra F., 1979. *Japan as Number One: Lessons for America*. Cambridge: Harvard University Press.

Vogel, Ezra F., 1993. *The Four Little Dragons: The Spread of Industrialization in East Asia*. Cambridge: Harvard University Press.

Wade, Robert, 1990. *Governing the Market: Economic Theory and the Role of Government in East Asian Industrialization*. Princeton: Princeton University Press.

Walker, R. B. J., 1984. *Culture, Ideology, and World Order*. Boulder: Westview Press.

Walker, R. B. J., 1990. "The Concept of Culture in the Theory of International Relations," pp. 3–17 in Jongsuk Chay, ed. *Culture and International Relations*. New York: Praeger.

Walker, R. B. J., 1993. *Inside/Outside: International Relations as Political Theory*. Cambridge: Cambridge University Press.

Walker, R. B. J., and Saul H. Mendlovitz, 1990. *Contending Sovereignties: Redefining Political Community*. Boulder: Rienner.

Wallerstein, Immanuel, 1974, 1980. *The Modern World-System I, II, III*. New York: Academic Press.

Wallerstein, Immanuel, 1979. *The Capitalist World-Economy: Essays*. Cambridge: Cambridge University Press.

Waltz, Kenneth, 1959. *Man, the State, and War: A Theoretical Analysis*. New York: Columbia University Press.

Waltz, Kenneth, 1979. *Theory of International Politics*. Reading: Addison-Wesley.

Wan, Ming, 2013. *The China Model and Global Political Economy: Comparison, Impact, and Interaction*. London: Routledge.

Wang, Hui, 2014. *China from Empire to Nation-State*. Cambridge: Harvard University Press.

Wang, Zheng, 2015. "China's Alternative Diplomacy," *The Diplomat*, January 30.

Wang, Yong, 2016. "Offensive for Defensive: The Belt and Road Initiative and China's New Grand Strategy," *The Pacific Review* 29(3): 455–463.

Wang, Fei-Ling, 2017. *The China Order: Centralia, World Empire, and the Nature of Chinese Power*. Albany: SUNY Press.

Watanabe, Akio, 1978. "Foreign Policy Making, Japanese Style," *International Affairs*, 54(1): 75–88.

Watson, Adam, 1992. *The Evolution of International Society: A Comparative Historical Analysis*. London: Routledge.

Webber, Douglas, 2001. "Two Funerals and a Wedding? The Ups and Downs of Regionalism in East Asia and Asia-Pacific After the Asian Crisis," *The Pacific Review* 14(3): 339–372.

Webber, Douglas, and Bertrand Fort, 2006. *Regional Integration in East Asia and Europe. Convergence or Divergence?* London/New York: Routledge.

Weber, Max, 1947. *Theory of Social and Economic Organization*. New York, Oxford University Press.

Weissmann, Mikael, 2012. *The East Asian Peace: Conflict Prevention and Informal Peacebuilding*. Houndmills/Basingstoke: Palgrave Macmillan.

Wendt, Alexander E., 1987. "The Agent-Structure Problem in International Relations Theory," *International Organization* 41: 335–370.

Wendt, Alexander E., 1992. "Anarchy Is What States Make of It: The Social Construction of Power Politics," *International Organization* 46(2): 391–425.

Wendt, Alexander, 1999. *Social Theory of International Politics*. New York: Cambridge University Press.

White, Hugh, 2010. "Power Shift: Australia's Future Between Washington and Beijing," *Quarterly Essay* 39: 1–74.

White, Hugh, 2012. *The China Choice: Why We Should Share Power*. Melbourne: Black.

White House, 2013. *Fact Sheet: The President's Plan to Make America a Magnet for Jobs by Investing in Manufacturing*. President Obama Achieves. https://obamawhitehouse.archives.gov/blog/2013/02/13/plan-revitalize-american-manufacturing

Wiesner-Hanks, Merry E., 2011. "Crossing Borders in Transnational Gender History," *Journal of Global History* 6(3): 357–379.

Wilson, Sandra, 2011. *Nation and Nationalism in Japan*. London: Routledge.

Wohlforth, William C., 2018. "Not Quite the Same as It Ever Was: Power Shifts and Contestation over the American-Led World Order," pp. 57–75 in Asle Toje, *Will China's Rise Be Peaceful? The Rise of a Great Power in Theory, History, Politics, and the Future*. New York: Oxford University.

Wolters, O. W., 1982. *History, Culture, and Region in Southeast Asian Perspectives*. Singapore: Institute of Southeast Asian Studies.

Woo-Cumings, Meredith, 1999. *The Developmental State*. New York: Cornell University Press.

World Bank, 1993. *The East Asian Miracle: Economic Growth and Public Policy*. Oxford: Oxford University Press.

World Bank, 2012. *Toward Gender Equality in East Asia and the Pacific. Key Finding*. Washington, DC: World Bank Group.

World Bank, 2018. *Worldwide Governance Indicators 2018*. The Worldwide Governance Indicators (WGI) Project. Washington, DC: World Bank.

World Values Survey, 2018. "WVS6 F00007942-WV6_Results_By_Country_v20180912," in R. Inglehart, C. Haerpfer, A. Moreno, C. Welzel, K. Kizilova, J. Diez-Medrano, M. Lagos, P. Norris, E. Ponarin, B. Puranen et al. (eds.). 2014. *World Values Survey: Round Six – Country-Pooled Datafile Version*. www.worldvaluessurvey.org/WVSDocumentationWV6.jsp. Madrid: JD Systems Institute.

WTO and IDE-JETRO, 2011. *Trade Patterns and Global Value Chains in East Asia: From Trade in Goods to Trade in Tasks*. Geneva: WTO Secretariat.

Wu, Fengshi, and Bo Wen, 2014. "Nongovernmental Organizations and Environmental Protests: Impacts in East Asia," pp. 105–119 in Paul G. Harris and Graeme Lang, *Routledge Handbook of Environment and Society in Asia*. London: Routledge.

Xi, Jinping, 2014. "New Asian Security Concept for New Progress in Security Cooperation." Remarks at the Fourth Summit of the Conference on Interaction and Confidence Building Measures in Asia, May 21, 2014. Shanghai: Ministry of Foreign Affairs of the People's Republic of China.

Yahuda, Michael, 1996. *The International Politics of the Asia-Pacific*. London: Routledge.

Yamamura, Kozo, and Walter Hatch, 1997. "A Looming Entry Barrier: Japan's Production Networks in Asia," *National Bureau of Asian Research Analysis* 8(1): 28.

Yan, Xuetong, 2006. "The Rise of China and Its Power Status," *Chinese Journal of International Politics* 1(1): 5–33.

Yan, Xuetong, 2011. *Ancient Chinese Thought, Modern Chinese Power*. Princeton: Princeton University Press.

Yan, Xuetong, 2014. "From Keeping a Low Profile to Striving for Achievement," *The Chinese Journal of International Politics* 7(2): 153–184.

Yan, Xuetong, 2018a. "Political Leadership and Power Redistribution," *The Chinese Journal of International Politics* 9(1): 1–26.

Yan, Xuetong, 2018b. *Moral Realism and Strategy for China's Rise*. Beijing: Social Science Academic Press.

Ye, Min, 2015. "China and Competing Cooperation in Asia-Pacific," *Asian Security* 11(3): 206–224.

Yeo, Lay Hwee, 2010. "Institutional Regionalism Versus Networked Regionalism: Europe and Asia Compared," *International Politics* 47(3/4): 324–337.

Zajak, Sabrina, 2017a. "Rethinking Pathways of Transnational Activism," *Global Society* 31(1): 125–143.

Zajak, Sabrina, 2017b. *Transnational Activism, Global Labor Governance, and China*. New York: Palgrave.

Zha, Wen, 2017. "Trans-Border Ethnic Groups and Interstate Relations Within ASEAN: A Case Study on Malaysia and Thailand's Southern Conflict," *International Relations of the Asia-Pacific* 17(2): 301–327.

Zhang, Yongjin, 1991a. *China in the International System, 1918–20: The Middle Kingdom at the Periphery*. Basingstoke: St Anthony's/Macmillan.

Zhang, Yongjin, 1991b. "China's Entry into International Society: Beyond the Standard of 'Civilization'," *Review of International Studies* 17(1): 3–16.

Zhang, Yongjin, 2001. "System, Empire and State in Chinese International Relations," *Review of International Studies* 27(1): 43–63.

Zhang, Yongjin, 2015. "China and the Struggle for Legitimacy of a Rising Power," *Chinese Journal of International Politics* 8(3): 301–322.

Zhang, Yongjin, and Teng-Chi Chang, 2016. *Constructing a Chinese School of International Relations: Ongoing Debates.* London: Routledge.

Zhao, Tingyang, 2006. "Rethinking Empire from a Chinese Concept 'All-Under-Heaven," *Journal of Social Identities* 12(1): 29–41.

Zhao, Tingyang, 2011. *The Tianxia System: An Introduction to the Philosophy of World Institution.* Beijing: China Renmin University Press.

Zimmerman, William, and Harold K. Jacobson, 1993. *Behavior, Culture, and Conflict in World Politics.* Ann Arbor: University of Michigan Press.

Zoellick, Robert, 2005. *Whither China? From Membership to Responsibility.* Remarks to the National Committee on U.S.-China Relations, September 21, 2005, New York.

Index

Abe, Shinzo, 29, 115, 181
Abenomics, 181
Acharya, Amitav, 31, 32, 76, 125, 166, 167, 197, 206
ADB, 163
AIIB, vi, 101, 176
Akamatsu, Kaname, 129, 134, 137, 138, 288
Alagappa, Muthiah, 32, 60, 196, 197, 203, 205, 206, 208, 288
alignment, 66, 74, 79, 89, 93, 94, 95, 99, 100, 102, 268
alliance system, 30, 95, 97, 200, 204, 206, 239
AMU, 194
APEC, vi, 80, 151, 154, 158, 159, 160, 162, 164, 165, 166, 168, 170, 174, 176, 177, 178, 179, 186, 187, 200, 288, 289, 294, 300, 301
APT, vi, 151, 158, 164, 169–171, 174, 176, 196
ARF, vi, 194, 196–198, 200, 202
ARMM, 214
Arrighi, Giovanni, 75, 145, 248, 288
ASEAN, vi, 11, 31, 32, 67, 68, 80–83, 105, 116, 124, 125, 139, 147, 151, 158, 162–171, 173, 175, 176, 178, 182, 185–187, 189, 192–208, 211, 213, 225, 226, 228, 263, 287, 288, 290, 291, 295, 297, 298, 300–302, 305
ASEAN centrality, 169–171, 185
ASEAN Concord II, 167, 186
ASEAN Declaration, 166
ASEAN way, 32, 68, 105, 124, 125, 167, 168, 186, 195, 197, 207, 208, 225, 226, 287
ASEAN+, 170
Asian democracy, 110, 121, 260
Asian financial crisis, 130, 135, 148
Asian modernity, 120, 121

Asian values, 105, 110, 120, 121, 250, 259, 260, 295
Asia-Pacific vision, 158
Ayoob, Mohammed, 228, 288

Ba, Alice, 193, 289
Baldwin, David, 228, 289
Baldwin, Richard, 186, 289
Battle of Dien Bien Phu, 63
Beeson, Mark, 289
Berger, Mark, 166, 186, 289
Bifurcation, 18, 126, 127, 151, 171
Bipolarity, 18, 87, 91, 93, 95, 97–103, 126, 189, 190, 209, 263, 269
BLOs, vi, 224
Bogor Goals, 165
BRI, 101, 144, 160, 161, 270
Buddhism, 110, 118, 119, 302
Bull, Hedley, 15, 56, 250, 264, 289
Busan, Barry, 15, 25, 32, 76, 251, 252, 264, 289

Cairo Declaration, 92
Cambodia-Vietnamese War, 64
Capitalism, 137, 155
Centripetal, 42, 43, 112, 120, 122, 257
CEPA, 172
Cha, Victor, 19, 30, 95, 96, 97, 103, 290
Chaebol, 256
Chang Mai Initiative, 170, 194
Chiang Kai-shek, 62
China Proper, 42, 55
Chinese World Order, 14, 30, 39, 40, 42–45, 49, 51–53, 55, 56, 66, 71, 73, 74, 87, 91, 112, 116, 195
CICA, 202, 203, 290
Clark, Ian, 15, 76, 251, 290, 291
classic realism, 88
Cochinchina, 46

Cohen, Warren I., 43, 44, 249, 291
Cold War, 18, 20, 30, 32, 45, 59–61, 67, 68, 78, 80–84, 87, 88, 94, 99–103, 112, 113–117, 119, 120, 121, 127, 147, 189, 190–193, 195–198, 202, 203, 205–207, 211, 227, 252, 268, 270, 288, 293, 294, 303
Cold War regime, 120
collective action, 82, 91, 184, 204, 218, 219, 222
collective identity, 32, 115, 119, 182, 270
collectivism, 122
colonialism, 72, 81
Columbo Plan, 164
common security, 190, 196, 207
communal conflicts, 66, 119, 125, 211, 223
Communism International, 98, 123
Communists, 18, 61, 63, 67, 72, 74, 82, 93, 97, 108, 119, 122, 190, 192, 197
confidence-building, 197, 202
Confucian authority structure, 110, 111, 116, 124
Confucianism, 110, 111, 119, 122, 259, 260
constructivism, 24, 32
continental East Asia, vi, 14, 18, 27, 40, 42, 45, 46, 49, 51–53, 55, 56, 70–73, 77, 78, 91, 94, 95, 97–100, 102, 106, 111, 112, 114, 117, 118, 121, 164, 166, 167, 174, 191, 192, 195, 249, 259, 267
continentalism, 52, 53
Correlations of War Project, 233
cosmopolitan law, 147
CPTPP vi, 158, 177
critical theory, 109
CSCAP, 198, 200, 291
cultural character, 107, 122, 123, 124
cultural theory, 28, 109
Cumings, Bruce, 17, 61, 138, 148, 149, 235, 246, 291, 304

Daoism, 118
De Bary, William Theodore, 15, 109, 291
democratic peace, 233, 238
Dent, Christopher M., 84, 186, 291
development financing, 144, 153, 161, 176
developmental peace, 238
developmental state, 73, 133, 145, 239, 243, 253, 260, 296

developmentalism, 132
domino, 94
Doyle, Michael W., 147, 233, 238, 244, 245, 291
DPRK, vi, 61, 198
DRV, 63
dual track dynamism, 222
Duterte, Rodrigo, 214, 231, 241

EAEC, vi, 158, 165, 187, 294, 302
EAS, vi, 80, 151, 158, 162, 169–171, 174, 176, 196
East Asia cooperation, 170
East Asian Business Council, 170
East Asian civilization, 15, 52, 105, 109, 110, 111, 248, 249
East Asian crescent, 49, 60, 91, 93, 94, 95, 97, 101, 102, 116, 121, 122
East Asian culture, 6, 69, 106, 108, 110, 120, 121, 126, 268
East Asian growth, 130, 131, 135, 138, 140, 143, 144, 145, 146, 147, 148, 153, 157, 172, 178, 268
East Asian miracle, 110, 129, 149, 253, 256
East Asian model of economic development, 122, 250
East Asian modernity, 110
East Asian nationalism, 117
East Asian peace, 20, 60
East Asian Peace, 85, 238, 303, 304
East Asian regionalism, 20, 101, 124, 151, 152, 153, 154, 155, 156, 158, 159, 160, 161, 164, 165, 167, 168, 170, 171, 172, 173, 174, 175, 176, 177, 178, 179, 180, 181, 182, 183, 184, 185, 200, 232, 240, 250, 268, 295
East Asian vision, 157, 175
East Indies, 46, 119
East Indies Company, 46
East Sea, 65, 71, 111
East Sea dispute, 65
East Sea rim, 71
ECFA, vi, 172
ecological citizenship, 222
empire building, 46, 50, 51, 55
enfeoffment regime, 41, 42
English school, 14, 22, 250–252, 264
environmental justice, 222

ethnopolitical conflict, 66, 68
ethnopolitical group, 67

Fairbank, John King, 14, 15, 42–45, 50, 56, 74, 109, 248, 249, 264, 292, 301
Far East, 13, 72, 78, 92, 248, 291
Far East Agreement, 92
FDI, vi, 137, 138, 142–144, 161, 179, 182, 281, 303
financial economy, 179
flying geese, 20, 132, 138–140, 142–145, 148, 149, 162, 163, 182, 296, 297
Fourteen Points, 78
Fravel, M. Taylor, 65, 85, 201, 292
French Indochina, 63
Friedberg, 19, 76, 290, 292
FTA, 159, 160, 165, 173, 175, 182, 194
FTAAP, vi, 158, 200
Fukuda, 73, 158, 163, 292
Fukuda Doctrine, 73, 163
Fukuzawa, 292
Fukuzawa, Yukichi, 26, 128, 292

Gaddis, John Lewis, 292
galactic polity, 46
Geertz, Clifford, 292
Gellner, Ernest, 116, 293
Geneva Conference, 63
geopolitical grouping, 82
geopolitics, 6, 8, 16, 17, 20, 21, 30, 69, 70, 74, 75, 76, 77, 81, 82, 83, 87, 146, 201, 209, 241, 242, 267, 269, 270, 288
George, Alexander, 58, 93, 107, 293, 296, 297, 299
Gerschenkron, Alexander, 144–145, 293
Gilpin, Robert, 75, 89, 91, 93, 101, 262, 264, 293
global international society, 15, 251, 252
globalization, 144, 146, 180, 219, 220, 262, 269, 295
Goh, Evelyn, 19, 76, 91, 95, 96, 97, 192, 204, 205, 238, 239, 293
Gong, Gerrit W., 15, 45, 51, 128, 251, 293
Gourevitch, Peter, 232, 245, 293
Great East Asian Sphere of Prosperity, 53
Greater China Three, 165
Gries, Peter, 117, 293, 294

group theory, 107
guerrilla war, 68
Gurr, Ted Robert, 66, 67, 233, 245, 294

Haas, Ernst, 159, 223, 228, 294
haijing (海禁), 49
Hall, Peter A., 155, 174, 186, 294, 300
He, Baogang, 14, 180, 186, 294
hedging, 83
Higgott, Richard
Hoffmann, Stanley, 294
Holsti K.J, 294
horizontal integration, 158
HRD Fund, 170
hub-spoke, 95, 96
Huntington, Samuel P., 108, 109, 121, 122, 128, 235, 245, 259, 294, 295
Hurrell, Andrew, 251, 295

ideational forces, 125
IISS, 200
Ikenberry, G. John, 25, 76, 89, 91, 95, 96, 103, 123, 145, 190–192, 204, 205, 208, 262, 293, 295, 297
illiberal democracy, 121
import substitution, 134
inclusion-exclusion logic, 178
Indochina War, 63, 64, 194
industrial diffusion, 20, 100, 132, 135, 138, 139, 182
industrial policy, 132, 133, 236, 253
industrial production, 72, 131, 134, 137, 138–142, 144, 145, 147, 151–153, 158
industrial revolutions, 46
Inoguchi, Takashi, x, 27, 28, 186, 295, 296
institutional vacuum, 56
intergovernmental, 152–154, 156, 159, 161, 162, 165, 166, 169–171, 173, 185, 197, 198, 200, 202, 226
internal conflict, 66
international order, 4, 6–8, 14, 21, 25, 32–34, 41, 45, 55, 61, 64, 70, 73, 75, 76, 80, 81, 83, 88, 89, 91–93, 95, 97, 99–103, 109, 112–116, 121, 126, 127, 156, 180, 189, 190, 195, 204, 205, 250–253, 262, 263, 267–269, 295, 298

international society, 9, 14, 15, 204, 248, 251, 252, 261–263, 270, 289
International structure, 18, 87, 88, 93, 100
internationalization of Japan, 28, 74, 114
interstate relations, 14, 15, 34, 35, 40, 42–45, 49, 51, 55, 56, 60, 63, 66–70, 77, 88, 91, 96, 117, 119, 123, 146, 147, 156, 209, 217, 228, 243, 259, 261, 305
intrastate conflict, 69
Iriye, Akira, 28, 52, 112, 113, 114, 296
ISIS, 198, 214
Islamism, 67, 68, 118, 119, 212–214
Islamic state, 67, 118

Japan-Korean Treaty, 53
JETRO, vi, 139, 142, 143, 161, 163, 295, 296, 304
JIIA, 198
Johnson, Chalmers, 73, 132, 133, 149, 235, 236, 237, 296
Johnston, Alastair I., 25, 117, 123, 287, 296

Kang, David C., 30, 43, 44, 59, 76, 112, 124, 238, 239, 248, 296
Kant, Immanuel, 144, 146, 147, 233, 238, 239, 245, 291, 296
Kantian peace, 146, 147
Kennan, George F, 93, 296
Kennedy, Paul M x, 75, 145, 296
Keohane, Robert, 88, 95, 153, 156, 186, 187, 191, 192, 210, 211, 251, 288, 296, 297
Kim, Samuel S., 252, 288
Koizumi, Junichiro, 29, 115, 181
Korean War, 17, 30, 60, 269

labor rights, 218, 219, 223
Lake, David, 76, 89, 91, 93, 96, 97, 99, 103, 253, 297, 298
Lasswell, Harold D., 106, 298
"learning to one side", 95
Lee, Kuan Yew, 43, 68, 112, 120, 124, 129, 228, 298
Leifer, Michael, 298
liberal international order, 25, 121, 204
Lipset thesis, 234

Lipset, Seymour Martin, 234, 245, 298
low intensity violence, 212, 214
low-intensity wars, 17

MacArthur Revolution, 113
Mahathir, Mohamad, 68, 120, 165
Mahāyāna Buddhism, 119
Maltti, Walter, 298
Mancall, Mark, 298
Manchuria, 52, 53, 54, 72, 77, 92, 93, 95
mandate of heaven, 112
Mao, Zedong, 62
maritime ban, 49
maritime East Asia, vi, 18, 53, 67, 91, 94, 95, 97–99, 102, 114, 116, 119, 120, 121, 131, 174, 192, 195
McCloud, Donald G., 46, 58, 299
Meiji moment, 114
Meiji Restoration, 26, 71, 111, 113, 118, 120, 132, 253, 261
Middle Kingdom, 42, 122, 305
middle powers, 6, 82, 83, 192
Mitrany, David, 223, 228, 299
Modernization, 119, 120, 122, 144
modern-state building, 220
Moravcsik, Andrew, 233, 239, 240, 245, 299
Morgenthau, Hans J., 250, 262, 299
multination state, 211, 215
multistate system, 41, 42, 44
Muslim, 68, 118, 213–216, 249, 259
mutual constitution, 43, 69, 262

NAFTA, vi, 155
national character, 107, 108, 112
nationalism, 116, 288, 291, 293, 294, 296, 298, 301, 302, 304
nation-state theory, 16
natural order, 118
Naughton, Barry, 122, 140, 299
neo-Bismarckianism, 25
neofunctionalism, 159, 223
neoliberalism, 155
neorealism, 19, 88, 288
New Asian Security Concept, 203
New Deal, 155
new institutionalism, 155, 156

new security concept, 190–192, 195–197, 203, 205, 206
NGOs, 222, 225
NIEs, 136
Nixon, Richard M., 74, 78, 79, 299
nontraditional security, 34, 206, 209, 210, 211, 217, 218, 221, 226, 232, 262
non-Western, 5, 126, 145, 252, 287
noodle bowl syndrome, 168
normal state, 28, 29, 73, 114, 117
normative structure, 6, 8, 76, 91, 95, 98, 105, 108, 112, 122, 125, 126, 127, 205, 263, 269, 270
North, Douglas C., vi, 13, 20, 63, 65, 67, 75, 83, 89, 97, 98, 101, 116, 120, 144, 153, 155, 156, 166, 184, 187, 223, 237, 241, 253, 290, 294, 299
Nye, Joseph S., 24, 124, 156, 210, 211, 290, 296, 300

ODA, 161
offensive realism, 24
open door policy, 77, 78
open regionalism, 153, 167

Pacific basin, 162, 164
Pacific business cooperation, 162–164
Pacific Forum, 198
Pacific War, 27, 53, 55, 72, 113, 163, 164, 291
PAFTAD, vi, 158
Palais, James B., 30, 109, 300
Pan-Asianist orientation, 52
Paris Peace Accords, 64
Paris Peace Conference, 64
Park Geun-hye, 241
Pax Sinica, 55
PBEC, vi, 151, 158, 162, 176
Pempel, T.J., 114, 180, 206, 208, 297, 300
perception theory, 107
perpetual peace, 146, 147, 233
personality, 106, 107
Pivot to Asia, 66, 80, 101, 174, 177, 179, 199, 200, 242
Plaza Agreement, 139, 180
political culture, 83, 107, 108, 110, 111, 113–117, 119–122, 124, 126, 222, 259
political cycle, 241

political development, 4, 78, 107, 108, 221, 257, 300
Potsdam Declaration, 92, 299
prefecture-county system, 41
preventive diplomacy, 197, 198, 201
primary institutions of international society, 251
product cycle, 131, 138, 141, 144
production networks, 20, 100, 130, 131, 132, 135, 138, 139, 142, 144, 146, 151, 156, 157, 158, 163, 167, 172, 178, 219, 222, 236, 237, 256, 270, 305
psychological character, 106
PTA, 172
public to private, 144, 160
Pye, Lucian W., 107, 108, 109, 110, 111, 112, 128, 248, 249, 264, 300

Qin, Yaqing, 24, 41, 300
quality of governance, 257

Ravenhill, John, 187, 287, 289, 300, 301
RCEP, vi, 151, 158, 159, 160, 171, 175, 176, 177, 301
Reaganomics, 155, 178
Realpolitik, 267
regime types, 34, 227, 233, 234, 239, 243, 244
regional identity, 32, 105, 116, 125, 187, 190, 193, 259, 302
regionalism, 152, 186, 187, 287, 288, 289, 291, 294, 295, 297, 301, 302
regionalization, 144, 152, 164, 180, 269
Reischauer, Edwin, 15, 109, 248, 249, 264, 292, 301
rent seeking, 82
responsible stakeholder, 123
rise of China, 14, 24, 55, 65, 66, 75, 76, 82, 100, 117, 129, 140, 160, 192, 199, 204
rise of modern Japan, 26
ROK, vi, 61, 143, 169, 197
ROV, 63
Rozman, Gilbert, 30, 288
rule of origin, 152
Russo-Japanese War, 77
Russo-Japanese War (1904–1905), 52

sakoku (鎖国), 49
San Francisco system, 73, 114
SCO, vii, 201, 203, 301
SEATO, 166
Senkaku/Diaoyu Islands, 65, 117
SFIA, 198
Shambaugh, David, x, 25, 75, 123, 297, 301
Shin, Gi-Wook, 30, 302
Shintoism, 118
Sino-Japanese War, 52, 53
Sino-Soviet split, 63, 99, 100
Smithian model, 145
Socialism, 120, 126, 155
soft power, 24, 123, 124
South China Sea, 17, 65, 66, 100, 241, 296, 299
South China Sea disputes, 66
Spruyt, Hendrik, 58, 291, 302
SPT, vii, 201, 203
SRV, 63
standard of civilization, 15, 251
Strait Settlements, 46
strategic compensation, 82
strategic defensive perimeter, 78
strategic triangle, 100
structural change, 75, 76, 253
structural realism, 76, 88, 262
structural theory, 88
structuration theory, 263
substantive economy, 179–181, 253, 268
swaegug(쇄국), 49

TAC, 194
Taiwan Strait, 17, 60, 62–65, 99
Taiwan Strait crisis, 62
Tambiah, Stanley J., 46, 119, 302
Terada, Takashi, 178, 187, 302
Thatcherism, 155
the English school, 14, 250–252
Theravāda Buddhism, 119
third wave democracy, 114, 121, 241
Three World theory, 23
Tianxia, 42, 44, 58, 305
Tilly, Charles, 69, 302
Tokugawa system, 45, 49, 53, 71, 72
Toynbee, Arnold J., 15, 109, 303

TPP, vii, 80, 158–160, 173–177, 181, 185, 242, 303
TPSP, 173, 174
track II dialogue, 198
transboundary river, 224
transnational activism, 210, 217, 221, 223, 227
Treaty of Shimonoseki, 52
treaty-port system, 49, 251
tribal conflict, 66
tribute system, 14, 43, 50, 112, 124, 252, 298
tripartite partnership, 218
tripolar, 99, 100, 143, 161
Tu, Weiming, 122, 128, 259, 303
Tucker, Nancy B, 85, 303

UNCLOS, 65
UNDCP, vii, 224
unipolarity, 100, 102
unit of analysis, 109, 248
UNTAC, vii, 64
USSR, vii, 17, 23, 56, 62, 63, 95, 100, 189, 268

Vietnam War, 16, 17, 60, 63, 64, 74, 84, 85, 163, 298, 302
Vogel, Ezra F., 135, 137, 303

Wallerstein, Immanuel, 20, 75, 101, 129, 144, 145, 303
Waltz, Kenneth, 88, 89, 99, 103, 232, 233, 234, 236, 237, 246, 250, 253, 262, 303
Wang, Hui, 42, 44, 56, 58, 101, 290, 295, 303, 304
Warring States system, 40, 41, 42, 49, 55, 56, 70, 71, 72, 111, 267
Washington Consensus, 130, 178
Watson, Adam, 15, 56, 250, 264, 289, 304
Wendt, Alexander E., 24, 29, 32, 109, 262, 304
Westernization, 122
Westphalia system, 44, 45, 50, 251
women rights movements, 220
world economic structure, 145, 157, 247
world economic system, 20, 144, 145, 155, 194

world society, 251
World Value Survey, 260

Yahuda, Michael, 18, 87, 95, 99, 100, 103, 297, 305
Yalta vision, 92, 94

Yan, Xuetong, 75, 76, 199, 305
Yoshida Doctrine, 28

Zhang, Yongjin, 15, 24, 41, 45, 56, 58, 76, 117, 251, 252, 264, 289, 294, 305
Zhao, Tingyang, 42, 58, 112, 305